Neo-Tech II Manuscript
for the

THE NEO-TECH DISCOVERY

The Entelechy of
Prosperity and Happiness
by
Frank R. Wallace

> **entelechy** n.: 1. a realization as opposed to a potentiality, 2. the actualization of form-giving cause as contrasted with potential existence, 3. a force directing life and growth.

for
Wealth
Personal Dealings
Business, Jobs, Careers
Art and Pleasure
Romantic Love

Ignorance Once Dispelled Never Returns

Neo-Tech forever dispels ignorance in curing the disease of mysticism and eliminating its symbiotic neocheaters. Once cured, a person flourishes naturally and easily to guiltless prosperity and abiding happiness. Once free from mysticism and neocheating, a person seizes iron-grip control of both the present and future to prosper forever. ...Once armed with Neo-Tech knowledge, a person overpowers all mysticism and neocheating that tries to harm or diminish his or her life.

Manuscript
for
Neo-Tech II

THE NEO-TECH DISCOVERY

complete with references to the
Original Neo-Tech Reference Encyclopedia

Neo-Tech/Psychuous Advantages
for guilt-free
Prosperity, Power, and Romantic Love
by
FRANK R. WALLACE

NEO-TECH IS DEDICATED TO
THE PRODUCER OF VALUES

You are the good, the innocent. Yet, you have been defrauded throughout history of your earned prosperity and happiness. You have been victimized by the politicians, theologians, and pseudo intellectuals. For they live off your efforts, repaying you only with falsehoods, unearned guilt, and demands for sacrifice. In your innocence, you have unnecessarily accepted their frauds, usurpations, and abuses. Without Neo-Tech, you could never know with certitude that you, not they, are potent and hold the power to control life. But now, with Neo-Tech, you can forever break free from their destructive hoaxes. You can take what all honest and productive human beings have rightfully earned, but seldom take: A guiltless life of prosperity, love, and happiness.

Neo-Tech is dedicated to you and to the discovery of the prosperity and happiness that belong to you.

Review Editor and Testimonial Curator: Gary L. Twitchell
Format and Typesetting Editor: Mike Trivisonno

13th Printing/July 1985 [5.5 BB] new version
14th Printing/October 1985 [7.2 BB] revised
15th Printing/January 1986 [7.8 BB] revised
16th Printing/May 1986 [15 BB] revised
17th Printing/January 1987 [22 BB] revised
18th-19th Printing/August 1987 [22 BB] revised
20th Printing/August 1988 [10BB revised, 8BB "11-3"]
21st Printing/November 1988 [10BB]
22nd Printing/January 1989 [10BB]

Foreign-Language Editions

available now	*available soon*	*available later*
Chinese	Arabic	Greek
French	Dutch	Polish
German	Fijian	Russian
Italian	Malaysian	Urdu
Japanese	Norwegian	
Portuguese	Serbian	
Spanish	Swedish	

23 25 27 29 30 28 26 24 22
ISBN # 911752-49-8
Library of Congress #86-81021
Copyright © 1985, 1986, 1987, 1988
by
Frank R. Wallace
All world-wide rights reserved
reproduction permissions required in writing
from
I & O Publishing Company

Neo-Tech Research and Writing Center

PREFACE

For nearly 2000 years, master neocheaters* have manipulated the destructive forces of mysticism to drain power and prosperity from all honest men and women. But today, for the first time in history, a newly discovered idea system called Neo-Tech reveals and eliminates those destructive forces while releasing a stream of physical, psychological, and material advantages. Neo-Tech integrations deliver emotional and material benefits to everyone possessing those integrations. Thus, anyone can use the Neo-Tech concepts to guiltlessly increase his or her wealth — now and forever into the future.

Furthermore, the Neo-Tech concepts can free any individual from all who waste one's time, from all who work against one's best interests, from all neocheaters and mystics who use non sequiturs** to diminish the lives of others. The Neo-Tech concepts provide the ways and means to limitless prosperity and happiness.

---

*__Neocheaters and mysticism__ are defined on pages xiii-xix.

**__Non sequitur__ must be defined here: The word non sequitur embodies the key survival tool of all professional mystics and neocheaters. Non sequitur is a Latin word meaning "it does not follow". Because the word is dead-language Latin, its meaning remains stable, immutable — unable to be changed or twisted by mystics and neocheaters. That is why the word is so valuable for uprooting neocheaters. Webster's 9th Collegiate Dictionary definition of non sequitur is, "a statement that does not follow logically from anything previously said". ...Great benefits accrue from understanding how mystics and neocheaters manipulate dishonest notions to usurp power and wealth from the value producers.

Non sequiturs are most blatantly used by the media genre of professional neocheaters. They manufacture non sequiturs by linking obvious facts and values to dishonest premises designed to attack and undermine producers and values. They constantly use such non sequitur/neocheating maneuvers to camouflage their destructive modi operandi with dishonest illusions of fairness and credibility. But with Neo-Tech, one easily identifies the dishonesty of their good-sounding non sequiturs designed to attack and undermine values. Such non-sequitur attacks are constantly used to usurp power and values not only by journalists but by the clergy, politicians, political cartoonists, certain professors, and self-appointed advocates of "causes". Non sequiturs are powerful tools for gaining strength and credibility without regard to honesty. And using non sequiturs to manipulate mysticism for usurping power and values is neocheating. With non sequiturs, no honest link exists between the facts being presented and the attack being promoted.

The above paragraph is from an article, "The Secret of Non Sequiturs", released at the first Neo-Tech World Summit. That article includes specific examples on the use of non sequiturs by professional neocheaters, religious leaders, politicians, and one's own self. That article also demonstrates how Neo-Tech demolishes non sequiturs to allow power, prosperity, love, and happiness to flourish in one's own self and others.

LETTERS FROM NEO-TECH OWNERS

The letters and testimonials placed on the left-hand pages are not to show the great values of Neo-Tech. You will discover that yourself. But the letters demonstrate the limitless variety of values arising from Neo-Tech for every individual and life style around the world.

All letters are important. For they document individual reactions to Neo-Tech while simultaneously aiding integration of the concepts.

Randal S.   C-9

Having anticipated receiving Neo-Tech, I promptly set to task reading (no consuming) the Instructions, Neo-Tech I and subsequently Neo-Tech II. For the first time in my life I was clearly able to label the force of malevolence (neocheaters) that I had known existed in life from childhood. The comprachicos who schooled me in self-doubt, the looters who stole my earned values, the grey figures who immortalized mediocrity and made virtue out of intellectual laziness. To nail them down and then to disarm them is the coupe de grace for all men (women) who could neither fight nor surrender. Heroic indeed!

Upon completing Neo-Tech II I did not immediately read III-V. Instead I began to assimilate the entelechy into a current concern regarding career. Here Neo-Tech proved itself in all regards by allowing me to logically and scientifically evaluate and correct errors. Upon returning to the last three packages, I found the matrix aspect of Neo-Tech which is providing me with the impetus for new challenges and a richer, guilt-free life.

Irl C.   J-9

These concepts have the greatest potential for meeting the needs of our society of of anything I have ever seen.

Keep up the good work and may you reach your highest goals.

INTRODUCTION

The integration of philosophy with psychology, physiology, and the material world is crucial not only to the Neo-Tech concepts, but to every individual on this planet. Yet, that key role of philosophy has until today remained essentially unrecognized by all the populations of this world. Why? The answer is below:

Philosophy

The philosopher's job is to provide human beings with practical tools for dealing with reality in order to live an easier, more prosperous, happier life. But almost all philosophers throughout history have defaulted in their responsibility and failed miserably in their job. Indeed, most philosophers have done all in their power to make life for human beings not easier and happier, but more difficult and unhappy by obscuring reality. As a result, almost everyone rejects the practicality of philosophy. Thus, almost no one recognizes the potential of this mighty tool.

Few people can formulate integrated philosophical systems on their own. Moreover, few people have the knowledge to reject or even identify the neocheaters and mystics who implicitly use philosophy to drain the lives of others. ...The first step in dismissing the mystics and neocheaters is to recognize that only two basic philosophical systems or choices exist:

One system arises from a mystical/altruistic premise that individuals should be sacrificed either to others or to "higher" causes. The Greek philosopher Plato (427 B.C. - 347 B.C.) identified and developed that system. Throughout history, all governments, religions, and neocheaters have implicitly used Plato's philosophy to usurp unearned power and values from innocent producers.

The other philosophical system arises from a reality/self-interest premise that the individual is the highest value in the universe. The Greek philosopher Aristotle (384 B.C. - 322 B.C.) identified and developed that system.

Neo-Tech identifies both the Platonistic and the Aristotelian philosophical systems and then clearly demonstrates how and why Neo-Tech guarantees prosperity and happiness. Neo-Tech (fully integrated honesty) shows how anyone can switch from being a loser with a mystical/Platonistic approach to being a winner with a Neo-Tech/Aristotelian approach.

Psychology

The Neo-Tech concepts deliver the psychological tools needed to achieve guiltless profits, power, and happiness. In addition, those concepts expose the deceptions of mysticism and neutralize the harm of neocheaters.

Physiology

The Neo-Tech concepts also integrate a wide range of physiological discoveries including body functions, diet, hormones, and physical fitness into a forward-march position that leads to increasing psychuous pleasures and happiness.

Larry L   C-5

Dear Neo-Tech Staff:

Since I was nine years old I knew that my lights were on but I was not home. I came home, however, during my first reading of Neo-Tech II some thirty-six years later. I would like to relate to you what happened to me while I was engrossed with Neo-Tech II. It was as though I was beaten to a pulp. I was slapped around and finally kicked to the floor all out of breath when I finally acknowledged that it was me that they were talking about. I was the lazy and envious person described throughout the pages of Neo-Tech that cut through me like a sword. I was the one that was not standing on my own two feet. I was the mystic. I was the Neo-Cheat. It was me that recognized "outside authorities" instead of the honest "producer of tradeable values" type person who was a prisoner that has been locked up somewhere inside of me. I was the promoter of Tarot, Astrology, Kabbalah, the occult and other forms of debauchery and time wasteing. It was me putting greater emphasis on death than on life and the realization of biological immortality. I even scored high on the Psyche Death check list — Leveraged Advantage # 98 — I got eight out of ten characteristics of a dying or dead psyche checked. Plato would have been happy for me. He never would have been proud. I would have never been proud of me either, but that was before Neo-Tech. Frank Wallace and associates and Neo-Tech revived me.

When I received Neo-Tech I was ready. Whatever I was doing simply was not working. And now I know that it was not productive, rational or reasonable. Neo-Tech is a part of me now and it is as though that I have been transplanted from an unrealistic hostile environment to a healthy one where I can <u>grow</u> and blossom indefinately. I am now of value to me, to my romantic-partner, and to others.

Stephen S.   J-131

Since January 1982, I have contemplated the contents and relevance of the Neo-Tech Discovery to my own personal life. I had a good initial enthusiasm to the material, but somehow I lost interest. In the last few months, however, I have gained a renewed interest in Neo-Tech and its applications. I have found that reading some of the books which you suggested under the "book analyses" section of Neo-Tech II gave me a good objective background and a new enthusiasm for learning more about the pursuit of personal happiness.

My advice to people just getting involved with Neo-Tech is to read some of the better books you have analyzed because they provide a wealth of excellent background material.

The reason I have a renewed, stronger interest in Neo-Tech is because I realize that without it I could never really acheive the potential guiltless, happy life that I desire. I now have the definite feeling that genuine happiness may indeed be on its way.

KEY DEFINITIONS

Pages vii-xxxvii provide the definitions needed to use the Neo-Tech concepts for gaining powerful advantages in all competitive situations. After studying these definitions, a person is ready to integrate the 114 Neo-Tech Advantages needed to gain prosperity, power, and love.

20 Key Words and Concepts
(order of appearance on pages vii-xxxvii)

Neo-Tech	Free Choice
Neo-Tech Concepts	Key Choice
Psychuous	Business vs. Mysticism
Psychuous Concepts	Man
Psychuous vs. Sensuous	Man's Nature and Survival
Life	Man's Biological Needs
Love	Morals
Sex	Altruism and Sacrifice
Mysticism and Neocheating	Objective Reality
Mystics, Neocheaters, and Nonmystics	Happiness

plus

31 Key Words Distorted by Mystics and Neocheaters
In Order to Usurp Values Earned by Others
(listed alphabetically in the table on pages xxxix-xlvii)

Achievement	Mysticism
Altruism	Objectivity
Biological Needs	Politician
Capitalism	Pride
Death	Producer
Egalitarianism	Rationality
Freedom	Reality
Government	Reason
Happiness	Romantic Love
Individualism	Selfishness
Laissez Faire	Selflessness
Life	Sensuousness
Logic	Sex
Man's Nature	Technology
Morality	Theologian
	Value

DISSOLVING THE CHAINS

By reading the following definitions, a person will understand how the manipulation of mysticism in others is the common bond linking all neocheaters: Now, for the first time, heads of states, religious leaders, elegant con artists, mafia dons, most attorneys, some Nobel-prize laureates, many leading academe, certain well-known media personalities, certain entertainment people, some bankers, and even certain business people (e.g., white-collar hoax executives) are inextricably linked together as soul mates. They all live by attacking values, producers, businesses, and products while producing no long-range, <u>net</u> benefits for others or society. In other words, such people live as neocheaters or as just plain cheaters by usurping, attacking, undermining, and destroying values produced by others. ...Neo-Tech ends that secret, parasitical bond by forever dissolving the chains of mysticism.

Jan M.   R-6058

Dear Drs. Flint and Wallace,

    I have had my N.T. Volumes I-V for about 3 months now. The first month was tough. I really needed to talk about N.T. but when I did, they all thought I'd gone off the deep end! I read and re-read the volumes--mostly II--at least ten times. My volumes are now loaned out so at last there are some people I know who also understand and embrace these concepts.

    North Dakota is not a very progressive state, at least not in ideas. Most people here are held captive by the Churches. This is very typical rural small town behavior. I have always been a non-conformist--a kind of black sheep in my strict Catholic family. As I got older, I got guilty and I tried desperately to conform my behavior to those that were around me. The more I conformed, the less happy I became. I wasted thousands of dollars and even more hours on books and programs trying to improve myself. I kept searching for something to help me feel better about my life. I was really desperate when I sent off the check for the Neo-Tech volumes. In fact, I actually thought I might have been duped by your company--a kind of mail order scam. You can not imagine my relief when I received your confirmation letter. I sure was not prepared for the powerful information that was packed in those rather un-impressive-looking manuals. I experienced the entire range of emotions-- from sheer terror to near-climactic euphoria. The letters from readers on their reactions to Neo-Tech were most valuable to me. Since it took several readings before Neo-Tech clicked, I would often find myself going over those letters and finding little pieces of myself in them. I would be motivated onward until finally it all made sense to me. I sure would be interested in even more of those letters since that is what is really helpful to me-- seeing how others have applied and used this information in their lives.

    After 37 years of living my life to suit others, I was very unhappy and frustrated. Neo-Tech has changed that for me. I now feel like I am capable of assuming effective control of my life. I have lots of work ahead but with this knowledge I know I will do it. I am seeking more information. I already sent for and just received the Neo-Tech Encyclopedia. I am ordering the complete Neo-Tech Library. I am hooked. Please continue your excellent work. Current world conditions sure indicate that this information must spread. It is the one and only thing that will save us from total annihilation or worse--domination by a severely repressive government. Our U.S. government is becoming one more so with each passing day. As far as I am concerned, you can not pass out this information fast enough. Saturate the world with Neo-Tech and do it quickly!

DEFINITIONS AND UNDERSTANDINGS

Neo-Tech can guide anyone to increased prosperity and happiness. But for full benefits, a person must understand the following 20 key concepts and words used throughout Neo-Tech:

NEO-TECH

Neo-Tech is a noun or adjective meaning fully integrated honesty. Neo-Tech allows the guiltless creation of earned power, prosperity, and romantic love:

Neo-Tech is a collection of "new techniques" or "new technology" that lets one know exactly what is happening and what to do for gaining maximum advantages in all situations. That technology is needed to be competent — to guiltlessly and honestly obtain the wealth and happiness available to everyone but achieved by so few. Neo-Tech provides the power to profit in every situation by nullifying neocheating and mysticism not only in others but within one's own self. Indeed, Neo-Tech eliminates the harm of all mystics, false authorities, neocheaters, and their infinite array of deceptions. Neo-Tech lets a person gather all power unto his or her own self while rendering mystics and neocheaters impotent.

With Neo-Tech, all effort is directed toward achieving fully integrated honesty needed to act in concert with reality. With mysticism, all effort is directed toward rationalizing non sequiturs or deceptions needed to satisfy some feeling, wish, or whim arising from one's self or some external "authority". ...Neo-Tech is rooted in effort, objective reality, and value production. Mysticism, by contrast, is rooted in laziness, random nothingness, and value destruction.

Neo-Tech is health. Mysticism is sickness. Neo-Tech is the opposite of mysticism. Neo-Tech heralds the end of mysticism and its symbiotic neocheaters.

NEO-TECH CONCEPTS

The Neo-Tech concepts are the most powerful thinking tools possible. And those tools will efficiently deliver prosperity, happiness, and romantic love to everyone who uses them. The Neo-Tech concepts are also the most effective mystic-eliminating tools ever developed. In addition, the Neo-Tech concepts effectively squelch all neocheaters.

PSYCHUOUS

Psychuous(SIGH-kyu-uhs) is a new word describing integrations that combine the activities of the mind, body, and emotions to continually increase prosperity, happiness, and romantic love. ...The psychuous concepts underpin Neo-Tech.

Psychuous Pleasures is the cessation of conflict among the mind, body, emotions by reconciling philosophy, psychology, and physiology so one's own actions harmoniously serve the material, emotional, and biological needs of the human organism. Using psychuous concepts, one experiences exquisite, lasting pleasures unknown to others.

Psychuous Sex is a fully integrated, rational approach to personal well-being. Harnessing one's potential through Neo-Tech is rewarded with prosperity, happiness, romantic love, and psychuous pleasures.

Mike M.   C-1026

Dear Neo-Tech friends,

This letter is to inform you of my continued satisfaction and amazement with the literature purchased during the Summit meeting. Satisfaction in the precision tool at my disposal and amazement at the powerful integrations revealed. I would also like to comment on the Summit itself.

So much of my personal life had been in turmoil as a result of mystical knots wrapping around me. 'Reasoning' my way through the 'complexity' of achieving guiltless happiness only entangled me further. Neo-Tech,Neo-Think allows me to cut through the crap with clearly formed facts,as well as, integrated actions. It has become fully evident that I had not the means to pull my life together. Life is truly the ultimate value and happiness is it's truest complement. The world as a whole desperately needs this information. It becomes more painful to watch the mental and physical oppression of millions now that I see how simple happiness can be accomplished. Mystics and their crafty lies are now very easy to identify and bypass. I am also relieved to know my children will not be shackled with flawed thinking processes as they grow and shape their world.

It makes me shudder when the beautifully simple truth is laid out in such a manner that it screams in ones mind. To think that all has been before us since man first contemplate his place in the universe. How many centuries such intelligent creatures have stumbled around the same. Once the door of ignorance opens however, the rest comes bursting through. As long as one remains strong in mind Neo-Tech,Think pulls all the old lies out of the thinking process.

Ira J.,   R1432

The most valuable information ever published. Provides accurate guidance to Truth seekers that will helps them preserve the real value of their wealth and a profitable money making strategy during these difficult financial times. Without this help from NEO-TECH the odds are stacked against you. Once you know, you can play the game of life safely, happily and confidently. I have stopped playing russian roulette with my well-being.

PSYCHUOUS CONCEPT

Neo-Tech reveals an entirely new set of concepts: Psychuous Concepts. Those concepts integrate prosperity, love, and reality with a person's physical, psychological, and intellectual nature. By understanding and utilizing the Psychuous Concepts, a person can experience great pleasures with guaranteed prosperity and happiness — for life.

And "for life" means exactly that for a person's entire life. The human mind is an organism that does not age if properly cared for. Since the human mind can grow forever, psychuous pleasures have no limits. But growth of the mind is not automatic. Instead, growth requires conscious effort. When a person defaults on that effort, his or her mind stops growing. When intellectual growth stops, the capacity for happiness and pleasure begins shrinking — the individual begins dying.

Moreover, human aging is a process of deterioration. Growth is the opposite of deterioration. Only when growth stops can aging begin. The human mind never has to stop growing. In fact, human life itself may never have to age. No scientific evidence dictates that a person has to age and die. Indeed, a person may be able to live indefinitely under fully integrated, fully rational, physical, psychological, intellectual, and emotional conditions. Before Neo-Tech, those conditions were never available or possible.

PSYCHUOUS PLEASURES
VERSUS
SENSUOUS PLEASURES

Sensuous relates to the five physical senses — touch, sight, hearing, smell, and taste. Sensuous is associated with the pleasurable gratification of one or more of those physical senses. Neo-Tech expands the meaning of sensuous to capture the essence of pleasure by including and integrating the most potent dimension, the pleasurable gratification of the human mind. That gratification includes the harmonious agreement of a person's love life with that person's material, intellectual, and emotional well-being. ...The word for that expanded meaning of sensuous is **psychuous**.

The conscious mind is the ultimate organ for experiencing pleasures, including sexual pleasures. The mind integrates all pleasures with all that a person *is*, *does*, and *thinks*. The mind is the organism that offers unlimited pleasure and happiness.

Expanding the meaning of sensuous to include the mind unveils a new, powerful dimension for achieving prosperity and pleasure: The word **psychuous** captures the essence of pleasure by including the conscious mind — the source of all objective values and pleasures. The five physical senses are important for experiencing pleasure via temporarily stimulating various sense receptors of the body. But the depth and intensity of pleasure

Gary W.   J-224

I wish to thank your firm and Dr. Frank Wallace for the profound
knowledge bestowed upon me by the Neo-Tech Information Packages.

I have quickly devoured most all of the information packages and
I am eager to see what's next. N-T has cleanly sliced through
the illusion of reality to expose the rich inner heart of all
life. I see the Neo-World forming with clarity in my mind.

I am filled with a strong sense of gratitude for being able to
finally see clearly what is happening in my daily experience. I
wish the best to all of you who are increasing the N-T exposure.

R.P.W.   C-1000, SOUTH AFRICA

Dear Mr Flint,

Having recently finished reading Neo-Tech Instructions followed by Neo-Tech 11 Manuscript for the Neo-Tech Discovery I have only one request please send me all available information on Neo-Tech and charge to my Diners Club card no. I authorise expenditure up to $1000 U.S. for whatever is available at the present time. The expiry date of my card is 11/87.

I have for many years been an ardent admirer of Ayn Rand and in fact have a complete set of all her writings but until receiving the Neo-Tech Discovery had begun to dispair that anything would ever come of her philosophy. I can only thank Dr. Wallace for his magnificent manuscript. I now feel confident that a better world will develop in the near future and offer my help in whatever way I can.

I am very much interested in the achievement of biological immortality and offer you my full hearted support. Please place me on your mailing list for any future information regarding this or any other publications by I & O Publishing Company.

lies within the conscious mind to the extent that a person has developed an integrated, psychuous mind. ...Sensuosity is a variable depending on the psychology of each individual. But, psychuosity is a consistent value based on the nature of man and woman. Psychuosity always has the same meaning and always comprises the most powerful of life's values.

SEX

In Neo-Tech, the meaning of sex includes intercourse as a brief but crucial highlight along a vast range of sexually rooted experiences and emotions. Indeed, the meaning of sex in Neo-Tech encompasses all sexual influences (often hidden but powerful) that weave through each person's life.

Ironically, sexual influences most dominate the lives of those who pretend to shun or repudiate the pleasure of sex (e.g., mystical celibates, religious ascetics, guilt-projecting preachers). Their very acts of avoiding or attacking sexual pleasure leave their lives far more dominated by sex than those who accept the responsibility of earning healthy, confident sex lives.

LIFE

The essence of conscious life is control — the ability to control one's present and future. Conscious life is the only entity in the universe that can control nature and future events. That control is possible to the extent that mysticism is absent and Neo-Tech is present. A person in control is happy and will prosper. A person out of control is unhappy and will fail. Neo-Tech puts a person in control.

LOVE

Three types of love exist: (1) sexual romantic love, (2) nonsexual friendship and family love, and (3) intellectual/artistic love such as love of Aristotle, Hugo, Chopin, Edison, Einstein. Contrary to myth, love is not inexplicable or beyond understanding. Love can be exactly defined and clearly understood.

Psychuosity encompasses romantic love, which integrates the mind and body of a man and a woman. That integration includes the emotional/intellectual development of values between that man and woman. Such a complex relationship requires planned, rational thought by each partner. Romantic love is one of life's most important and practical achievements: Romantic love is a major source of personal growth, efficient living, happiness, joy, and pleasure.

Yet romantic love is often dismissed as blind, mindless, irrational, immature, transitory, impractical. But the opposite is true. And similar false notions have led to the misunderstanding of words such as "romantic", "romanticism", and the "Romantic era". How did those false notions begin? "Romantic" and its related words originally implied freedom, individuality, and *rational* ideals based on integrated honesty...not *irrational* whims based on mystical illusions. But over the years, the concept of romanticism became inverted by the mystics and falsely associated with the irrationalists and the

Brendon R.   R-2367

I cannot describe to you the enormous value that your book has been in my life, it has been the best investment I've made to date.

The most important experience I've had relating to the information in your book is the realization of the unlimited power and potential in me. The achievement of my dream is not a dream anymore.

The second most important experience is the increased awareness of the people and institutions (my environment) draining my hope & happiness and how there roots have infiltrated my whole life.

Kenneth H.   R-3039,   IRELAND

Dear Sir,

Just recently I was accepted for the post of Trainee Manager of an expanding Insurance Company. A year ago I think it would have been unlikely that I would have been accepted for this job, indeed I probably would not have had the confidence to apply in the first place. This and other positive changes in my life, I put down to the knowledge I have recieved from Neo-Tech.

sentimentalists of the 19th Century Romantic Period. Philosophers, poets, writers, and artists such as Rousseau, Wordsworth, Blake, Van Gogh were considered romanticists. But they were not romanticists at all. They were existentialists, mystics, and sentimentalists who basked in the intellectual and political freedom of romanticism. The actual romanticists were individuals like Spencer, Hugo, Chopin, Gould, Edison (and earlier romanticists like Aquinas, Michelangelo, da Vinci, and other honest, hard-working idealists). Such individuals created every major value since the Renaissance. Yet, while they were sometimes considered rationalists or even idealists, they were seldom considered romanticists as they actually were.

The "Oxford English Dictionary" (1972) traces the usage of "romance", "romanticism", and other words whose meanings today are distorted or inverted.* Etymologies trace those distortions as far back as the 17th and 18th Centuries. Such word distortions diminish the thinking tools needed to understand and implement the most important and powerful human actions. But the Neo-Tech/Psychuous concepts return the word "romantic" and other important words to their accurate meanings that render the neocheaters impotent.

Romantic love involves an emotional, intellectual, and sexual involvement with another person. And romantic love offers the deepest of all happiness and the greatest of all pleasures.** But as with all major values, romantic love is not automatic. Romantic love must be earned through rational thought and planned effort. And then, that love must be maintained and expanded through constant honest effort — through constant discipline, thought, and control (the DTC method).

The attributes men seek in women for romantic partners are too diverse to generalize. But through the ages, civilizations, and cultures, women seek in men a single attribute, however interpreted. That attribute is *strength*. ...Neo-Tech delivers maximum strength to every human being.

MYSTICISM AND NEOCHEATING

Mysticism is defined as: 1. Any mental or physical attempt to recreate, evade, or alter reality through dishonesty, rationalizations, non sequiturs, emotions, deceptions, or force. 2. Any attempt to use the mind to create reality rather than to identify and integrate reality.

---

* Other valuable words whose meanings have been distorted or inverted include individualism, capitalism, selfishness, pride, technology, rationality, logic. Neo-Tech corrects all such distortions. Neo-Tech also identifies those who purposely distort key words in undermining their victims' thinking tools in order to neocheat them. [Reference: Table on pages xxxix-xlvii]

** All emotions fluctuate. Even the strongest romantic love will wax and wane. At times, even the most ardent lovers can feel diminished love for each other. But within an upward fluctuating pattern, romantic love can constantly renew and build to higher levels.

L.J. R-4171

Gentlemen:

Surely a higher education, more useful than a B.A.

Yergie S. R-1842

Thanks to Dr. Wallace for his concern and his workings for the good of the people. Now I have something to look forward to, before I thought we were just headed for destruction and everyone out to cut each others throat. Congratulations, now I know someone is working to help.

G.W. C-1001, UNITED KINGDOM

Dear Mr Flint,
I have recently recieved and read Neo-Tech I-V. As a long time member and recruiter for the Church of Scientology who resigned from the church over policy five years back. Neo-Tech was a vital slap of reality which I have found most rewarding. Of course its difficult to dismiss a deep held belief in ones spiritual nature instantly, however, the practical benefit of being a Scientology "Clear" is minimal, when compared with the real benefits I've achieved just from reading through the neo-tech discoveries. I know this neo tech viewpoint should stand me in good stead. The few dollars payed are nothing, considering the many thousands I'd spent in the Church over many years. Neo tech was undoubtedlly the best purchase I've ever made, and I mean ever!

Does this mean that I'm standing on my head? Well I want every scientologist to find out about Neo cheaters neo tech and Biological Immortality, these radical ideas, with the lodgical approach must be the way ahead.

To me and I dont want to seem funny. its like meeting Mr Spock from Star Trek. asking him how Vulcans changed from savages to a lodgical and highly respected Race. I'm sure he'd say Dr Wallaces Neo tech !

I wish you every success. and as a free lance writer in the U.K. I'm at your service .

Mysticism is a disease — an epistemological disease that progressively undermines one's capacity to think, to identify reality, to live competently. Mysticism is also a collective disease that affects everyone who looks toward others, or the group, or the leader for solutions to his or her own problems and responsibilities. The symptoms of mysticism are dishonest communication, out-of-context assertions or attacks, use of non sequiturs, jumbled or nonintegrated thinking and speaking. Those symptoms are most commonly exhibited by neocheating politicians, clergyman, union leaders, media commentators, university professors, entertainment personalities. Such public neocheaters are the Typhoid-Mary spreaders of mysticism. In fact, through the ages, the most virulent spreaders of mysticism have been those neocheaters who wangle respect and values from the value producers of this world.

Mysticism is a disease: a disease that blocks awareness and brings stupidness. But mysticism is also the tool that neocheaters use to justify or rationalize the use of force, fraud, or dishonesty to usurp values from the producers. For example, mysticism is used to create false standards and guilt designed to beguile individuals into surrendering their earned values, power, and happiness.

Mysticism also means keeping the mind open to irrational ideas and then imposing them onto others. ...Mysticism is the fertilizer of deception.

Mysticism is a rebellion against life, effort, and the conscious mind. Mysticism leaves people with sour government faces and is the neocheater's tool for plundering the value producers.

Mysticism is based on a false and destructive idea: the primacy of emotions over reality. ...Mysticism is the opposite of Neo-Tech.

Mysticism is the only disease of the conscious mind. But as with drugs and alcohol, mysticism is seductively comfortable, like a warm, old friend — until the destructive consequences and hangovers manifest themselves.

Neocheating is defined as: Any intentional use of mysticism designed to create false "realities" or illusions in order to extract values from others. Neocheating is the technique for expropriating unearned money or power by manipulating mysticism in others. Neocheating is the means by which politicians, clergymen, union leaders, many journalists, and many academe usurp power and values from the innocent producers.

MYSTICS AND NEOCHEATERS VERSUS NONMYSTICS

Mystics violate morality, for they purposely harm their own and other people's lives. By choosing to evade or fake reality, they undermine their ability to identify and integrate reality, to think clearly, to produce values, to live competitively — to survive. As a result, they increasingly lay responsibilities for their well-beings onto others. Thus, they routinely lay blame or guilt on others for their own problems and failures. ...Everyone must resist, must fight mysticism both from within and from without. Those who surrender — quit resisting, quit fighting — allow mysticism to take over their lives. When that happens, they become a part of the unhappy, dishonest world of mystics and neocheaters.

Wallace K.W. R-6410

I have read numerous books on growth over many years. None have inspired me to the heights that Neo-Tech I-V have done. I had mixed emotions until my second reading and than something took place--like a new awakening - I can honest-ly say, it has given me hope. Not only for myself, but for my fellow-man!

It seemed a little strange at first, that I would be taking a 180° about face in my thinking. But as time passes, I can now say that I totally agree with Dr. Frank R. Wallace, John Flint and all of the writing and thinking that takes place at the I+O Publishing Company.

Like all good things, we always wonder what took so long in it coming about. As it unfolds, I wondered why I didn't think along these lines years ago. It all seems so basic, and yet, so earthshaking.

To summarize, I wish to thank all of those who took part and are taking part in this great cause. I believe we will see a worldwide change within several years. I definitly want to be part of it.

John S. CB-104

DEAR MR. JOHN FLINT,

    I AM INTERESTED IN ACHIEVING BIOLOGICAL IMMORTALITY FOR MYSELF AND MY LOVE ONES. AFTER READING NEO-TECH I FELT AN ENORMOUS BURDEN LIFTED FROM MY LIFE. NEVER HAD I THOUGHT THAT MISCONCEPTIONS DERIVING FROM OUR PRESENT EDUCATION SYSTEM, GOVERNMENT ECT. WOULD HAVE SUCH A DETREMENTAL EFFECT ON MYSELF AND COUNTLESS OTHERS. THANKS TO DR FRANK WALLACE AND HIS CONSTITUENTS MY VERY EXISTANCE AND DESTINY ARE CRYSTAL CLEAR TO ME NOW. NEO-TECH IS BY EVERY SENCE OF THE WORD A MASTER PIECE AND IS DESPERETLY NEEDED BY EVERY ONE. MANY OF US ARE MERELY SCRATCHING ON THE SURFACE OF OUR CAPABILITIES BUT NEO-TECH WILL ENABLE US TO UNLEASE EVERY RESTRICTION THAT HAS BEEN HOLDING MANY OF US BACK FROM AQUARING ALL THAT IS NECCESSARY FOR US TO BE HAPPY. IN CLOSING I WOULD LIKE TO SAY THAT I AM GLAD THAT I EXPOUNDED ON MY INNER SENCE OF CURIOSITY AND ORDERED NEO-TECH.

Mystics and nonmystics can and often do share similar problems, feelings, thoughts, and emotions. The difference is that the nonmystic will (1) take responsibility for his or her own problems and (2) reject the destructive notion that "realities" spun from the mind can replace objective reality. On the other hand, mystics will (1) avoid the responsibility, effort, and honesty needed to identify and integrate reality and (2) use their feelings or imaginations to recreate "new realities". They attempt to fill their desires the "easy", mystical way. But the mystical way is unreal — the hard way that never works.

Mystics make problems where none exist. They focus on the visible symptoms to avoid identifying the hidden mystical source of their problems. They make "realities" out of what they feel, think, wish, or want rather than on what actually is or exists. Thus, they blind themselves to what is happening and become increasingly incompetent. They are irresponsible, immature people. As a result, such mystics and neocheaters cannot achieve or retain the major values of life: genuine prosperity, romantic love, abiding happiness. Mystics avoid the responsibility of a conscious being and, thus, miss the rewards of life.

As pervasively evident throughout TV network news, many involved in media journalism are profoundly dishonest manipulators of mysticism who live by purposely creating problems where none exist. They do that by dishonestly attacking and undermining values to gain unearned power and values. Many are consummate neocheaters who find the media the easiest, most effective format for mass deception.

Neocheaters do more than violate ethics and morality. They constantly try to expand their usurpations of values by manipulating mystical illusions and non sequiturs. Moreover, neocheaters design their illusions to present themselves as the benefactors of society. At the same time, they enviously present the real producers (e.g., aggressively alive entrepreneurs, innovators, business people, industrialists) as the malefactors of society.

But the opposite is true: The neocheaters are the mean, the guilty, the malefactors of society. And the value producers are the compassionate, the innocent, the benefactors of society. Yet, as long as most people allow themselves to accept inversions of truth and mystical illusions, the neocheaters will continue usurping values.

Some neocheaters usurp credibility by exploiting popular causes that sound good — causes that in proper context may be noble if handled honestly. Examples include the environment, nutrition, health, animal rights, human rights, peace. But neocheaters exploit such causes to usurp credibility and power in order to attack competent producers, their honest businesses, and their valuable products. ...The two-headed essence of all mystics and neocheaters is dishonesty and laziness.

Other neocheaters (politicians, clergymen, many journalists and academe) survive by attacking values, businesses, producers, and earned profits as enemies. They attack by making those who create genuine values for others appear as guilty and wrong. Simultaneously, they live by promoting

Donald R.   R-4444

"Every day acquaintances, authoritorian bureaucrats, manipulated by parents, drained by bosses gypped by merchants, intimiated by pushy or monied people, misled by professional people, stunted by dishonest and incompetent educators, used by friends, abused by strangers, fouled up by bureacrats, fooled by mystics, and hurt by government---"

Yup--I have been "sandbagged" by all of these neocheaters from day one until recently.

Just to know that I was not alone , and that others were in the same situations is a horrible comment on our Western Culture, a culture based on a subtile, and pervasive use of the bicameral mind of man.

Frank R. Wallace, the firms he has organized, the Neo-Tech Research and Writing Center, and allied companies, have supplied the mental tools (detection and solutions) by which the "regular guy", producers and employees from corporate president to garbage man can foil and turn aside the neocheaters: identify them, watch their operations (and best of all) render their "put-ons" harmless. Platonistic philophy has been secretly used by neocheaters for years; Aristotilian philophy has been supressed by neocheaters for centuries.

Thanks to Neo-Tech R. & W Center for its complete "history" of how Dr. Wallace came to realize and understand the "game world of poker" and evil parallels in the world in which we live. The producers, no matter where they are or what they do, are no longer defenseless with the knowledge of Neo-Tech. "Go , go, Neo-Tech.!!!"

ELLIS S.   C-1002

Dear Dr. Wallace,

   Sir, I want to condradulate you and your associates on a fine piece of work. The entire Neo-Tech package is a precise tool for prosperity and power, now and in the future.
   When I first purchased your package, I was shocked at what I read. At that time, I was pretty much into church. Your package had described different people, that I knew, with amazing accuracy. It even described alot about myself and the way I felt about things. But still I had put your information aside because it shook my beliefs.
   Some time later, I picked up your package again. I began reading more with an open mind. I began to understand how and why things happen. I also began to see the truth and honesty in your work.
   During the last several months, I have begun studying your work again (Neo-Tech I-V). I guess, a little older, and a little wiser, I now understand the power behind your work. You have truly created a masterpiece.

mysticism, altruism, external "authority", collectivism as friends. They promote those destructive forces by making them appear innocent and right.

Mysticism is central to the neocheater's ability to thrive by attacking values. For only through mysticism would anyone accept the neocheater's upside-down world of undermining, attacking, and destroying values.

Mystics base their actions on what they feel, wish, want, or imagine rather than on what actually exists right in front of them. That is why neocheaters can easily manipulate mysticism. Neocheaters manipulate mysticism to usurp values earned by others. As a result, the mystics and neocheaters eventually destroy all values of life (earned prosperity, love, and happiness) for themselves and everyone involved with them.

Nonmystics are innocent and moral. They accept the responsibility to think objectively and act consistently to support themselves by producing values for others. With a loyalty to honesty, they act in concert with reality. They are evolved people. They strive to honestly integrate their words and actions with reality, regardless of anyone's dogma, dictates, or opinions. As a result, nonmystics benefit everyone and society.

* * *

The mystic's life is irrational and unhappy with perhaps some scattered islands of rationality and happiness. By contrast, the nonmystic's life is basically rational and happy with perhaps some scattered islands of irrationality and unhappiness. ...On turning to one's inner self, mystics find unhappiness, anxiety, and hatred whereas nonmystics find happiness, equanimity, and love.

CONSCIOUSNESS AND FREE CHOICE

Consciousness allows human beings to escape the automatic controls of nature. At the same time, only through consciousness can a person be subjective and mystical. Thus, only through consciousness, can a person choose to act in discord with nature. Unlike all other animals, conscious beings can choose to act better or worse than their nature to benefit or harm themselves and others. Choosing to deny or contradict nature or reality is mysticism, which is an unnatural, irresponsible abuse of the conscious mind. But, conscious beings can also choose to act better than their nature to gain power and advantages over all else in the universe. Because consciousness allows choices and actions beyond preset nature, only human beings can choose to be honest or deceptive, objective or mystical, responsible or irresponsible, competent or incompetent, striving or lazy, productive or unproductive, beneficial or harmful, noble or evil. ...With consciousness, anyone can choose either alternative at any time.

All other animals have no choice but to automatically respond to nature. They cannot be deceptive, irresponsible, mystical, or purposely harmful to themselves and others. They have no such choices, thus, they bear no responsibility for their actions. ...Animals cannot be mystical, dishonest, or self-destructive.

With consciousness, only human beings can freely choose to live better or worse than their natures.

Dear Dr. Flint,   S. Beebe,   C-108

I purchased the Neo-Tech manuals in early 1984 and to be perfectly honest I had been so steeped in mysticism for 24 years that my main reason for purchasing the Neo-Tech package was to find a get rich - no work method and I had very seriously thought about becoming a preacher (Mystic) up to that point. As a matter of fact, when I first received my information package. I glanced through it and was shocked at so much of what I saw that I threw it in a box and didn't even look at it for over 2 years (two). Shocked is probably an understatement, and I'm not sure if I'm glad of what I did, but I know I couldn't have handled it at that time (it, being the reality expressed in the Neo-Tech package.) I spent 1 long year in 85-86 growing up and learning to face reality (this was at the age of 55) then when I ran across Neo-Tech II - V; I had lost #I, it blew me away because it made things very clear to me, I realized that I had ~~first~~ finally learned to consciously think, and the power that I have recieved for myself in the last few months has been incredible. I have never been happier

Free choice determines the future of all human beings: Through mystical choices, people diminish themselves and their potentials to live happy lives. But through Neo-Tech choices, people reject mystical choices. Thus, in turn, they prosper and live happily, far beyond nature's preset course. In fact, only by choosing the integrated effort of Neo-Tech over the automatic laziness of mysticism can people build lasting prosperity and happiness.

THE KEY CHOICE

The choice between exerting effort or defaulting to laziness determines the course of all important human actions. The three choices constantly confronting every human being are to (1) exert integrated effort, (2) default to camouflaged laziness, or (3) act somewhere in between.

The choice to exert integrated effort or to default to camouflaged laziness is the key choice that determines the character, competence, and future of every human being. That crucial choice must be made by everyone, continually, throughout life. ...That key choice determines the:

1. direction of an infant's life beginning at the first moment of consciousness.
2. development of a child's implicit nascent philosophy which determines that child's developing psychology.
3. development of an adult's implicit and explicit philosophy which develops that person's psychology to determine the quality of his or her life.
4. philosophies that guide entire nations, eras, and civilizations with the resulting cultures, economies, and degrees of enlightenment or darkness.
5. evolvement or regression of human consciousness, power, and prosperity.
6. prosperous survival or eventual destruction of human life on this planet.
7. development or rejection of human biological immortality.

That same basic choice determined the direction of all original philosophers: For example, the key immoral philosophers, Plato and Kant, chose to formulate sweeping, out-of-context abstractions in conjuring up all-encompassing mystical idea systems that were "validated" with brilliantly deceptive inner logic. Thus, their basic choice was a default to laziness. For they chose the neocheater's "shortcut" to unearned power or "greatness" by formulating out-of-context, non-sequitur, "higher-cause" philosophies.

Such specious philosophies are designed to assault the supreme value of the conscious mind. Their negative, attack-oriented "greatness" contrasts sharply to the positive, life-oriented greatness of the key moral philosophers: Aristotle and Rand. For, they chose to exert hard efforts and fully integrated honesty to build full-context, rationally integrated systems of universal value for all people of all times.

Those choosing to live through automatic laziness survive by usurping or attacking values produced by others. Those usurpers and attackers include essentially all politicians and theologians as well as many dishonest professionals, attorneys, psychologists, academe, elitists, journalists, philosophers. Well-known usurpers and attackers of values include

John R. R-1946

The Neo-Tech Concepts are so purely rational that I was shocked when I first read them. Never before had I studied a work so clear and objective as this one. So many times I had begun reading "a great work, by a great author" and found contradictions, denunciations of the human mind, and attacks against free will. What a refreshing change it was for me to read the Neo-Tech information.

As I read, all of my years of confusion began to melt away, and a new sense of freedom and power started growing within me. I read several of the recommended books and then reread Neo-Tech. Finally, I realized that I was, in a sense, starting over again. Using the knowledge from these pro-life sources, I was becoming reintegrated with my true, rational self. I was reviving my long, lost ego that had been trampled and torn by many years of denial and sacrifice. I began to see that I had been wickedly deceived by government, schools and teachers, parents and siblings, and most of all by the so-called experts of society. I always sensed that I was being deceived in some way, but I had concluded that this deception was just part of the human condition. Thank you, Dr. Wallace for proving my conclusion wrong

Plato, Hitler, Stalin, FDR, the Pope, Al Capone, Pol Pot, Fidel Castro, Ralph Nader, Picasso, Immanuel Kant. By contrast, those who choose to live through integrated effort can thrive by producing or building values for others. Those producers include working people, business people, industrialists, scientists as well as honest professionals, artists, musicians, philosophers. Well-known value producers include Aristotle, Ray Kroc, Henry Ford, Edison, Einstein, Pierre S. du Pont, Andrew Carnegie, Jay Gould, Galileo, Michelangelo, Rachmaninoff, Ayn Rand.

That choice between laziness and effort determines if one becomes a neocheating, unhappy attacker of values or an honest, happy producer of values.

BUSINESS VERSUS MYSTICISM

Business is the profitable development, production, and marketing of values that benefit others. Any and every aspect of business succeeds to the extent that effort, thinking, planning, and action are free of mysticism...or fails to the extent that mysticism is injected into any decision. Business ultimately flourishes in the absence of mysticism or dies in the presence of mysticism. Mysticism is the creating of problems where none exist; business is the solving of problems wherever they exist. Business represents life; mysticism represents death. Mysticism is nonbusiness; business is nonmysticism.

Since the early days of Phoenician commerce, envious mystics and destructive neocheaters have striven to besmirch the value producers and their business enterprises. Legions of pseudo-intellectuals, say-much/do-little underachievers, envious nonproducers, and mystic-manipulating neocheaters, especially in the media and academe, constantly attack businesses and their creators. With specious pejoratives, the attackers imply that business people lack care, humanity, compassion, social concerns. Such implications are opposite the truth. Indeed, only through business and its creators do societies advance and individuals prosper.

Hiding behind their altruistic platitudes, the neocheaters and mystics are the ones who default on productive effort, do not care, and lack humanity, compassion, social concerns. For all they can do is cleverly attack values. And their negative attacks are directed toward undermining those heroic efforts required to produce jobs and values for others. Indeed, the mystics and neocheaters strive desperately to conceal the intellectually superior, universally beneficial, cheerfully benevolent, nonmystical nature of business. For business is the antithesis of mysticism, the epitome of rationality and morality, and the furthest evolvement of human intellect.

Business is the highest evolution of consciousness, responsibility, and morality. No other animal is even remotely able to function on a business level. The essences of business are honesty, responsibility, integration, abstraction, objectivity, long-range planning, effort, discipline, thought, control. Business creates essentially every major human value, ranging from the development of language, mathematics, the arts, and all commercial breakthroughs up to the electronic revolution...and now finally Neo-Tech.

Randy S. M.   R-3912

Dr. Wallace and Associates;

    Since recieving the Neo Tech Information Package(I-V) in November of 1985 I can very honestly state that my life and the lives of my family cannot ever again be the same. Neo Tech is, indeed, THE Discovery which places one squarely into the future. A future undreamed of by me until recently.

    To the uninitiated it must seem incomprehensible that between the black and white covers of "The Neo Tech Discovery" lies more solid, unvarnished truth than all the aisles of any modern book-store.

    Neo Tech has touched virtually every aspect of my life;it has freed me from the guilt foisted by Chritianity (I had renounced the church years before but only the Entelechy removed the residual guilt), it dispelled the doubts I silently held about my own intellectual capabilities, and it has taken Romantic Love and Sex in new and deeper levels of pleasure and satisfaction.

    These benifits and many more personal gains were realized within months of aquiring Neo Tech information, but indeed, the greatest benefits of Neo Tech to any man or woman come with constant study and application of the broader-based principles of Neo Tech. Only by consistently measuring reality against this standard and then integrating Neo Tech values with one's own standards and situations can a person gain the long-range, all-encompassing, multi-dimensional aspect of Neo Tech. Neo Tech has been effective in evaluating employers and prospective employers, in gaining insights in the under-pinnings of the psychology of a competitor or associate, as a rapid sorting mechanism for business opportunities and as a quick-lock guidance systems in dangerous or uncertain situations.

    I am currently using Neo Tech to protect my son from the comprachico-variety neocheater- the public school system. In confronting very fundamental issues involved in the schooling of our eight-year old Third grader we unearthed:one manipulating, coercive school room teacher; one pragmatic non-sequitur-slinging principle and a Neo-Freudian clinical psychologist,who, although he had never even met our son,dismissed his failings in the class-room as a projection of his anger over being deserted by his father (he is my step-son). The supporting cast in this drama includes political-climbing school board members and a remote, apathetic and grossly over-paid administrator. No average parent can successfully tread this labyrinth of Neocheaters--only those armed with titanium-hard NeoTech can identify, isolate and neutralize these mind-killers. Our two sons will grow up armed to the teeth with Neo Tech; they will grow, prosper and live forever into the future with all the advantages that Neo Tech and, when it is released, NeoThink have to offer. And for all of us the day when RIBI releases Biological Immortality.

    Thank-you, Frank R. Wallace, I&O and all who helped bring NeoTech to an otherwise dying planet!

Fittingly, I & O is the first company to successfully introduce a fully integrated system of ideas and values directly into the stream of public thinking and action. That is being done by subjecting Neo-Tech to organized business disciplines in markets far beyond the small, closed circles of elitists and academe.

Without being subject to the intense, disciplined efforts of business and marketing, Neo-Tech would have languished undeveloped, perhaps for centuries, trapped in those small, closed circles of less-evolved, nonbusiness intellectuals. But by applying hard-nosed business disciplines to marketing Neo-Tech ideas, I & O Publishing Company is demonstrating in real life the extraordinary, practical benefits of Neo-Tech to every human being. Marketing Neo-Tech through a high-effort, business structure provides the fastest, most efficient distribution of Neo-Tech advantages to every value producer in this world.

Until now, the most widely circulated system of ideas has been the Bible. But biblical ideas are mystical, dishonest, malevolent, destructive, and for centuries have provided the philosophical ammunition to diminish happiness, drain prosperity, and neocheat productive people on a grand scale. By contrast, Neo-Tech ideas benefit all honest people. Neo-Tech ideas are objective, honest, benevolent, productive. Neo-Tech provides the practical tools to eliminate mysticism and neocheating throughout the world while enhancing prosperity and happiness for everyone. For that reason, life-enhancing Neo-Tech ideas will increasingly replace life-diminishing, biblical or mystical ideas as the source of philosophical standards and values for all honest, productive people — for all people who count.

Business people create values through intellectual efforts involving the widest-range integration of facts and knowledge. Successful, growing businesses always require honest long-term planning combined with constant integration of time with effort. ...Few people have any idea or appreciation of the constant, hard-driving effort and difficult integrations required for an individual to create and maintain value-producing jobs for others.

By contrast, mystics and neocheaters avoid all such long-term, wide-range, integration efforts. Instead, they operate on a dishonest, anti-intellectual level — on spurious, out-of-context terms in attacking producers with force, coercion, false guilt in order to usurp values from them. The master neocheaters gain power by constant destruction of values rather than by production of values. To realize that fact, a person needs only to examine the words of any Hitler, Pope, charismatic politician, network anchorman, high-profile humanities professor, or advanced-degreed underachiever. Their essential words are always in a negative mode or an envious attack mode. They rise in power not by the long, hard, positive efforts that build values but by the quick, glib, negative ploys that undermine the producers and their values. ...That fact becomes obvious on comparing the words of honest business people to neocheating media people.

Mystics and neocheaters are guilty losers who harm everyone. But business people are innocent winners who benefit everyone. Honest

P.S.D.   C-1003, UNITED KINGDOM

Dear Dr Wallace

THANK YOU!

Around 4 to 12 on 14th september 1987 I realised the Possibilty of eternal life (B.I.).

Ignorance exsists only through laziness. at this moment in time MANKIND IS paying the ultimate price for laziness that is death.

AMAZING HOW PEOPLE ACCEPT ILLOGICAL IRRATIONAL DEATH. YET REJECT LOGICAL RATIONAL NEO-TECH.-!

Due to laziness, encoraged greatly by the mystics, that have surrounded me since birth, I find myself unfit physically and with an immature personality. (lack of experiance of life, Lack of disipline, Shyness etc)

But my conciousness had developed to the Level where I could accept NEO-TECH instantly.

Douglas P.   R-2123

The greatest discovery to benefit all of Mankind forever!

business people do not even know how to think, much less talk or operate in the destructive, out-of-context, envious attack modes of mystics and neocheaters. Instead, such business people cheerfully focus on reality — on benefiting others by creating and trading values. But, without Neo-Tech, those business people are unable to protect themselves from the neocheaters' destructive ideas and actions.

Master neocheaters rise above others without earning their way — without exerting the long-term, hard integration efforts needed to build values for others. By nature, neocheaters are unproductive, hostile, immoral, guilty and without power, once exposed. By contrast, business people are productive, benevolent, moral, innocent — and the only source of genuine power and prosperity in the universe.

Two worlds exist: One world is that of the mystics, neocheaters, master mystics, and master neocheaters. That unhappy, sour world is for the living-dead — for those who choose to (1) detach themselves from reality, (2) remain ignorant of reality and what is actually occurring, (3) survive by usurping values from others. That destructive world consists not only of lethargic mystics but of aggressively active, master neocheaters and their minions or followers. Such neocheaters stage furious but meaningless or destructive activities in their need to appear busy and important to themselves and others. ...The world of mystics and neocheaters is destructive, unhappy, meaningless.

The other world belongs to the producers. That happy, cheerful world is created by individuals who prosper by producing values for others. That purposeful, active world consists of those workers, business people, industrialists, professionals, artists who produce more than they consume. The world of producers is exciting, prosperous, meaningful.

The integrated efforts of producers such as businessmen are directed toward building values for others. In sharp contrast, the efforts of neocheaters are directed toward draining values from others. Their activities are wasteful, manipulative, destructive in everything ranging right up to political summit meetings and papal tours. Those neocheaters include not only politicians and clergymen but the say-much/ do-little academe who conceal their lack of value by constantly flaunting credentials to impress themselves and others. On establishing specious credibility, they extract values from others by promoting spurious ideas that undermine or attack value producers and objective values.

Those two worlds will never meet. For, they are moving in opposite directions: one toward death, the other toward life. Any conscious individual, however, can choose at any time to reject mysticism and exchange the unhappy world of value destroyers for the happy world of value producers. ...The choice is to exist in the dead world of mysticism or the alive world of Neo-Tech.

MAN

The word *man* has two meanings: 1. man meaning a male (gender use), 2. man meaning a human being or mankind (generic use). The English

Jan G.   R-3856,   NEW ZEALAND

I always dreamt of success, to have the things I wanted out of life. I read many self-help, positive thinking type books. And when they didn't work, I thought there must be something wronge with me! I was also a very emotional person, and spent a great deal of time feeling sorry for myself. But I was able to pump up my false ego by reading the tarrot cards, it gave me this invisable power that made me feel special.

Then I sent away for my Neo-Tech package. I didn't know what to expect, but I thought it would involve a 'selling of the soul' experience, along with other preconceived notions.

When I received my Neo-Tech package, I was confused to say the least. I was expecting to be told what to do — from getting out of bed on the right side, to manipulating people for my own profit. I searched the pages for the 'magic words' or instructions — but there was nothing. Instead I was shown how to THINK for myself. WOW!

As I read, it was like looking in a mirror, and I didn't like what I saw. I saw my life for what it was — I was doing 'Nothing' and going 'Nowhere'.

But with the knowledge and the understanding of Neo-Tech, I truly have direction, and a certain self-satisfaction in everything I do. I used to think financial security was what I wanted but now I'm looking forward to financial abundance! And the time to enjoy it!

I always used to say that the world is my oyster. All I have to do is find out how to open it! And Neo-Tech has proven itself to be my opener!

language does not distinguish the words "man, his, him, and he" used in the male gender from those same words used in the neuter or generic sense. Consider "Man and His World": The meaning of "man" and "his" is ambiguous without some clarifying context or explanation. Generic words such as "human being" often cannot be smoothly or appropriately substituted. For example, "Humans and Their World" does not sound right, read well, or retain the same shade of meaning as "Man and His World". Throughout Neo-Tech, the distinction between the generic word and the gender word is clarified by context. Also, throughout Neo-Tech, the often-used phrases "nature of man" or "man's nature" always refer to man in the neuter or generic sense.

While many physiological differences exist between man and woman, the human mind is neuter: No differences exist between man and woman in capacity for intelligence or potential for character.

MAN'S NATURE AND SURVIVAL

The nature of all animals evolves around their survival mechanism. But what is the distinguishing nature of man? He has the ability to think consciously in concepts; no other animal can think consciously or think significantly beyond percepts. Furthermore, man can logically integrate two or more concepts into new and still wider, more abstract concepts. That logical integration of concepts is called reasoning. Man's reasoning ability is his survival mechanism. But unlike all other animals whose survival mechanisms work automatically, man's reasoning mechanism works volitionally. Man must *choose* to exert the effort required to reason. Man undermines or damages his or her reasoning ability by nonuse or misuse of the mind through mysticism or neocheating. At the same time, that mysticism and neocheating always reduces his or her quality of survival, well-being, self-worth, happiness.

Reasoning is the nature of man — the distinguishing nature that elevates the value of man above all other life ...above all else in the universe. Reasoning through logic is man's survival mechanism.

MAN'S BIOLOGICAL NEEDS

The biological needs of all animals are fixed by the nature of the organism. Except for gradual evolutionary changes over many millennia, biological natures and needs remain consistent and unchanged for the primate species, which includes man.

Man is unique among animals: He has a conceptual mind. And a conceptual mind is part of his biological system. Hence, man's biological system not only includes physical needs but also psychological, emotional, and intellectual needs that must be filled to deal competently with reality.

Neo-Tech/Psychuous/Aristotelian actions complement human nature. Thus, they fill human biological needs. But mystical/altruistic/Platonistic actions contradict human nature. Thus, they cannot fill human biological needs. The profound difference between Neo-Tech/Aristotelian thinking and altruistic/Platonistic thinking is indicated in the table on pages xxxix to xlvii.

Michael L. Singapore, C-10

Two weeks after very extensive studying of the manuscript and the accompanying NEO-TECH INSTRUCTIONS with Special Information Packages, I exposed a neocheater and made $2000/- - or rather, recovered this sum of money he had cheated me of previously.
I also made up my mind to stop worshipping in church and realised for the first time what conmen ministers of religion really are!

Reginald O. C-1004

Dear Dr. Wallace -- Dr. Flint and all other Neo-Tech Achievers.

I hate with a purple passion to admit that I have been reamed, steamed and dry cleaned by the mystics, neocheaters and all other creeps. I knew something was wrong but I just couldn't define it until I sent for Neo-Tech. It makes one boiling angry to think that we have spent most of their productive lives in the grips of parasites. We are honest dedicated hard working people and now know how these parasites work to control our every action. The blood suckers thrive on our efforts and talents and do not produce nothing. They are lower than a fishes belly at the bottom of the sea.

U-BET I can recognise them now. I am awake and ready to challenge them at every turn. What a sly, cunning, under-handed way to try and apply their external authority. It makes one fighting mad to know how we have been deceived in the disguise that it is for the good of all mankind.

Dr. Wallace, I was very facinated when I received your first brochure on just how you discovered Neo-Tech through your gambling experiences. I have been a gaming gambler for years and played the game straight and took my chances. What a eye-opener when I got Neo-Tech and especially your first publication Neo-Tech I The Neo-Tech Discovery thru playing poker. I feel I can hold my own in any game now. Thank you very much.

Neo-Tech is the only answer to combat all external authorities and in just a short time we will have ALL the cheaters on the run. There is no way they can compete with us once we know their game and how to get rid of them.

I want all I & O People to know how much I appreciate your very dedicated work for all the suffering people of the world. You are doing a outstanding job and I thank your very deeply from the bottom of my heart.

Very Respectfully Your,

P.S. Yes, you certainly may use this letter if you see fit for any other publications.

MORALS

Since morals and morality require conscious choices, man is the only animal who can be moral or immoral. Thus, man is the only animal who can consciously or purposely make moral choices: to think or not to think, to be mystical or nonmystical, to produce or usurp...to benefit or hurt oneself and others.

The meaning of *moral* in Neo-Tech is simple and direct: Whatever is consciously done to help fill human biological needs is good and moral (e.g., the productive actions of honest people). Whatever is consciously done to harm or prevent the filling of human biological needs is bad and immoral (e.g., the destructive actions of mystics and neocheaters).

Honestly using one's reasoning nature is always beneficial and moral; dishonestly using one's reasoning nature is always harmful and immoral. ...Volitionally harmful acts always arise from mysticism — from dishonesty, rationalizations, evasions, defaults.

Yet, acting on fully integrated honesty (Neo-Tech), not reason itself, is the basic moral act. When Genghis Khan, for example, chose to use reasoning for a specific military move, then in an out-of-context sense, he chose to act morally by protecting himself and his troops (thus filling human biological needs). But in the larger sense of fully integrated honesty, Khan's total actions were grossly immoral in choosing to use aggressive force in becoming a mass murderer (thus negating human biological needs). The highly destructive, irrational immorality of Genghis Khan's overall dictatorial military actions far outweighed any narrow, out-of-context "moral" actions. ...Genghis Khan was enormously evil as were Lincoln, Hitler, Stalin, Mao.

IMMORAL CONCEPTS: ALTRUISM AND SACRIFICE

Genghis Khan an altruist? Stalin and Hitler* too? Yes, they were altruists as were Jesus, Mao, Schweitzer, Nixon, Nader, Pope John Paul, and almost all other professional mystics and neocheaters. And as demonstrated in the Neo-Tech/Psychuous Concepts, all current religions and governments exist through altruism.

The dictionary definition of altruism is: "Uncalculated consideration of, regard for, or devotion to other's interests sometimes in accordance with ethical principle." At first glance, the definition of altruism seems loving, kind, and good. In which case, how could Genghis Khan and Hitler possibly relate to that definition?

---

*Hitler an altruist? He was the ultimate altruist in both word and deed: "The Aryan is not greatest in his mental qualities as such, but in the extent of his willingness to put all his abilities in the service of the community. In him the instinct of self-preservation has reached the noblest form, since he willingly subordinates his own ego to the life of the community and, if the hour demands, even sacrifices it."

Adolph Hitler, "Mein Kampf", translation by R. Manheim, Houghton Mifflin, Boston, 1943, page 297.

Michel A. C-5002, France

After searching through books on positive thinking, success, personnal fulfilment reading biographies of people who succeeded I never found a work as powerful, and disclosure of truth as Neo-Tech. The reading of this manuscript brings me a premotory vision as no man in my surrounding has ever felt.

Thank you to the whole team of Dr Wallace

Don F.   C-1007

Dr. Flint,

I wish to start by thanking you and your team, especially Dr. Wallace for opening my eyes to reality. It was a hard task, but you have succeeded in changing my thinking on a lot of issues.

Let me begin by saying that I have been a student of the Bible for 11 years. Claiming to the protestant and Christian faith, I have taught and spoke at many Christian locations in my local area. I have taught Sunday school classes, preached, wrote lesson on biblical studies, led and directed musicals. As you can plainly see I have been actively involved in my faith. I am also self taught in Greek and biblical syntax.

Having a mind of curiosity and my Neo-Tech book has probably saved my life. I must confess though, at first I found your books very disturbing. It was challenging the very existence of the very God I worshipped. So I didn't take your word for it, I had to do some research for myself. My reading itinerary for the past few months and for next few as well has been a huge load. The information I discovered is what helped me understand the fate of religion and other cults of this world. The hopes I had was falling to the way side. Julian Jaynes book[1] is the book that has really 'opened' my eyes. His book alone did not do it though. It was a combination of many books.

Close examination of altruism reveals that its ethical principle and implications are human sacrifice*. Thus, the altruist accepts as ethical principle that human beings and their values can be sacrificed to others. And those human sacrifices can be made to anyone or for the sake of anything — the gods, the tribe, the ruler, the fatherland, the system, the party, the "good", the poor, the cause...for the sake of enhancing any neocheater's power or prosperity.

All current political and religious systems depend on the principle of altruism...the principle of forced or coerced sacrifice of victims to others. Altruism (as in Biblical mysticism) holds sacrifice as a good in itself, regardless of the means (e.g., force, coercion, fraud, guilt, deception, charisma), regardless of the recipients (e.g., dictators, presidents, popes, theologians, welfare clients), and regardless of the victims (e.g., war dead, taxpayers, business people, value producers).

Sacrifice is the opposite of productivity: Productivity creates values. Sacrifice destroys values. Sacrifice is contrary to human biological nature as demonstrated throughout Neo-Tech. Upholding the ideas of sacrifice or altruism involves accepting the nonreality of mysticism. And accepting such mysticism always requires evasive rationalizations. Indeed, mysticism, altruism, and sacrifice are purposeful reasoning defaults that are always harmful to human beings, thus, are always immoral.

---

*Auguste Comte (1798-1857) was the first philosopher to articulate the ethical principle of altruism as sacrifice. His altruistic ethics held *sacrifice* as the goal of moral actions, regardless of the means, cost, or beneficiary. He projected selflessness and sacrifice as the ultimate good while positing self-interest as the antithesis of that good. (Reference: Comte's "System of Positive Polity", 1877).

But Immanuel Kant (1724-1804) consciously and methodically laid the philosophical groundwork for the concept of altruistic self-sacrifice as a moral principle. Kant used brilliantly orchestrated, highly integrated, philosophical attacks on logic, reason, and the human mind. Kant is among the most destructive of all master neocheaters. His philosophy provides ingenious systems of noncontextual, inner logic that offers beautiful-sounding rationalizations for all violations of individual rights and destructions of values. Kant's works are essential for Fascism, Marxism, and every murderous neocheating regime of the twentieth century: Plato begot Kant, who begot the socialist's philosophical father, Georg Hegel (1770-1831). In turn, Hegel begot Karl Marx and spawned mass-murderers Lenin, Hitler, Mao. And, Plato begot the philosophical father of religio-conservatives — Jean-Jacques Rousseau (1712-1789). In turn, Rousseau spawned equally bloody mass-murderers: Robespierre, Pol Pot, Khomeini. ...All that blood, suffering, and destruction arise entirely through neocheaters manipulating unreal, arbitrary illusions of mysticism.

Stuart D. R-6464

Neo-Tech provided the missing link. Suddenly my life has a new purpose, a driving force and a confidence I never knew I had is slowly developing within me.

Neo-Tech fills me with excitement for the future and the present. It is without doubt the finest purchase I've ever made in my life.

Harold S. E. CB-103

Dr. Flint,

You have created an honest, productive force in this mystical ridden world. Since childhood, I have been using N.T. concepts — unknowingly — to defend myself and loved ones from the value stealers. One of my favorite sayings as I observed the state our world is in is, "I wish I could open up a college that gives a degree in good old 'common sense.'" Well Dr. Flint, you have managed to create a correspondence college that deals in "common sense", and you offer the course in an understandable and readable format called Neo-Tech. A warm, secure feeling pervades my entire person knowing that N.T. is finally linking and consolidating people worldwide; uniting to reorientating the masses and guiding them toward using their own consciousness to think and provide for themselves.

Altruism and sacrifice are rationalized through mysticism. And mysticism is a reasoning default that accepts fake realities or nonrealities such as sacrifice, faith, dogma. Thus, all advocates of altruism are mystics or neocheaters by nature because they accept or manipulate the mystical concepts of sacrifice.

But why do people default on reason? Why do they evade reality to become advocates of altruism who promote sacrifice? Professional advocates of altruism are always, in a direct or indirect way, recipients of the sacrifices they promote. The booty is often unearned power. But the booty may also be or include unearned material goods, glory, adulation, love, respect, pseudo self-esteem, neurotic or psychopathic satisfactions. In any case, professional advocates of altruism depend on the sacrifice of others to fill their material needs, their self-esteem needs, their images of importance, their neurotic wants. In one way or another, all professional altruists are neocheaters who live off the forced or coerced sacrifices of productive people.

In addition, altruism and sacrifice are the vortex of all concepts, ideas, and philosophies that drain productive people of their earned values and happiness. In the long run, altruism and sacrifice fill the needs of no one. Instead, they always end up draining everyone. For that reason, no professional mystic or altruist can be happy or experience psychuous pleasures.

Over the past 2000 years, altruism and sacrifice have destroyed untold values and millions of human lives. As identified by the Neo-Tech/Psychuous concepts, all current governments and major religions exist on the principles of altruism and sacrifice. But Neo-Tech shows: 1. how to negate all neocheaters; 2. how to avoid being victimized by mysticism or sacrificed to altruism; 3. how to forever collapse the 2000-year-old hoax of mysticism and eliminate its symbiotic neocheaters; 4. how to live prosperously, guiltlessly, and happily to the benefit of everyone.

OBJECTIVE REALITY

Although Neo-Tech occasionally uses the words *objective reality*, the word *objective* is unnecessary or tautologous with the word *reality*. For, only one reality exists. And it exists independently of anyone's feelings, thoughts, or perceptions. Reality is reality. Anything else is nonreality or nothing. Still, throughout Neo-Tech, the word *objective* is occasionally used with *reality* to underscore the notion of objective reality as opposed to some subjective or mystical notion of reality. Indeed, notions such as subjective reality, relative reality, true reality, higher reality, or reality for this situation or that situation have no meaning. ...Only reality exists; nothing else exists.

HAPPINESS

Happiness results from dealing competently with reality. Happiness is a state of intellectually knowing and emotionally feeling the following:

C.W.D.   C-95

Dear Dr. Wallace,

I have recently read Neo-Tech I-V and am extremely pleased with it. Having been a long time admirer of Ayn Rand most of what you say is not so startling to me as to others not exposed to "Aristotelian" based philosophy. What you've done is to take the objectivism of Rand and expand on it, and further to organize all this knowledge into easy to assimilate little packets of truths. I'm sure that it will be a great help to me as I begin to internalize the concepts over time. My congratulations on a monumental piece of work, and hopefully this will ~~become I~~ be the genesis of a world-wide philosophical revolution.

Peter N.   R-2262, AUSTRALIA

As to NEO-TECH II, I must congratulate you on the clarity and the excellent presentation of the various concepts and book reviews. I must admit that I have never come across such clear and concise presentation of any subject before and would appreciate additional book reviews, if available. - As to Biological Immortality, I am certainly most interested as a doctor and health practitioner. To counteract the ageing process with an equal renewal process, similar to aerodynamics where lift equals gravity or perhaps orbital velocity overcoming gravity altogether, - is certainly the most exciting goal to aim for.

With very best wishes,

Short-Term Happiness
(Positive or Negative Sources)
The situation is good.
The situation is right.
The situation is of value.

Long-Term Happiness
(Positive Sources Only)
Life is good.
People are good.
Oneself is good.
Oneself is right.
Oneself is of value.
Oneself is growing in a positive direction.
Oneself is producing values needed to live independently.
Oneself is capable of understanding reality.
Oneself is competent to reject mysticism in self and others.
Oneself is worthy of living.

Short-term happiness from positive sources can add to a person's long-range happiness. But short-term pleasures from negative or irrational sources (e.g., drunkenness, drugs, promiscuous sex, prosperity through dishonesty or fraud) can deliver only temporary feelings of power, well-being, and happiness. Then the inescapable consequence of reality will always assert itself, reversing those "good" feelings to yield ever greater unhappiness and anxiety.

Long-term well-being and happiness come *only* from (1) a continuing development and evolvement of one's own mind and character, and (2) one's increasingly accurate knowledge and control of reality and self.

Achieving happiness is the ultimate moral purpose of human life.

MEANINGS OF OTHER IMPORTANT WORDS

To benefit fully from the Neo-Tech/Psychuous Concepts, a person must also understand the connotations of 31 key words. Many people use these words with false, altruistic, mystical, or Platonistic connotations. The following, five-page table contrasts those random, subjective Platonistic connotations to the consistent, objective Aristotelian connotations used throughout Neo-Tech. Those 31 words are:

alphabetical listing

Achievement	Laissez Faire	Reality
Altruism	Life	Reason
Biological Needs	Logic	Romantic Love
Capitalism	Man's Nature	Selfishness
Death	Morality	Selflessness
Egalitarianism	Mysticism	Sensuousness
Freedom	Objectivity	Sex
Government	Politician	Technology
Happiness	Pride	Theologian
Individualism	Producer	Value
	Rationality	

H.S. C-1005

Dear Mr Wallace,

My husband ordered the neo-Tech I-II. As soon as he began to read volume II, he could not stop! Now and then he read me a few phrases aloud and suddenly a TON of guilt fell of my back and cried of relief!!

I have always lived totally selfless in order to be liked, to be accepted. That was my mistake! Result: at 30 years of age I collapsed. From then on I lived like a vegetable, had barely enough strenght to go trough each day. No doctor could ever find anything. Since I read N.T. I dare to be alive again, to laugh, to feel happy!

I did also the almost impossible effort of cutting the rope with our only child, the nearly destruction of our small family.

I am 48 years now and thought I would not make it much longer. Now I feel alive again and will improve all the time. My husband says, it's a miracle. I always felt so damned lonely in the way I lived, honestly, productive and innocent, until I read N.T. It is like meeting humans for the first time in my live. It is like being in a club of people who live and feel like me.

How can I ever thank you Dr Wallace, you Giant genius (and Team).

Yours sincerely,

xxxix

TABLE D-1
CONNOTATIONS OF IMPORTANT WORDS AND EXPRESSIONS
(The meanings of all words in this table are expanded and clarified throughout Neo-Tech)

Key Word	Dictionary Definition*	Dishonest Altruistic-Platonistic Connotations (Used in most of today's literature)	Honest Objective-Aristotelian Connotations (Used in Neo-Tech)
Achievement	(2a) A result brought about by resolve, persistence or endeavor.	The source of hang-ups and unhappiness. Profit-motivated rhetoric of businessmen and work-ethic executives. Requires effort and, therefore, is pleasure depriving. Causes loss of freedom.	The source of self-esteem and long-range happiness. A human necessity and the prime source of man's values. The building block of civilization. The essence of human living.
Altruism	(1) Uncalculated consideration of, regard for, or devotion to others interests sometimes in accordance with an ethical principle.	A benevolent life-style based on selflessness and sacrifice that reflects love and concern for one's fellow man and his needs. Self-sacrificial altruism is the ultimate ethical good.	The philosophy in which sacrifice of self and human values is the good. But altruism or sacrifice always yields a net loss to everyone and denies individuals the chance to live their own lives for their own sakes.
Biological Needs (man)		Basic needs filled existentially by outside forces (e.g., government, society, God).	Basic needs filled from within the individual by the individual.
Capitalism (also see Laissez Faire)	(1) An economic system characterized by private ownership of capital goods and by investments that are determined by private decision rather than by state control. Prices, production and distribution of goods are determined by a free market.	A system of exploitation of the weak by the strong...devoid of love and good will. Capitalism dominates most Western governments. Capitalism, big business, and fascism are synonymous.	Laissez-faire capitalism is the only political system that does not use force. Based entirely on mutually agreed upon exchanges of values. The only system consistent with man's nature and well-being. A system that offers freedom and individual rights to all. A system that permits maximum individual growth while providing maximum benefits for all. Western political systems have pragmatically and improperly used various aspects of capitalism, but no nation has ever tried laissez-faire capitalism.

*The numbers in parentheses below represent the definition number in Websters Third New International Dictionary.

Jerry H.   R-2209

NEO-TECH is without a doubt the most honest and profound concept to which I've ever been exposed. I've just started going over the entire package for a 2nd time and feel as if I'm in a process of "de-brain washing" myself from all the rubish I've had crammed down my throat for 40 years. What a relief! I was so confused before about life in general that I wasn't able to muster an intelligent argument and win against neo-cheaters. While going through the material the first it dawned on me that all my life I had been taught to doubt my own intelligence and look for external guidance. All the while there was a massive conflict, a rebelion going on subconsciously and I always assumed "something was wrong with me"! So here I am, 42 years old, and for the first time in my life I feel that all my dreams are attainable IF I WORK TOWARD THEM. (No small task).

Someone has spent an incredible amount of time reading and thinking to uncover the foundations of NEO-TECH. I want to thank all of you from the bottom of my heart for your great efforts. I think NEO-TECH is about as important as the invention of the wheel.

In closing, my life is in a process of change, I feel as if I'm waking up from a long sleep. I feel a little scared and a little nervous, but I know that to be happy I have to cut the ties that bind me to the neo-cheaters, go out into the world and stand on my own two feet. Thank you again, Dr. Wallace

Jeff C.   R-1686

Clear, Powerful, & Intelligent.

Wyour F.   R-2062, AUSTRALIA

Incredibly Revealing.

TABLE D-1
CONNOTATIONS OF IMPORTANT WORDS AND EXPRESSIONS
(The meanings of all words in this table are expanded and clarified throughout Neo-Tech)

Key Word	Dictionary Definition*	*Dishonest* Altruistic-Platonistic Connotations (Used in most of today's literature)	*Honest* Objective-Aristotelian Connotations (Used in Neo-Tech)
Death	(1) A permanent cessation of all vital functions; the end of life.	A biological necessity for the good of the species. A necessity to give opportunities to younger people.	A biological phenomenon obsoleted by human technology that has advanced beyond the benefits of evolution. Medical abilities to improve life are now superior to the natural processes of nature. Nature's death mechanism in man is now unnecessary and undesirable.
Egalitarianism	(1) A social philosophy advocating the leveling of social, political and economic inequalities. (2) The suppression of all distinctions between individuals and groups.	The highest ideal...the highest moral and social goal for all societies. The leveling of all differences among people and the equal sharing of all property and material goods.	A philosophy that works toward eliminating all individual (and property) rights. Reduces all individuals to the lowest common level. A goal that is destructive to the well-being and happiness of all human beings by depriving them of their biological needs.
Freedom	(1) The absence of necessity, coercion or constraint or from the power of another.	Being free from self-responsibilities.	Being free from initiatory force and fraud (i.e., being free from government, religion, crime).
Government	(1) The act or process of governing; authoritative direction or control.	A necessary power to control people for their own good.	An unnecessary power or force that would vanish in a laissez-faire capitalist political system.

Joseph B.   J-213

Neo-Tech came along at a good time for me (although I desperately needed it 30 years earlier). Neo-Tech offered an intellectually honest, integrated framework on which to organize and clarify many of the ideas that had been arising for me. Subsequently, I explored other home-grown U.S. gurus, wholistic health, the human potential movement, and hard-money economic advisors. For many years I was guided by my belief that I could find a satisfactory accommodation between mysticism and my own intellectual integrity. I willingly suspended judgment enough to look into one ism after another, but I maintained enough intellectual honesty to gradually reject each one as its prospects for delivering what it promised began to diminish in my mind.

In reading Neo-Tech II-V (and concurrently reading or re-reading some of the books discussed in Neo-Tech II) I experienced a crystalization of ideas taking place -- ideas that have been important to me much of my life, but for which I've found little support from people I've associated with, began to link themselves to and become integrated with the structure of ideas developed in Neo-Tech. I began to feel less like an alien on the planet. I also felt an uprising of anger about the negative influences religion and altruistic ideas have had on my life.

As a child I was under heavy pressure from my father and church members to adopt the doctrine and practices of a strict fundamentalist religion. From age 4 on up through the years, I can remember feeling that the religious ideas didn't make sense but were not open to questioning with my father or in the church. The people advocating the religious ideas did not exemplify the kind of intellect or social orientation that I aspired to. But until I was in my teens, I yielded to social pressure and conformed enough to keep the zealots off my back.

Ed P.   C-69

I have been in receipt of the Neo-Tech package for over 4 months now, have read it through & through, which has in turn turned my life upside down, had me spinning end over end forward in great leaps & bounds. Sensational stuff.

TABLE D-1
CONNOTATIONS OF IMPORTANT WORDS AND EXPRESSIONS
(The meanings of all words in this table are expanded and clarified throughout Neo-Tech)

Key Word	Dictionary Definition*	Dishonest Altruistic-Platonistic Connotations (Used in most of today's literature)	Honest Objective-Aristotelian Connotations (Used in Neo-Tech)
Happiness	(1) A state of well-being characterized by relative permanence, by dominantly agreeable emotions ranging in value from mere contentment to deep and intense joy in living and by a natural desire for its continuation.	A feeling of contentment or relief arising from good luck, good fortune, or selfless acts. Happiness is equated with altruism.	A psychological state of knowing that oneself is dealing effectively with reality and morally, satisfying his or her nature. The goal of human life is happiness, which is earned by making rational choices to satisfy one's material, biological, and psychological needs.
Individualism	(1a) The ethical principle that the interests of the individual himself are or ought to be paramount in determination of conduct.	An inconsiderate state of selfishness that should be avoided in self and prevented in others...by force if necessary.	A rational, moral state. A prerequisite for functioning properly and effectively. Required for prosperity, freedom, romantic love, and long-range happiness.
Laissez Faire (also see Capitalism)	(2) A philosophy or practice characterized by a deliberate abstention from direction or interference, especially with individual freedom of choice and action.	A cruel, dog-eat-dog philosophy. An everyone-for-himself social state that must be prevented or eliminated by government control or force in order to make everyone serve the public "good".	Translated from French means, "to let do" or "to let the people do as they choose". The philosophy that is consistently pro-freedom, anti-force, and anti-government oppression. The philosophy that fully acknowledges and respects the individual's right to his own life and property.

Joan P. C-104

>The Neo-Tech mental "tools" have
>added power to the vague concept
>of the "Life Force" concept that
>the well-known artist-philospher,
>George Bernard Shaw, was search-
>ing for before he died. Read (a play)
>please, "Back To Methusela" by him,
>and his preface and epiloque.
>Your Neo-Tech has brought me such
>life that I feel as if I am immortal.
>Is it possible? I have experienced

such a healing as cannot be described in words. And I have experienced a creative flow, a living stream of truth in my inner life and outer life. What more could a human being ask for?
I sure would like to meet other members. Please help me.

I had a sense of humor that was dying. I could feel it slipping away. Neo Tech has brought it back to life in full force. My confidence is spreading to other areas, too. For instance to job confidence, and to romantic areas, hopefully. There is nothing in this world so powerful as the healing force of Neo-Tech. The "mouth responsibility" that I have now is almost void of errors....What an incredible feeling it is to be a winner. I haven't felt that since I was a child.

The charm of children is that they win a lot, regardless of the attempt to defraud and mislead them. They know, as I knew, the difference between the truth and the lies. If they are hardy enough to withstand the "attacks" on their intelligence, they survive, the way I did.

What a fantastic experience it is to be able to love again.
Miraculous is not an exaggeration. No drug in the world could beat Neo-Tech concepts; they are metaphysical, yet they are as solid and strong as steel! And I now feel that I am worth my weight in gold.
To feel the integrating, the connecting, force of Neo-Tech is to be re-born
Respectfully yours,

Key Word	Dictionary Definition*	Dishonest Altruistic-Platonistic Connotations (Used in most of today's literature)	Honest Objective-Aristotelian Connotations (Used in this book)
Life (Human)	(1b) A principle or force that is considered to underlie the distinctive quality of animate beings.	A means to serve a "higher" good or cause.	An end in itself. Individual consciousness is the highest good and cause in the universe.
Logic	(1c) A science that deals with the canons and criteria of validity in thought. The science of correct reasoning.	An outdated, impotent process for discovering truth. Intuition and mystical routes are superior to man's fallible mind as a means to "truth" and higher "knowledge".	The only route to valid knowledge. The process that each individual must properly use to survive and prosper.
Man's Nature		Designed to be directed by "higher" powers to serve "higher" causes (e.g., mankind, God, country, ruler)	Designed to deal with reality for the rational benefit of the individual. The free and rational individual provides the maximum benefits to self and to mankind.
Morality	(3) Conformity to ideals of right human conduct.	Subjective, variable rules for serving "higher" causes. Can be automatic or inborn.	Objective, consistent rules for filling the individual's biological needs. Always requires a conscious choice.
Mysticism (and religion)	(3a) Vague speculation: a belief without sound basis.	A superior or ultimate form of knowledge from "higher" powers. Based on faith and dogma. "Realities" created from thoughts, feelings, or emotions.	A non entity that has no meaning or existence in reality. The creation of problems where none exist.
Objectivity	(1b2) Existing independent of the mind: relating to an object as it is in itself or as distinguished from consciousness of the subject.	A restrictive condition that demands time and effort at the expense of the "free", subjective world of automatic "knowledge" and willed "reality".	The precondition for honesty, knowledge, and beneficial human actions. That which exists independent of consciousness.
Pride	(1) The quality or state of being proud. A sense of one's own worth. A lofty self-respect.	An undesirable state of vanity, egoism, and conceit. A sinful state.	A desirable human state reflecting self-confidence and pleasure relative to one's productive achievements. Pride is a fuel for further achievement and self-esteem.
Politician	(1) One actively engaged in conducting the business of government.	A public servant who performs a valuable and beneficial service.	A nonproducer who performs specious services that can neither benefit the individual nor, in the long run, fill anyone's objective needs.
Producer	(1) One that produces: esp. one that grows agricultural products or manufactures crude materials into articles of use.	A person who works for "higher" causes.	A person who competitively fills human biological needs.
Rationality	(2) The quality or state of being agreeable to reason.	A forced, unnatural, uncomfortable state of man.	The natural state of man.
Reality	(1) The quality or state of being real.	That which is perceived by the mind...any mind. Reality is a variable that depends on consciousness (subjective "reality").	That which is reality is reality. And only one reality exists. ...Reality exists independently of consciousness. (objective reality).
Reason	(2a) Orderly, sensible thinking.	An outmoded form of thinking. An inferior source of knowledge compared to the automatic "knowledge" received from feelings, intuition, and mystical insights.	The only source of knowledge. Involves the integration of concepts and knowledge with reality. The only route to productive, beneficial actions.

Carolyn D.   J-132

Dear Dr. Wallace:

Needless to say, your Neo Tech Discovery is a major breakthrough for mankind.

We are now in the process of developing a new company in the Atlanta, Georgia area. We are looking forward to the practical application of Neo Tech in our daily, progress and the long range benefits of the standards of capitalism.

Again, Neo Tech is a magnificent human achievement. We sincerely appreciate the priviledge of a progressive and productive commercial business guided by the Neo Tech concepts and future developments.

Robert G. R-4190

I DIDNT KNOW WHAT TO EXPECT WHEN I SENT FOR NEO-TECH DISCOVERY, SOME EASY WAY TO ACHIEVE RICHES I SUPPOSE

WELL I WASNT DISAPOINTED, THE RICHNESS CAME IN A DIFFERENT WAY, A NEW WAY OF THINKING THAT WILL COMFORT ME FOR THE REST OF MY LIFE

Wesley B   C-2

The purity and clarity in the Neo-Tech package, has made it the best ever information that has ever rolled off a Printing Press anywhere in the world today. Heartiest congratulations again to Dr. Frank R. Wallace and the staff of I & O Publishing Co. Keep up the GREAT WORKS.

Key Word	Dictionary Definition*	*Dishonest* Altruistic-Platonistic Connotations (Used in most of today's literature)	*Honest* Objective-Aristotelian Connotations (Used in this book)
Romantic Love	(7a) Characterized by a strong personal sentiment, highly individualized feelings of affection or the idealization of the beloved or the love relationship.	An unrealistic notion based on fantasies and quixotic ideals. An immature relationship for adolescents, premarital lovers, and naive newlyweds.	A serious, sexual-love relationship based on rational values and emotional growth. The most important and valuable of all human relationships. Offers unlimited potential for pleasures and happiness. The complete integration of the mind and body in a love relationship.
Selfishness	(1) A concern for one's own welfare or advantage at the expense of or in disregard of others.	A destructive, immoral state for man. The cause of human suffering. The opposite of love. An inborn human flaw and evil that must be suppressed by forced-backed government or religion.	The desired moral state for man. When in the context of *rational* self-interest, selfishness is man's logical and only means of achieving well-being and happiness for himself and others.
Selflessness	(adj) Having no concern for self.	The desired, moral state of man.	A destructive, immoral state for man.
Sensuousness	*Sensuous*: (3) Producing an agreeable effect on the senses. Conductive to physical comfort or contentment.	An individual's vanity for attractiveness and selfish happiness. Reflects self-pleasure. Projects egotistical sexual attitudes that are socially immature.	The translation of personal pride into physical actions that project the sexuality and attractiveness of one's own body.
Sex	(3) The sphere of interpersonal relationships, especially between male and female most directly associated with, leading up to, or resulting from genital union.	"Playboy" view: An instrument of selfless animalistic fun. Casual, interchangeable, and irrelevant. Religious view: a questionable or negative activity, except for procreation purposes.	The combined physical and psychological inner actions between man and woman for achieving rational pleasures and happiness.
Technology	(2b) The application of scientific knowledge to practical purposes in a particular field.	A major cause of today's problems and misery. The cause of pollution, war, and waste. Should be slowed, stopped, reversed, or eliminated so man can return to nature.	Man's creative outlet for moral actions in improving the quality of human life. The main source of all accumulated human values and the building block of civilization. The route to man's future well-being, happiness, and immortality.
Theologian	A specialist in theology.	A moral person who fills spiritual needs.	A deceptive nonproducer who performs a destructive mystical function that militates against filling objective human needs.
Value	(1) A fair return or equivalent in goods, services or money for something exchanged. (8) Something intrinsically valuable or desirable.	Something relative that can never be defined in absolute terms. A fluid entity that varies from person to person and from culture to culture (e.g., "all values are only relative to a given culture", Eric Fromm, Webster's Third New International Dictionary.)	An entity that is objectively good for the human organism. Objective values are absolutes and include productivity, honesty, justice, self-esteem, psychuous pleasures, psychuous sex, and romantic love.

MYSTICISM HARMS EVERY VALUE
IT TOUCHES — ESPECIALLY LOVE

After attacking values for 2000 years, professional mystics and neocheaters aim their most subtly destructive attacks on value production, romantic love, and happiness: First they undermine the concepts of values, love, and happiness with clever inversions of facts that sound good or valid. Then, for example, they undermine the concept of love by promoting the false idea that totally rational behavior between couples would yield cold, passionless relationships. But the exact opposite is true: Consistently honest, rational behavior offers the greatest capacity for love and passion. By contrast, emotionally reacting, irrational behaviors destroy love and passion.

Successful romantic love requires acting on reality rather than reacting on feelings. Only through fully integrated honesty (Neo-Tech) can one guiltlessly experience the full range of positive emotions and passion. By contrast, mystics act on feelings rather than on reality. That leads them toward incompetent actions that cause them to lose prosperity and romantic love. They experience life with increasing anxiety, unhappiness, deadness.

Neo-Tech demonstrates that professional mystics and neocheaters avoid the honest thought and hard competitive effort needed to produce values desired by others. Instead, they live by faking reality to extract power and values from others through deception, coercion, force. ...Unchecked mysticism destroys all values, especially love and happiness, through arrays of irrational illusions and dishonest actions ranging from chants and poetry to genocide.

NEO-TECH DELIVERS MONEY/POWER/ROMANTIC LOVE

Those who live by fully integrated honesty (Neo-Tech) are by nature sexy, happy, prosperous winners. For they ultimately hold all honest power. Moreover, with Neo-Tech, they hold the supreme aphrodisiac. By contrast, mystics and neocheaters contradict their nature through their laziness, dishonesty, and parasitism. They are unsexy, unhappy, envious losers. Thus, they become increasingly impotent, tired, powerless.

Only through fully integrated honesty (Neo-Tech) can one increasingly earn competence, self-esteem, happiness. ...Through Neo-Tech, one soars to spiralling heights of money/power/romantic love.

MYSTICISM AND NEOCHEATING VANQUISHED

With the discovery of Neo-Tech, all mystics and neocheaters are in the final sentence of the final chapter of their long, destructive history on planet Earth. They are finished forever. But ironically, for the first time in history, all mystics and neocheaters have through Neo-Tech a powerful, invincible tool to purge their own mysticism, to solve their own problems, to evolve into happy, productive human beings. ...Happy days are here for everyone, forever.

THE NEO-TECH DISCOVERY

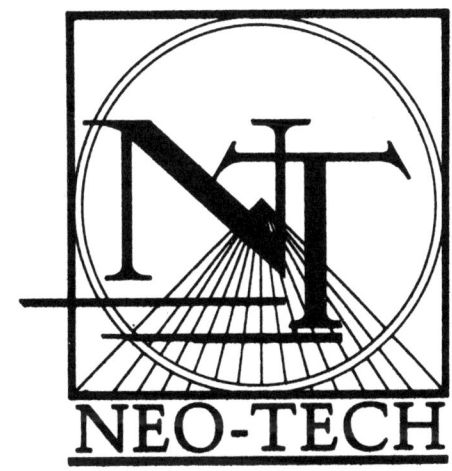

William O. R-8005

Neo-Tech is the ultimate mind expanding intellectual writing of the twentieth century. At first it shocks the reader, especially those entrenched with mysticism. Those who seek the truth overcome and begin the mind healing process. It is true that the mind is a powerful self-healer as Dr. Wallace claims.

I have had the Neo-Tech manuscripts now for just over a year. My life has been profoundly affected in a most positive and healthy way. My thinking processes have become quite clear and many emotional mysteries of my past have become solved due to many hours of introspecting. Religion (Catholicism) is no longer a part of my life or thinking nor are any other forms of mysticism.

As a result of my new found acute awareness of Neo-Tech and the mind's power of consciousness, I have made some profound observances in myself as well as many others. I sense and am aware that there are many stratified layers of consciousness or conscious functioning between bi-cameral animalism and stark awareness of absolute reality. I suspect that for some humans (maybe all) there are limitations to how high one's thinking may experience along the stratification. I am also beginning to see, for myself at least, that I am capable of experiencing many of these "levels" of consiousness in the same day and even from moment to moment.The world functions within split levels of consciousness

My awareness of reality and my ability to think clearly and take guiltless steps in directing my life have soared beyond my wildest expectations. If anyone thinks for one moment that human personalities and character cannot change, they surely haven't yet experienced a Neo-Tech person. A day does not go by without my thoughts turning to Neo-Tech. Each day I heal more and grow stronger. My thoughts, obervations, experiences, and concious awareness are now reaching beyond the bounds of the Neo-Tech Discovery.

Peter B. R-3693

Just amazing — to think that I have been stupid and blind these seventy two years. I cannot find enough words to describe my deepest appreciation to Dr Wallace — no contest — Thanks a million.

Manuscript
for the

NEO-TECH DISCOVERY

Table of Contents	Page #
Preface	i
Introduction	iii
Dissolving the Chains	v
Definitions and Understandings	vii-xlvii
Table of Contents	li
The 114 Neo-Tech Advantages	1-393
Negative Testimonials	396
Appendices	397-400
Listing of the 114 Neo-Tech Advantages	401-403
Notes and Update Addendums	405-407
Index	408-424
Neo-Tech Reference Encyclopedia and the Original Manuscript	425
Neo-Tech, The Business and Goals of I & O	426

Micheal L.   C-54

THE NEO-TECH DISCOVERY IS A WHOLE NEW DISCOVERY OF AN INTELLECTUAL JOURNEY INTO THE FUTURE OF MANKIND.

IT SUPPORTS INDIVIDUAL RIGHTS AND INDIVIDUAL CHOICE, IT ALSO ALLOWS INDIVIDUAL SUCESS AND INDIVIDUAL FAILURE, FOREMOST NEO-TECH ARMS YOU WITH THE TOOLS TO SEEK OUT AND DEFEAT NEOCHEATERS. THREE CHEERS FOR BIOLOGICAL IMMORTALITY AND CAPITALISM.

Rolly O.   C-102

Dear Dr. Flint,

Having Neo Tech I-V is the greatest thing that has ever happened to me in my life time. Barely few weeks after reading Neo Tech I-V, my life style has been greatly transformed from darkness into a 'refined life'. I must confess that each time I read Neo Tech, I always feel very reluctant to keep it down, in fact, Neo Tech is my 'Other-self'.

I am extremely excited at the discoveries, the whole concept is without any blemish, it is very interesting, useful and eye opening after my 26 years slumber. I am greatly impressed. Thanks a lot to Dr. F. Wallace and I & O Publishing Company, Inc. for this great achievement.

Neacheaters and mystics will no longer thrive at my expense.

Victor A.   R-2797

THANKYOU, DR. WALLACE!

YOU SAVED MY MARRIAGE.

THE NEO-TECH/PSYCHUOUS ADVANTAGES

The easiest, quickest way to gain Neo-Tech/Psychuous advantages for prosperity, power, and romantic love is simply to forge ahead: Read all Neo-Tech Advantages in order. Do not make prejudgments. Wait until you have completed all 114 Neo-Tech Advantages. Forget judgments made by others. Do your own thinking; make your own judgments.

Grab the values from those concepts to which you can relate. Put aside temporarily those concepts you are uncertain about or disagree with. By the end of this volume, all the concepts will come together into a clear, harmonious understanding — into a powerful, practical matrix. You will then have integrated control over all competitive situations through the Neo-Tech/Psychuous concepts. You will also know exactly what is happening and exactly what to do. You will forever know how to conquer mysticism in self and others. You will forever know how to quell all neocheaters. You will forever hold the power of unlimited prosperity and romantic love.

* * *

All advantages in this manual are backed by the original Neo-Tech source — the "Neo-Tech Reference Encyclopedia".

Neo-Tech Advantage #1
THE NATURE OF MAN AND WOMAN

Anyone can experience financial prosperity, psychuous pleasures, and long-range happiness by satisfying his or her biological needs (i.e., physical, psychological, emotional, intellectual needs). Psychuous pleasures require the freedom to satisfy one's own healthy needs and to set one's own standards...to live without being obligated to fill someone else's needs or to follow someone else's standards (e.g., standards of spouse, government, church). But in freedom, a person's actions must be rational to be beneficial. Irrational or mystical actions will always diminish a person's well-being and happiness.

Tom G. R-6550

    Neo-Tech is great! I am in the process of my second reading but it has already influenced my thinking, prosperity, and happiness. I have been searching for a philosophy for some years and have tried some off-beat ones such as karate (good for fitness but lots of mysticisim). Religion never impressed me and I had turned to other forms of mysticisim (positive thinking, magick) which only hastened my losing touch with reality. <u>BUT NOT ANYMORE!</u>
    I realize now how I have let others make me feel guilty so they can have their own way. I now analyze everything I see on television and in the movies and read as to Neo-Tech, neocheating, and mysticisim.

    I especially enjoied the ideas on romantic love and have stopped being so shy and will put myself into more situations to meet potential partners. Mouth responsibility also impressed me. I have put myself down humorously for quite some time now due to lack of self-esteem, but realize now that only hurt my self-esteem more.

    Again, I was very impressed with Mr. Wallace's masterpiece and intend to intergrate it into my life. I am still battling some internal mysticisim but have only had one month to undo a lifetime (29 years) of bad learning.

In asking, "What is the nature of man and woman?", a person might also ask, "What is reality?" and "What is required for prosperity, love, and happiness?" Losers will answer from a mystical, Platonistic basis. Winners will answer from a rational, Aristotelian basis:

1. WHAT IS THE NATURE OF MAN AND WOMAN?
Mystical Answer (Platonistic)
Human beings are by nature evil, irrational, and destructive. They are subordinate to "higher" causes. Human beings must be controlled by some higher authority or government and forced to serve others or society.
Factual Answer (Aristotelian)
Human beings are by nature good, rational, and productive (or mankind could not exist). Human beings are competent to fill their needs and to achieve happiness. By being free to act according to their own nature, they will best serve themselves and society without force or coercion from any authority or government.

2. WHAT IS REALITY?
Mystical Answer (Platonistic)
Reality is what the mind thinks or imagines. Wishes, will, or faith can create or alter reality. "True" reality is unknowable.
Factual Answer (Aristotelian)
Reality is what exists. Reality exists independently of anyone's thoughts, desires, will, or wishes. All reality is knowable.

3. WHAT IS REQUIRED FOR PROSPERITY, LOVE, AND HAPPINESS?
Mystical Answer (Platonistic)
Sacrifice, humility, and service to duty are needed for prosperity, love, and happiness in the hereafter.
Factual Answer (Aristotelian)
Productivity, self-esteem, and rational action are needed for prosperity, love, and happiness here on earth.

[Complete answers to the above three questions are developed throughout the Neo-Tech/Psychuous concepts.]

Human beings survive by using their minds rationally to deal with reality. They must know reality to produce the values needed to prosper. Only by being left free to satisfy their nature can human beings serve themselves and others best. ...A future of prosperity and happiness can be secured only by people free and willing to live according to their natures.

Neo-Tech Advantage #2
THE CHILD OF THE PAST
The child of the past exists in every adult. Lost within faded memories, that child keeps searching for a life of adventure, discovery, value, happiness.

The Neo-Tech/Psychuous concepts let the reader turn inward to discover that child. And then the reader can break free from those who are hurting him or her...from those who are wasting his or her time and resources. That child of the past will kindle a new life of adventure, discovery, value, happiness.

John P.   J-161

>   Thank you for showing me how to become a real person at last. Neo-Tech has eliminated whatever doubts or confusion that existed within my own philosophical outlook. I cannot imagine that I shall ever read a more important document and hope soon to introduce my brother to this remarkable discovery.

Kenton C.   R-262

> THE INITIAL READING OF THE INFORMATION IN NEO-TECH HAS SERVED AS AN EFFECTIVE CATALYST FOR PEELING AWAY SUCCESSIVE LAYERS OF PREVIOUSLY UN-QUESTIONED BELIEF SYSTEMS. IT HAS BEGUN TO PRODUCE A SENSATION OF DEEP VITALITY AND ENERGIES THAT WERE EMBEDDED WITHIN ME, BUT WERE DILUTED THROUGH SUBTLE FEELINGS OF GUILT AND INADEQUACY. A POWERFUL TOOL FOR ANY SERIOUS PERSON SEEKING TO FULFILL GOALS OF TRUE HAPPINESS AND WORTH.

Harry H.   C-98

> Words seem inadequate to describe the absolute truths contained in the concepts.

Neo-Tech Advantage #3
CARVING ONE'S OWN DESTINY

While the past is gone forever, it offers valuable experience and reference points that can greatly enhance one's present and future. But many people consume too much time living in the past. Those people often cripple their potential by living and thinking in terms of concrete, past experiences. Thus, they fail to grasp the broader concepts and principles necessary for productive growth into the future. People who live in the concrete past often lose the ability to control their futures. Those who achieve long-range prosperity, happiness, and psychuous pleasures are well aware of the experiences and knowledge gained from their past. But, they live in the present while continuously laying the groundwork for growing into the future.

Rational producers can view their personal futures with confidence in the knowledge that they have the power (via their own rational minds and efforts) to control their own destinies no matter what external variables impinge on them. With the exception of being trapped in an inescapable totalitarian slavery situation*, rational individuals can carve their own destinies while achieving great prosperity, romantic love, and happiness no matter what external forces surround them. Indeed, the rational mind can be more powerful than all those irrational minds that constantly work to diminish everyone's life [Re: Table 7, Neo-Tech Reference Encyclopedia].

The rational mind can also vanquish the destructive effects of religion and the God concept. Likewise, with the rational mind one can spring free from the guilt pushers and free loaders as well as from "friends" and relatives (including parents and nondependent children) who do not offer overall values to one's personal life.

The variables of nature (e.g., weather, tides, earthquakes, hurricanes, floods) can have chance impacts and short-range effects on a person's life. For most productive people, however, natural variables have little or no effect in their long-range lives. Other natural forces such as the faint celestial forces (minute gravitational and electromagnetic forces from planets and from stars beyond our sun) have no effect on anyone's life, except for the illusionary, psychologically damaging effects on those who allow their thinking or

---

*A no-hope, no-escape situation would occur only with total control by master neocheaters. That would mean a Leninist-style, never-ending terror totalitarianism with no hope for change within one's lifetime or no place to escape to freedom. Under such conditions, life for the moral, productive individual would be intolerable, unbearable, and not worth living. The only viable options would be (1) maintaining personal integrity and freedom by surviving without slavery through underground or guerrilla existences, or (2) suicide. [Re: Concept 111, Neo-Tech Reference Encyclopedia].

Louis B.   R-1899

The Concepts contained in Neo Tech contain the most liberating knowledge for the human mind I have read anywhere in my 78 years. This knowledge comes to me a little late, but I shall use it for myself and others for the remainder of my life.

I live in the so-called Bible Belt. It is almost impossible to talk with the people who live in this area about how they are being fooled and swindled by their ministers and churches. Even those who are more intelligent and better educated will not listen.

G.A.H.   R-4438,   UNITED KINGDOM

Before reading Neo-Tech I felt moderately happy, moderately successful and moderately optimistic for the future. Now I know that success involves more than good luck and knowing the "right" people. I feel like I've opened a door into a whole new world of success + happiness. There's so much involved in this - I feel like I've only skimmed the surface and already my life is much more satisfying. Congratulations and thank you to all involved!

actions to be stunted or undermined by immature beliefs such as astrology. [Re: Concept 31 in the Neo-Tech Encyclopedia exposes mystical frauds such as astrology and UFOs. The Encyclopedia also reveals the harmful effects those frauds have on prosperity, romantic love, and long-range happiness.]

Neo-Tech Advantage #4
DOGMA AND RULES ELIMINATED

All Neo-Tech/Psychuous Concepts develop from the three basic elements of human nature — the physical, intellectual, and psychological nature of man and woman [Re: Concept 7, Neo-Tech Reference Encyclopedia]. All individuals are uniquely different with widely variable tastes, desires, personalities, characteristics, and needs. Neo-Tech offers no fixed rules or dogma for any individual to follow.

Neo-Tech deals with principles and concepts. Anyone can choose to use any number of the 114 Neo-Tech/ Psychuous Concepts. Since each of the 114 Concepts developed by Neo-Tech are linked to the basic nature of man and woman, the application of any single concept will deliver certain specific values. The application of each additional concept will deliver additional values. The more Neo-Tech/Psychuous concepts the reader uses, the greater will be his or her prosperity and happiness. To fully utilize any concept, however, an individual must first integrate that concept through one's own mind according to his or her own unique character and values. ...But the unbeatable power of Neo-Tech comes from grasping, integrating, and then using *all* 114 Advantages as one mighty, unbreakable unit.

Neo-Tech Advantage #5
GOOD AND BAD ACTIONS
BLACK AND WHITE MORAL ABSOLUTES

Rational or good actions increase one's prosperity, happiness, and psychuous pleasures. Irrational or bad actions undermine those values. While each individual's life and values are unique, certain basic actions never change in terms of good or bad actions. The rightness or wrongness of those basic actions do not vary according to anyone's opinion, or from person to person, or from generation to generation, or from culture to culture, or from solar system to solar system. Objectively good or bad actions are based on the biological nature of human beings and are definable in absolute terms. But other actions are amoral and cannot be judged in terms of good or bad because they are a matter of personal preference determined by individual differences.

Likewise, objective morals are not based on opinions of the author or anyone else. Objective morals are not created or determined by anyone. No one can deem what is moral and what is not moral. The same moral standards exist for each and every human being throughout all locations, cultures, and ages. Those standards are independent of anyone's opinions or proclamations. ...Natural, black-and-white moral absolutes exist as follows:

Luciano A.   R-2244,   AUSTRALIA

Dr. Wallace,

After reading Neo-tech, something amazing happened to me. I suddenly woke up from a 25 year sleep! All is crystal clear and refreshing. Life now becomes LIFE with capital letters. Neo-tech should be made available to all good productive people. The information within the pages delivers amazing power. I want to get my hands on all of Dr. Wallace's works and all the Neo-tech library. I want to tell everyone that Neo-tech in infinitely the most valuable information ever published. It answers all questions with OBJECTIVE TRUTH not mystical blurb. It is clear and concise. Can't find any faults with neo-tech

Neo-tech is more than priceless —
It IS IMMORTAL!

Thankyou Dr. Wallace
for Neo-tech

A chosen action that is objectively good for the human organism is morally good or right.

A chosen action that is objectively bad for the human organism is morally bad or wrong.

Feelings and emotions, on the other hand, cannot be considered as absolutes or morals. A person's life style, desires, needs, and preferences can vary greatly without altering that person's character or without making that person morally right or wrong. Still, moral absolutes do exist. And following or violating moral absolutes determines a person's character and self-esteem. The two moral absolutes essential for prosperity and happiness are:

1. Integrated honesty for knowing truth and reality
2. Integrated efforts for self-sustaining productivity

Habitually violating either of those two moral absolutes preclude genuine prosperity and happiness. Related to those absolutes are the following moral issues:

Honesty
Self-esteem
Individual rights
* * *
Sacrifice
Use of force
Ends justifying the means

The list below shows how each *moral* issue separates into either a moral, pro-life, pro-individual category or an *immoral*, anti-life, anti-individual category.

Objective morals are based on reality, reason, logic. Subjective "morals", on the other hand, are unreal, random, and based on feelings or wishes. All such unreal "morals" require force, deception, or coercion to impose them on others. Subjectivism, mysticism, existentialism, and "do your own thing" are all attempts to deny objective morals by implying that no standards exist and everything is of equal value (thus denying objective morals and values).

MORAL ISSUES

Moral Issue: Honesty.

Prosperity and Happiness Approach

Conscious striving for self-honesty. Unyielding loyalty to honesty. Productive effort. (Moral)

Failure and Unhappiness Approach

Pragmatic compromise and evasion of honesty. Parasitical laziness. (Immoral)

Patrick B. R-3689

Neo-Tech I-V is some of the most interesting material I have ever read. It has influenced my thinking and attitudes more than anything I can remember. Like a good science book it says 'this is how things are, but don't just believe me, go and see that it is so for yourself!'. So you look, listen, and think, and you realise IT MAKES SENSE.

Neo-Tech is very important to me for two reasons:- Firstly it is information which makes clear sense, which is unusual. Secondly the information in Neo-Tech can be used to measure the logical content of other information and ideas. This latter point, I believe, is the power of Neo-Tech.

R. B.   C-117, AUSTRALIA

I WISH TO CONGRATULATE & THANK DR FRANK WALLACE &
I & O PUBLISHING COMPANY FOR PUTTING TOGETHER AN
UNFORGETTABLE & BRILLIANT PACKAGE OF NEW IDEAS &
KNOWLEDGE, THAT HAS HELPED ME TO BOTH UNDERSTAND
& APPRECIATE THE WORLD IN WHICH WE AS HUMANS COHABIT.
YOUR ATTENTION TO DETAIL & STRENGTH OF PRESENTATION
ARE OUTSTANDING QUALITIES OF THIS EPIC WORK. IT HAS
REALLY MADE A RESURGENCE IN MY QUALITY OF LIFE &
ATTITUDE TO ALL ASPECTS OF LIVING.

Moral Issue: Self-Esteem.

Prosperity and Happiness Approach
Productive and creative actions that increase effectiveness in dealing with reality. (Moral)

Failure and Unhappiness Approach
Nonproductive or destructive actions that diminish effectiveness in dealing with reality, living independently, and using the mind. (Immoral)

Moral Issue: Individual Rights.

Prosperity and Happiness Approach
Recognition of the inalienable right everyone has to his or her own life and property. (Moral)

Failure and Unhappiness Approach
Denial of individual or property rights in order to violate and plunder the life and property of others. (Immoral)

Moral Issue: Sacrifice*.

Prosperity and Happiness Approach
Refusal to sacrifice is by nature life enhancing and thus is morally right. (Moral)

Failure and Unhappiness Approach
Sacrifice is "noble" when done for a "higher" cause or, better yet, no cause. (Immoral)

Moral Issue: Use of Force.

Prosperity and Happiness Approach
Prohibiting the initiation of force, threat of force, coercion, or fraud against any individual for *any* reason is the foundation of morality. (Moral)

Failure and Unhappiness Approach
Use of force (especially government force) is acceptable against individuals, especially if the result serves the social "good" or a "higher" cause. (Immoral)

Moral Issue: Ends Justifying the Means.

Prosperity and Happiness Approach
In regards to force, the ends *never* justify the means. All moral actions are based on principles that prohibit initiatory force, threat of force, coercion, and fraud as a means to accomplish ends, no matter how "noble". (Moral)

Failure and Unhappiness Approach
Ends can justify the means. Force and coercion can be pragmatically used. Individual rights can be violated or sacrificed for the "good" of society or for "noble" ends. (Immoral)

---

*Sacrifice occurs when a value is diminished or destroyed for a lesser value or a nonvalue.

Achous K. C-5001, France

Reading Neo-Tech has enlightened me on the subjects of politics, religion, love and economic problems.

Neo-Tech opens the way to another form of culture and thinking.
It is an essential philosophy to the road to freedom.
The way is opened; one must go forward as fast as possible.

Rodney S. R-2987

Finally free from most of the guilt-producing nonsense learned during my life. I also feel more self-confident and sleep better realizing my true worth.
I now know how to evaluate relationships with other people in any area of my life, but I would like to learn how to effectively deal with the non-producers.

Pat R. C-318

NEO-TECH III is staggering. Easily the most important information I've received in over twenty years. Alone worth many times the cost of the entire NEO-TECH package.

Neo-Tech Advantage #6
ABANDONING THE NEOCHEATERS

All destructive, nonproductive authorities and other neocheaters would become powerless if the producers withdrew their support and cooperation by simply saying "no". If all the victims of neocheaters and mystics said "no", those oppressors would lose their power to plunder and destroy.

Consider this quote from "A Discourse of Voluntary Servitude" by Etienne de la Boétie, written in the 16th Century:

> "The oppressor has nothing more than the power you confer upon him to destroy you. Where has he acquired enough eyes to spy upon you if you do not provide them yourselves? How can he have so many arms to beat you with if he does not borrow them from you? The feet that trample down your cities, where does he get them if they are not your own? How does he have any power over you except through you? How would he dare assail you if he had not cooperation from you?"

Stanley Milgrams in his book "Obedience to Authority", demonstrates through the famous electrical-shock experiments done at Yale that the majority of average, honest citizens will follow authority to do destructive, immoral acts up to the point of injuring, even killing other people. As quoted from Milgrams's book:

> "...ordinary people simply doing their jobs, and without any particular hostility on their part, can become agents in a terrible destructive process. Moreover, even when the destructive effects of their work become patently clear, and they are asked to carry out actions incompatible with fundamental standards of morality, relatively few people have the resources needed to resist authority."

But what is that external authority? It is a myth that has no basis in reality. Such external authority always develops into a destructive machine when the majority unthinkingly or out of fear accept, obey, and follow the commands and wishes of that authority. In reality, no one has any real authority over anyone else. Once that fact is realized, a person can say "no" and break the destructive habit of obedience to the myth of authority. Then the neocheaters would be abandoned by the producers, left to founder with no power to survive.

Felicia C. J-189

This is surely the **best** investment I will ever make. I have to admit I was a little overwhelmed by the lengthy content of Neo Tech II thinking it would take forever to get through all those pages. When my curiosity finally peaked I sat down & began my journey down the road to a successful and fulfilling life - my long range goal.

Three <u>weeks</u> after I opened the first page I finished Neo Tech I-II. Since then I have felt much stronger in all aspects of my life. Right in front of my eyes I have become more assured of myself because I know that I can achieve anything that I want - Neo-Tech has become my "Bible"!

I know I will be referring back to Neo Tech many times in the future.

Neo-Tech Advantage #7
PROSPERITY AND HAPPINESS GOALS

Life is the universal standard to which all people are subject. And **life** — conscious human life — is the standard on which every Neo-Tech/Psychuous Concept is based.

How does the standard of life relate to prosperity and happiness? Human beings must meet specific needs to function at their best (i.e., to function as the living organism is designed to function). Filling those needs produces prosperity, pleasure, and happiness.* The Neo-Tech/Psychuous Concepts provide the knowledge for filling those biological needs — physical, psychological, and intellectual needs. And in filling those biological needs, personal prosperity and happiness become the natural, rational goals of human life.

An important purpose of Neo-Tech is to demonstrate that three requirements for prosperity and happiness always exist: (1) a healthy physical state, (2) a healthy self-esteem or self-love, and (3) an honest, efficacious handling of objective reality in producing maximum values for others. A person can meet all three requirements by using the Neo-Tech concepts in producing values to earn prosperity. But to earn prosperity through productivity requires rational thought and constant effort. ...By nature, a prosperous, happy life is an active, challenging life. [Neo-Tech Advantage #11 provides a self evaluation test to determine if one has oriented his or her life as a value producer or as a value destroyer.]

---

*Throughout Neo-Tech, the words prosperity, pleasure, and happiness are always used in a rational context. For, irrational prosperity or pleasures are based on destructive actions (e.g., profit by fraud, victory by force, success by deceit, drunkenness, sadism). Such actions may provide a transitory sense of well-being or happiness, but can never deliver abiding prosperity, pleasures, or happiness.

Neo-Tech Advantage #8
HAPPINESS TEST

A person sets up prosperity and earns happiness from within. Happiness cannot be taken from the material world or from another person. Happiness depends on genuine self-esteem, which is a product of a person's own life and choices. Happiness is a deeply personal, inner matter. Thus no one can judge another person's happiness by outward appearances alone. A person may be miserable (such as a nonproductive mystic), but project a happy, cheerful, gay appearance. Another person may appear unsmiling, even stern or cross (such as an extremely busy business executive), but if he or she is a productive person with self-esteem, that person will be profoundly happy.

To achieve long-range happiness, an individual must be mentally healthy. Many people, including most psychiatrists and psychologists, erroneously believe that mental health depends on how well a person adapts to the views and opinions of others, the majority, or society. That belief places conformity

Gilbert O. C-70

After being on this earth 57 years, I AM BROKE.... Thanks to Neo-tech, I now know why.

I have been a producer and giver all my life, but have been used by many people, in business and in my personal life. (many under the guise of FRIENDSHIP ????)

Neo-Tech has helped me sort many things out and I have found, after being a person of integrity and honor all my life,- - - I do not have a single friend with tradeable values. It is not easy starting all over again at 57, but thanks to Neo-Tech, I AM starting to do it.....

I NEED MORE OF YOUR WORKS...

John R.   R-1946,   CANADA

Neotech gives the reader a completely different viewpoint and a way to think things through to their ending. Makes you realize that a lot of supposedly worthwhile ventures are truly "worthless". Made me rethink my relationship with my girlfriend and my family. I got the biggest kick out of "Neotech" when attending church (not recommended) and applying it to the sermons and to the reverend's admonitions about standing in the rear of the church. Felt a wee bit like Eric Flame!

Neotech seems weird at first, then obnoxious, then "maybe there's something there" then "definitely something there", and finally "like it or not that's truth and logic carried in its purest form". Entertaining and educational. Really makes you wonder about the so-called "producers", and the real "producers". Perhaps more should have been devoted to "Neotech's" effect on our planet earth.

John K. RP-106

Firstly, I would like to start off by saying how much I have enjoyed, and will continue to enjoy Neo-Tech I-V. When I read my first copy in 1986, at the "tender" age of Twenty, I instantly appreciated, but completely misunderstood the basic message of Neo-Tech and attempted to convince others of the rightness of my new-found philosophy by "preaching" to them about it instead of demonstrating by becoming successfull. Now a scant two years later(two years of pervading poverty and unhappiness) I have reread the material and it is as if I had read it upside-down the first time! Now I understand the message and have begun to rearrange my life. Iwill be attending a Recording school in the Fall and this is the basis of my second point.

as the standard for mental health. But, instead, mental health depends on a loyalty to honesty, *regardless* of the views and opinions of others or one's own feelings. Indeed, the individual must deal honestly with reality to gain the productivity and self-esteem required for quality survival of the mind and body — for prosperity and happiness.

Productivity and self-esteem build on each other. They are not, however, in a cause-and-effect relationship. The **cause** is character evolvement, development, and maturity; the **effect** is both productivity and self-esteem. And that **effect** delivers prosperity and happiness.

The human mind and body, by nature, function harmoniously. But when an individual accepts mystical ideas or takes irrational actions, the mind and body clash and contradict each other (e.g., the acceptance of religion-inspired guilt clashes with the sexual needs and natures of men and women).

With Neo-Tech, one can easily determine the direction that an individual is moving: (a) toward prosperity, happiness, and life, or (b) toward conflict, unhappiness, and death. [Re: Table 3, Neo-Tech Reference Encyclopedia]

Neo-Tech Advantage #9
REWARDS FROM LIFE

Nearly everyone desires the rewards available from life. But, few people achieve those rewards. And people who buy into or promote altruistic, self-sacrificing approaches to life *never* experience those rewards. The main reasons for prosperity limitations and failures are (1) the lack of knowledge and (2) the acceptance of mysticism. But the Neo-Tech/Psychuous concepts provide that knowledge for eliminating mysticism to achieve full-range prosperity and happiness.

Many clichés about prosperity and happiness (from "authorities" and unknowns) sound right and click into people's minds as packages of truth. But those clichés are generally misleading, false, or destructive. For example, the works of Sigmund Freud, Herbert Marcuse, and Wilhelm Reich suggest that sex dominates human life. Their views help promote the false notion that all human life is oriented around sex. While sex is important to life and happiness, such an all-inclusive life orientation around sex is a myth. Life is oriented around the quality survival and well-being of the living organism — not around sex. Survival is man's fundamental **physical** need. And self-esteem is man's fundamental **psychological** need. A person's life is oriented around those physical and psychological needs — not around sex. ...Still, sex plays a major, pervasive role in human life and happiness.

Neo-Tech Advantage #10
THE HIGHEST CAUSE — THE CONSCIOUS INDIVIDUAL

The highest cause in the universe is the well-being and happiness of the human individual. The individual — a minority of one — is the smallest, the

Cyril T.   R-6312

Dear Dr. Flint,

      I own both the Neo-Tech Discovery and The Grand Event Neo-Tech/Neo-Think System. I have lost count of the number of business aids and self-help books that I have purchased and read. But, one day, out of the blue came a leaflet about Neo-Tech and I thought I may as well try this one as well. At first I thought I had purchased another load of rubbish but I persevered and I read it and I re-read it and I listened to the tapes and I re-listened to the tapes and I gradually realised that I had a formula at last that will lead to success where all other efforts have failed ~~Its no~~ good wishing I had it before when it would have made all the difference because the important thing is that I have got it now. What a difference it has made and is making to my whole attitude to business and life. Its in front of me now on the shelf and its keeping me in front of all the Neo-Cheaters. Thanks, old chap, and greetings to all you Neo-Tech people.

      Sincerely,

Donald S.   R-469

I'm glad you published Neo-Tech. I'm glad I had the sense to purchase it

most important, most unprotected of all minorities. If individual and property rights are fully protected, then all rights are protected for everyone — for Blacks, Chicanos, women, factory owners, factory workers, farmers, homosexuals. Rights for minority groups is a meaningless, racist concept. In fact, that concept is a tool used by politicians and other neocheaters to usurp power and unearned values by actually violating the rights of individuals. Only individual rights is a meaningful, valid concept. The following table contrasts the collectivist, anti-individual, neocheating view to the free-individual, Neo-Tech view.

COLLECTIVIST VIEW VS. FREE-INDIVIDUAL VIEW

Collectivist, Neocheating View
(Platonistic Oriented)

- The uncontrolled, free individual is bad and harmful to human life. Morally, the individual must be controlled by external "authorities".

- Group or government force is necessary to control the individual to make him do good.

- The human individual is subordinate to society or to "higher" or "nobler" causes.

- The use of force to compel individuals to comply with the "will" of society is proper.

- The moral purpose of life is self-sacrifice in serving "higher" goals.

- Self-sacrifice is a virtue and morally right.

- Altruism is a prime good.

- Pride is a character flaw.

- Duty to authority is everyone's obligation.

- Service to one's country by conscription is necessary and proper.

- Property belongs to society, the "people", or the government.

- Social science is a valid, valuable science.

- Populations consist of various groups of people, societies, and cultures.

Free-Individual, Neo-Tech View
(Aristotelian Oriented)

- The uncontrolled, free individual is good and beneficial to human life. Morally, the individual must be free and remain free from external "authorities".

George C.   R-6254

   Though I wasn't 100% conscious of it all the time, Neo-Tech is what I have been waiting
for my entire life. I have lived for 39+ years on this planet using many Neo-Tech
concepts to guide me, having read several Ayn Rand books at an early age and taken
them to heart. For Dr. Wallace to do what he has done with the research/books is
very much appreciated, to say the least.
   I owned my own business or businesses for most of my adult life and was successful
in them. But, as has happened to others and as Neo-Tech explains, I allowed myself
to get chewed up and spit out by the mystical, altruistic Neo-Cheating attitudes &
people who, unfortunately, comprise the majority of society (at least right now). I
bear no grudges because I had choices to make all along the way and, as time passed,
I increasingly made those choices that were not good for me. At one point I even
bought into the Neo-Cheating syndrome because I felt like a lone soldier fighting
a much larger army and I got tired of the battle.

Wayne S.   R-6344

If I could say everything I wanted to about Neo Tech, then I would have to write a book.
All I can say here is that without Neo Tech I would never have discovered the truth about the way we think or the way we live, worse I would have 'died'.
YOU NEED NEO TECH, WE ALL NEED NEOTECH

Mike F.   R-1815

Excellent!!! My understanding of life is very different now. I look forward to being a free individual as I have never been before.

- Both the individual and society function best when the individual is free from any group control, government force, or external "authority".

- The human individual is the highest, noblest possible good or cause in the universe.

- The use of initiatory force against any individual for any reason is immoral.

- The moral purpose of life is to achieve rational happiness.

- Self-sacrifice is morally wrong.

- Altruism is a prime evil.

- Pride is the result of moral virtue.

- No one owes duty to anyone or anything except to one's own children (until they can function as independent human beings).

- Service to one's country or to any cause is proper only on a voluntary basis. Any form of conscription is sacrificial slavery and morally wrong.

- Property is an earned entity. Thus, it can morally belong only to individuals (or their businesses) who produced values to earn that property.

- Social science is not a science and has no validity, especially because it denies the individual as the prime entity of human life.

- Populations, societies, and cultures consist of specific individuals.

Neo-Tech Advantage #11
SELF-ESTEEM AND THE ULTIMATE REWARD

Happiness of man and woman is not based on sex or pleasure, but on self-esteem. Self-esteem acquired through honesty and productivity is the requisite for romantic love and psychuous pleasures. Within a romantic-love relationship, psychuous sex adds an intensity to human pleasure unattainable elsewhere in life. Psychuous pleasures are the rewards for day-by-day, rational, productive actions. Psychuous pleasures, financial prosperity, romantic love, and long-range happiness are the rewards of a productive, honest life.

Self-esteem is a person's estimation of his or her self-worth. Self-esteem is based on the ability to live independently, happily, competently. Self-esteem is dependent on one's effectiveness in dealing with reality.

P.M.C. R-6382

Dear Sirs,

Neo-Tech has unearthed a wealth of information which has not reached most of the population.

I have been unable to read Neo-Tech until now because I was trapped in my specialised responsibility on night duty for the past six months. Now that I have gone through the package, I have discovered how badly we have been decieved by those heartless neo-cheaters. What a betrayal by those people who claim to look after our interest. Instead they keep us shackled to the endless misery of dead-end jobs while skilfully clawing back huge chunks of our hard earned wages in one form of tax or another.

Undertaking this vast project, and assembling the material, we owe a huge debt of gratitude to Dr Wallace, Dr Flint and their devoted team — who sacrificed their time to provide us with these new values in order to detect and destroy this menace of neo-cheaters.

        Victor T.   R-2026, ENGLAND

Astonishing. Has made me re-examine my views on accepted dogma. Has opened the door to a whole new way of thinking.

A high level of self-esteem requires a commitment to objectivity and honesty. But objectivity and honesty do not occur automatically. One must constantly work hard to be objective and honest. And one must always work to maintain those qualities or they will slip away.

Self-esteem is that emotion of feeling worthy and competent to live in this world — of feeling in control of life. That feeling depends on having a value-producer orientation or value-destroyer orientation as listed in the following self-evaluation test:

SELF-EVALUATION TEST

Value-Producer Orientation

☐ I earn my livelihood by producing values tradeable in the free market.

☐ I am a student gaining knowledge necessary to become a producer of values tradeable in the free market.

Value-Destroyer Orientation

☐ I do not earn my livelihood by producing tradeable values. I live off of values produced by others.

☐ I am a student learning how to manipulate people and use government, religion, or other forms of mysticism to usurp a livelihood from the producers.

Orientation for Positive Changes

☐ I will stop living as a usurper and learn to become a producer of tradeable values in order to earn my prosperity and achieve happiness.

☐ I will withdraw my support from those neocheaters who through direct or indirect force or coercion live off my efforts.

Neo-Tech Advantage #12
UNJUST CRITICISM AND GUILT

Personal *emotions* comprise an untouchable ownership and privacy. Emotions are subject neither to criticism nor judgment (only *actions* can be criticized or judged as right or wrong). Feelings and emotions can have a rational or irrational basis, but they are never "right" or "wrong". Emotions are spontaneous, automatic reactions that are not in the immediate or direct control of a person. No one ever needs to feel guilty about any emotion.

A person is responsible only for the actions he or she takes. Those *actions* include the words that egress from one's mouth (mouth responsibility: what one chooses to go in and out of the mouth determines a person's

John C. J-165, ENGLAND

The Neo-Tech Information Package, I must say, transcends anything I have ever read. It is a tour-de-force. Apart from anything else, I feel like a totally new person; like pure, fresh blood has been injected into my system. I can now see things differently. Another important aspect of the change, is the realisation that generalised information have been distorted to suit the interests and aspirations of external authority.

Neo-Tech is what humanity needs but, it is important that the right people should have it in the first instance. It is my belief that, if everyone had Neo-Tech and sincerely apply its principles, humanity would know all happiness, and live in harmony ever after.

competence, self-esteem, weight, health, appearance, happiness).

Also, since feelings and emotions are often subjective, making moral judgments of others on the basis of personal feelings or emotions is unsound and unfair. For example, most of the negative-judgment vilifications that neocheaters publicly make (especially neocheating journalists and cartoonists) against such great value producers as Jay Gould, John D. Rockefeller, Howard Hughes, and Aristotle Onassis are based primarily on emotions of resentment and envy. In time, the misinformed public begins to accept the mystical-based cancer seeds, the emotional-based judgments, the big-lie assertions of the media. The public generally accepts the neocheater's assertions, no matter how groundless, dishonest, unjust.

The facts are, however, that individuals like Jay Gould, John D. Rockefeller, and Howard Hughes were moral men of great integrity. And, they were major producers of values. Indeed, they were major benefactors to mankind whose values will live forever as opposed to those quickly-forgotten malefactors who enviously attacked them.

***

Almost all successful businessmen not involved with governments are, by nature, honest in their private and business dealings. Moreover, when those businessmen avoid, evade, even pay off government bureaucrats, politicians, and other neocheaters merely to be left alone in order to keep producing, they are neither dishonest nor immoral. Instead, they are morally trying to protect their capacity to produce values for others. They are meeting their highest responsibility in protecting themselves and others from the immoral force of government parasites and neocheating "authorities" who live through value destruction.

Producers of values neither like nor sanction neocheaters, usurpers, and plunderers. But can honest producers say "no" to the powercrats or neocheaters who threaten them? In the long run, producers can and must say "no". They must refuse every usurping neocheater if they are to survive. Indeed, most businesspersons are innocent heroes struggling to produce values for others despite increasing government coercion, attacks, and usurpations.

Contrary to the efforts of the academia and media to make such businesspersons appear guilty, the facts are the opposite: government powercrats, politicians, bureaucrats, most lawyers, and many of the media journalists and university professors are the guilty ones. For, they are the neocheaters; they are the ones who are destructive, corrupt, dishonest; they are the ones who exist by deception, force, coercion, dishonesty, fraud.

Without governments and their neocheaters, all the corrupt systems of forced regulations, forced mediocrity, fake litigation, destructive taxes, corruption, and wars would not exist. But without the value producers, civilization itself would not exist. Without the producers, all civilization would perish. Or, expressed another way, without mysticism all neocheaters would perish. Everyone else would flourish.

Neil M. R-6337

Since I bought Neo Tech I was unemployed now I own two businesses, have just bought a new house and new car. On those personal achievements I owe much of my success to Neo Tech. However the things that I now want to achieve would be impossible in a normal life span. For this reason biological immortality is so very important to me.

J.V. and B.H. R-3359

Dear Doctor Flint,

We have been studying the Neo Tech Discovery and most of your other products for 2 1/2 years and feel that we are overdue in expressing our gratitude and giving you our comments.

We are a couple in our mid thirties with three young children. We have found the Neo Tech Concepts to be invaluable in our child rearing, romantic relationship and careers. We can now confidantly deal with any person or situation knowing that our guidelines are integrity, the pursuit of happiness and the avoidance of Neocheaters. Tremendous amounts of money and time have been saved by the avoidance of guilt-induced `charitable' donations and so-called. `duty' to one's community.

The Neo Tech writings were particularly gratifying in that neither one of us had previously found religion to be of any value. It is incredibly encouraging to find an oasis of sanity in this mystical world. We are finding evidence of bicameralism at every turn but we are optimistic that I & O Publishing will succeed in its goal of making this world a more rational one.

Mark F. J-752

Like many people I fear death intensely. Sometimes this fear gets the better of me. Before reading Neo Tech, I succombed to the practice of rationalising this fear through various fairytales, particulaly the God concept. It has been my atitude in the past to accept death as a necessity, and pass the thought out of my mind. For the sake of getting on with my productive life, this is something I still do to a certain extent.

I fully accept now that my Bicameral tendancies are not going to save me from departing from this world. All the slogans and Gods in the world cannot help me. One cannot receive assistance from that which does not exist. After digesting Neo Tech, I abandoned all external authorities in favour of the only valid authority – My own consciousness.

Neo-Tech Advantage #13
SENSE OF LIFE

A sense of life is an integral part of everyone's subconscious philosophy and psychology. Every person has a fundamental view or sense of life. While usually existing on a subconscious level, a person's sense of life largely determines his or her major actions. Sense of life falls into two opposite categories:

    1. An objectively rational, self-interest, benevolent, individualistic sense of life that is characterized by:

        a. the knowledge that human achievement is the highest value.

        b. the knowledge that the human mind is competent to know reality.

    2. A mystically irrational, altruistic, malevolent, anti-individual sense of life characterized by:

        a. a belief that non-man-made values (e.g., nature, the universe, the cosmos) and mystical "values" (e.g., God, the State, society) are superior to man-made values.

        b. a belief that the human mind is impotent to know reality.

The altruistic, malevolent sense of life finds virtue in sacrificing real, individual values to unreal, mystical "higher" causes such as God, the fatherland, nature, society. That altruistic, malevolent sense of life keeps one from acting in his or her long-range best interest to achieve power, prosperity, and happiness. Those achievements, by nature, require a rational self-interest, pro-individual sense of life combined with effort and honesty.

Neo-Tech Advantage #14
SELFISH VS. SELFLESS VIEW

Most productive people subconsciously hold a self-love, pro-individual sense of life, but outwardly express various selfless views deemed virtuous by theologians, politicians, much of the media and academia, and other altruistic promoting neocheaters. A major step toward personal prosperity and happiness is to break free from the neocheater's foisted guilt. That guilt-free break is achieved by discovering the moral virtue of one's own rationally selfish, pro-individual sense of life that always benefits self, others, and society to the maximum.

Destructive altruism is easily rejected on identifying that the rationally selfish view is the only benevolent, honest, and beneficial view for human beings. By contrast, the irrational, selfless, altruistic views promoted by neocheaters throughout history are malevolent, dishonest, and harmful to all human beings.

Altruistic selflessness is the prime moral wrong that works to destroy everyone's values, well-being, and happiness. Rational selfishness, on the other hand, is the prime human virtue that objectively benefits everyone and society.

Lazaro J.   C-121

Dear Dr Flint,

After reading Neo-Tech I-V twice, I knew I had to write to you and tell you that Dr. Wallace and you are geniuses, and that your work will go down in history as the dawn of a new chapter in the emancipation of the individual and the true progress of the Human race.

The idea of achieving biological immortality withing our lifetimes, captured all my hopes and expectations of a life long dream of mine.

I do believe that through the efforts of your organization, this will be possible, and I have no words to express my appreciation for all you and Dr Frank R. Wallace are doing for all of us individuals.

Thank you from the bottom of my heart.

Joseph I.   R-901

DEAR DR. FRANK R. WALLACE:

THANK YOU FOR EDUCATING THE INNOCENT PRODUCTIVE MIDDLE CLASS WHO HAVE BEEN DEFRAUDED THROUGHOUT HISTORY.

Neo-Tech Advantage #15
AVOIDING SACRIFICE

An honest producer can outwardly practice altruistic sacrifice, but he does so always at the expense of his own productivity and happiness, while reducing his value to others and society. An altruistic producer is a psychological contradiction. Such a person represents a personal tragedy who is unnecessarily sacrificing to clever neocheaters his or her own efficacy, well-being, and happiness.

On the other hand, professional mystics and neocheaters function by forcing or coercing the producer to sacrifice increasingly larger portions of time, property, and earnings to themselves and other nonproducers. As a result of making "careers" from other people's sacrifices, those value destroyers never learn to exert the honest thought and effort needed to produce tradeable values required to become happy, independent individuals with genuine prosperity and self-esteem. By their defaults, mystics and neocheaters lose the possibility of earning abiding prosperity and happiness, despite their desperate efforts to feign importance, self-worth, well-being, and happiness. ...With Neo-Tech, one cannot only avoid sacrifice, but can smash the facade of all professional mystics and neocheaters.

Neo-Tech Advantage #16
RETAINING HAPPINESS

For two thousand years, altruistic ethics (oriented around the state, society, or God) have been the prime tool of neocheating powercrats (rulers, dictators, politicians, social "intellectuals", theologians). That tool is used to sacrifice the well-being and happiness of producers to various "higher" causes, such as God, the State, society. Those powercrats apply force and coercion to extract their livelihoods from productive individuals. Neocheating powercrats always operate from behind masks of altruistic higher causes such as fighting wars, fighting drugs, fighting depression, fighting inflation, fighting poverty, fighting pollution, fighting nonbelievers, fighting technology, fighting for the common good, fighting for all sorts of "noble" causes. They do this "fighting" with an air of self-righteousness as they extract their livings from the value producers.

Altruistic ethics are always promoted by neocheaters. Those ethics throw into unresolvable contradictions every innocent, productive person who accepts the ethics of sacrifice while at the same time seeking happiness by being productive. That constant ethical contradiction diminishes and can eventually destroy a productive person's capacity for happiness. On the other hand, any productive person can avoid sacrificing his or her growth and happiness to neocheaters by consciously rejecting their false, mystical ethics of altruism and "higher causes".

Dennis R. C-76

It has been about three months now since I have received the Neo-Tech information package (Vols I-V). I must say that it was some of the most interesting reading I have ever done. I have read Neo-Tech II three full times now and I have read some of the concepts many more times. I've considered myself an agnostic for a long time now but now I can honestly say that I am an atheist. Your concepts have indeed changed my life. I am more productive at work and at home and I have gained more respect from the management of the company that I work for. My self esteem has improved a lot. I can't thank you enough.

John L. J-195, CANADA

Even though I have read Neo-Tech only once (to this date) I can see what has happened to me over the last several years. I lost my children, company, everything, through being cheated, and my stupidity. These situations will not be repeated again, thanks to Neo-Tech

James S. R-2630, Singapore

The publication of your Neo-Tech Information Package by Dr. Frank R. Wallace at a time when people all over the world are confused and unable to discern between reality and myth, fact, and fiction, truth and falsehood -- is a real gem and a beacon. It offers us the opportunity to view human personalities from angles few people ever attempt to do. It is like traveling to the untrodden corners of the earth to understand how man evolves and looking at human nature with all its imperfections and flaws, uniqueness.

Neo-Tech Advantage #17
OVERCOMING ALTRUISTIC ETHICS

Neo-Tech defines evil as any action designed to physically, intellectually, or emotionally harm human beings. Such is the evil rooted in altruism and related philosophies of sacrifice. Altruistic-rooted evil is sometimes subtle, but is always pervasive and affects all areas of an individual's well-being and happiness.

All nonvalue, "liberated" approaches to sex arise from an altruistic sacrifice of the personal importance and value of sex. After perhaps initial increases in pleasure and "freedom", the longer-range trend for people "liberated" around such altruistic sacrifices is toward impotence and frigidity. Only after repudiating altruistic sacrifice can people discover their full potential for prosperity, happiness, passion, love.

The most harmful neocheaters operate through government, religion, public education, and dishonest journalism. Such people must always fake self-esteem to justify their destructive existences. They do that by slyly attacking businesses, their products, and those who through heroic efforts create productive jobs for others (a supreme moral virtue). For, by attacking through the bizarre, inverted ethics of altruism, even the most destructive neocheaters can fake a moral superiority over great producers and their works. Indeed, attacking values is the only way those neocheaters can gain a drug-like relief from their anxieties caused by living destructively. They get relief by destroying values. That destruction gives them a sense of power — a faked self-esteem needed to survive — needed to ward off suicide. ...With Neo-Tech, the producers finally have a fumigant to rid their lives of mystics and neocheaters.

Neo-Tech Advantage #18
BENEFITS AND PLEASURES FROM ROMANTIC LOVE

Every relationship can be evaluated in either "good for me" or "bad for me" terms. Love partners, for example, can evaluate their relationship by how much it increases or decreases their well-being and happiness.

A sacrifice-free, romantic-love relationship allows both partners to fill their physical, emotional, and intellectual needs more effectively. That increased efficacy provides major personal benefits and increased pleasures from life. And, over the long term, a person can honestly love only those who deliver benefits and pleasures.

Neo-Tech Advantage #19
RELIGIOUS VS. "PLAYBOY"
VS. PSYCHUOUS VIEW OF SEX AND LOVE

Three basic views of sex and love exist:
1. The religious-procreative view.
2. The recreational-fun-noncommitted view (e.g., the "Playboy" view as partly developed by Hugh Hefner in his *Playboy* magazine).

Douglas S. R-3998

Dear Dr. Wallace;

Thank you for bringing Neo-Tech to the world while there is still time to save it. I have read the Neo-Tech Discovery just once, but already feel benefits from it. I plan to read it again soon.

At first, the Discovery looked like the writings of yet another cult. But, as I read on, the truth began bringing me back to the real world; like going from darkness to daylight. I began to notice a weight being lifted off my shoulders as guilt was leaving me.

Now that I realize I _am_ a worthwhile person, biological immortality does appeal to me. I want to work and create and produce as long as I can. I also look forward to the time when I can have a body that is straight and comfortable and well functioning so I can live a full life and enjoy a romantic love relationship. (The medical profession I have come in contact with is either unwilling or unable to deal with this satisfactorily.) I am angered at how much time has been wasted by listening to the mystics' and praying and waiting for things to get better, and of course, that _way_ they don't!

Thank you once again, Dr. Wallace (and your associates).

Sincerely,

3. The psychuous-sex view as developed by the Neo-Tech/
   Psychuous concepts.

The contradictions and guilt generated by the religious view of sex make psychuous pleasures and romantic love impossible. Today, the guilt caused by the religious view is more cleverly hidden. Still, that subconscious guilt eventually leads to the same loss of pleasure and happiness. An even more devastating loss evolves from performance anxieties caused by the "Playboy" view coupled with the demands to be a "sensuous" person by someone else's standards.

The diminished self-esteem caused by the fun-only "Playboy" view creates anxiety and boredom to steadily diminish sexual pleasures and capacities. That process, if allowed to continue, ends in impotence or frigidity. Much of the impotence in men today is linked to self-esteem problems. Many insecure men who depend on a macho act for pseudo self-esteem collapse into impotence when confronted with healthy, confident, sexually liberated women who see through their act as laughable or childish.

Only the third view, the psychuous-sex view, agrees with human nature and permits growth of abiding, open-ended pleasures and genuine sexual pleasures for both men and women. But most innocent people subconsciously perceive sex through a combination of those three views. The result is various degrees of satisfaction as the negative effects of the religious and "Playboy" views undermine one's natural, healthy view of sex.

Despite the psychological harm the "Playboy" view causes, Hugh Hefner and his *Playboy* magazine contributed greatly to the well-being of men and women by countering the oppressive guilt of religion and control by government. Moreover, the Playboy Corporation provides funds to defend individual rights related to sexual matters through the Playboy Forum and the Playboy Foundation [Re: Concept 122, Neo-Tech Reference Encyclopedia].

Overall, *Playboy* magazine has helped lift sexual guilt and repression from millions of human beings. For *Playboy* magazine recognizes that everyone has the right to live for his or her own pleasures and happiness. That benevolent, guiltless view of life has always left *Playboy* magazine and its founder, Hugh Hefner, open to unjust attack. Such attacks emanate from envious, anti-life people and neocheating organizations seeking unearned power, including most women's-lib organizations such as NOW.

Playboy magazine has made major contributions toward lifting sexual guilt and repression by projecting sex as a healthy, pleasurable activity. But, *Playboy's* values are diminished by its erroneous, "casual-fun" viewpoints on sex, love, and women.

Ironically, even the religious view does not diminish one's self-esteem as much as the "Playboy" view over the long term. For most religions do hold

Nicholas T.   R-5660

DR WALLACE:

I HAVE NOT BEEN AS EXCITED WITH LIFE AFTER READING NEO-TECH II AS I HAVE BEEN SINCE FALLING IN LOVE WITH MY WIFE 14 YEARS AGO. AFTER READING THE CONCEPTS FOR ONLY A FEW DAYS, MY MIND BECAME SO ACTIVE THAT I COULD NOT GET TO SLEEP FOR MORE THAN 4 HOURS A NIGHT AND I ALSO COULDN'T EAT DUE TO CONSTANTLY THINKING OF NEO-TECH II !!

THE POWER AND CONFIDENCE I FEEL IN MYSELF IS UNBELIEVABLE. I CAN LOGICALLY THINK OUT PROBLEMS NOW WITHOUT BEING INTIMIDATED BY THEM. I FEEL THAT I HAVE MATURED MORE IN THE PAST MONTH THAN ALL THE 52 YEARS OF MY PREVIOUS LIFE!

I ALWAYS *HAD* A FEAR OF MEETING NEW PEOPLE BUT NOW I ACTUALLY LOOK FORWARD TO IT. REGARDLESS OF THEIR IMPORTANCE, I FEEL AS THOUGH I'M ON AN EQUAL LEVEL WITH THEM.

I CAN HONESTLY SAY NEO-TECH IS THE ONLY HOPE FOR A TRULY HAPPY & PROSPEROUS FUTURE. THANK YOU FOR OPENING MY EYES

Robert H.   R-1406

My life has never been the same since I became a "Neo-Tech man" 2 yrs. ago. I now possess an inner power, peace of mind, certainty, confidence, positive life-philosophy that I, until 2 yrs. ago, could only dream of. Best of all, I'm still growing, and always will!

sex as serious and important for procreation [Re: Concept 39, Neo-Tech Reference Encyclopedia]. But the overall effect of religion has been to deprive most human beings of happiness and pleasure. They do that through projection of unearned guilt and by wiping out the objective links between morality, pleasure, value, and sex. Indeed, religion has always striven to deprive the human race of not only its material well-being but of its psychological well-being and happiness [Re: Concept 43, Neo-Tech Encyclopedia].

Many potentially rewarding romantic-love situations are needlessly destroyed either by the religious trap of guilt or by the "Playboy" trap of treating sex as an unimportant, casual-fun activity. Only the psychuous view guiltlessly combines the mind and body to allow men and women to fully experience their earned pleasures, love, and happiness.

Neo-Tech Advantage #20
REQUIREMENTS FOR PSYCHUOUS PLEASURES

The requirements for psychuous pleasures depend on human biological needs — on human material, physical, psychological, emotional, and intellectual needs. Since biological needs change only with extremely long-term evolutionary change, the requirements for psychuous pleasures will not basically change for as long as the current human race exists. ...Those requirements for psychuous pleasures are:

Physical

The development of physical awareness is needed to integrate the body, emotions, and intellect into a harmonious human being. Contrary to the erroneous religious and "Playboy" views, no separation or dichotomy exists between the mind and body. For, by nature, the mind and body always function as an integrated whole.

Psychological and Emotional

The development of self-esteem is needed to feel worthy of pleasure, love, happiness.

Intellectual

The development of an efficient, rational mind is needed to produce the desirable, tradeable values required for quality survival.

* * *

The Neo-Tech/Psychuous Concepts throughout this manuscript show how one can meet the above requirements.

Neo-Tech Advantage #21
PSYCHUOUS PLEASURE VS. SENSUOUS BEHAVIOR

Sensuous behavior can increase psychuous pleasures. But since psychuous pleasures involve the whole person in both sexual and nonsexual experiences, those pleasures are *not* dependent on sensuous behavior.

Most individuals can and should increase their sexual attractiveness. But some people reduce their natural sex appeal by faking sensuousness. And

Tyoler B. J-155

I recieved Neo-Tech I & II and they were perhaps the most enlightening books I have ever read. I was shocked, terrified. My whole life was, and is, at stake.

Ken P. J-18

Neo-Tech is giving me an open-ended ever-increasing sense of control of my life and surroundings.

Lloyd W.

I believe as stated in NeoTech V the unmatched virtue of man's most magnificent creation - business.

My life is one of being productive and particularly as I get older and realize my greatest passion - ambition I am self employed and work an average of 12 hours each day but placing priorities where they belong.

disaster results when a psychuously unattractive person (e.g., a nonproducer, neocheater, mystic, or any other destructive person) habitually tries to conceal his or her defaults by faking sensuousness. As that person's unattractive defaults become harder to hide, the demand for a put-on image (e.g., playboy, evangelist, powercrat, jet-setter, machismo) mounts until the image breaks. At that point, the value destroyer's chance for psychuous pleasures and happiness plunge to near zero.

Neo-Tech Advantage #22
PSYCHUOUS EXPERIENCES

The Neo-Tech/Psychuous concepts deliver a rainbow of new, valid ideas that allow a person to dump the mystical ideas of sacrifice and altruism, allowing that person to guiltlessly experience psychuous pleasures and prosperity.

For example, psychuous sex is an intense mind-body experience. Yet, psychuous sex does not always produce intense *physical* reactions. That would be too exhausting, too demanding, and eventually boring. Psychuous-sex intensity is measured by emotional depth and expression...not by overt physical reactions.

Nonproductive people often fake pleasures they cannot experience. But the habitual faking of sexual pleasures will cause a malcontentment with sex that leads to impotence or frigidity.

On the other hand, productive people can experience continuously growing psychuous pleasures, not only from sex but from all rewarding activities, especially work. [Re: Table 4 in Neo-Tech Reference Encyclopedia traces the development of psychuous pleasures from birth.]

Neo-Tech Advantage #23
PSYCHUOUS CAPACITY

Capacity for psychuous sex, the most intense human pleasure, always arises from the same base — from dealing honestly with reality. And that is the same base from which long-range prosperity and happiness arise. Thus, any action that enhances psychuous sex, prosperity, and long-range happiness is good and healthy. Likewise, any action that diminishes psychuous sex, prosperity, and long-range happiness is bad and unhealthy. That "good for me" or "bad for me" standard can be used to classify any action as good or bad, beneficial or harmful, healthy or unhealthy, moral or immoral. [Re: Concept 10, Neo-Tech Reference Encyclopedia; Table 5, The Sexual Quality Test; Table 6, The Sexual Capacity Test.]

Neo-Tech Advantage #24
OTHER BOOKS VS. NEO-TECH

Most people can recall reading inspiring, mind-over-matter, positive-thinking books and articles that offer rules for self-improvement. Generally the inspiration and determination to follow someone else's non-sequitur rules remain for various periods of time...until that person returns to his or her own self and situation.

Frazine F. R-6054

Neo-Tech has helped me to focus the knowledge I had acquired
over the past 50 odd years into a much more usable form.
It has helped greatly in my relationships with all people,
including family members, with whom I must interact. I feel
fortunate that I was made aware of Neo-Tech and acted to
acquire it. Thanks.

Sergio C.   J-144

Neo-Tech has validated some feelings I have long held but seldom shared with anyone.
① That there is virtue in true selfishness since I believe if one seeks lasting rewards through selfishness then one will not harm one's fellowman.
② That the individual is responsible for self.
③ Praying is an abdication of personal responsibility

Edwin M. R-2515

Since reading the manuscript, my life has done a 180 degree turn.
I've come to realize that there are only two types of people on this
planet, PRODUCTIVE INDIVIDUALS and NON-producers.
It is such a great feeling to know that I   have this subtle, but
extremely powerful power in my hands.

Likewise, reading about rules for improving financial, business, or personal situations and the actual improvement of such situations are two different activities. Nevertheless, gaining knowledge through reading is a prerequisite for most productive achievements. Yet, most "self-improvement" books promote altruistic premises and "mind-over-matter" mysticism (e.g., "positive-thinking" approaches) that are self-defeating. By contrast, Neo-Tech operates on provable premises and self-interest ideas that let anyone achieve permanent advantages, prosperity, and happiness.

Specifically, Neo-Tech operates on the premises that the conscious individual is by nature (1) good, (2) the highest value in the universe, and (3) competent to understand and deal with reality. By adopting those premises, one can enjoy guiltless freedom and an immediate advantage over the neocheaters operating through society, government, and religion. ...By adopting those Neo-Tech premises, a person can achieve great prosperity and psychuous happiness.

Neo-Tech Advantage #25
VALUABLE BOOKS

Many recent books about achieving happiness, pleasure, and love contain valid, valuable information. But many of those books are slanted toward gaining approval of the neocheating media and culturally influential pseudo-intellectuals. Many authors struggle to gain approval of the neocheaters by maligning material achievements and disparaging the potency of the human mind. One must know how to dismiss that "striving for approval" approach in order to glean any useful knowledge and values from those books.

But many books can be more damaging than helpful to readers because their authors project major psychological, philosophical, and even physiological errors. Those errors are often subtle and remain undetected by most readers. [Eight of the best selling "sensuous" sex manuals are summarized in Table 11 of Neo-Tech Reference Encyclopedia in decreasing order of values. Those books are analyzed in greater detail in Appendix C of the Neo-Tech Reference Encyclopedia. The first two books on that list, for example, have excellent value and are recommended reading as a supplement to the Psychuous concepts. The next three books are of value, but contain various errors that demand dogmatic adherence to the authors' tastes and standards — or else, the authors imply, the reader will be guilty of "unsensuous" behavior. The last two books could be harmful to many readers, even fatal.]

Except for Alex Comfort's "The Joy of Sex" and "More Joy", the popular "how-to-be-sensuous" books are surprisingly limited and puritanical in their views. A number of those books seem, on first glance, to be projecting a free, liberated approach to sex. But on closer examination, they are at times rigid, restricting, dogmatic, reactionary, antisexual, and anti-individualistic.

Gordon R. R-3932, AUSTRALIA

Dear Dr. Wallace,

Thankyou Dr Wallace for the Neo-Tech Discovery and its Revelations.

At last, after 30 years of searching, I believe I have found a source of vital knowledge, information and concepts, that have enabled me to form, the basic foundation for a new begining and direction, in my life.

For me, Neo-Tech has opened my eyes with wonder, as I begin to move from darkness into light and see my life start to fill, with a new purpose and meaning.

True ambition to me, is a profound desire to live a happy, useful and productive life and as a result, be able to contribute something of value to others in our society, which will improve the harmony of the world in which we live, for now and future generations.

Wishing you and all those associated with you, continued progress and development of the Neo-Tech cause, to which I intend to participate, as an individual member of the growing Neo-Tech Army.

John K. B. R-4077

SIR.
THE BEST INVESTMENT I HAVE EVER MADE
I REALLY ENJOYED THE LOGIC BEHIND THE ENTIRE
THING

Some books reflect the authors personal or sexual problems and actually point the way to eventual impotence and frigidity. Major exceptions to such books exist — such as the books by the farsighted pioneer of modern sexuality, Havelock Ellis (1859 – 1939). Also reflecting sexual health rather than sexual problems or hang-ups are the books of Albert Ellis (although his books fail to recognize the crucial importance of value selectivity). Alex Comfort's books, "The Joy of Sex" and "More Joy", and the O'Neills' book, "Open Marriage", also project healthy views recommended for reading as supplements to Psychuous Pleasures.

Because of its title, most people erroneously think "Open Marriage" advocates promiscuity or multi-affairs in marriage. But instead, the opposite is true. In refusing to understand "Open Marriage", the religious mystics remain unknowledgeable. Thus, those mystics are particularly scathing, gossipy, and dishonest in their attacks on the O'Neills and their book. Those dishonest attacks even overwhelmed the O'Neills, causing them to succumb to those value-destroying attacks.

Some books not only harm their readers, but undermine the lives and happiness of those authors who believe and follow their own mystical notions [Re: Table 12, Neo-Tech Reference Encyclopedia]. Authors, however, who do *not* believe their own published advice are so deeply dishonest that they quickly wipe out their own self-esteems.

On the other hand, honest, valid books can greatly benefit the authors as well as their readers. For example, Havelock Ellis (1859 – 1939) delivered liberating and important values to his readers. But also, his honest work gradually freed Havelock himself from the crippling effects of Christian, anti-sexual ethics. Those ethics dominated his youth and left him sexually inept in adulthood. Paralyzed by masturbation terrors, he remained a virgin until the age of thirty-two when he married. During his twenty-five-year marriage to an overt lesbian, Edith Lees, they seldom engaged in sexual intercourse, although each loved the other dearly. With the help of several mistresses, all of whom apparently loved this handsome and compassionate man, Havelock Ellis finally became a competent lover. Well after his fiftieth birthday, Ellis began to greatly enjoy sexual intercourse. In his late sixties, Ellis reached his sexual zenith in becoming a passionate lover of his beloved mistress, Franoise Laffité-Cyon, with whom he achieved great happiness and sexual fulfillment until his death at eighty years of age.

Neo-Tech Advantage #26
HARMFUL BOOKS

Erich Fromm's best selling book, "The Art of Loving", is among the most subtly damaging pieces of literature since the Bible in undermining human well-being and happiness. For the independent-thinking reader seeking knowledge, however, nearly every well-written book, even dishonest and harmful books, can be valuable for extracting new understandings of either positive or negative views. For example, the reader gains valuable knowledge in discovering that Erich Fromm's central (but initially disguised) theme is that "real love" means loving everyone causelessly and equally.

Pierre A. C-5003, France

To read Neo Tech is to render mysticism, neocheaters and politicians.

Neo Tech is really the greatest discovery of the century.

Thanks to you Mr Wallace I have become a completely different man.

Neo Tech has become my reference book that I keep reading without weariness

Mitch W. J-83

Now, I'm on my way to be free and to become the producer that I know that I am. The road ahead is very bright, even though the responsibilities are awesome. We must break the shackles and chains of tradition that for milleniums have crippled the creativity and productivity of man. I only say to you and all those associated with Neo-Tech, & I&O Publishing, "hold on to the torch and never let it go"!

Any discrimination in love is condemned by Fromm as unloving selfishness. That dishonest, egalitarian theme wipes out the objective standards of human values, love, worth, and especially justice.

Fromm's false theme implies that no one has to earn love, value, or worth. If the person is your lover, husband, wife or child, that person should have no more of your love and valuation than a beggar in Calcutta, or a Hitler, or a Charles Manson...they all should be valued and loved equally. In other words, according to Fromm's theme, all human beings, regardless of their earned values or characters, should be diminished until they are equal in value to the lowest, meanest, unhappiest human being on this earth. That same destructive, unjust theme is promoted repeatedly by the Bible in both explicit and implicit terms.

Albert Schweitzer goes a step further in suggesting that one should love all living entities equally. That means a person's love for one's husband, wife, or child should never exceed the love that person could give to a stranger, or to a tree, a blade of grass, a weed. Indeed, certain Asiatic philosophies take still another step in declaring that all nonliving entities must also have equal love. In other words, the love for one's spouse or child should not exceed the love one could feel for a pebble on the beach. ...Such is the meaning of love to the Fromms, the Schweitzers, the Bible, and other neocheating promoters of egalitarianism and altruism.

But an even more malevolent theme has recently developed in the rhetoric and actions of today's neocheating "ecologists" and "environmentalists". They, by using the force of government, place the "well-being" of birds, insects (including mosquitoes), trees, plants, and inanimate "landscapes" *above* the lives, well-being, and happiness of human beings [Re: Concept 101, Neo-Tech Reference Encyclopedia]. Those anti-human themes are extensions of the altruistic philosophy advanced through books such as the Bible and Fromm's "The Art of Loving".

And beyond? What does a future of growing egalitarianism and altruism hold? Constant exposure to the increasing atrocities of altruism and egalitarianism gradually numbs people into silently accepting higher and higher levels of injustice, human suffering, crippling of minds, killing, violence, terrorism. Fewer and fewer people object or even care about those mounting atrocities. Before Neo-Tech, those who consistently upheld individual rights to life and property were fading in both intensity and numbers. In that way, conditions were developing for the ultimate egalitarian end result — an eventual worldwide, Marxist-style or religious-style slaughterhouse. But Neo-Tech is reversing that trend — slowly today, rapidly tomorrow.

The final egalitarian "purification" is always the mass liquidation of human life. That "purification" starts with the exploitation and then sacrifice of the productive middle class and ends with their physical slaughter. Those who live by honest principles, those who uphold freedom and justice, those

Cornelius B.   R-4958, SOUTH AFRICA

Dear Dr. Wallace,

Since receiving and studying Neo-Tech some months ago, I discovered a subconscious awareness of the Neo cheating in everyday life; in religious institutions, government and just about every walk of life. That in itself is invaluable because I can make more accurate decisions concerning my life and react more swiftly in rectifying a negative situation without being afraid or hesitate, in doing so.

After being advised against selling my block of shares by a number of "well to do" business men, I analized my situation trying to determine what is really happening in the market, and after realizing that the market is dishonest and overvalued, I sold my shares and made a good profit, only days before the big crash. Today I can thank Neo-Tech for giving me the ability to see things as they realy are. Before I would have followed advice blindly because of lack of self-confidence and surely would have lost everything.

My life is arranged into a number of projects and I am trying to use the Neo Tech way to improve each. These are, my family life, my career advancement and my intellectual advancement. Every phase of my projects, I approach with truth and honesty, and if I deal with any person or institution and find any Neocheating type, I just disregard any contact with such and look for the contacts that are more in line with the Neo Tech way.

The result? I had more success in achieving and have even seen people change overnight with regard to their attitude towards me.

Maybe I am not yet where I want to be, but having Neo Tech to assist me, I have no doubt that getting there will be so much more worth while.

Thank you for Neo Tech

Jeffery M.   R-5008

This is my first letter to the Neo-Tech folks and it is a pleasure to write. I received my *Neo-Tech Discovery* package late last year. It was quite refreshing and freeing to have many of my life's views so well described. I have always held very strong views on individuality and of capitalism.

Though I had been a mystic, for a number of years, Neo-Tech helped me to reorganize my life's priorities. My view of the universe had been that of a part-time astrologer. Neo-Tech has shed a lot of light on questions unanswered by other mystics. Astrology is no longer a part of my life nor any other mystical nonsense. Nonsense is the best description for that sort of stuff. It was amazing how much mind-trash I had going on! I was especially interested in the romantic love concepts contained in Neo-Tech. That, too, was as a breath of fresh, clean air. I am living a much more satisfied and fulfilling life, thanks largely to Neo-Tech's philosophies.

who love life, those who will not surrender their minds and lives to others, those who produce the most values for others — they, as the best, are eliminated first. The mass destruction of the best, the innocent, the virtuous producer of values has been occurring with increasing intensity in various African and Asian countries. And the same would happen throughout the Western world, including the United States, if altruism and egalitarianism grew to their natural conclusions. ...Neo-Tech will prevent that from happening.

But, only those holding genuine power — the value producers — can cure the disease of altruism. The value producer can stop altruism cold by saying "no" to the sacrificial demands of mystics and neocheaters. Indeed, through Neo-Tech, all value producers can guiltlessly, decisively reject all mysticism, altruism, egalitarianism. When the producer says "no" to the neocheaters, their mystical hoaxes will become powerless and then crumble. Never again can those neocheaters trick or coerce the value producer into supporting them.

The Neo-Tech/Psychuous concepts provide the tools to expunge all professional mystics and neocheaters from our planet forever.

Neo-Tech Advantage #27
MYSTICISM AND DESTRUCTION

All religions and most political systems contradict man's nature because they are based on mysticism and altruism. Those systems require the individual to contradict his or her nature through sacrifice. Under the spell of mysticism, one loses increasing portions of prosperity, life, love, and happiness to various imaginary "higher causes". And such losses are for no real reason except to support those neocheaters who survive by manipulating dishonest, destructive, mystical notions. ...Mysticism and sacrifice contradict the nature and needs of human beings. All mysticism and religion, therefore, work to undermine self-esteem and psychuous pleasures. Such destructive mysticism, in turn, leads to incompetence and unhappiness.

The more an individual surrenders to mysticism, the more that person becomes incompetent and tries to escape reality. For such a person, life increasingly becomes a source of conflict and pain. To the extent that one accepts mysticism is the extent that a person withdraws from life and loses contact with the pleasures that life inherently holds. A unifying characteristic of mystics is their view that (1) life is inherently miserable, unfair, unhappy; and (2) people are inherently bad, harmful, and malevolent to others. Yet, in reality, the opposite is true: (1) Human life is inherently pleasurable, fair, happy; and (2) people are inherently good, beneficial, and benevolent to others. ...All forms of mysticism (from astrology to religion) arise from ignorance, fraud, deceit, and the need to destroy values.

Mysticism is perpetuated by neocheaters who must undermine honesty in order to usurp their livings and pseudo self-esteems through value destruction. Such people must disregard or undermine the "burden of proof" concept. For that concept is the protector of all honesty. The "burden of proof" concept requires that whoever makes an assertion has the burden to

Andrew C., AUSTRALIA

After obtaining a copy of Neo-Tech I, at first, couldn't believe that I had in my hands exactly what I had been looking for. I was overcome by an imense excitement. Reading Neo-Tech ignited my mind and know, my mind is exploding.

Neo-Tech has caused my original ideas to undergo a phenomenal compounding that is still taking place.

Irma N. R-4361

I've enclosed a letter which contains some of my responses to NEO-TECH. Certainly you may publish (in part) whatever seems relevant to your purposes. I trust it will be effectively supportive. There is so MUCH to learn -- and to do. But being on the "winner's side" of the issue is so heartening. It dispels all fears. And if not "all", then let us say, MOST. Certainly the fears that doubt and superstition can play! These ancient deterrents to man's liberty must be the first chains that we must drop. Hooray! They CAN come off. It takes constant vigilance however, certainly after a lifetime of being fodder for the world's successions of CHEATERS. I think I was under the influence, at one time or another, of almost every one of them, not even excluding the CP, and Scientology. The harm these cheaters did would have been fatal but for Neo-Tech and its basic principles coming to the "aid" in the nick of time.

Here's to that "victory" of spirit and body---of PERSON---that can be achieved with the tools of Neo-Tech. Their use, when done consciously, is effective beyond one's fondest dreams. I've seen the "visionaries" flee in horror from me when I asserted my conscious individual perception of issues. I think I've become a kind of social pariah. Well, hooray again! Who needs parasites?

On to a world without contaminated men and women. WHAT WILL THAT WORLD DO WITHOUT ITS TRUE VALUE CREATORS?

supply objective proof before any credibility is granted to that assertion.

People who promote mysticism either ignore the "burden of proof" concept or subvert the concept by passing off non sequiturs or specious rationalizations as "proof". In any case, mysticism by nature is the opposite of honesty, rationality, objectivity, reality, and Neo-Tech.

Neo-Tech Advantage #28
WHO CREATED EXISTENCE

The questions "Who Created Existence" and "Why of the Universe" are ancient, mind-subverting gimmicks of positing invalid, intellectually untenable questions that have no basis in reality. That false-question maneuver has been used by theologians and other mystics for centuries. The gimmick works by taking an invalid or meaningless idea and then cloaking the idea with specious but profound-sounding phraseology. That phraseology is then used as an "intellectual" prop to advance false, irrational concepts or doctrines. Consider, for example, the "Who Created Existence" and the "Why of the Universe" questions so often used by poets and theologians to advance the God or higher-power concept. On closer examination, one realizes that invalid questions such as "who made the universe" are meaningless and unprofound. For this type of infinite-regression question answers nothing and is anti-intellectual. Such a question cannot or need not be answered once one realizes that **existence exists.**

On realizing that by nature existence simply exists, one then realizes that the "Who Created Existence" and "Why of the Universe" questions cannot or need never be answered because no causal explanations are needed for **existence** or the universe. Existence is axiomatic. It just exists; it always has and always will exist. Nothing created it and no other explanation is needed or valid. ...What is the alternative? No alternative is possible or needed, unless one accepts the contradiction that existence does not exist!

Neo-Tech Advantage #29
TECHNIQUES OF MYSTICISM

Books such as Fromm's "The Art of Loving" established the following technique that most of today's popular, mystical-based books use to gain credibility, public acceptance, and salability: Obviously valid facts and concepts are first presented to capture the interest and confidence of the reader [Re: Concept 36, Neo-Tech Reference Encyclopedia]. Those valid concepts are then woven throughout the false, mystical notions to lend an air of validity to the whole work. Essentially all religious and altruistic doctrines depend on similar techniques of using out-of-context facts, non sequiturs, slogans, "truisms", and parables to "validate" their false, specious doctrines.

Cleverly manipulative writers such as Fromm and deceptively manipulative organizations or "modern" churches such as Ron Hubbard's Church of Scientology can be even more dangerous and harmful than the

Randall H. J-124

Dear Mr. Flint: I have been reading and studying Neo-Tech I
and Neo-Tech II for a couple of weeks, and I think it is a
revolutionary philosophy that could change the ruinous course
that countries of the earth are headed toward.

George D. R-3005, CANADA

Absolutely Excellent!!!! It straightened out my mind and increased my income by allowing me to rationally think things out. I can now focus on the matters that count instead of wasting my time trying to figure out things that are immaterial.

Joe C. C-73

I believe Neo-Tech has all of the information one needs to springboard his or hers career by ending all mysticism! I'm 100% interested in achieving biological immortality.

overt, old-time religion or the neurotic, televangelists' born-again approaches. Today, most individuals reject the more obviously vicious, hellfire-and-brimstone aspects of the Bible and "old-time" religion. Still, even the most commonly rejected, blatantly malevolent aspects of the Bible and religions continue to do their damage by infusing subconscious guilt into those trying to live by Judeo-Christian ethics.

Similarly, the news media constantly mislead their audiences by using out-of-context facts and non sequiturs to create stories that seem valid, but are not. In that way, the media mystically manufactures "news" that subtly or overtly attacks objective values and their producers*. Constant exposure to propaganda against objective values and heroic producers leaves people increasingly indifferent toward upholding truth and justice. That mystical-based indifference produces lethargy and ennui not only toward objective values and producers but toward life itself.

By manipulating subjective mysticism with biased reporting, much of today's neocheating media successfully obscure the value of productive individuals and their benevolent power. That constant obscuring of truth undermines everyone's view of great human achievements such as the automobile, supermarkets, and major technological advances. The persistent attacks against objective human values by politicians, theologians, social "intellectuals", and the media gradually diminish the strength, confidence, and happiness of the productive middle class, leaving them increasingly vulnerable for exploitation by the professional mystics and neocheaters.

Using the techniques of Fromm and the media, many current authors of social literature use specious cliches, non sequiturs, concrete-bound specifics taken out of context, rationalizations, and guilt-inducing half-truths to manipulate the middle-class producers into sacrificing their self-interests to an array of "higher" causes. [Table 13 in the Neo-Tech Reference Encyclopedia shows how such mystical-based books harm an individual's well-being and happiness. Table 14 compares techniques used by authors of destructive books to techniques used by authors of books that deliver objective values.]

Neo-Tech Advantage #30
THE GOD CONCEPT — A TOOL OF DESTRUCTION

The God concept and all religions are products of mysticism and altruism. Mysticism is the opposite of reason. Mysticism underlies all volitionally destructive actions. Mysticism undermines the capacity for reasoning,

---

*Despite the dishonesty and hypocrisy widely practiced by much of the news media, no government controls or regulations should ever be placed against the press or the communication media. Moreover, any possible form of control or regulation against any communication (written, visual, or oral,) should be permanently abolished.

John B. J148, England

   I am glad to express the change its teachings have brought to my life. In fact, words are inadequate to describe how every line has affected my life. I am very grateful to both the writer, Mr. Wallace and the I & O establishing Company.

                 Mark B.   R-507

   These books are the most important I've read in my life. I have been used by Neo-cheaters all my life. The new sence of freedom is beyond anything I could have imagined.

                 R. Frank A.   C-206

Dear Mr. Flint:

      I have personally begun to work on the collapsing of mysticism in Canada. Of course I have started this work on myself.

which is the survival tool for all human beings. ...The mystical-oriented mind is the exact opposite of the business-like mind.

For over two-thousand years, the God concept has been the most effective tool of the nonproducers, neocheaters, and mystics for usurping a material and psychological living from the producers. The God concept is such an effective tool because it manipulates major thinking defaults into convenient well-organized packages of specious "truths". Professional nonproducers can with relative ease use various God-concept frauds to deceive or cajole innocent producers into sacrificing their earned values to them, the nonproducers. Most God-concept frauds promote the "virtues" of humility, egalitarianism, selflessness, "higher" causes, and sacrifice. Such specious "virtues" are designed to generate guilt for lowering the self-esteem of producers to the level of the nonproducer. Once burdened with false guilt and humility, the producer will more readily hand over or sacrifice his earned values to the nonproducers.

Throughout history, the many God-concept variations have provided nonproducers and neocheaters with effective tools for extracting a living from the producer*. For survival, nonproducers depend on the producer to sacrifice his or her created or earned values to them. They also extract values through government force (e.g., taxation, wars) and through government coercion (e.g., bureaucratic regulations, antitrust laws, victimless-crime laws). ...All professional mystics and neocheaters rely on the unearned guilt foisted on producers through various altruistic or God-concept hoaxes to extract material and psychological "livings" from those producers.

The God concept, religion, and mysticism are also the tools needed to establish totalitarian dictatorships, including both theistic and "atheistic" dictatorships**. Russia, for example, was the most religious, mystical country in Europe during the early 1900's. That heavy mysticism provided an ideal psychological setup for the acceptance of the most destructively irrational, mystical-based political system — Marxism/Leninism. Acceptance of an irrational, Kantian-based philosophy such as Marxism was needed to negate values and individual rights, to rationalize the enslavement of entire nations, to slaughter millions of human beings for a meaningless, mystical

---

*On a morality scale, most criminals rank several notches above such destructive neocheaters as politicians and theologians. The criminal does not attempt to establish himself as a morally righteous person or palm off his actions as morally good. And most important, the criminal does not use altruism or the God concept to foist guilt on his victims.

**No dictatorship is really atheistic. Various dictatorships only replace one mystical authority called God with another mystical authority called the State. Philosophically they are all equally mystical, destructive, and immoral.

Richard H. C-82

After fifty years of being in the dark (caused by mysticism & neocheaters) I am begining to see the light, thanks to Neo-Tech. Although the fog is clearing now I still have a lot to learn from Neo-Tech. I never realized that there were others that had the same doubts and questions about life as I do.

I first purchased Neo-Tech I-V in 1984. This was when II was titled "Phychuous Sex" (1st copy manuscript #187CE) and now I have purchased the "Neo-Tech Discovery". They are both masterpieces of work, but I must say the "Discovery" is a bit easier to read and understand.

I can never thank you enough for your wonderful blueprint for life. My only regret is that I didn't have this information as I was going through grade school and public school. I know my life would be much different now.

higher "authority" — the state. ...Thus, the God-concept tools of altruism and mysticism are needed not only to establish the murderous religious regimes of an Ayatollah-led Iran but the murderous "atheistic" regimes of a dictator-lead Soviet Union and Red China.

Stalin, Mao, and their neocheating colleagues used various altruistic, God-concept tools to justify slaughtering millions of innocent, middle-class producers in the name of a higher "good". In the "atheistic" regimes, the external "authority" or higher "good" is simply switched from a God-labeled government to a state-labeled government. Both are manipulated through mysticism by neocheaters. The same God-concept dishonesties are used by all neocheaters in all countries to transfer the producers' earned property and values to the nonproducers and value destroyers.

In order to live, the nonproducer must usurp values created by producers. That dependence deprives the usurper of self-esteem, leaving him or her resentful and envious toward producers. Such feelings of worthlessness, resentment, and envy can build until the usurper would subconsciously just as soon be dead. Out of such resentment and envy, that person would like to drag everyone else to the grave with him or her, especially the producers and their values. Indeed, that is what happens when totalitarian leaders assume power. Out of envy and hatred, they eventually destroy themselves and anyone else they can destroy.

Stalin, Hitler, and Mao, for example, were personally responsible for staggering property destruction while systematically slaughtering many millions of innocent, productive human beings. Castro, as another example, publicly stated that he, a man who has never produced or earned values, would like to drop a nuclear bomb on New York City, destroying the greatest concentration of earned, man-made values on this planet. Such mass destruction would help prop his pseudo self-esteem by making him feel important. ...All mass murderers throughout history required the tools of altruism and mysticism to rationalize their purposeful destruction of values and life.

In literature and other forms of communication, dealing with the God concept falls into four categories [Re: Table 15, Neo-Tech Reference Encyclopedia]. The first three categories involve the harmful promotion of the God concept and other mystical frauds. The fourth category involves the beneficial exposé of the God-concept and other mystical frauds. Neo-Tech falls into the fourth category in identifying the route to guiltless prosperity and happiness.

Neo-Tech Advantage #31
ASTROLOGY, UFOS, AND OTHER MYTHS

As with all forms of mysticism, acceptance of myths varying from astrology and UFOs to religion and the God concept cripples a person's thinking process. And a crippled thinking process undermines a person's financial well-being, psychuous pleasures, and long-range happiness.

John P.   R-2998

Neo-Tech has helped me get the confidence I need to become a sales leader in my Insurance Profession.

Better yet, I'm gaining new confidence each day as I work for greater accomplishments, knowledge, & well-being. It helps to re-read sections of the manual to have clearer understanding

Teri R.   R-449, CANADA

THE INFORMATION PACKAGES WERE EXCELLENT. THEY REQUIRED MANY HOURS OF STUDY DUE MAINLY TO MY LIMITED EDUACTION. THE MAGNITUDE OF MY EXCITMENT IS HARD TO DESCRIBE. DAYS CANNOT ARRIVE FAST ENOUGH NOW AND TIME IS SO LIMITED. I HAVE A NEW CONFIDENCE NOW AND WILL STRIVE FOR MY SELF ESTEEM. NEO-TECH ALLOWED ME TO RECENTLY RID MYSELF OF A NEOCHEATER WHO HAD TAKEN ADVANTAGE OF ME TO THE TUNE OF $140,000.00 I FIND THE TECHNIQUE FANTASTIC.
   THANK YOU SO VERY MUCH

Many popular myths depend on proclaimed "scientific" evidence to create illusions of credibility. Astrology devotees promote the "scientific" notion that the infinitesimally faint celestial forces that impinge on human beings affect and even control their minds, actions, behavior, and destiny. As "proof", for example, they state how the gravitational forces of the moon cause the oceanic tides. But facts and logic show that man alone controls his own destiny. And his mind can easily override all the forces of nature combined [Re: Table 7, Concept 22, Neo-Tech Reference Encyclopedia]. Indeed, in a free society, the human mind is a much stronger controller of an individual's future than all the overt, direct forces of nature, government, and religion combined.

A person's own choices, not his environment, control his or her destiny. Except for natural catastrophe or brute-force totalitarianism, the forces of nature and social environment when pitted against the rational human mind have little or no influence over a reasoning individual's long-range future.

For a person to allow his future to be influenced by even the most direct and powerful forces of nature (such as the weather, the wind, the rain) would be to relegate the potency of his or her mind and actions to a low position indeed. But to assert, as astrologers do, that a human being and his mind can be controlled by the faintest forces in nature (the celestial forces from outer space) is to relegate the human being and his mind to a most inept position. To view the human mind as being that feeble or impotent, even though the view may be only subconscious or implicit, undermines a person's confidence and self-esteem. And, more serious is what happens to the confidence and self-esteem of those who let themselves be controlled or influenced by nonexistent forces, such as God.

Many people erroneously believe that the governmental and religious forces that surround them are more powerful than they are. With the destruction that those forces have always inflicted on mankind, such an attitude is understandable, but invalid. Government and religious forces, while always exerting destructive influences, need not be the controlling forces on any individual's present or future. By using the mind and acting on reason, a person can usually avoid or minimize the effect of government and religion on his or her personal self in order to live independently, productively, and happily.

Direct forces of government, religion, or even nature (e.g., floods, tornadoes) can at times have devastating effects on any individual. The government can confiscate or plunder a person's property. The government can jail or kill people. Religion can destroy a person's mind or happiness. The church will also torture and kill masses of innocent people whenever it holds direct political power (e.g., Dark Ages, Inquisitions, Jonestown, Ayatollah Iran, Witch Trials, crusades). But none of those potential or real

Tonye J.M. F-100, FRANCE

After reading and rereading Neo-Tech and all the concepts I realized immediately how much the Neocheaters were stifling me. "Bravo". Wallace is a genius and I admire his enormous work. He deserves all the significant appellations I could add in praise to that of other Neo-Tech owners. My hope now is to protect myself from the Neo Cheaters and live only by the concepts of Neo-Tech.

Down to the Neocheaters

Bruce B. R-3067, AUSTRALIA

IT GIVES ONE A FEELING OF COMPLETE INVULNERABILITY. TO KNOW THAT RELIGIOUS POISON IS NOT GOING TO INFECT YOU. I CAN ONLY FEEL SORROW WHEN I SEE THAT FOOLISH OLD MAN, ALL IN WHITE, KISSING STONE SHRINES AND THE GROUND. HOW BLOODY RIDICULOUS. I ALSO DESPAIR WHEN I SEE THE WASTED ADULATION THAT IS HEAPED ON THE ROYAL FAMILY.

forces basically control human lives or destiny. The human mind, along with the choices made through an individual's life, controls the life and future of a productive person (unless government or religious forces directly cripple or destroy that person).

***

Accepting "scientific" myths such as UFO's (unidentified flying objects from intelligent outer space) will diminish a person's self-esteem and reduce that person's capacity for psychuous pleasures and happiness. As with astrology (and with ESP, PK, and other forms of "scientific" mysticism*), the outer-space UFO advocate must first establish a scientific-sounding base to create an illusion of credibility. A scientific-sounding UFO base is accomplished by taking out of context the valid hypothesis that millions of earth-like planets exist in outer space in which advanced civilizations of living beings have developed technology far beyond our own civilization [Re: F. R. Wallace, "We the Creators of All Heavens and Earths", I & O Publishing]. And many of those civilizations most certainly would be capable of communicating or even journeying across many light years to reach earth. For living beings of such advanced civilizations would have achieved biological immortality long ago.

The above hypotheses are statistically valid and almost certainly factual. From statistical considerations, many millions or billions of earth-like planets with intelligent civilizations do exist throughout the universe. Many of the existing civilizations are undoubtedly far in advance of our own, have achieved biological immortality, and are capable of contacting earth. Yet, logic and statistics dictate that other civilizations, even though capable, would not contact earth.

The main reason for believing that no outside civilization has ever contacted earth is that no one has ever found hard evidence that even suggests intelligent beings from outer space have ever contacted earth. All claims of evidence to date have been spurious, false, or scientifically unsound. If intelligent beings from outer space ever had contacted earth, the evidence would have been immediately and spectacularly conclusive because of the highly advanced state of any civilization capable of developing the energy

---

*Most forms of mysticism reflect wishful desires to discover outside forces or "authorities" to take over the thinking tasks of the human mind. The mystic's wish is to be automatically and effortlessly guided to knowledge and through life by external forces. But that is not possible. No outside force can take over and do what the mind and the individual must do for oneself. Consider the president of the United States following the stupidity of astrology. Or consider the government of the U.S.S.R. directing funds for "research" efforts in ESP, psychokinesis, PK, and other pseudo sciences: Indeed, the intellectual impotence of those governments and their leaders is revealed. In reality, such governments are silly and their leaders are clowns, ready to be laughed out of existence by the competitive forces of Neo-Tech.

Stefan J. R-3835

I THINK EVERY PERSON HAS SOME DOUBT ABOUT RELIGION AND GOVERNMENTS, BUT ACCEPTS IT BECAUSE "IT IS SUPPOSED BE LIKE THAT".

AFTER READING NEO-TECH I-V I HAVE TO SAY THAT THOSE QUESTION-MARKS, AND MANY MORE HAVE BEEN MADE SO CLEAR, AND IN SUCH AN EASY WAY.

AFTER MY FIRST READING OF THE NEO-TECH PACKAGE I CAN ALREADY "FILTER" OUT CERTAIN PEOPLE AROUND ME, AND I'M STARTING IMMEDIATELY TO READ IT A SECOND TIME.

BUT THE BEST THING SO FAR IS IN THE WAY YOU LOSE ALL YOUR GUILT-FEELINGS IN ALL AREAS OF LIFE.

MANY THANKS.

Robert W. R. C-126

Dear Dr. Wallace:

Neotech is without a doubt the most profound explanation of life and reality I have ever seen.

and technology required to contact earth from even the closest earth-like planet in our own galaxy.

Furthermore, although many highly advanced civilizations throughout outer space undoubtedly have the technological capacity to contact and travel to earth, the following logic indicate none would: The technological advance of any civilization can be measured by the amount of energy harnessable by that civilization. Energy capacity is a direct measure of scientific knowledge and technological development. The energy requirements for outer space communication and travel are far beyond the total energy capacity available on earth at our present level of technology. Thus, a civilization capable of contacting earth would have to be advanced far beyond our civilization. That would mean that any such civilization would be well past the *Nuclear-Decision Threshold* [Re: Table 51, concept 116 of the Neo-Tech Reference Encyclopedia], which is the point that every advanced civilization must successfully pass through to survive. Our civilization is at this point today. The *Nuclear-Decision Threshold* is the point at which energy, knowledge, and technology have advanced to where sufficient, man-made energy (e.g., nuclear energy) can be generated to physically destroy all life on the planet. From that point, all civilizations must follow one of two courses:

(1) To exist within an irrational, altruistic, Platonistic philosophical system that accepts the use of force to achieve mystical "higher" causes. Such systems will eventually lead either to all-out nuclear warfare* or to a retreat into an anti-technological Dark Ages in which most knowledge and technology are lost. In either case, most of the world's population will die and all civilization will be destroyed because of meaningless mysticism.

(2) To exist within (or change to) a rational, business, nonforce, Aristotelian philosophical system in which force plays no role, allowing civilization to safely advance beyond the *Nuclear-Decision Threshold*.

Thus, any civilization advancing significantly beyond that threshold would by nature exist within a consistent, nonforce, Aristotelian/Neo-Tech society. That in turn would mean a free-market business society from which initiatory force is eradicated as uncompetitive, impotent, and immoral. In any

---

*Ironically, the unilateral peace and disarmament movements are not only dishonest, mystical, and usually promoted by neocheaters, but they are the very forces that move the world toward nuclear annihilation. By contrast, a well-prepared, rational society can effectively protect itself against nuclear war as well as prosper into the future. For, a prime moral obligation is self-protection. Thus, the development of an effective SDI or "Star-Wars" defense system is the most rational, moral act any country could perform in protecting its citizens and their property. (Also, see page 377 for the profound right to self-defense.)

Detier B.   F-101, FRANCE

I just love Neo Tech you have realised a work of great importance for the salvation of Humanity

Lindsay G.   R-2042, AUSTRALIA

Finally, as a writer of contemporary fiction, my ideas and philosophy have undergone a much needed awakening and strengthening based on the rational and value-oriented concepts of Neo-Tech.

Knowledge of Neo-Tech is power when applied correctly. I feel that what I have already received brings me in touch with a new frontier in thought and action

I believe I have only just begun to benefit from the concepts in Neo-Tech and a rereading of the complete package will be undertaken to achieve further advantages.

Kruger A.   R-2078, SOUTH AFRICA

A TOUR-DE-FORCE.

such advanced society, all forms of mysticism would by nature have been discredited and discarded as stupid and destructive. Such a business-minded society would be free of politicians, theologians, neocheaters, coercive governments, and other usurpers and parasites. Actions would be based on reality-oriented logic exercised by free individuals harmoniously living in accord with their rational best interests. And commercial biological immortality would be available to everyone.

In such an advanced society, no logical reason would exist and no apparent benefits could accrue by expending the excessive time and energy required to contact Earth or similar, outer-space civilizations. Such an undertaking would *not* be scientifically interesting or profitable for a civilization so far advanced in knowledge and technology.

In other words, as a civilization approaches a technological stage so advanced that other civilizations could be contacted, then the need, interest, and benefits to do so would cease. All such societies would by nature exist within Neo-Tech, rational, self-interest cultures. All individuals in such societies could fill all of their physical needs, psychological needs, and growth needs within a practical sphere of space (although capable of reaching any point further into outer space). Moreover, such advanced civilizations would have access to the interstellar computer system most certainly present throughout the universe. Throughout that computer system, all important knowledge would be organized and available for exchange among all advanced, Neo-Tech civilizations — perhaps through a gravity coded system.

In summary, probably thousands or millions of highly advanced civilizations exist in outer space that have the technological capacity to contact Earth. But being nonaltruistic, business-minded societies, they would have no logical motive or incentive to expend the time and energy to do so.*

For our own civilization to advance significantly beyond our current *Nuclear-Decision Threshold* would require a shift from the current

---

*Perhaps the only rational motive for an advanced civilization to communicate much beyond their immediate star system would be the pending death of their primary energy source — their sun — via an explosion-type burnout. Those beings would probably explore and colonize planets in nearby solar systems. The positions of stars in our own Milky-Way galaxy are constantly shifting relative to each other. Thus, our planet could at times become a "nearby" star system (e.g., less than ten light years) to a highly advanced civilization that must abandon its own solar system because of a impending solar explosion or other catastrophe. In such a case, our planet could become the object of exploration and even colonization from outer space. Statistically, however, such a combination of events would be extremely unlikely.

Bob J.   C-317

The road ahead is very bright, even though the responsibilities are awesome. We must break the shackles and chains of tradition that for milleniums have crippled the creativity and productivity of man. I only say to you and all those associated with Neo-Tech, & I & O Publishing, "hold on to the torch and never let it go"!

Machado R.   R-2347

NEO-TECH OPENED UP A NEW WORLD TO ME, THE REAL WORLD! NEO-TECH HAS MADE IT SO EASY TO RECOGNIZE THE UNSAVORY CHARACTERS THAT WALK & STALK OUR WORLD!

Vern A.   R-2077, CANADA

A most scientific concept that will revolutionize the world.

Platonistic/altruistic philosophical base to a Aristotelian/Neo-Tech philosophical base [Re: Table 51 in Concept 116, Neo-Tech Reference Encyclopedia].

Paradoxically, at our current level of civilization, we can gain considerable economic, technological, and scientific benefits from investigating outer space and exploring our solar system and beyond. And, on switching to a rational Neo-Tech society, our civilization will advance significantly beyond the *Nuclear-Decision Threshold*. Then our knowledge, technology, and well-being will advance so rapidly and far that when our energy capacity reaches the potential for contacting civilizations in far outer space, the logical reasons or incentives for such contact (economic, social, scientific) will fade. For, within a Neo-Tech society of self-ruling individuals, the potential of each individual can be fully realized. And that unrealized potential of conscious beings represents the total creative power available throughout the universe. On meeting that potential, nothing further out in space is required, especially after business-driven scientists learn to access the interstellar computer available throughout the universe.

The answer, therefore, to the outer-space, UFO question reduces to:

1. Probably many highly advanced civilizations exist throughout outer space that currently have the capacity to contact and even travel to Earth.

2. No valid, scientific evidence has ever been found that suggests intelligent, outer-space communication or visitation has ever occurred on Earth.

3. Logic indicates that advanced civilizations with the energy technology to contact Earth would not do so because there would be no economic, social, or scientific incentive to do so. For, once an advanced civilization has dug well-defined holes into space by exploring, understanding, and exploiting those areas, the need and incentive to dig more and more holes, deeper and deeper into space at greater and greater costs steadily diminishes to zero.

Neo-Tech Advantage #32
EXISTENTIALISM AND ITS INFLUENCE

A dominant form of mysticism and Platonistic philosophy in Western civilization is existentialism and its many variations such as Gestaltism, transcendental meditation, Zen Buddhism. Existentialism is really nothing more than clever irrationalism, often cloaked in pragmatic non sequiturs or good-sounding rationalizations. For that reason, the meaning of existentialism is impossible to understand clearly. For it means nothing. Expressed in countless different ways, existentialism is the philosophical

Ralph O.   C-15

Dear Mr. Flint,

   I am interested in achieving biological immortality for myself and loved ones. Neo-Tech has helped make me a man with new ideas for advancing myself to financial and psycological well-being. The Neo-Tech information package has been long awaited. Since I was seven years old I wanted to know the meaning of life, the purpose of my existance. I searched everywhere knowledge and wisdom was said to be. Whatever group I got involved with the real truth seemed to be missing. That which was being taught I felt was incomplete. Not until I read Neo-Tech did I stop struggling to put it all together. Now none can decieve or cheat me unless I let them. I do recognize the profound importance of Neo-Tech to everyone's future and wish to work toward Man's highest goal.

Les E.,   R-1251

The work is fantastic!! New, exciting, invigorating — am using it every day to make $$!! Thanks!!

form projected by (1) most media commentators, (2) almost all politicians and theologians, (3) neocheating social "intellectuals", including many teachers, university professors, and (4) know-nothing personalities and entertainers acting as "authorities" on the basis of feeling rather than knowledge.

In the past five decades, those four groups of people have effectively spread existentialism among the nonproductive elements of society. More recently, those same groups are successfully pushing existentialism onto the working middle class. As a result, the worker's productivity and self-esteem diminish as they increasingly swap their earned happiness and freedom for the existentialistic ideas of mysticism, egalitarianism, and altruism. Their surrender of self-responsibility and self-control opens the way for increasing government control of their lives.*

Many people are drawn into the chameleon-like forms of existentialism through an assortment of highly publicized, illusionary benefits designed to suit almost anyone's taste. Touted benefits include discovering "real truth", "peace of mind", "happiness", new "freedoms", "self-awareness", increased "sensitivity", "discovery" of one's true self, and a wide variety of health and nutritional "benefits". Other benefits touted by groups such as Scientologists include various mystical routes to "freedom" and "happiness" through self-awareness via clearing hang-ups or engrams [Re: Concept 39, Neo-Tech Reference Encyclopedia]. But beneath all such jargon and claimed benefits,

---

*Government control always means the control of individuals by force. Communism, fascism, socialism, and democracy are political systems that survive by force and repression. Democracy, however, is generally less destructive or less malevolent than the other three systems of oppression. All four political systems operate on the same concepts of government authority for the unearned power of neocheaters backed by "legalized" force and Platonistic, existentialist philosophies needed to usurp livings from the producers.

Contrary to popular myth, democracy is rooted neither in justice nor in the protection of individual rights, but is rooted in the principle of authorities with power to force the deemed "will" of the majority onto specific individuals. (The United States was not founded as a democracy, but as a republic that was a hybrid between democratic and free-choice, free-market principles. Today, most of the remaining nonforce, free-choice elements of freedom in the United States are being replaced with fascist or socialistic elements of force.) A business-like, free-market system is the only political system based on objective values, justice, and free choice rather than on feelings, force, and coercion. Of all political systems, only the nonforce, free-market system rejects the concept of "authority" by force, threat of force, or coercion. And only free markets fully recognize the sovereignty of the individual and the right to his or her own body, life, and earned property.

Roy J,

Several weeks ago I received my manuscript of Neo-Tech. Thanks!

First off, I am a Southern Baptist preacher and I first ordered Neo-Tech in 1980. I returned it, for I was not ready then.

Finally, I ordered again this year because you continued to send me advertisements in the mail. Thanks again!

When I received this time you had included the Neo-Tech instructions. These helped more than you will ever know. Also, this time I was ready for Neo-Tech.

I have resigned my church effective June 3, 1984. I have gone to work in sales. I am now at concept 92 and enjoying the new knowledge I am gaining.

I did not realize how effective guilt was until I began reading Neo-Tech II.

I now want as many as possible to get Neo-Tech. This information must get into the hands of all producers that are ready for it.

I want to learn more from Dr. Wallace I have never met nor heard of a man like him before. Already he has saved me from Christianity and the Church of Scientology. Thanks again Dr. Wallace.

existentialism is nothing more than a wimpish irrationality that promotes stupidity. Indeed, existentialism promotes the negation of reality. [Re: Table 16, Neo-Tech Reference Encyclopedia defines existentialism and identifies some of its manifestations being thrust onto the productive middle class by mystics, politicians, and other neocheaters.]

Existentialism and religion both grow from mysticism, and both lead to the oppression of the individual. Existentialism and religion both reflect fear of the independent individual and even greater fear of individual pride. Most mystics denounce pride as negative, bad, sinful. But, individual pride is the result of moral virtue, which requires the rejection of the dishonesty inherent in mysticism. Pride is the reflection of self-worth, which requires the negation of mysticism. And that negation or rejection of mysticism through the reflection of self-worth is what all mystics, existentialists, and neocheaters fear and attack.

Neo-Tech Advantage #33
THE SEVENTEEN-HUNDRED-YEAR OPPRESSION OF HUMAN HAPPINESS

About 300 A.D., Christian theologians discovered the ultimate neocheating technique to control human beings. That technique was to link guilt with sex [Re: Section Four Neo-Tech Reference Encyclopedia]. With that technique, the Christian church rose to its height in power, causing Western civilization to crumble into the mystical Dark Ages as human well-being and happiness sank to the lowest level in recorded history.

The history of Christian oppression of individual rights, happiness, pleasure, and sexuality is outlined below:

CHRISTIAN OPPRESSION OF
HAPPINESS IN MEN AND WOMEN

100 A.D. — 385 A.D.

*Roman Empire still appeared vibrant, but was surrendering to a new religion...Christianity. Rome plunged into altruism and asceticism.
*Roman pagans began persecuting those Christians who became altruistic fanatics and used any means to meet their goals of destroying the life-enhancing and productive aspects of Roman civilization. Those neocheating Christians had the dual objective of wiping out the pleasures of human life as well as the high standard of living enjoyed by the Romans. (Some Christians, however, did form tightly-knit anarchist groups for effective resistance and protection from the oppression of the bureaucratic Roman government.)

C.L. W.   C-106

Dear I & O.
    I am now on my third reading of Vol. II and feel I must write. The first reading was quite chilling and exciting, now on my third its awesome. Where before I saw normality I now see cheating, its amazing they are everywhere, what is really awful is to realize you have been a cheater.
    I have spent 15 years in search of something and thought I had found lifes answers on several occasions, but having read Dr. Wallace I realize I have not only been cheating but have been completely mugged. Oh how sad it is, millions are kept down poor and starving, guilt is foisted on everyone at all levels it is pitiful.
    We have seen religious leaders fall down from grace. Usually called lust, we see the Pope foisting guilt on millions. Now when I look at the so called leaders of religion, I see great actors living in luxury. I see people around me wishing for their luck to change and praying for miracles that never happen — everyday is the same: wishing, praying. I've done it myself — its easier than taking full responsibility.
    I am 34 years of age, married with one daughter who thank goodness (I nearly said thank god) we have not pushed into any religious belief — she's free, thank you.

          Michel T.   F-102, FRANCE

I am happy to be the owner of Neo-Tech. I have found joy in living again. These books are extraordinary. Neo-Tech has opened my eyes.

385 A.D. — 1000 A.D.

*The rise of the unkempt ascetics (hippies) in Egypt. Based on Christian self-torture and denial (e.g., St. Simon).

*Christianity discovered a fast, neocheating route to power — the foisting of guilt on innocent producers. As an effective rallying symbol, they found and elevated to martyr-level status an obscure historical individual who died three centuries earlier. That individual was an illiterate, hallucinating, unproductive hippie who lived off a group of mystical followers and possibly neocheating manipulators. That individual, their new symbol, was named Jesus Christ.

*Christians became more preoccupied with sex than ever as they struggled against lust (e.g., by burning off fingers to resist temptation). Thinly veiled, neurotic eroticism steadily increased within the church.

*St. Augustine (born 354 A.D.) promoted guilt through his books: (1) *Confessions* — self-accusations of his pagan, lustful youth. He converted to a Christian in 386 A.D., then gained power through neocheating by hatefully using guilt to turn the goodness and pleasures of man against himself. Stated that we are born between feces and urine; (2)*The City of God* — his major work — speculates how babies might be born from women "uncankered by lust and sex". Demonstrates passionate hatred for human life. St. Augustine became a master neocheater in achieving respect and power by making problems where none existed, then destroying values (rather than creating them).

*By the 5th Century, marriage came under church domination.

*The decline into dark ages coincided with the rise of Christianity. Collapsing under the Christian stranglehold, 6th Century Rome was repeatedly ravaged and looted. One million population was reduced to fifty thousand. The city lay in rubble and ruins. The Senate ceased for lack of qualified men. The hygiene, science, and culture of Rome was abandoned as Christianity took hold.

*By 585 A.D., Catholics argued that women did not have mortal souls and debated if women were even human beings.

*Sex was reduced by Christianity to an unromantic, harsh, ugly act with penance easily and hypocritically granted to men whenever required. Women became pieces of disposable property.

*Clergy and popes turned to prostitutes and neurotic sex. (e.g., The Pope of 904 A.D. practiced incest and was a lecher with children).

*By the 9th Century, Christianity dominated. Women were considered property of men. The church sanctioned wife-beating. Men were merely fined by the church for killing women. Noblemen had the "natural right"

Douglas I.   R-646

I have been a natural artist all my life and never really sold anything — since my experience with Neo-Tech — I am painting and selling — I have created a cartoon that is in process of close publication. I built an office and studio in an older building — set up in a swap meet (flea market) circuit — I have a pholio of stocks in a penny stock market — on the + side.

If you ask me a year ago — to do these things — there would be 100 excuses why it wouldn't work.

You notice I don't say — this may be published or I hope the stocks make money — I think I can sell my art work.

Your Neo-Tech is very deep for a person with my limited education — but I look up meanings of words — am in the process of taking a course in writing — a book is in process

I have noticed I do not know why — I do things with a better judgement. Except it has to come from your Neo-Tech information.

Steve P.   C-319

Certain concepts were not clear to me at first — but in rereading I have noticed I am unconsciously using these concepts — I present myself better to other people — I was layed off from my job — without a worry about what I am going to do — I have created a + money factor of things before I would not have attempted.

to ravish any peasant woman on the road and to deflower all brides of their vassals.
* For the Catholic clergy, sex without values (e.g., prostitute sex, orgy sex, even forced rape or sadistic sex) was not a serious offense, but sex with values (e.g., loving or valuing a woman) was a high sin with severe penalties. For, love and valuing resist control by "authorities", therefore, must be squelched.
* St. Jerome stated that he who too ardently loved his wife was an adulterer.
* Christian marital sex was performed only in one position and then only to conceive a child. Sex was never to be performed during penance nor on Sundays, Wednesdays, Fridays, holiday seasons.
* The major Christian sin was not sex, but pleasure.

1000 A.D. — 1500 A.D.

* Courtly love reflected happiness and contradicted the malevolence of religion. Churchmen feared and fought courtly love (e.g., St. Thomas stated that to kiss and touch a woman with delight, even without thought of fornication, was a mortal sin).
* The struggle was between oppressive religion and renaissance free-thinking. Also, the struggle was between papal power and the new Aristotelian ideas.
* In the 1300's, an ominous new interest in witchcraft and exorcism began to appear in the church. Priests fulminated about the evil powers of women who formed sex pacts with the Devil.
* By 1450, the dichotomy was complete and the dogma was established by the Catholic church that all physically desirable women were evil witches. The church was losing its power, and this was their means to fight the rediscovering of human joyfulness brought on by the emerging Renaissance.
* Renaissance noblemen in the 15th Century equated beauty to good. To counter this trend toward good and beauty, the church attacked through the Pope. The Catholic church developed a new breed of neocheating malefactors not known before...the inquisitors who were backed by a series of papal pronouncements and bulls. The Pope set up two theologians (Jacob Sprenger and Henry Kramer) to act as inquisitors. Sprenger and Kramer wrote a widely influential book dealing with the "evils" of women and witchcraft. They advocated hanging "evil" women by their thumbs, twisting ropes around their heads, pushing needles under their nails, and pouring boiling oil on their feet in the "devout" hope of forcing confessions of their "wickedness". That led to the burning to death of tens of thousands of innocent women during the Renaissance.
* Crosscurrents and contradictions — the "lady ideal" projected by the happy Renaissance spirit and the "evil witch" projected by the malevolent spirit of the church.

James Mc. R-2081

I congratulate you on your excellent work in communicating the value system at ground zero! This is vital if the balance is to shift in time to avoid another dark age.

Charles A.   R-1960

Dr. Wallace,
After the reading of NEO-TECH, my whole outlook on life has changed dramatically for I view life as a means to an end. Neo-Tech has clearly shown the unproductive politicians that exists and their altruistic morals that are the real culprits in todays economy that have brought so much pain, suffering, and our lowered standard of living by extracting wealth from the uninformed

Douglas H.   R-2091, CANADA

I have found Neo-Tech I + II Truely priceless

*King Henry VIII was the first major figure to combine love and marriage. He waged a long battle with Bishop Wolsey and Pope Clement VII about his divorce and subsequent marriage to Anne Boleyn.
*Renaissance enlightenment made sex seem not so sinful and disgusting as the church insisted. The middle class began to associate sex with love.

1500-1700

*The Reformation combined the enlightened Renaissance (by considering sex in marriage as wholesome and free of guilt) with the malevolent Christian position that continued to burn women as witches.
*Martin Luther battled Catholic asceticism by advocating the enjoyment of every pleasure that was not "sinful". Luther lived in a lusty "eat, drink, and be merry" style. He fought Rome and claimed that celibacy was invented by the Devil. He insisted that priests could marry and asserted that marriage was not a sacrament at all, but a civil matter. Luther asserted that sexual impulses were both natural and irrepressible. He broke from Rome and married. He cheerfully loved his wife and held pleasurable sex in marriage as good. Luther's reformation rapidly spread across Northern Europe.
*John Calvin (the father of the Bluenoses) was the opposite of Martin Luther. Calvin was sour, malevolent, and had a ferocious theology based on human depravity and the wrath of God. He was an unhappy ascetic who had ulcers, tuberculosis, and kidney stones; he considered life of little value. Calvin set up a brutally strict theocracy in Geneva that allowed no dancing, fancy clothes, or jewelry. The death penalty was imposed for adultery. Even legitimate love was stringently regulated. Engagements were limited to six weeks. No lingering at romance was allowed. Weddings were grave with no revelry. The Calvinist marriage had two functions: (1) to produce children, and (2) to reduce sexual desires.
*Most Puritans, however, were quite unlike the inhuman joylessness of Calvin. But a few vocal fanatics such as John Knox in the United States continued to pile misery onto others. His Blue laws of the 1650's were against Sunday amusements, smoking, drinking, gambling, fancy clothing. He also promoted public whippings, scarlet letters, executions for adulterers, and the Salem "witch" executions (executed 26 women and two dogs in 1692).
*Early Puritan traits were mainly stern expressions masking mischief and romance. Church trial records show much "sinning" existed. But only sex outside marriage was attacked. Puritans were very much for sex inside marriage and condemned the virtue-of-virginity concept. Most Puritans were tenderly romantic and good lovers.

E. T.   R-1964

Overall, Neo-Tech is a work of art. Neo-cheaters, who I wouldn't have recognized before, have been exposed. Now, Neo-cheaters cannot control my life; I will now take advantage of their (ex: the govt) newcheating moves to increase my value. I now have the power to reject the harmful flood of information and threatening social contacts. Thanks to Dr. Wallace, innocent victims can now rise from the ashes and become true winners.

Thomas K.   R-4186

Several months ago, city hall bureaucrats were trying to stick me for fees for services I did not receive, nor even wanted. They did the same thing six years ago, when it took me several months to get them off my back. I used the press in that battle after they had turned my water off, without notice. It was very time consuming and created a lot of stress. This time, I was fully aware that the official I was dealing with was talking in non sequiturs. Right after he left, I wrote him a letter which clearly explained that his statements were completely irrelevant to the issue, which, in this case, is an agreement I have with the city dating back nearly thirteen years. I sent a copy of the letter to his superior, the city manager. The matter was cleared up within a week.

Thanks to Neo-Tech, I was able to spot the non sequiturs immediately and take action from a position of strength, instead of being confused by the bureaucrat's statements.

*The image of the sexless Puritan with a stony heart is false. For example, the 17th Century Puritan John Milton (*Paradise Lost*) projected a healthy view of married sex. He displayed idealistic, romantic views about marriage. Moreover, Milton sent tracts to Parliament urging modern-day, easy divorce. Milton's *Paradise Lost* projects a benevolent view of Adam and Eve in a romantic-love context. Milton rejected St. Augustine's malevolent views of life, sex, and pleasure.
*16th Century Puritans combined the ideals of romantic love with the normality of sex in marriage. Woman's status improved under Puritanism (e.g., if beaten, women could separate and even divorce.). Property rights and inheritance laws improved. Marriage became a civil contract.

1700-1800

*The rationalists in this new Age of Reason rejected the gloom of Christianity. They scrapped the church's portrait of woman as evil.
*18th Century love rejected Christian anti-sexual values and idealized the mythical Don Juan, who was impeccably mannered, lustful, haughty. Love was reduced to mere sensuality and pleasurable sport with the motive to seduce and then desert.

1800-1900

*Religious Victorian men, on the other hand, were patriarchal and stern. But they played that role at their own sexual expense.
*Out of religious Victorianism arose a great hunger for a fantasy sex life. Flagellation, pornography, and prostitution rapidly increased.
*Capitalistic economics were greatly accelerating the dissolution of medieval religious ties along with their unjust social customs and racism.
*The religious Victorian home was threatened by talk of female suffrage, divorce reforms, and free love.
*Victorianism was a reactionary, desperate delaying action (in collusion with the church) against the inevitable changes made by an emerging industrial civilization. Religion-oriented Victorians tried to fight change via religious coercion, government force, and police activities.

1900-1950

*Margaret Sanger staged a historic fight for birth control claiming that a woman's body belonged to her alone. She published birth-control information in 1914 and opened birth-control clinics in 1916. Outraged Catholic elements had her arrested and jailed.

Dennis V. R-5282

Dear John,

I am seventeen years old and have just completed my first reading of Neo-Tech I-V.

When I first recieved the Neo-Tech advertisement sheet, I was so thrilled at what I thought it had to offer. I saw it as a book that would teach easy techniques in which to make money and get girls. I figured I would be rich by the time I left high school, and would soon become the biggest stud on Long Island. Of course it turned out that I was mistaken in many ways. Neo-Tech does not give step-by-step techniques, but it does give something more important → objective reality based on facts and statistics. It taught me that there is no **real** long-range pleasure in being a "big stud", and that if I want to be rich, its going to come about through hard work. I found out what life is <u>actually</u> about, and how the government, neocheaters, and all mystics exist on lies that distort or totally avoid reality. And I finally learned the truth about the God concept.

I used to be a **DIE-HARD** christian in which I would curse anyone for not totally devoting their lives to Christ. I hated Catholics because of their hypocracy towards what they themselves preached (humility, pray in a private place, etc). I had accepted the Bible, as what Frank Wallace would call "a package of truth"; I believed it as true reality, that would remain unchanged. So you could imagine my shock on reading Neo-Tech. It put down everything I believed in. I felt I had thrown away $100 for nothing. But being the open minded person I am, I read Neo-Tech's side of the story. It was so logical and comprehensive, that I began questioning the religion in which I have grown up with all of my life! I actually prayed for a sign that would tell me if I was doing the right thing. I asked "God" to prove his existence by giving me a massive miracle, or I would abort him from my life completely. (As you probably guessed, I am now 100% Atheist.) I now know "heaven" was created from the fear of death. And when an error-free method for biological immortality is developed, the idea of "heaven" will become useless and will eventually fade.

(continued next page)

1950-1980

*Modern sexual revolution toward openness and honesty has caused the church's malevolent influence over sexuality to wane. In a last desperate effort, the "modern" church rapidly adopted the existentialist or fun view of sex in order to diminish the value and importance of sex, thus keeping control by undercutting people's self-esteem. Without self-esteem, one cannot experience abiding happiness or psychuous pleasures. Without self-esteem, a person will continue to be controlled by neocheaters using their tools of mysticism.

1980-PRESENT

*An ominous rise of overt mysticism, born-again Christianity, and fundamentalist religions signal a turn back toward malevolent views of life, love, and sex. A revival of fundamentalism and theocratic concepts are conditions ultimately sought by all mystical leaders. No matter what their deceptive facades, mystical leaders are all destructive neocheaters who ultimately want to reign with murderous power. But today, for the first time in history, mysticism and neocheating are being effectively identified and eliminated by the spreading Neo-Tech matrix.

Neo-Tech Advantage #34
AESTHETIC PLEASURE

The aesthetics (art, music, drama, and literature) are rational, self-interest pursuits that add important increments of emotional fuel and psychuous pleasures to a person's life. Moreover, aesthetic pleasures are important to the growth of one's psychological and spiritual* well-being. Aesthetics reflect a person's most important values in a concrete way, providing a powerful emotional fuel to seek ever greater personal growth and achievements.

A false but common belief is that a person's response to art (music, literature, fine arts, performing arts) is a mystical experience that has no basis in reality and serves no practical purpose. But the exact opposite is true. A positive response to art is a starkly real phenomenon that reflects a person's deepest, most important values. Those values can be either objective or neurotic values. That is why some people can respond positively to art that reflects neurotic values, nonvalues, or even value destruction. Moreover, response to aesthetic values fills important psychological needs and pleasures.

---

*The word **spiritual** as used throughout Neo-Tech has no mystical or religious connotations. Spiritual means one's sense or view of life combined with one's assertiveness toward living.

- I now look at the Bible as a fun book to read for sparking up the imagination as does Ulysses, Novels by Stephen King, or anything to do with fantasy. No mystic can ever control me through "God" again.

But not only has Neo-Tech helped take away mystical views from my life, it has also brought up my high school grade average nearly 20 points from what it used to be before Neo-Tech. In my first three years of high school, I had an approximate average of 67%. I had fallen into a deep depression as a result of all the mystics and neocheaters that surrounded me. But because of Neo-Tech, I have become a happier, more self-confident, productive individual. My average is now 87% and rising. Neo-Tech was the insentive and the morale booster that I needed to study harder and improve my life.

Finally, I would like to thank those who introduced me to Neo-Tech, and entered me into their world. I'm happy to have recieved such information at such an early age, I have lots of time to build my own empire and hopefully have Biological Immortality in my lifetime (If the world isn't blown up by that time). Neo-Tech has changed my views on life and the people that surround me. The first reading has knocked down the walls of mysticism, the second reading shall put me on my way to life!

<u>Thank You!!!</u>

Another false belief is that art is entirely subjective and cannot be evaluated on an objective basis. With sufficient knowledge, all art can be judged by precise, objective standards. Objective evaluation can include sense of life, the theme expressed by the artist, execution skill, overt style, presentation integrity.

Psychological pleasure derived from an art work comes from the similarity of the artist's values and sense of life to one's own values. Admiration of an art work, on the other hand, comes from the viewer's evaluation of the artist's skill, style, and integrity. An individual can dislike the values, the sense of life, or the theme of an art work, but can admire the artist's skill or style.

One dominant myth propagates that most great, universal artists (i.e., composers, painters, sculptors, novelists) lived in poverty and were not recognized during their lifetimes. Indeed, that myth serves as a handy excuse for pseudo, dilettante, or government sponsored "artists". The truth is that such "artists" never put forth the great learning, training, and execution efforts needed to develop the ability to produce works of art saleable in free markets.

With few exceptions, most universally enduring artists throughout history were fully recognized during their lifetimes, often early in their careers. Most great, objectively creative artists collected and enjoyed their earned financial and emotional rewards throughout their professional lives. Their work was objectively valuable and recognized as such, making their products highly marketable not only in their lifetimes but throughout the ages. Furthermore, the objective value of an artist's work is almost always in direct proportion to the rational thought and effort that artist put into developing and executing his skill. Success is not the result of being naturally gifted or of being lucky. Both of those notions are false and mystical.

Still another myth about art is that if a person dislikes a work of art, then the person does not understand the work. In most cases, if a person does not like or enjoy a work of art, the work is either (1) poorly executed or (2) contradicts that person's inner values.

And a final misconception is that poetry is an art form that enhances love and the quality of one's life. Poetry is generally an invalid art form that can be destructive to romantic love, prosperity, and long-range happiness [Re: Concept 136, Neo-Tech Reference Encyclopedia; also see Neo-Tech Advantage 104 in this volume].

As a concluding note: Since art can reflect powerfully emotional values to the beholder, art can be loved, appreciated, and enjoyed for those values. The art work itself, however, is an extension of the artist and thus can

Terry P.   C-13

    I did some investment counseling for my father last month. Considering liquidity, yield, safety, and risk my fathers investments will quadruple in five years. My decision was based on some of the Neo-Tech data along with other information. I am the sole heir of that money. It is reasurring to know that I will be a millionaire some day. Now, my father is studying some of the Neo-Tech data. He's pleased and I am pleased.

                John   D. R-2665

Removed the blinders from my eyes, w/o guilt; the only obligation I have is to myself.
    Should have read completely 3 yrs. ago when received. I'm glad I cleaned the closet.

                Mark B.   C-4

Dear Dr. Flint;

I acquired the Neo-Tech information package several years ago when I was a college student, but never sat down to read the information until this past month. Frankly, I am overwhelmed. Every day I feel as if new and exciting horizons are opening up before me. As someone with a background in chemistry and a keen interest in the medical sciences, the whole concept of biological immortality has taken my imagination by storm and I have become so excited that I am often unable to sleep at night.

never be spiritually possessed or owned by anyone else, even though the physical ownership and copyrights can be transferred or purchased.

Neo-Tech Advantage #35
VALUE OF EMOTIONS

Emotions and feelings are among a person's most valuable assets. All pleasure and happiness are experienced through emotions. Negative emotions are reliable warning signals that a person is acting mystically or contrary to his or her nature and well-being.

Emotions deliver the ultimate human rewards and penalties. Such emotions depend on the life a person chooses to create and live. A person's emotional content will be either happy or unhappy, depending on the extent which that person has rejected or accepted mysticism. Rejecting mysticism means accepting sole responsibility for understanding and dealing honestly with reality. A person must reject mysticism to effectively solve life's problems and develop the competence needed to earn prosperity, power, and love. That, in turn, delivers the self-esteem and emotional content needed to experience abiding well-being, psychuous pleasures, and romantic love. ...Everyone controls his or her wide-range emotions (i.e., being fundamentally happy or unhappy) through one's constant, volitional choice to be honest or dishonest — to be Neo-Tech or mystical.

Human pleasures and happiness are experienced by sensory and emotional means. To fully experience pleasure and happiness, a person must develop an integrated awareness of emotions along with a mystic-free, guiltless acceptance of those emotions. But first, a person must solidly establish the psychological, philosophical, and productivity positions to provide the self-esteem necessary for romantic love and psychuous pleasures. Then that person must reject mystical guilt to fully experience his or her earned emotions of happiness, pleasure, love.

Happiness, pleasure, and love can be experienced only through emotions. To the extent that a person represses emotions* is the extent that the person denies that emotional part needed to experience earned pleasures and happiness — which is the entire moral purpose of human life.

---

*Repression of emotions is the attempt to deny emotions. Such repression is harmful and entirely different from the suppression of emotions, which can be a valuable, necessary process. Suppression of emotions is an act of discipline in consciously putting aside emotions to experience them later at a more appropriate time or in a more controlled manner. In suppressing an emotion, one is not denying the emotion and remains fully aware of it. Suppression is an important tool for preventing destructive, mystical reactions in oneself.

Mary A.D. R-6799

Dear Dr. Wallace & Mr. Flint:

Neo Tech has really opened my eyes as to the kind of mystic I have been for over 50 years. My life has been controlled by Neo cheaters and mystics -- but now, thanks to you and N.T. my eyes are open and I am forging ahead with MY life. I am now standing on my own feet and controlling my future. I feel free of encumbrances that have chained me for years.

I am re-reading many concepts that directly affect my life and am constantly learning. My life has always been "giving" to others, but now I can say NO! and start to gain self esteem and financial prosperity.

Thank you for helping me to grow and develop into the person I know I can be.

Keep up the marvelous work.

Sincerely,

Oliver W.L. R-4170

THIS INFORMATION IS ESSENTIAL TO THE WORLD.

The human organism must experience emotions in order to psychologically live. If a person continually diminishes self-awareness or represses emotions, that person will steadily lessen his or her capacity to feel emotions. To compensate for that deadening of feelings (thus a deadening of life), that person must take increasingly stronger measures to feel something until the only feeling left to feel is pain. But that person must feel something, so he or she strives to feel pain. And the easiest, quickest route to feel pain is through destructive actions rationalized through mysticism.

Also as a person diminishes self-awareness, the initiation of longer range, positive actions becomes increasingly difficult. At the same time, the person increasingly succumbs to mysticism in selecting more and more destructive actions in order to feel something. Destructive actions taken to feel something include manipulating others, initiating force (political or criminal) to control or plunder others, using drugs or alcohol, promiscuity, injurious masochism or sadism, vandalism, thrill killings, mass murder, waging war, genocide.

Neo-Tech Advantage #36
EMOTIONS AND REALITY

Emotions are a real part of every person and, therefore, are a part of reality. To know and deal with undistorted reality, a person must first know one's self, which includes knowing one's own emotions. A person must learn to be aware of feelings in order to prevent destructive emotional reactions. A person must also know one's own emotions in order to effectively share them in a love relationship. For, the value of a romantic-love relationship is measured by pleasure, happiness, and emotional closeness.

Neo-Tech Advantage #37
CHRISTIAN CONDEMNATION OF EMOTIONS

Emotions are not subject to condemnation, guilt, or right or wrong judgments...only *actions* are right or wrong.* Next to the mystical concept of original sin, perhaps the most pervasively damaging, unjust concept projected by the Christian ethic is the moral judgment of emotions. Especially malevolent and harmful are the condemnations of emotions such as found in the Sermon on the Mount: "But I say unto you, that whosoever looketh on a woman to lust after her, hath committed adultery with her already in his

---

*An individual, however, is always responsible for all of his or her actions. Even if the action is an accident or honest error, one always remains responsible for every action. Thus, by nature, one must eventually pay for all errors, even accidental or innocent ones. Innocent errors, however, do not carry the serious long-range consequences of uncorrected volitional or dishonest errors.

Carl R. C-5000

Through this monumental creation of Neo-Tech, you have produced untold of values for myself.

I'm still only scratching the surface of the implications contained in these Golden Volumes (I'm only half way through Neo-Tech II), but I feel at once a release from the years of mysticism I have succumbed to (as a result of the deaths of my parents) as well as a surge of energy and clarity I haven't experienced since being a child.

I thought it was all a hoax when I first ordered, but now I can't believe how fortunate I am to have gone ahead.

Following the Dr. Atkins diet, along with Dr. Cooper's aerobic program has helped tremendously. I was never sure what the best things were to do for my health but following this program has proved successful.

I'm fascinated, excited, and breaking through my self-imposed limitations.

heart.". By condemning human emotions, Christian neocheaters discovered an effective tool to condemn everyone...to make everyone guilty, keeping them more controllable for usurping power and values. Since everyone by nature possesses a full range of automatic feelings or emotions that cannot be directly controlled, shut off or stopped, nearly everyone is victimized by Christian-style "sin" and "guilt".

While everyone innocently experiences negative, irrational emotions, no one ever has to act on such emotions. And since only human actions are subject to choice, only human actions are subject to moral judgment.

Neo-Tech Advantage #38
FEAR OF EMOTIONS

Many innocent people repress emotions because of false guilt. In doing so, they never get to know themselves. Once the following two facts are realized, one can eliminate any fear or guilt about one's own emotions:

1. Immediate emotions are beyond a person's direct control. Thus, emotions are not subject to moral judgment or condemnation and should never be associated with guilt. Only volitional actions can be wrong, condemned, or associated with guilt.

2. Emotions never have to be acted upon. Thus a person never needs to fear irrational emotions. A person can feel hatred toward anyone, even the desire for violence, rape, or murder — a person can *feel any emotion*, rational or irrational, without being guilty of anything. A person becomes guilty only if he or she chooses to act on irrational emotions to harm oneself or others.

Neo-Tech Advantage #39
EMOTIONS OF FEAR
AND THE VALUE OF FEARLESSNESS

Objective fear is a valuable protection mechanism. By contrast, irrational fear is destructive whenever it stops a person from taking needed actions. Fortunately, the paralyzing effects of irrational fear can be overcome with direct, conscious effort. For example, if a person takes a rational action that he or she fears (if no actual danger exists), that fear will dissipate.* Irrational fears can cause inaction that prevents deserving, productive people from developing prosperity and happiness. A fearlessness to live is perhaps the most financially and emotionally rewarding character trait that an honest, productive person can develop.

---

*Recommended for effective treatment of most phobias: Callahan, Roger J., *The Five Minute Phobia Cure*, Enterprise Publishing.

Scot S.   R-4016

A strange growth of unstoppable power will lurk through the bones and sinew of anyone who reads this. A person cannot return the same once he takes a trip through these pages of total, integrated honesty.

For this reason I have decided to quit my job as a teacher and go into business for myself producing tradeable values for others.

Kevin T.   C-56

have received the copy of "Neo-Tech Discovery" which you recently forwarded to me, and I am most pleased with it.

It has actually clarified many points for me and has completely overcome any confusion which I felt was present after I had read and re-read the original Reference Encyclopedia. I now feel totally confident about the whole work, and can only say that is it brilliant. In retrospect, it would have been preferable for me to have read the "Discovery" BEFORE the Enclopedia, but of course this was not available at that time. I now find that I have an unquenchable thirst for more and more of the same,

"Far better it is to dare mighty things, to win glorious triumphs, even though checkered by failure, than to rank with those poor spirits who neither enjoy much nor suffer much, because they live in the gray twilight that knows not victory nor defeat."
— Theodore Roosevelt*

Neo-Tech Advantage #40
FEAR OF REJECTION AND RISK TAKING

Fear of being hurt or rejected prevents the development of many romantic-love relationships. That fear keeps a person defensive, which in turn prevents emotional openness with his or her partner. That openness is necessary for developing romantic love and psychuous pleasures.

The achievement of romantic love involves a willingness to take risks. And the fear of being hurt by being open is unfounded. To the contrary, a person is always hurt by faking emotions or by concealing emotions from one's self or a loved one. Denial of feelings traps a person into emotionally repressive situations that diminish the potential for love and happiness. Being emotionally honest and open is the safest, happiest way to live. ...Being emotionally open, however, does not mean gratuitously projecting emotions onto others or blaming one's emotional or personal problems on others. ...Blaming others for one's personal problems is an irrational, unfair, and mystical act that keeps a person from solving his or her own problems.

Consistently acting on rational premises and being loyal to truth builds confidence in a person's own rightness and worth. This, in turn, helps remove the fear that prevents people from venturing into new growth areas such as romantic love. Rationality, fairness, and truth act as powerful protectors when venturing into unexplored areas, ranging from business to love relationships.

Neo-Tech Advantage #41
INDEPENDENT JUDGMENT VS. OPINIONS OF OTHERS

Acting on what *others* think rather than on one's own thinking not only undermines integrity and judgment, but diminishes self-esteem. That, in turn,

---

*The anomaly of a worthwhile quote from a politician is explainable by realizing that "mighty things" and "glorious triumphs" in the minds of value-destroying politicians can mean something entirely different from "mighty things" and "glorious triumphs" in the minds of value-creating business people (e.g., being a "great" and powerful politician or dictator via force and manipulation is quite different than being a great and creative artist or industrialist via honest, productive effort and earned ability)

John E.N.   R-4077

I have just completed a second reading of the entire package. All the concepts and ideas seem to leap off the pages and into my brain. I have been selfish more or less all of my life and now I know - thanks to your fantastic work - why I was and still am much more satisfied and happy when I am being selfish than when I let the neocheaters dominate my life - There is <u>NO doubt</u> in my mind what so ever that the Neo-Tech discovery is truly one of the <u>GREATEST</u> <u>WORKS</u> <u>OF</u> <u>ALL TIME</u> and should have far reaching effects for decades - no centuries to come!!!!

M.A.G.   C-1009

A year ago I ordered Neo Tech - a manuscript that should have been written 2000 yrs ago because it would have prevented many men to make mistakes and live a happy life in harmony with each his own goal.

gradually represses the best qualities within a person. In a free or semi-free society, everyone has the basic choice of acting on his or her independent judgment versus acting on the basis of what other people think, do, or say. In a totalitarian society, however, no such choice exists. The authorities terrorize everyone by coercion, force, and threats into acting on the basis of what some "authority" thinks or wishes (e.g., the dictator). By preventing people from acting on their own judgments, totalitarian governments deprive individuals of their natural survival mechanisms by undermining the independent use of their minds. Being unwilling or unable to act on one's own judgment, the individual is controlled by others — by the whims, wishes, and demands of neocheating "authorities".

Neo-Tech Advantage #42
CASUAL VS. SERIOUS SEX

Psychuous sex is always linked to values...to an exchange of rational values between partners. A continuous exchange of values that enhances personal worth and psychological visibility is the basis for psychuous pleasures and romantic-love. But, sex without serious values (i.e., casual sex) cannot deliver psychuous pleasures and is eventually self-destructive.

The difference between serious and casual sex is not always obvious on the surface. But the difference always appears at the base of every relationship. While the actual sexual activity of serious sex can and often does have interludes of lightness and fun, the meaning behind every act is serious and important. But sex on a nonserious, unimportant, or casual basis done for "fun" only is a diminishing experience that erodes self-esteem and sexual competence. On the other hand, a serious sexual affair will always produce growth and values so long as the relationship is based on mutual values, honesty, and respect. In a value-based sexual relationship, psychuous pleasures are linked to a mutual reflection of each partner's personal values and worth.

Unlike casual sexual relationships, serious relationships have no bounds or limits to personal values that can be exchanged. The value of a serious romantic relationship can grow so great that a person would give, if necessary, all of one's possessions, even one's own life, to protect his or her love partner.

Neo-Tech Advantage #43
MULTIPLE PARTNERS, VALUE SYSTEMS, AND INDIVIDUAL DIFFERENCES

The value of relationships outside of a primary love relationship can vary greatly depending on the motivation and nature of those involved. The various relationships can be classified according to their type and value [Re: Table 20, Neo-Tech Reference Encyclopedia].

Few people if any can benefit from a multi-partner relationship not only because of the painful, emotional conflicts but because of the time and effort

Susanna C.   C-300

Gentlemen:

Having recently finished my first reading of Neo-Tech II, and starting over lest I miss a single 'important thought,'

I can only say how very angry I am (in a healthy way) in allowing myself to be usurped by others when, in my mind, I always knew the realities as you so eloquently and intelligently pointed out.

Because I do have (and always have had) a high regard for human consciousness - specifically others, it is a wonderful feeling to now guiltlessly include myself. A thin but powerful obstructive line to be sure. Such a small price to pay for 'peace' and prosperity.

Sincerely,

J.J.M.   R-6052

I COULD NOT WAIT TO GET MY HANDS ON MY NEO TECH BOOKS. WHEN THEY FINALLY ARRIVED I COULDN'T PUT THEM DOWN.

WHAT THIS WORLD NEEDS IS MORE DR WALLACES! WHAT A GLORIOUS WORLD WE WOULD LIVE IN.

PLEASE, DR WALLACE, KEEP UP YOUR EYE OPENING INFORMATION

inherently required to develop a valuable, romantic-love relationship with just one partner. Furthermore, the amount of time required to develop valuable multi-partner relationships could deprive an individual of the time needed to fully develop other areas of life such as a rewarding career or productive work. [Re: Concept 41 and 42, Neo-Tech Reference Encyclopedia]

The biggest negative of multi-partner relationships evolves from the nature of psychuous sex: Romantic love works best when structured around long-term, monogamous relationships. Why? Because continuous efforts and experiences with an exclusive partner deliver the most intimacy, growth, and values. Thus, the most erotically exciting and sexually satisfying experiences by nature evolve from long-term, monogamous/psychuous relations. ...And today, the rise of incurable herpes and deadly AIDS adds a new dimension to the rhapsody of monogamous, romantic-love relationships.

* * *

All individual values, including sexual values, fall into two categories — (1) nonjudgable or amoral values that arise from each person's unique personality development, and (2) objectively right or wrong values that arise from a person's volitional character development. Many Neo-Tech/Psychuous concepts deal either directly or indirectly with the second category. Those values are self-determined and reflect a person's view of:

- Self and others.

- Rights of individuals.

- Value of human life.

- Work, productivity, creativity, achievement.

- Acquiring knowledge and loyalty to honesty.

- Acquiring personal pleasures and happiness.

Other Neo-Tech/Psychuous concepts deal with the nonjudgmental or amoral values that reflect unique individual preferences such as the:

- Physical and psychological features that a person finds most attractive and stimulating in a love partner.

- Combination of values that deliver the greatest curiosity, excitement, satisfaction.

- Most satisfying or pleasurable styles, methods, techniques.

Bobby P.   R-5926

Dear Gentlemen

Thank you very much for making these books available to me. They have come to me just at the right time. This has been my first year in college and your books have helped me to make a lot of decisions, properly.

My mother and father had raised me to be a cheater (mostly my mom). I often lied, begged for pity, broke trusts and was very lazy. I had no real friends just other cheaters. I very much relied on religion and thought I had to do nothing but wait and it would all come to me without work.

Thank you very much for setting me straight. I now have good friends & a beautiful lover. I have started to do real work again on myself, my degree & other areas, especially producing values. I have lost about 40-50 lbs. and have begun working out at the college gym. Most of all I am now running my own life instead of telling others how to run theirs!!

Thank you for showing me the correct path.

Each individual has his or her own sexual value system. Such values evolve from subconscious ratings of past experiences, personal preferences, personal desires. Those values can vary widely from person to person. Many sexual values depend on the individual's unique personality and tastes. And those values are not subject to judgments of right and wrong, better and worse, moral and immoral...they merely reflect personal differences.

Contrary to advice in most books on sex and marriage, an important task of every couple working toward romantic love and psychuous pleasure is <u>not</u> to seek compromises between their unique sexual values, but to openly become aware of each other's sexual values. Once aware of one's own as well as one's partner's sexual values, the differences can be used to intensify pleasures. That is best done by satisfying the other partner's sexual values without compromising one's own sexual values. In that process, each partner becomes increasingly valuable and uniquely irreplaceable to the other. Such relationships become increasingly secure as romantic love grows without restrictions or bounds. Divorces in those rational, non-mystical relationships diminish toward zero as values and happiness grow with time and effort.

To gain honest Neo-Tech advantages, one must always be aware of the great physical, intellectual, and psychological differences among individuals. People exhibit strikingly different characteristics in: physical structures, ways of thinking, areas of knowledge, mental capacities, views of life. As a person develops his character, an unevenness in being honest versus being mystical occurs. For example, a person may find that the honest integration of facts is easier in certain areas of life. In other areas, that person surrenders to the "easy-way-out" mystical trap. Such unevenness in honesty is caused by a person's past and present choices and actions. That volitional behavior, in turn, determines the rate of *personal evolvement* and the quality of *character development*.

A major mistake that many people make is to expect other people to be like them. People are *not* alike. Furthermore, most individual differences are *not* subject to right or wrong judgments. Amoral differences are merely differences — not right or wrong entities. Another error is the belief that a person can change the basic nature of another person. Basic changes occur only from within the individual's own self. No one can really force or pressure such changes.

Neo-Tech Advantage #44
RELATIONSHIP ERRORS

Casual, nonintimate, or fun-only sex does not always start from a neurotic base. Casual sex may begin as an immature sexual view during adolescence. Or casual sex may begin as a notion to experiment with "new" sex in order to

Boni M.   R-4746

When I first read your Neo-Tech Manuscript Vol. I-5 I was astounded! It was as though a lifeline had been tossed to me. The concept that a person should not live life feeling guilty made me stop & think.

Also I am still learning to think rationally, but I hope I'm getting better at it.

Robert P.   R-1231

Before I ever recieved and read the Neo-Tech information I could honestly say that I was walking around in a trance. I was existing but I was not really living life as I wanted. I was doing things because other people thought it was the right thing for me to do. I seemed to be existing for other people and I wasn't very comfortable with that.

However, throughout my life, though brief at 27 years of age, I had always questioned everything. I didn't know the answers to many of these questions but I knew within myself that I would find the answers to these questions somewhere, someday. The Neo-Tech information has answered these questions and many more. Institutions I was taught to believe as right and positive(ie.,religion, government) are negative, very destructive forces which must be eliminated from society so that man may live as he should. It is easy to recognize and control the Neo-cheaters to my advantage. It is done so easily, <u>naturally</u>! It is so easy to think, reason naturally and make logical, competent decisions now than before.

As I began to read and assimilate the material a transformation began to take place. I had always felt an unnatural tension or pressure flowing through me. As I began to understand the material this tension gradually disappeared. My body and mind felt natural to me for the first time in my life. My whole physical and financial outlook has changed. And I know its going to get better!!

In closing let me express my thanks and appreciation for making available this information to me. The Neo-Tech package,along with the supplemental reading material, are the most important experiences I have ever had. It has changed my life-for the better! I can't understand how I survived this long without it. Thanks again.

broaden one's sexual experiences or to diminish sexual inhibitions and taboos. Indeed, casual sex, swinging sex, orgy sex may accomplish those ends. But, the eventual cost of casual sex, fun-only, or exploitive sex to one's self-esteem is high. One experiences such sex only with grave consequences to his or her self-esteem, sexuality, and happiness. By contrast, one experiences a limitless broadening of erotic sexual experiences with enhanced self-esteem through the Neo-Tech/Psychuous concepts.

Human beings are always capable of correcting errors. The harm caused by past, casual-sexual experiences can be reversed by restructuring sexual standards around the consistent, value-oriented foundation of Psychuous Sex.

Neo-Tech Advantage #45
ACHIEVING PSYCHUOUS PLEASURES

By defaulting on the basic human responsibility of achieving personal happiness and psychuous pleasures, a person lets his or her future turn downward toward death. Through that default, life and time slip away, increasingly unrewarded and unfulfilled. By that default, the exciting potential for life (which everyone senses at least some time during his or her life...usually in early childhood) will fade, never to be experienced again — unless revived by Neo-Tech.

Such defaults are contrary to human nature, unnecessary, and rooted in the mysticism continually promoted by neocheaters. By contrast, the experiencing of an exciting, value-generating life and the achievement of prosperity, power, and psychuous pleasures are accomplished through self-responsibility...through a commitment to rational efforts and a loyalty to honesty [Re: Neo-Tech Reference Encyclopedia].

A value-oriented, romantic relationship offers limitless pleasures ranging from joy and spontaneous fun* to erotic thrills, adventure, psychuous pleasures, and profound happiness. Equally important, such romantic relationships can greatly enhance each partner's productivity, values, and prosperity.

Psychuous pleasures can always grow, even during crisis or turmoil. Psychuous sex lets a person physically confirm the value of his or her life, especially during difficult or crisis periods. Psychuous sex allows a person to be acutely aware of his or her worth, pleasures, and happiness. But psychuous pleasures go far beyond sexual intercourse. In fact, sexual intercourse itself plays only a small (but crucial) role in psychuous pleasure, which is integrated with all aspects of human life.

Romantic love and psychuous pleasures add so much to human happiness that to settle for something as unchallenging and limited as casual, fun-only sex is to treat one's self poorly. Limiting the potential for pleasure to such a narrow, shallow range of experiences undermines a person's entire life.

---

*Joyful, child-like spontaneous fun is entirely different than the contrived, boring, mechanical "fun" of fun-only sexual relationships.

Tom S. CB-1000

Dear Neo-Tech,

I am a 17 year old guy that has found an extremely beneficial company's publishings to be lifesaving.

Now, instead of buildings upon problems I disect them and always find one of these three, 1. Neocheater 2. Mystic 3. Lazy person. Life is so great, just, and fair because I no longer listen to the stranglehold comments of government and religion. There is absolutely no difference between the White House and the Kremlin, Baptists and Catholics, etc., they're all the same crap!

Bruce N. CB-101

It's hard to believe that a single publication could have such a major impact on how one looks at life and oneself. The affect on me has been remarkable. The highlight of my summer vacation was reading the Neo-Tech package. It's as if I had a total housecleaning of my mind, ridding myself of all the unnecessary garbage accumulated over my 45 years.

Neo-Tech was able to change my thinking processes. Now I'm more attentive to detail, with a greater interest in reading, listening and reducing commentary to its "real" meaning. It's like having a dull blade sharpened; or a mind that was dulled by mysticism and neocheating to one sharpened with objective reality. The mist has been lifted from mysticism!

I have much to thank you for, and appreciate Dr. Wallace's exceptional works and your business concepts. Thanks to Neo-Tech, there is optimism and strength from within. It's nice to know that one can obtain this strength (power, prosperity, happiness, and romantic love) from honesty and anti-mysticism.

Neo-Tech Advantage #46
END OF A GOOD RELATIONSHIP
VOLUNTARY AND INVOLUNTARY

A serious romantic relationship can last and grow forever. But if growth stops and cannot be revived, the relationship should end before the growth potential of either partner diminishes. If a good relationship does end, however, each partner can and should retain the values and benefits of all past growth.

Voluntary termination of a psychuous relationship requires a carefully considered, mutually reasoned decision to avoid the tragic mistake of terminating a good relationship unnecessarily. A decision to terminate should include a thoughtful plan to avoid harm to either partner while preserving the growth and values already achieved.

Involuntary termination of a good relationship through death is final. Still, the living partner must continue growing. Involuntary termination of a good relationship can also be initiated through errors of one or both partners. Each partner must fight to save a good relationship from being destroyed by errors. Each must identify the errors and reject destructive mysticism that always seeks to destroy values by creating problems where none exist.

When ending a previously good relationship, no matter how much pain or hurt is involved, great efforts should be made to leave one's partner in a positive, uplifted condition. That effort can deliver long-term benefits to both partners, including a preservation of past growth and values, along with a freer, guiltless position from which to seek a new relationship and happiness.

But terminating a hopelessly destructive relationship is quite different. Just frankly stating the necessity to end the relationship and then walking away from it completely and forever is often the healthiest, least painful method for everyone. A complete and decisive physical and emotional break leaves both partners freer to reestablish separate lives more quickly for new growth and renewed happiness.

Whenever love dies, reasons always exist. But the reasons are not always obvious. A person can better prepare for a future relationship by identifying the reasons for failure through high-effort, honest introspection.

Neo-Tech Advantage #47
LOYALTY TO HONESTY
THE WAY TO HANDLE PROBLEMS

Honesty is not automatic. It always requires explicit, conscious effort. Being honest is hard work...very hard work. If, in difficult emotional situations, one is not aware of the concentrated effort required to be honest, that person is probably not being fully honest. At that point, he or she can easily plug into effortless mysticism. For with mysticism, a person can easily rationalize out-of-context scenarios to avoid the effort required to understand reality and solve one's own problems.

Jon S. R-4776, CANADA

Until I learned of Neo-Tech, I always described life as "the time between the times," i.e. the time one has between the time of one's birth and the time of one's death. Biologically, of course, life does begin at birth but the concepts of Neo-Tech and biological immortality have changed my past definition. Life that is really life, life as it is meant to be - happy and prosperous - does not truly begin at birth nor, as the saying goes, does life begin at 40. Real life, I've now discovered, begins when one starts to explore Neo-Tech. It is my hope that your institute will be successful in seeing that there is no end to this journey of discovery and exploration.

Ricu R. C-305

INFORMATION HAS BROUGHT ME INTO TOTAL CONSCIOUSNESS OF LIFE AROUND ME AND HAS ASWERED MANY QUESTIONS, AND FREED ME OF ALL GUILT, CONTROL, AND NEOCHEATERS

I SEE NOTHING BUT PROSPERITY, HAPPINESS AND A BETTER UNDERSTANDING OF WHAT A HUMAN BEING CAN ACHIEVE CLEARER THAN EVER BEFORE.

THIS WORK IS A MASTER PIECE OF TIME AND ENERGY. LOOKING FORWARD TO NEO THINK AND ALL FUTURE CORRESPONDENCE.

Developing the skills for being honest is neither automatic nor easy. Honesty requires high-effort concentration, discipline, and awareness. Because of the constant effort required to be honest, many people default to mysticism and thus lose the essential tool for solving problems — for achieving prosperity, power, and happiness.

Fully integrated honesty evolves from the great efforts required to be consistently honest. By contrast, mystical dishonesty evolves from self-deceptions and defaults — from a self-chosen laziness that relegates honesty to a low priority, especially when feelings are involved. ...With mysticism, honesty becomes arbitrary.

A commitment to honesty with one's romantic-love partner is essential for achieving psychuous pleasures. In an open relationship, each partner is free to follow those actions self-judged best for his or her own rational well-being. Each must also be equally free to make and correct his or her own errors. Both must strive to meet their individual needs for growth. Both must accept the fact that neither has any physical or psychological ownership over the other. With total freedom and self-responsibility to guide one's own life, each partner develops an ever-growing accumulation of strengths. Those new strengths allow each to continually feed fresh love and enriching values to the other.

With each partner feeding new strength and values into the relationship, each benefits from the other's unique experiences. With such constant values coming from free and independent sources, the excitement between partners can grow continuously, often by large leaps, toward increased psychuous pleasures and abiding happiness. With this never-ending, spiraling growth, each partner becomes increasingly valuable to the other. Thus, fewer and fewer circumstances could threaten or replace such a romantic-love relationship.

Like money in the bank, newly added values accumulate with interest. And with time, the strength of such value-built relationships becomes so great that no outside force, no matter how valuable or appealing, could compete. ...Such self-built, continually added strengths and values offer the only genuine security for any romantic-love relationship.

By contrast, sexual affairs hidden from one's love partner are deceptive and, therefore, dishonest and destructive. Moreover, such affairs are usually too restricted by their secrecy to deliver continuously growing values. ...Honesty and rationality are the foundations of psychuous pleasures and romantic love.

Honest disputes without physical aggression or psychological injury can be valuable. Verbal disputes can cut through emotional blocks to release repressed feelings and foster communication. But undisciplined let-it-all-hang-out anger and negativity are immature, unhelpful, destructive. Also, disputes become destructively dishonest when one or both partners silently save up the "worst" faults or problems of the other in order to use them later as manipulative weapons. ...Saving up faults is a common, immature tactic used to break up or end relationships.

Steve G.   C-315

    I was, at first, shocked and amazed but the more I read the more my eyes were opened.

    Neo-Tech is worth thousands of dollars to any individual. I have spent a lot of money in the past on books that were just garbage and because of this I was reluctant to buy neo-Tech. I took the chance and changed my whole outlook on life as a result.

    I know I will have to read neo-Tech again and again before I fully understand everything contained within the concepts.

    Frank Wallace, and everyone in I&O have put together a marvellous package. I look forward to neothink and works on music, sport etc.

    The world is looking good again!

Glenn M.   C-316

Congratulations on your excellent work.

Most impressive!

Within a romantic-love relationship, the problems that do arise provide opportunities to discover new strengths and values for richer love and pleasures. Even if certain problems seem unresolvable, they can be mutually understood if discussed honestly. And the more explicitly problems are understood, the more satisfying will be their resolutions. Moreover, with sufficient information and honest efforts, all disagreements can eventually be resolved without compromises by either partner.

An efficient approach for resolving conflicts is to reduce the disputed differences to writing and then find the common premises always revealed by self-honesty [Re: Communication Map in Tables 26a and 26b, Neo-Tech Reference Encyclopedia]. Explicitly breaking down problems into communication maps usually generates happy agreements. Even if a problem cannot be completely resolved, the honest communication will (a) draw each partner closer, and (b) develop greater competence in solving future problems. [Re: Table 26b, Neo-Tech Reference Encyclopedia]

Neo-Tech Advantage #48
GUILTLESS FREEDOM TO BE ONESELF

For a healthy romantic relationship, each partner must grant the other guiltless, free choice to enter any growth relationship (in principle, including sexual) with any person of value. In growing romantic-love relationships, however, the circumstances for an outside, rational *sexual* relationship are essentially nil. But one must always have guiltless freedom of choice to enter such outside relationships.

Acceptance or approval by people other than one's romantic-love partner is *not* a requirement for success, happiness, or psychuous pleasures: To achieve psychuous pleasures, a person must be free to be one's own self and choose one's own actions. Trying to be different from one's rational self is a distortion of human nature and contrary to romantic love.

Likewise, a person cannot change another person's nature. For, one's nature can be changed only from within that person, not from without. Of course, a person can develop his or her own character and correct errors as new knowledge is acquired. Such changes are the process of personal growth. And such growth comes through volitional choices to honestly integrate new knowledge.

A person is what he or she is. To pretend to be anything else is to present a false illusion requiring dishonest role playing. A person diminishes any personal relationship to the extent that a false illusion is presented.

Carl R   CB-200

THROUGH THIS MONUMENTAL CREATION OF NEO-TECH, YOU HAVE PRODUCED UNTOLD OF VALUES FOR MYSELF.

I'M STILL ONLY SCRATCHING THE SURFACE OF THE IMPLICATIONS CONTAINED IN THESE GOLDEN VOLUMES (I'M ONLY HALF WAY THROUGH NEO-TECH II), BUT I FEEL AT ONCE A RELEASE FROM THE YEARS OF MYSTICISM I HAVE SUCCUMBED TO, AS WELL AS A SURGE OF ENERGY AND CLARITY I HAVEN'T EXPERIENCED SINCE BEING A CHILD.

Patrick W.   R-2092, ENGLAND

Neo-Tech Beyond doubt the most powerful & valuable investment of my life. The work is brilliantly integrated, consistent & continuously valuable to me.

Dr Wallace leaves me without words to express my admiration for such an achievement.

Enlightened & happy to have the answers.

S.A.G.   R-5513, France

Super, at last the key to happiness!

A person must present oneself as "This is me. Take me or leave me as I am". Only from that position can a person proceed with the genuine growth required for romantic love, psychuous pleasures, and abiding happiness.

Accepting a "take me or leave me" position does not mean specific errors should be accepted or uncriticized. A person can and should change erroneous views and destructive traits (such as mysticism and dishonesty) through character development. Furthermore, each partner must be free to constructively point out harmful errors in the other as well as to be open to criticism about one's own self. Moreover, each partner should expect continuous growth in the other. ...But if a person does not accept the nature of his or her partner, the romantic-love relationship will deteriorate.

Two dangers exist in criticizing one's romantic-love partner:

The first danger is that criticism may unintentionally turn into an invalid attack on the partner's basic self. And attacking a partner's basic self can end the relationship. Still, if certain aspects of a partner's basic self are unacceptable, ending the relationship may be the best, most rational action.

The second danger concerning criticism involves *avoiding* valid, specific criticism for fear of causing problems or rejection. Avoiding criticism cuts off important areas of communication necessary for personal growth. Both partners must be free to express themselves to the other: their compliments and criticism, their likes and dislikes. Valid praise and criticism should not be held back, but should be expressed in specifics to avoid insincere flattery or manipulative criticism (i.e., using criticism as a tool to pressure a person).

Allowances must be made for errors. Through misunderstandings or wrong premises, one partner may erroneously criticize the other. And to the degree erroneous criticism occurs, the relationship will be diminished until the error is corrected.

Most people have large capacities for self-improvement and correcting errors, especially in an atmosphere of benevolent freedom. Having guiltless freedom to make discoveries along with errors and subsequently being able to correct those errors lets each partner develop into his or her best possible self with the most values to offer the other partner.

Mistakes and errors need not do permanent damage. When faced and dealt with, most errors become self-revealing solutions that create new areas of strength, knowledge, and growth. ...Guiltless freedom is essential for converting one's errors and problems into assets.

Don M. C-306, CANADA

Thanks to the Neo-Tech discovery I can now imagine a world where everyone is honest--devoted to producing tradeable values.

Now let us see!

This would mean:

- no need for Law Enforcement
- no need for a military
- no need for big government

therefore ?

- no need for taxes?

With the old mystical expressions demystified such as:

"Everyone has to die sometime!"

no longer valid

no longer do I have the death wish:

"If I have to go sometime, I might as well go happy"

Now released from this terrible concept

I have stopped drinking alcohol "cold turkey"

The inspiration that we were supposed to get from religion but never did

is now mine!

Now we must concentrate our effort on protecting and

prolonging that which is the most important

single element in the universe

SOARING CONSCIOUS/ LIFE

Concentrated Research into:

- Prolonging life
- Preserving life
  - Safety on the highways
  - Safety in the work place----etc.

Neo-Tech Advantage #49
THE INJUSTICE OF JEALOUSY
GT JEALOUSY VS. BT JEALOUSY

Neo-Tech identifies two types of sexual jealousy: *good-thought* (GT) and *bad-thought* (BT).* Both types are based on the erroneous assumption that one has a claim on his or her love-partner's life, especially that person's sex life.** The feelings of jealousy arise when the unreal presumption of possessing one's partner seems challenged. GT jealousy is characterized by the retention of basically *good thoughts* about one's partner, even when pain or anger is generated. Most people can experience various degrees of GT jealousy about their love partners. GT jealousy does not always mean the jealous-reacting partner is insecure or possessive, especially if the jealousy is experienced only as a passing feeling. GT jealousy, even if severely painful, rarely inflicts deep or permanent damage on either partner or the relationship.

---

*Although sexual jealousy is common and perhaps exists to some degree in most people, such jealousy is neither natural nor psychologically healthy. Such jealousy often stems from insecurity or self-esteem problems. Sexual jealousy is not synonymous with the valid desire for sexual privacy and romantic exclusivity experienced in most value-oriented, love relationships. ...By contrast, nonsexual jealousy (NS) differs from sexual jealousy (GT or BT types). NS jealousy involves relatively harmless, natural desires for values possessed by others. Often NS jealousy is erroneously called "envy". Envy is not a desire to possess values of others, but is a malevolent desire to **destroy** values earned by others. Envy is rooted in the fear of exposing one's own inadequacy, incompetence, impotence. Productive people can experience harmless NS jealousy, while nonproductive people often experience destructive envy [Re: Concepts 133 and 134, Neo-Tech Reference Encyclopedia].

Note: No value judgment is or can be made on emotions alone. Only the choice to react rationally or irrationally to an emotion can be judged good or bad. The above judgments are based on jealous reactions, not jealous emotions. The choice to act rationally in avoiding a jealous reaction will help dissipate that harmful emotion. But the harmful, irrational choice to react jealously always feeds and amplifies that emotion.

**No one can ever really own another person's life, including that person's sex life. Every individual exclusively owns each and every segment of his or her own life. In relationships, people volitionally share, not own, various aspects or segments of each other's lives. In a romantic-love relationship, by nature, many more life experiences are intimately shared and integrated (but not owned) than in other types of human relationships. Also, while certain segments of a person's life can be temporarily rented or hired as in a voluntary employer-employee relationship, no part of a person's life can be actually owned by anyone else.

Albert R.

As I was reading Neo-Tech, I could feel the chains that bind me breaking one at a time. Your books are most enlightening and at times shocking. I realize now that neo-cheaters and external authority have controlled me and binded me my whole life. Neo-cheaters no longer control me, and external authorities are slowly disappearing.

Kevin P. R-2551

I am overwhelmed by Neo-Tech. At first I thought it was going to be a magic formulea of how to get rich.

I think the realisation that the responsibility for everything was totally upon my own shoulders was the first "shock". But I soon got to work and have improved things for myself 2000% in just 12 weeks, and I feel as if I haven't even started yet!

Likewise, GT jealousy seldom cuts deeply into the emotions because positive feelings about one's partner dominate the underlying emotions.

BT jealousy, on the other hand, is a destructive, mystical reaction that conjures up, often out of nothing, unjust *bad thoughts* about one's partner. Those bad thoughts are often well concealed, but are insidiously destructive to the emotions of both partners. In contrast to GT jealousy in which good thoughts are retained about one's partner, BT or bad-thought jealousy prevents the jealous partner from knowing, accepting, remembering, or believing the values in the victim partner. Instead, unreal bitterness, cynicism, or malevolence against the victim partner is conjured up by BT jealousy. Such negative illusions are usually rooted in past experiences not even related to the victim partner. The victim partner usually senses a "bad-person" feedback from the BT jealous person. That causes the victim to respond with increasing puzzlement or astonishment followed by anger, dislike, and a sense of injustice. Those negative emotions usually keep building until they eventually outweigh all the good feelings and values between the partners. At that point, love and the relationship die.

The Neo-Tech/Psychuous Concepts identify and can overcome both types of jealousy, especially the GT type. BT jealousy is more difficult to overcome because the cause is a cancerous mysticism that becomes deeply rooted in one's emotions. Cognitive-based psychotherapy* may help overcome BT jealousy and its destructive effects. But the only certain cure is to use mystic-breaking, integrated honesty to self-command *all* actions. Without that integrated honesty, one will continue reacting to the emotions of jealousy.

---

*Effective cognitive psychotherapy is objectively oriented around the cognitive nature of human beings (rather than mystically oriented around behavioral and social natures). To be effective, a therapist must understand the relationships between reason and emotions, between self-esteem and mental health, between mysticism and mental illness. Unfortunately, few psychologists or psychiatrists are oriented around objective standards, even fewer work with or even understand the relationship between self-esteem and mental health. And only a minute fraction, if any, in the profession understand mysticism as the prime disease of the human mind and the only disease of human consciousness.

(Footnote continued on next page)

Tom K.   R-357

I'VE SPENT YEARS AND YEARS OBTAINING A LITTLE BIT OF INFORMATION FROM EACH OF HUNDREDS OF BOOKS. I'VE NEVER READ SUCH A COMPLETE SOURCE OF PERTINENT INFORMATION. THESE CONCEPTS ARE DEFINATELY ONES TO FOLLOW AND TO LIVE BY.

Dan B.   R-404

In reading Neo-Tech I note honesty, forthrightness that has not been allowed to surface heretofore.

Hugh P.   R-1624

No material that I have read during my 67 years approaches the depth, quality and force of NEO-TECH.

The fraudulent God concept, for instance, enslaved me for most of my life. I am now free of the influences of the theologians.

And I no longer hold bureaucrats and politicians in high esteem.

James W.   R-1514

Neo-Tech teaches you to see the REALITY of events as opposed to the illusions the parasites project

The bad thoughts of BT jealousy along with its hostile possessiveness and obligatory demands become increasingly unreal, unfair, and burdensome to the victim partner. Such jealousy will eventually destroy any love relationship no matter how strong were the original love and values. BT jealousy is an unfair, hostile foisting of one's own personal problems or inadequacies onto the victim partner. The mounting obligatory demands and hostile possessiveness of BT jealousy destroys a love relationship by penalizing the victim partner for the very values he or she offers. In fact, the more values offered, the greater are the penalties — the greater are the possessive attacks and obligatory demands. Indeed, BT jealousy, possessiveness, and obligatory demands are not only unreal and mystical, but are always unjust since the victim is penalized to the extent he or she offers values to the jealous partner.

The jealous partner ignores the free-choice position necessary to build a healthy, permanent romantic-love relationship. The jealous partner accepts the false idea that outside relationships or associations are by nature threatening [Re: Concept 63, Neo-Tech Reference Encyclopedia]. Furthermore, the jealous partner erroneously judges his or her partner in terms of unrelated, outside experiences and relationships rather than in terms of their own relationship [Re: Concept 63, Neo-Tech Reference Encyclopedia].

Through mysticism, jealousy destroys values by focusing on what is *not* given or not available...while ignoring, abusing, tearing down, or destroying what is given or is available. Through Neo-Tech, the non-mystic

---

(Footnote from previous page continued)

That is why most psychiatrists and psychologists have poor "cure" records. Most such therapists are ineffective or harmful in helping their patients find real, long-range solutions to their problems. Ineffective therapy not only costs the patient much time and money, but increases the long-range damage by camouflaging the problem under illusions or feelings of relief, well-being, improvement, or cure. Those illusions are like drugs: they give temporary feelings of euphoria on which the patient becomes increasingly dependent. But the problems always reemerge in other forms, often in forms more destructive than previously experienced.

To benefit from therapy, the patient must first determine the therapist's honesty, integrity, and criterion for mental health. If, on questioning, the therapist's treatment is not clearly based on the biological nature of man and a criterion of self-esteem, the patient should seek another therapist. A wrong or an incompetent therapist can cost a patient's long-range happiness, even his or her life. Also, the need for ever using psychotherapy, especially in overcoming internal mysticism is questioned in Neo-Tech Advantage #73 entitled, "The Nature of Emotions". In fact, most neuroses are self-chosen indulgences in mysticism for which therapy is of little value. Usually, only a self-chosen maturity and honesty to break that mystical indulgence (cause) will end the symptomatic neurosis (effect).

Michael B.   R-3598,   ENGLAND

To me it was an explicit explanation of everything that had hitherto been vague and ambiguous. — That self-responsibility for ones own destiny can be the only basis for morality. Any other ethical theorizing is hocus-pocus and a poisonous confidence-trick played by those who have a vested interest in devitalizing and emasculating others; thus revenging themselves upon life itself.

Altruism is a pitiless instrument, with its aid mystics can play the tyrant.

Thank you Neo-Tech for freeing me from slavery from condoning and subsidizing the despotic irresponsibility of mystics.

Kathleen H.   R-2236

A couple of months ago, we purchased a copy of Neo-Tech from you. We could not let such an inspiring, comprehensive achievement go unacknowledged.

In this Age of Confusion, it is the work of people like yourself, and many other great minds that lend hope for the future of mankind. Through your efforts, you have now reached a few more minds in the philosophical and intellectual vacuum that has been pervasive in this country (and the world) for far too long.

We look forward to receiving any information concerning your future endeavors, as well as Neo-Think and any other of your writings.

Please regard us as strong supporters in your battle.

Respectfully yours,

appreciates and focuses on what values are given or are available and then builds from that position — and only from that position.

"Testing" is simply another form of jealousy in which one partner translates his or her insecurity into testing the victim partner for proof of love or fidelity. Such "testing" is unfair, immature, and continually escalates until the values of a relationship are destroyed.

Neo-Tech Advantage #50
THE POISON CORE OF JEALOUSY

BT jealousy will eventually destroy even the deepest love relationships. Jealousy gradually poisons the friendship aspects of love. Once that friendship is gone, no link remains to hold together the nonsexual aspects of the relationship.

Within the person projecting bad-thought jealousy, a core of bitter, poisonous emotions develops (although often initially hidden). That core increasingly releases bad feelings toward the victim partner which, in turn, unfairly diminishes the victim's freedom and happiness. Recognizing the presence of that poison core is the first step in keeping BT jealousy from destroying a relationship. But once that core is formed, it is difficult to free oneself from its destructive effects.

The problem of BT jealousy cannot be wished away. For the poison core usually develops from mystical defaults deep within the jealous partner's subconscious [Re: Table 27, Neo-Tech Reference Encyclopedia]. Unless identified and removed, that poison core will dissolve the pleasure, happiness, and love in any romantic relationship.

Such a poison core generates hostile actions that are often subtle and unrecognized at first. But that jealous partner increasingly takes unjust advantage of the victim partner's innocence, values, love, and goodwill. Such injustice constantly wounds the victim partner and will eventually destroy all love and friendship. Unlike the nonjealous lover who usually experiences pain whenever his loved one is in pain, the BT jealous lover will often gain a satisfying sense of security on being able to inflict pain on the victim partner. That malevolence of BT jealousy eventually negates any value of the relationship.

A person should avoid listening to false accusations or unjust innuendos leveled against oneself or others by a jealous, envious, or gossipy person. Even though the conscious mind can reject known false charges, such accusations still enter nonanalytical pockets of the subconscious mind. That, in turn, causes subsequent emotions to automatically reflect negative feelings toward oneself or the person being falsely accused. A person is helpless in avoiding those unjust, harmful, subconscious reactions. Likewise, a person is essentially powerless to avoid the guilt or bad feelings resulting from false implications coming from a BT jealous partner. As long as that relationship continues, the jealous partner can increasingly inflict deep psychic damage to

Nichole S. F-108, FRANCE

What a wonder Neo Tech is! What a wonderful world it lets us see. It's staggering! It is true that Neo cheaters pollute. I see them better now because Neo Tech is a magnifying glass spread over the universe, the details are startling. How honesty is so rare; thanks to the Neo Tech Army which is on the move, man will become free and happy. What a relief to see the world from an angle of supreme happiness. With all the efforts of the Neo Tech people our world will become an Eden. Man's wisdom will have finally arrived. Let Biological Immortality rule.

Clyde P. R-422

BEST INVESTMENT I HAVE MADE TO DATE! THIS INFORMATION HAS FREED ME FROM A 10 YEAR ADDICTION PROBLEM OF ALCOHOL AND MARIJUANA. I AM NOW WELL ON MY WAY OF DEPROGRAMING MYSELF OF FOURTY YEAR'S OF YIELDING TO THE EXTERNAL AUTHORITIES OF FAITH AND GOVERMENT, WHICH I NOW KNOW WAS LEADING ME TO DEATH!

the victim's subconscious. The victim partner suffers damage proportional to his or her exposure to the poison core of a BT jealous partner. Usually the only release from that damage is for the victim partner to terminate that harmful relationship.

By contrast, a non-mystic, Neo-Tech partner will ask: "Judge me by what you know about my deeds and actions. Do not judge me on your feelings, wishes, imagination, or what others say. And I will always grant you the same".

Neo-Tech Advantage #51
UNNECESSARY AGING

As people grow older, their views of life often grow increasingly negative. Their hopes and dreams often turn into disillusions. On aging, such people gradually lose the capacity to experience the joy inherent in life. Their anticipation of life continually diminishes as their used-up, shrinking futures become evident and the inevitability of death draws closer. ...But Neo-Tech reverses that dying process by allowing life and happiness to grow with age and experience.

Age is no factor in achieving psychuous pleasures, except for the possible lack-of-knowledge limitations of adolescent sex [Re: Concept 80, Neo-Tech Reference Encyclopedia]. Moreover, psychuous pleasures can continually increase with age as one widens his or her values, knowledge, and experience. In building psychuous pleasures, a person's psychological growth can far outweigh so-called physical aging effects. Emotional and physical pleasures as well as prosperity and happiness can increase indefinitely for any honest, productive individual applying Neo-Tech knowledge.

For most people, both sexual and nonsexual pleasures unnecessarily diminish with age. Negative philosophical and psychological changes occur as their futures fade and their spans of remaining years shrink. They despair and become sour with age while increasingly surrendering to the mystics' come-to-God or waiting-for-death attitudes. They surrender to the altruistic myth that older people should sacrifice themselves, their careers, their lives to "make room" for youth. With that surrender, a person's happiness fades.

Despite what many physicians erroneously advise,* no mystic-free, productive person has to decline in physical, mental, or sexual activity with

---

*Many physicians are incompetent, especially in the area of sex and aging. But most make themselves appear as all-knowing and infallible to their patients. Blindly following the advice of an incompetent physician not only can damage a patient's physical well-being, but can cost the patient his or her happiness and life. Health, well-being, and happiness are not the responsibilities of physicians, but are the prime self-responsibilities of each individual.

Bud S. R-1182

I learned a lot by reading your 1 to 5 Neo Tech. I am a Senior Citizen 70 years old but look 20 years younger. I have discovered the Fountain of Youth. A while back in my reading. I have used books reading since I was 19 years old, but I have never really learned anything until I used you Neo Tech for information I needed to see things in the clear. I can only thank you.

age. All mystic-free, productive people can experience increasing happiness and quality of life with age because of increasing knowledge, growth, and experience. By applying the Neo-Tech/Psychuous concepts, one can not only avoid the unnecessary, mystical decline toward death, but can continually elevate his or her quality of life and psychuous pleasures through that increased knowledge, growth, and experience.

Sex never renews itself spontaneously. Left unattended, sex gradually diminishes in both quality and value. But with Neo-Tech, the quality and value of sex is continuously renewed and expanded by constantly investing conscious thought and effort into further developing personal values and pleasures. The Neo-Tech/Psychuous concepts allow never-aging growth on all levels of conscious human life (i.e., on physiological, psychological, and philosophical levels). With Neo-Tech, one never needs to age...or die.

Neo-Tech Advantage #52
PARENTS AS SCAPEGOATS

Most people dutifully profess love toward their children and parents. But often the past and present psychological differences, conflicts, demands, and "duties" make genuine love and enjoyment between parents and their children impossible. An important step toward emotional growth is to realize that no one has a duty to love anyone, not even parents, children, husband, wife.

Genuine love occurs only voluntarily, through a mutual exchange of objective and emotional values. Genuine love between parents and children can and does occur in those relationships in which objective values grow and are exchanged. Occasionally, parents may be partially responsible for some problems experienced by certain adolescents and young adults. Too often, however, parents are blamed for their grown children's faults, defaults, sexual shortcomings, and other problems for which those grown children themselves are responsible. Blaming parents only hides or avoids the self-responsibilities and efforts needed to correct one's own personal problems.

Major problems between parents and children often develop from the parents' failure to respect their own children: their failure to treat children as human beings with individual rights. Parents, for example, commonly initiate force and physically assault their children under the euphemisms of spankings, protection, discipline. [Re: Concept 114, Neo-Tech Reference Encyclopedia.] If children are not granted respect, they may never develop respect for themselves, for their parents, or for values themselves. Such children often develop into tomorrow's mystics and neocheaters. They then

Sean F.   R-4348, Australia

Reading your original promotional material (NTP News Report: F.Wallace-Interview. 1986) filled me with a deep feeling of suspicion. It's hard sell over-the-top, too good to be true exclamations were laughable to say the least. I concluded that Neo Tech must be either a philosophical breakthroug or more probably, a grand con-trick. However, my sheer curiosity & fear of ignorance caused me to reach for the cheque book. Was I to be victim or victor ?

Three-quarters way through Neo-Tech II and I had the answer. I was reading revelation after revelation, not from God, but from a man called Wallace. This was too contentious, too profound, too neat, to be a hoax. I was thrilled to be reading this at age 26 rather than 66.

As a trained chemist, I have always been suspicious of the God concept, and N.T. not only swept away any lingering sympathy for religion, but also integrated theology with the evils of politicians, mystics and other assorted parasites.

On the whole, I found N.T. to be a fascinating and elegantly written, arranged and presented piece of work, which is certainly the most valid philosophy for life I have come across.

I would like to thank Dr. Wallace and everybody at I&O, for making Neo-Tech available to me. I have already realised the benefits of possessing N.T. knowledge, for example by simply dismissing doorstep Jehovas-Witnesses with reasoned argument, but probably more significantly by my increased confidence and optimism, which has helped me in planning my own business venture.

Finally, the concept of a Neo-Tech way of life, incorporating biological immortality , is indeed very desirable, however, we must remember that those people who first choose to explore N.T. knowledge are by nature the restless the dissatisfied and the curious fraction of mankind. The rest of society include the apathetic, the lazy, and the non-thinking and completely deluded people who are quite content to career down the path of dreary subsistence. These people represent the majority, and these are the ones who must be inspired into believing that Neo-Tech is not just desirable, but possible.

I believe this represents the real challenge to I&O in realising a Neo-Tech future.

Peter G.   R-1240

I feel as if I've lived for 45 years of darkness and suddenly have been enlightened.

survive by usurping their living as politicians, trouble-making lawyers, destructive bureaucrats, criminals, theologians, media journalists, or educators who hold little respect for honesty, productive business, or individual rights.

By contrast, the two most valuable gifts parents can give their children are (1) respect as conscious human beings with individual rights, and (2) supportive environments that promote honesty, assertive effort, integrity, independence, and the skill to perceive reality accurately.

Neo-Tech Advantage #53
ADOLESCENT, PREMARITAL, AND NONMARITAL LOVE

Sexual feelings begin long before puberty. As noted by Havelock Ellis, Freud, and Kinsey, very young children and even babies two and three months old have sexual experiences (both through self-stimulation and through handling, caring, and fondling by parents). Valid sensuous/sexual pleasures can be experienced between child and parent, especially between mother and child during nursing or nude cuddling. While such pleasures are loving, healthy, and beneficial, those pleasurable values for both the child and parent are often inhibited by incest fears and taboos.

Adolescent sex never need be approached with inhibition or forbiddance. But few adolescents have sufficient emotional development, knowledge, or desire for deep emotional involvements and serious mutual commitments with sexual partners. For adolescents and adults alike, sexual involvement should always be judged from a "good for me"/"bad for me" standard. Serious sexual experiences that deliver growth and happiness through exchanges of objective values are usually good for everyone involved, regardless of age. But sexual relations that are casual, not grounded in objective values, or neurotically based are bad for everyone, regardless of age. For casual sexual relationships undermine self-esteem and block psychuous pleasures.

Adolescents having sexual relationships before they are able or desire to involve themselves in serious value-exchanging relationships will undermine their future capacity for romantic love. The loss of self-esteem resulting from casually giving away one's personal self militates against psychuous pleasures, romantic love, and long-range happiness. For, casual or manipulative sex undercuts self-esteem. But, by understanding the concepts of psychuous sex, one can identify and correct past sexual errors while creating conditions for psychuous pleasures.

Marriage itself is no criterion to commence sexual relations. In fact, avoiding sex until marriage would usually be irrational and potentially harmful to future happiness. In any romantic-love relationship, satisfactory sex is required for full emotional intimacy and growth. In addition to achieving

Bernard M.   R-379, CANADA

Dear MR. Flint,

Sincere congratulations to you and to Dr. Wallace for the work: <u>NEO-TECH</u>. It is a <u>great</u> achievement!

David P.   R-1663

Dr Wallace is a Genius

A. G.   R-395

I agree completely with the observations in the manuscripts.
The boxing-in of the dispersed enemy was a euphoric experience.

I have searched all my life for this information.

For this freedom, I feel a great debt owed to you.

It is my sincere wish that your company efforts succeed.

emotional growth, value-oriented premarital sex helps eliminate harmful anxieties for sex performance often experienced in virginal marriages. That release from sexual anxieties lets each partner concentrate on those nonsexual aspects required for long-lasting, value-producing, romantic relationships.

Nonmarital sexual relations can provide a full range of sexual values and psychuous pleasures. [Re: Concept 68, Neo-Tech Reference Encyclopedia.] Serious nonmarital sexual affairs offer important life-lifting values while avoiding the sacrifice of happiness that dominate closed marriages based on duty and sacrifice rather than honesty and values. Moreover, nonmarital sexual relationships generally allow more time and freedom for self-development and creative work, which in turn, provides increasing values, happiness, and strength to the relationship.

Most valid, growing romantic-love relationships can and do lead to marriage*, usually flourishing, lasting marriage.

Neo-Tech Advantage #54
SEDUCTION TECHNIQUES:
CASUAL, SERIOUS, MUTUAL

The first known sex manual was written about 2 B.C. by a Roman named Ovid. His manual stressed seduction techniques for *casual sex*. In addition, the manual aggressively promoted the Don Juan and "Playboy" fun views of sex while teaching various role-playing games and manipulative techniques for the seduction of women.

The Don Juan and "Playboy" approaches to sex use hypnosis**, manipulations of sex partners, and pragmatic dishonesty of professing

---

*Marriage in this context does not necessarily mean "legal" marriage, but means any serious long-term, romantic-love relationship mutually agreed on by each partner. "Legal" marriage has no bearing on the success or failure of a relationship. The mutual decision for sharing life in a serious, sexual-love relationship is the fundamental entity for building a romantic-love relationships that deliver psychuous pleasures and long-range happiness.

**Rapid hypnosis and self-hypnosis techniques can be easily mastered (e.g., see Bibliography Summary Table B-2 in Neo-Tech Reference Encyclopedia for D. Elman's book, "Exploration in Hypnosis", Nash Publishing. Note: Amateur hypnosis can do psychological damage and is not recommended in any form). Indirect, subtle forms of hypnosis are the most important tools in a Don Juan's seduction repertoire. Ironically, a subconscious form of negative-feedback self-hypnosis is the primary mechanism that leads to impotence and frigidity not only for Don Juans, but for almost everyone who dishonestly manipulates sex partners

Francois E.   F-111, FRANCE

After reading Neo Tech for the second time I have just lost 32 yrs of illusion. In november 1987 I realised that I had given 32 yrs to others. That for 32 yrs I did nothing but serve the neocheaters who were my family, my friends and my colleagues.

I was always available with time money etc ---- and never did anything for me or mine.

Today it's over. I am being reborn at 33 yrs old. My wife and my true friends don't recognize me anymore.

I was transformed into a producer of values conscious of my own capacities. True values according to my own ideas and concepts. In four months I eliminated the neocheaters around me that were preventing my development.

Ended is neocheating.

"sincerity" and "seriousness" when strategically advantageous for conquest. But most modern-day Don Juans can only feign lust while actually being terrified of their own sexual inadequacies. Many macho Don Juans have never experienced psychological orgasms and remain psychosexual virgins all their lives — they never develop a capacity for delivering or receiving psychuous pleasures [Re: concept 45, Neo-Tech Reference Encyclopedia].

Behind every sexual relationship is either a healthy or an unhealthy motive, although often hidden or subconscious. A person should become aware of a partner's motive for a sexual relationship. Hiding unhealthy or neurotic motives for a sexual relationship is eventually harmful to both partners.

Negative, after-reaction emotions are natural warning signals from the human nervous system. If a person does something that is "not good for me" physically or psychologically, the nervous system will let that person know with hangover reactions of pain or discomfort. After-the-fact feelings transmitted from the nervous system always signal if past actions were objectively "good for me" or "bad for me".

No matter how irrational or immoral if enacted in reality, fantasies are never immoral, wrong, or harmful when experienced or expressed without external action. For, fantasies are never harmful as long as they remain in the non-action fantasy stage.

Seductiveness (in the traditional, casual-sex sense) and sensuousness are two different qualities. Traditional seductiveness involves sly trickery to accomplish an end (e.g., sexual seduction) — often for neurotic macho-like purposes (e.g., to bolster a weak self-esteem.)

Sensuousness, on the other hand, involves openness and self-expression free of guilt.* Sensuousness is a healthy trait, while seductiveness is

---

*Self-expression is reflected in a person's body movements. The combined effects of guiltless relaxation and awareness of bodily pleasures allow the muscular motions to function in a free-movement, animal-like fashion...in the graceful, pleasurable way the human body is meant to move (such as in the gracefully sensuous movements of cats through their free, guiltless nature). A human being is a beautifully graceful animal when the total muscle system is functioning in a guiltlessly relaxed, free-flowing state. That state is reached by using Neo-Tech to expunge the unnecessary guilt, tensions, and problems laid on everyone for 2000 years by the professional mystics and neocheaters.

Matt T.   R-352

Neo-Tech II is unusual because it is a product of a ruthless application of reason, and this has a beauty all its own. It is a great work of art.

Randal S. M.

To merely pick up the manuscript of The Neo-Tech Discovery is to know that something awesome has been unleashed and that, at last, it is guarded by a single-minded purposeness that can sustain and prosper in the crucible of man's intelligence. I look foreward to reading more, experiencing more and contributing to this brave adventure.

Sincerly,

Gaye B.   R-65

For over 30 years I was genuinely involved in religious study with a goal of being a teacher-lecturer. I truly believe that the psychological effects you mention happened to me.

Now, I sincerely believe that Neo-Tech is absolutely essential for awakening us from mesmeric-manipulating methods of the Neocheaters.

generally an unhealthy trait. Sensuousness honestly used to enhance personal appeal adds to long-range pleasure and happiness. Seductiveness used to manipulate sex partners undercuts self-esteem and happiness.

But, seduction techniques for *serious sex* can be honest and beneficial. Those techniques are more accurately described as "sensuous projections" and differ from casual seduction techniques that depend on deceit. Sensuous projections are done through both verbal and body communication. The presentation of a person's body and words can be sexually provocative if projected with calculated thought. Those techniques are nonmanipulative and can be mastered through understanding the nature of psychuous sex. Men and women using the Neo-Tech/Psychuous concepts can quickly achieve effective sensuous-projection techniques. The techniques involve integrating clothes, cosmetics, hair with one's body, face, voice, expressions — all combined to project sexual attractiveness. Once acquired, those advantage-gaining techniques are available for life.

A basic right, indeed a self-duty, of every human being is to be sexually attractive. Natural attractiveness is a given that has no moral virtue. But self-made, sexual attractiveness is an admirable, moral virtue that requires continuous thought and effort. Keeping one's self sexually attractive throughout life is a highly rational act of self-responsibility that delivers increased power, prosperity, and romantic love. ...Contrary to the cancer seeds planted by mystics and neocheaters, self-made sexiness does not reflect any lack of values or promiscuity. But, to the contrary, self-made sexiness reflects a respect for values and self.

The primary attraction between two people moving toward rational, romantic-love relationships is their character traits, not their personality traits. Likewise, character development is the chief element in successful romantic-love relationships. And a romantic relationship based on psychuous sex usually develops into a *mutual* seduction process. During that process both partners project mounting sensuous, sexual attractiveness between them. Non-manipulative seductions are innocent projections of sexual attractiveness combined with trust, honesty, and care. That kind of seduction helps both partners plumb rich, personal depths with each other — physically and emotionally.

Neo-Tech Advantage #55
PHYSICAL BEAUTY, ABUSE OF PARTNER, POTENCY LOSS, SEXUAL ROLES

Because of their greater ease in initially attracting sexual partners, individuals with great natural, physical beauty must be cautious of the tempting traps inherent in easily obtainable sexual love:

Lowell B. R-1850

Dear Mr. Wallace,

I would like to thank you for your Neo-Tech II information package.

My first value was to stop smoking. I had tried many times and many ways, including hypnosis, but was never able to get past the first day. It has been eighteen days now since my last smoke and I am very sure that I will never be a slave to a cigarette agin.

Randal H. R-4843

Dear Dr. Flint,

   Prior to receiving the Neo-Tech Discovery in June of 1987 I had been unemployed for two years, my wife worked and the rent we paid for a seedy and run-down little house in a lower class neighborhood was making my landlord rich, to make matters worse, my marriage of 17 years was on the rocks and sinking fast; life was without purpose, merit or hope.

   In just six short months (it is now December 1987), I have become fully employed, now own my own home in an upper class neighborhood consisting of four bedrooms, two baths, family room with fireplace, formal dining room, den/computer room and other luxery extras. My marriage, while not yet fully repaired is fast recovering. I will be starting my own business at the begining of the new year and fully expect to be financially independent within the next twelve months. My life now has a well-defined focus and a definite purpose.Although the financial rewards are nice, nothing can compare with my newly-acquired sense of real personal power; a feeling that grows daily.

A few people, because of their stunning natural beauty, are not directly subjected to nature's vigorous sexual competition. To achieve love, sexual pleasures, and happiness, most people recognize early in life that they must become competitively attractive through high-effort development of character and competence. In adulthood, those who grew up accepting the challenge to self-develop can easily outcompete those natural beauties who earlier in life never experienced those pressures to develop. As a result, many people with great natural beauty sadly grow old remaining undeveloped, immature, incompetent, unable to love or be loved.

Achieving psychuous pleasures and romantic love require the same discipline, thought, and effort for every individual, regardless of innate physical appearances. Likewise, a person must be cautious of involvement with people of exceptional, natural beauty whose personal lives reflect low-effort, low-productivity. Such individuals often let their natural beauty substitute for the long-term effort required to develop characters of competence, self-esteem, and sensuosity required for romantic-love.* Physically beautiful people of low productivity often default on their sexual-character development to become not only boring, value-draining people, but also poor lovers with low self-esteems.

Physically attractive people can easily develop "lady-killer" or "man-killer" syndromes in their relationships. Being a seductive "killer" can temporarily boost a weak ego by feeling a power to destroy values and hurt others. But that syndrome leads the perpetrator into life-wasting, destructive relationships. Indeed, a person who mistreats or manipulates his or her love partner usually suffers much more in the long run than the abused partner. For that abused partner will have new chances for love and happiness. But the chronic manipulator loses his or her capacity for love and is left with a future of increasing unhappiness, sexual incompetence, romantic failures, and ultimate loneliness. ...And the inevitable sexual impotence or frigidity evolves either consciously or subconsciously:

<u>Conscious Loss of Potency</u>
Anxieties caused by pressures from "expected" sexual performances cause impotence and frigidity. Impotence also occurs through put-down statements from a partner. Such statements or actions occur either willfully

---

*Often displaying similar development problems are homosexuals. For they can easily acquire promiscuous, low-effort sexual affairs without subjecting themselves to the pressures of heterosexual competition. ...Such competitive environments exert healthy pressures needed for developing strong, mature, responsible adults.

Godwin H.   R-4000

I received Neo-Tech information package on 30-3-87 after reading it, I found the information packages to be excellent. They made clear why people can be controlled through their bicameral minds and that the ultimate goal is biological immortality.

Neo-Tech taken as a whole, has helped me understand how I have been cheated and deceived in all areas of my life.

Neo-Tech has been a new awakening for me, and a new life.

Dr. Wallace has put together the information necessary for mankind to shape his future and ultimate destiny.

Yana D.   J-45

the thoroughness, lucidity and practicality of the package was, to say the least, astounding. Reading Neo-Tech inspired me, galvanized my ideas and gave me a sense of professional direction and encouragement that I doubt many written treatises could ever do.

The sapping of energy and creativity by the "collectivist monster" as well as the systematic plunder of values by them from productive, creative individuals must end, and my own goal is to help assure that this barbaric set up ends sometime during my own lifetime.

and maliciously or through error or ignorance. But the effects of such damage are often limited to that particular relationship. Thus, once the problem is identified, the victim can promptly abandon that destructive relationship. Decisively rejecting a "castrating" or "frigidizing" partner usually restores full sexual capacity.

Subconscious Loss of Potency

A less obvious, more dangerous pressure subconsciously corrupts the mind. That pressure comes from listening to false or undercutting statements about the sexual performance of one's own self or others. Such statements, no matter how false, involuntarily lodge in the subconscious mind. That happens even when the conscious mind rejects such statements as false [Re: Concept 77, Neo-Tech Reference Encyclopedia]. By that mechanism, a subconscious undermining of a person's sexual potency or character can occur in one of two ways: (1) by innuendo and other indirect forms of communication, or (2) by sexual or character put-down humor. Even if the conscious mind rejects such put downs, the choice to grant credibility by voluntarily listening lets the subconscious mind accept such specious, harmful information as valid.

The nonanalytical, subconscious mind does not evaluate assertions or distinguish between true and false or serious and humorous information. Thus, on entering the subconscious, the false, undermining information gradually works its damage on the mind and nervous system. For that reason, a person should avoid listening to put downs, attacks, or gossip concerning the character or sexuality about oneself or anyone else. ...Such is the ear and mouth responsibility of everyone.

A person, however, should always be open and receptive to constructive, factually valid criticism about oneself or others.

Impotence and frigidity also develop when a man tries to oppress a woman, or vice versa. A person's willingness to accept such oppression blocks the possibility for psychuous pleasures. Such mutual acquiescence to oppression leads to impotence and frigidity in both partners.* By contrast, a man's psychosexual dominance and a woman's act of *sexual* surrender harmonize with the physical and psychological nature of human beings [Re: Concept 47, Neo-Tech Reference Encyclopedia]. That dominant/surrender interaction permits both partners to achieve the guiltless freedom and emotional closeness necessary for psychuous pleasures.

---

*Chronic mistreatment of a partner almost always involves the tacit willingness of the abused partner. The willingness to mistreat or be mistreated is so profoundly unnatural that psychuous pleasures are impossible in any relationship open to such mistreatment.

Ronald A.   R-3040

I HAVE NOT YET FINISHED THE ENTIRE MANUSCRIPT, BUT WITH WHAT I HAVE READ SO FAR, I RECOGNIZE THE VALUE OF THE INFORMATION I NOW POSSESS. A NEW SELF-CONFIDENCE SURROUNDS ME AND I KNOW THAT I NO LONGER HAVE TO <u>FEAR</u> THE NEO-CHEATERS OF THE WORLD.
MY LIFE HAS TAKEN A NEW, <u>SUCCESSFUL</u> TURN AND I CAN FEEL THE MOMENTUM AT WHICH IT IS PROGRESSING. ALL I CAN SAY IS WHAT ROBIN WILLIAMS ALREADY SAID,
"<u>REALITY</u>... WHAT A CONCEPT!"

Buckley G.   J-178, AUSTRALIA

Thanks to Neo-Tech, 1984 has been a magic year for me — I now realise that I have been extremely fortunate and can take great pride (without any feelings of guilt) in the facts that I am married to an intelligent wonderful person and that I have been in business for 24 years.
After many months I am still studying and learning from the package.

Milan M.   J-145, CANADA

The contents of the Neotech package left me surprised and enthusiastic at the same time. Surprised, because I never thought any such work existed, and enthusiastic, because it provided me with answers that would have taken me a long time to arrive at by sifting through and digesting an endless number of materials.

On the physical level or even on the fantasy level, the dominant/surrender sexual roles can and should be reversed between the man and woman whenever desired. But on a psychological level, those sexual roles cannot be reversed.

Neo-Tech Advantage #56
PSYCHUOUS PLEASURES

Essentially all growth in government power depends on their leaders constantly diminishing or blocking psychuous pleasures in more and more people by continually undermining individual rights. For, only through those rights can people achieve psychuous pleasures through their own efforts, free from mystics, "authorities", and neocheaters. Individual or property rights* are necessary for a person to live as he or she is designed to live — to live according to one's biological nature. Still, those rights have been systematically violated to varying degrees by all governments and religions throughout history.

Today, for the first time in history, Neo-Tech/Psychuous concepts are available to the public. Neo-Tech forever breaks the stranglehold of guilt and sacrifice foisted on the producers by all political and religious neocheaters. Today, Neo-Tech can break that stranglehold to free all productive individuals. Neo-Tech will allow all producers to discover prosperity, psychuous pleasures, and abiding happiness that belong to them. Neo-Tech will release them from the neocheaters who have always lived off the efforts and earnings of others. If value producers use Neo-Tech to reject the guilt foisted on them by the professional mystic and neocheater, they will free themselves not only for psychuous pleasures but for financial prosperity, abiding happiness, and biological immortality [Re: Concepts 145, 146, Neo-Tech Reference Encyclopedia].

Neo-Tech Advantage #57
NATURAL PHENOMENA

Most people call natural phenomena such as various survival and mating behaviors "instinct". But "instinct" is a mystical term that does not exist in humans or in animals. The term "instinct" implies inborn or innate knowledge, which is a false, meaningless notion. The use of "instinct" to

---

*Individual rights and property rights are the same and inseparable. Private property is a natural extension of every human being. And that extension is essential for a person to effectively produce values for others in order to achieve prosperity and happiness. Without property rights, individual rights have no meaning. By contrast, with property rights fully protected, individual rights are fully protected.

Mike M.   R5250

Neo-Tech has changed my life so much that it is hard for me to believe that I've only had it 2½ months!

Before Neo-Tech, I was lazy and irresponsible. I smoked pot, drank alcohol, snorted crank, and lived on cofee and soft drinks. I worked at a minimum wage job and was ready to flunk out of college. Obviously my life was a mess! I was commiting slow suicide.

Neo-Tech turned my life around. I quickly quit all drugs, doubled my income, and for the first time in my life, I will finish an entire quarter of college without skipping a single day of class. Also, my grades are now all A's and my boss tells me that I may soon be running his business!

Its hard to believe that anything can have this kind of affect on a person but its amazing what a difference it makes to see life through eyes that only see what's real. No longer clouded by mystical ideas, I can consistently make decisions in my logical best interest. I've come a long way in a short time and I have a lot further to go. One thing is for sure, the rest of the journey will be exciting and fulfilling!

<u>Thank You!</u>

Arvo J.   R-1833

Definately the most valuable and
interesting reading that I have
ever experienced. Biological Immortality
should be of interest to any and all
life loving people on this planet.
Dismissal of 'mysticism' would provide enhancment of progress for
 all of humanity,

explain behavior is to explain nothing. Moreover, the "instinct" explanation closes further investigation into that which is not yet understood or known. "Instinct" is a mystical, anti-intellectual, anti-scientific term. For, accepting that catchall term as an explanation precludes further intellectual and scientific efforts to discover the reasons for various behaviors. Accepting "instinct" as an explanation for any human behavior constitutes accepting the mystical concept that knowledge can be inborn or innately acquired without the self-integrating efforts required for acquiring all knowledge. Likewise, all living species function through definable, understandable biological actions and reactions, not through undefinable, mystical "instincts". To explain anything as "instinct" is a default to the mystic's desire for automatic, inborn, effortless knowledge.

Neo-Tech Advantage #58
PERSONAL APPEARANCE AND NATURAL BODY FUNCTIONS

Achieving and maintaining good physical fitness and appearance are necessary for developing psychuous pleasures and long-range happiness. On the other hand, physical appearances *not* within one's control are unimportant for achieving psychuous pleasures and happiness. The difference, for example, is between being sloppy and ugly. The natural, physically ugly person can choose to develop character beauty. He or she can then experience the full range of psychuous pleasures and happiness. But careless or sloppy people can never fully experience psychuous pleasures and happiness as long as they choose to remain careless about self or life. For by not caring about self or life, they obliterate their self-esteem and desirability, while cutting themselves off from love and happiness. ...How can anyone ultimately care about those who do not care about themselves?

Consider people who let themselves grow fat.* Such people have chosen to travel on a death curve [Re: Table 32, Neo-Tech Reference Encyclopedia]. Traveling that route, a person's unhappiness and probability of death increases with increasing fatness. In turn, that route devastates a person's self-esteem.

Certain natural body functions are inconvenient, painful, unpleasant. For example, menstruation and child birth labor are not convenient or pleasant body functions, even though they are completely natural. Such inconvenient

---

*Many fat people have self-inflicted, metabolic problems that make permanent weight reduction difficult (even with near-starvation, carbohydrate diets). To effectively lose weight, such people must permanently restrict carbohydrates from their diets via high protein diets (as outlined in Dr. Atkins' book, *Dr. Atkins' Diet Revolution*, McKay). But those high-protein diets are safe only for aerobically fit people as identified in the footnote on the next page. [Re: Concept 91, Neo-Tech Reference Encyclopedia].

James S.   R-2428

Real informative. It has really made me aware of the way neo-cheaters operate.

I am really glad that I obtained a copy of Neo-Tech. It has helped me out a lot in my life. I can feel the power that I have derived from all the information that I have read & studied.

I wish more people could take advantage of Dr. Wallace works.

I see so many people that are ruled by, the Govt, Religion, Polititions, and other non-producers that I am glad that I can reason & make my mind more often to ferrett out all what is going on in the world. Dr. Wallace has done a super endevor & has a lot of people like me to thank him for all he has done to rid the world of the non-producing Neo-cheaters.

Robert Mc.   R-2451

Neo-Tech is one of the greatest pieces of literature that I have read. The information is invaluable.
Thanks,

or painful body functions should be diminished by any practical, safe means. For example, safe and painless child birth methods are now available. And new menses techniques can conveniently eliminate most of the unpleasant effects of monthly menstruation. [Re: *Our Bodies, Ourselves*, the Boston Women's Health Book Collective, Simon & Schuster].

Neo-Tech Advantage #59
PHYSICAL FITNESS, DIET, ADDICTIONS

People who let themselves physically deteriorate or grow obese lose the capacity for psychuous pleasures from both physical and psychological capacities.

Nearly anyone at any age in any physical condition can achieve optimum physical fitness by gradually increasing physical stress with an aerobic-type program totaling less than two hours per week of running, swimming, bicycling, or brisk walking as described in Dr. Kenneth H. Cooper's book, *Aerobics*.* Permanent, optimum body weight can be achieved through low-carbohydrate diet as described in Dr. Robert C. Atkins' book, *Dr. Atkins' Diet Revolution***. Both books taken together are major contributions to human health and well-being that deliver attractiveness, vigor, and happiness.

---

*The best reference for physical fitness through an aerobics program is Dr. Kenneth H. Cooper's book, *Aerobics*, Bantam Books. Dr. Cooper is the originator and developer of the aerobic, physical-fitness system [Re: Book Analysis 2, Neo-Tech Reference Encyclopedia].

The best reference for weight control through a low carbohydrate diet is Dr. Robert C. Atkins' book, *Dr. Atkins' Diet Revolution*, David McKay Company. [Re: Book Analysis 27, Neo-Tech Reference Encyclopedia]. Despite the distorted attacks on Dr. Atkins' diet by many "nutritionists" and some in the medical profession and the A.M.A., Dr. Atkins has developed the most scientifically sound dietary information offered to date. Dr. Atkins' contribution to human well being can significantly extend and improve the lives of those who choose to be *both* physically and aerobically fit. His dietary approach is tailored to the natural carnivorous physiology of human beings. In addition to reaching and maintaining optimum body weight, the low carbohydrate diet can reduce or eliminate the most common forms of chronic fatigue (hypoglycemia or low blood sugar). Dr. Atkins' diet, therefore, can increase a person's capacity for psychuous pleasures and life itself. **But because of the high-cholesterol content, Dr. Atkins' diet is recommended only for those becoming and remaining aerobically fit. ...Any high-protein, low-carbohydrate diet cannot be safely separated from aerobic fitness.

Dexter O.   R-615

IT WAS VERY REFRESHING TO READ SOMETHING BASED ON RATIONALITY INSTEAD OF SENTIMENTALITY. NEO TECH'S GREATEST VALUE, TO ME, IS IN PROVIDING A STABLE, SENSIBLE PHILOSOPHICAL BASE, THAT'S RATIONAL, AND WITICH CAN BE USED TO GUIDE ME THROUGH MY DAY-TO-DAY DECISIONS, AND USED AS A STABLE DATUM TO WITICH OTHER INFORMATION CAN BE COMPARED AND EVALUATED.
                              THANKS

Robert T.   R-1782

YOU HAVE FOUND THE KEY MOTIVATORS IN LIFE

L. P.   R-1527

Dr. Wallace, I certainly have enjoyed your Neo-Tech teachings and concepts. It is fantastic! Unbelievable! I am still a neophyte, but my confidence and personality have changed dramatically. I can see there are greater things possible in the future.

Dallas W.   R-1054

A revelation to human happiness. Never have I felt so free & powerful as I have become from reading Neo-Tech.

A physically fit body is needed to enjoy the full range of psychuous pleasures. The easiest, most efficient way to get and stay in optimum physical condition is to accumulate 30 aerobic points per week according to Dr. Cooper's conditioning system and to eat less than 40 grams of carbohydrate per day according to Dr. Atkins' diet system. **(Both books should be read and understood before embarking on the combined aerobic-fitness/low-carbohydrate diet.)** A trim, fit body adds a major increment of pleasure to nearly every facet of living, especially to work, romance, and sex.

Addictions to sugar, drugs, alcohol, caffeine, nicotine not only undercut physical fitness, personal appearance, personality, and health, but will steadily diminish a person's self-control, self-esteem, and happiness. Such addictions are rampantly common, yet widely unadmitted. Addictions and compulsions also undermine honesty because they constantly require dishonest rationalizations. That dishonesty, in turn, reduces self-esteem, competence, productivity, and psychuous pleasures. ...The Neo-Tech/Psychuous concepts provide a powerful philosophical/psychological base for eliminating all mysticisms that promote addictions and compulsions.

Contrary to popular opinion, no natural conflict exists between the mind and body (or between the intellect and emotions). By nature, the mind and body are designed to work in beneficial harmony with each other — and they do when each is used according to its biological nature.* When the mind and body are not used according to their biological natures, then conflict, pain, and damage result.

An individual has much more voluntary control over his or her physical and mental health than most people realize. Over the long range, a person has almost total control over his or her mental, emotional, and physical well-being. By choosing to consistently use the mind rationally in becoming an honest, productive, independent human being,** a person *can* control his

---

*Objective human standards must be based on the biological natures of men and women functioning as the human organism is designed to function. By integrating logic with the nature of existence, then the biological function of the mind becomes obvious: to identify and integrate reality so human beings can become self-sufficient and independent (materially, intellectually, psychologically, emotionally). Fulfilling integrated biological needs is necessary to experience the self-worth and competence needed to achieve increasing prosperity, psychuous pleasures, and abiding happiness.

**Human beings genuinely prosper only through the rational use of their minds. By dealing logically with reality, they achieve self-sufficiency and independence by producing values for others.

Dear Dr Wallace,

Stephen C.   C-55
United Kingdom

I have read the Neo-Tech packages 1-V twice now since receiving them in August this year.

I am thoroughly impressed with the contents and your findings. Although such logical concepts are not fully realised yet, I can now see a clear path ahead of me with the adoption of those concepts. The reality of these "new" concepts are somewhat frightening when one realises all the altruism and mysticism that surrounds us and has surrounded us for many centuries. My profession is that of taxation consultancy. In this field of knowledge, I see Master Neo-cheating, mysticism and altruism every single day. I experience it in my day to day functions when dealing with tax officials, lawyers, accountants and other Government officials. When I first started out in tax practise I was respectful of our tax system and acted in accord with the Government's commandment;

"Thou shalt pay-over all taxes"

After a few years of consultancy I began to realise the result of the above commandment on the lives' of my clients' and my own life. Now, such commandment represents "legalised theft". The creation of a law, such as tax law, that extracts values from producers' (and sometimes non-producers) with reasons of "public good" or "higher causes" is absolutely immoral and is one of the greatest crimes, against human development, to be committed.

I have no respect for any Government (and their paid agents), any higher cause or any public good enforced upon and against an individual's right to prosperity, romantic love and happiness. The Government of this country (Labour Party) has adopted an altruistic-platonistic connotation which states;

"Everyone must pay their fair share."   (in taxes)

The above statement is invalid and is an altruistic malignancy. What would the above statement possibly mean in monetary terms? I therefore reject such mystical statement as invalid and a non-existence. I was quite surprised with the concepts on religion. Throughout life I have been a part-time believer in God. I never knew whether or not he existed but I do suppose that within my subconscious mind I always believed because other people believed. I thought that it was "good for me" to believe in order that no harm come to me and my loved ones i.e. I would thus not be regarded as a sinner. The one question that has frustrated me for many years was;

continued next page

or her own psychological and physical well being. Every individual always has the choice to rationally solve problems or to default on that responsibility. Those who chronically default on that self-responsibility have no way to earn prosperity, self-esteem, psychuous pleasures, romantic love, or abiding happiness.

Some knowledge has been developed toward understanding the psychosomatic links between the mind, body, and various ailments. The mind-body links are probably much more significant than currently realized. With advancing medical knowledge about controlling body functions and the nervous system, people may someday vanquish even cancer and heart disease through the long-range, controlled use of their minds and bodies.* But, little valid information has been published concerning the mind and a person's potential to control one's well-being. Specific Neothink* books on this subject will be published over the next few years, including the definitive diet book titled, "The CAS Happiness Diet". That diet eliminates the three most widely used drugs that undermine human life, health, and happiness — Caffeine, Alcohol, Sugar.

Neo-Tech Advantage #60
ALCOHOL, MARIJUANA, SUGAR, TOBACCO, AND MYSTICISM:
EFFECTS ON ROMANTIC LOVE AND PSYCHUOUS SEX

Alcohol, marijuana, mysticism, and other reality-distorting agents have both short-range and long-range harmful effects on health and happiness. Even in moderate amounts, alcohol, drugs, and mysticism distort reality. Distortions of reality are harmful because the human organism depends on accurate perception of reality to be competent, competitive, and to make the non-mystical judgments necessary for prosperous, happy survival. The illusionary values of alcohol, drugs, and mysticism arise from their reality-distorting effects. Indeed drugs, alcohol, and mysticism can feel like old, comfortable, warm friends. But, in the long-term, they deliver only harm, incompetence, and unhappiness. And their distortions can initially be so well rationalized that the alcohol or drug user can easily choose to remain unaware of the mounting damage until permanent loss of happiness, energy, and life become inescapable.

Damage from alcohol, drugs, and mysticism can range from a quick overdose death or suicide, to an unhappy truncated life, to the more subtle psychological and physiological damages that occur even with moderate use

---

*The consistent rational use of the mind to control the long-range development of one's life is the opposite of the mystics' specious shortcut notions of "mind over matter" or their wishful thinking of (1) the mind willing "reality" or (2) others showing them the "truth".

"If God is true, then where is he when needed in times of trouble. Why has he not shown himself or provided any evidence of his existence?"

Now, through Neo-Tech, I have found the answer to end all of the wasted efforts of mind in wondering of God's existence. The answer to this question is that "there is no answer and never was" thus this question does not exist and such so-called God does not exist.

With Neo-Tech, neo-cheaters and altruists and mystics will perish. Recently, I applied a Neo-Tech concept on a master neo-cheater in my day to day duties as a taxation consultant. This particular neo-cheater is a lawyer. By directly applying the concepts of Neo-Tech 1 ("Contrasting Characteristics, page 9") I easily removed his "mask of mysticism". In removing his neo-cheating, mystical mask I revealed his true self...., a "traditional cheater". What I had revealed frightened me. I am astounded that by applying Neo-Tech concepts, I exposed this lawyer in such an easy but most powerful manner. On exposure, this former master neo-cheater was reduced to a "nervous and stiff" traditional cheater. I am truly amazed!

For years I ranked second to "professional" mystics (e.g. certain lawyers, accountants etc). Through Neo-Tech I have realised some areas from which I can prosper. Ideas to be actioned are now formulating fast. There is so much to learn and prosper from and with Neo-Tech, this can now be accomplished. For years I have consulted in taxation in accordance with the "pre-packaged" truth (tax laws). Now, there is no "pre-packaged" truth and tax planning takes the form of "what is good for my clients" which is also "good for myself".

I am truly thankful to Frank Wallace and I & O Publishing for the discovery of Neo-Tech. It has already shown me where I have gone wrong in my business, marriage and my duty to my young children. Although I have not yet fully-grasped and understood many of the Neo-Tech concepts I do realise that I am feeling a strong and positive change in my attitudes and actions toward business, marriage and my children.

There is no doubt in my mind that I can achieve Biological Immortality. I am very determined to achieve Biological Immortality. I would also like to obtain the "Neo-Tech 2 Reference Encyclopedia" and the "Original Neocheating Manuscript" and "Neothink/Neo Power" when available. Can you also advise me where I can obtain copies of the books noted in Neo-Tech References. I would be pleased to receive any other material from you. I am interested in assisting you in any productive way with the "Neo-Tech Research and Writing Center".

Thank you and I look forward, very much, to hearing from you all again.

of mysticism, alcohol, and drugs. For example, even a few alcoholic drinks cause irreversible damage to certain brain cells by a dehydration that causes a sludging together of red blood cells. Such sludging clogs the blood capillaries; thus, the amount of oxygen reaching those brain cells via the minutest capillaries diminish. Some of those oxygen-starved brain cells die each time that dehydration or sludging occurs. Damaged or destroyed brain cells do not regenerate. Any single occurrence of alcohol brain-cell damage is not measurable. But the effect is cumulative, gradually yielding measurable, permanently damaging effects.

Likewise, marijuana disorients the electrical brain patterns to diminish one's quality of thinking and order of priorities. For example, marijuana tends to convert demanding action and ambition into passive dreams and laziness. More serious, that movement from effort and ambition to passivity and dreams may be cumulative. Furthermore, the mystical-dream effects of marijuana destroy competence. Also, investigations by Masters and Johnson show that male marijuana users experience drops in testosterone of 40% and more. Reduced testosterone causes reduced sex drive, an atrophy of male sex organs, a softening of muscle tissue, and a wimpish decrease in aggressiveness. In addition, marijuana can enter the fetuses of pregnant women to possibly influence the sexual development of unborn males; for testosterone is essential to the sexual development of males. ...Drugs such as cocaine and heroin are simply more aggressive forms of suicide.

Despite the damaging effects of alcohol and drugs, no rational or moral reason exists for government to restrict, control, or forbid by force the sale or use of alcohol or drugs in any way whatsoever. No one or no government has the right to initiate or threaten force against any individual who is not violating the individual or property rights of others. Individuals have the basic right to do anything with their lives they choose, including damaging themselves by using alcohol and drugs, just as they have the right to damage themselves with sugar, tobacco, religion, promiscuous sex, mysticism, and suicide...so long as they do not initiate threats, force, or fraud against any other individual.

Any use of force to accomplish a "good" always, by nature, does much more long-range harm to society than any intended good. Moreover, those who use or advocate such force seldom have honest or innocent intentions, no matter what their external appearances. And in using force to prohibit drugs, the enforcers are not only morally wrong, but their policies of force drive drug prices far above their free-market values. Those artificially high prices, in turn, allow organized crime to flourish through the extremely high-profit margins guaranteed by the government enforcers.

Rick T.   R-1797

The first autobiography that my 2nd Grade son was required to read, a book of sickening generalities regarding Martin Luther King sent me into an immediate depression. His first autobiography wasn't on any of the truly great and productive men of all races and (over)
— greeds. On the contrary, a book instead, that glorified the mystic, the non productive and promoted guilt in ample quantities. My reaction was outrage! However, your works helped me focus upon the moment more clearly. Armed with the knowledge that a beacon of truth does still emanate, I settled down and realized that my son has a choice in his future. He'll have the advantage of a mother and father who have uncovered the "mystery of the universe", the neocheater. The choice will be his; but most importantly, he'll have a <u>choice</u>. Heart felt Appreciation,

Indeed, those government-created, sky-high prices cause the addict to push drugs onto others, especially onto vulnerable children and adolescents. The addicts must push drugs in order to obtain the cash needed to pay for the grossly inflated drugs. Thus, government oppression of individual rights through force creates hundreds of thousands of young, new addicts each year **because** of anti-drug laws. In addition, the desperate, dying addict will rob, mug, commit mayhem, murder — he will do anything to raise the money required to buy the government-inflated drugs.

Government policies against the sale and use of drugs help no one while creating more addicts, causing the addicts to steal the property and harm the lives of millions of innocent people every year. And finally, as in prohibition, the anti-drug laws are by far the greatest boon and source of wealth to organized crime. The government through its power-usurping oppression creates huge, lucrative markets from which organized crime prospers and grows.

* * *

Drugs cause many psychological and physical problems that diminish prosperity, romantic love, and psychuous pleasures [Re: Table 33, Neo-Tech Reference Encyclopedia]. Other diminishers of prosperity and happiness include mystical religious and political activities as well as lying, self-lying, praying, promiscuous sex, and the use of tobacco, sugar, and caffeine.

Breaking sugar, tobacco, and caffeine habits quickly improves a person's quality of life. A person's self-esteem also significantly increases by eliminating habits that are destructive to the conscious mind and physical body. ...The surest way to stop smoking is to make a nonnegotiable decision to stop smoking completely and forever...and then stop completely and forever without using any crutches such as increased eating, snacking, sweets, sucking Lifesavers, or excessive bragging. A person who uses such crutches will almost always return to smoking sooner or later. The decision to stop must be decisive, irrevocable, uncompromisable, and forever.

Likewise, caffeine in coffee and cola is a stimulant drug. Aside from the negative psychological effects of being controlled by a habit, prolonged and excessive use of caffeine can physically damage parts of the body such as the kidneys and pancreas and can adversely affect carbohydrate metabolism. That, in turn, can add to the damage and unhappiness caused by sugar consumption. Except for mysticism, the most common drug, the sedative drug sugar, causes more unhappiness, illness, and deaths through body mutilation (fatness), metabolic damage, physical and psychological harm than all other drugs combined.

But the most pervasive and destructive of all diseases is mysticism. In fact, for 3000 years, mysticism has been far more destructive on human life than all the other diseases on this planet combined.

Jack G.   R-1762

AFTER READING NEO-TECH MY WORLD BLEW UP IN MY FACE. EVERYTHING THAT I BELIVED IN WAS NOT THERE ANY MORE.
I HAD THE POWER TO CHANGE ANY THING I WANTED TO. I NO LONGER FEAR ANY THING OR ANY BODY.
THANKS FOR GIVING ME THE FREEDOM IN THIS WORLD TO LIVE HAPPY.

Marshall P.   R-280

NEO-TECH SUPPORTS MY MOST FUNDAMENTAL IDEAS. IT WILL BE PASSED ON TO MY CHILDREN, AS REQUIRED READING.
I FEEL MOST, IF NOT ALL, OF THE CONCEPTS EXPRESSED IN WALLACE'S BOOK WILL HAVE TO BE DEALT WITH BY EVERYONE SOMEDAY. THESE IDEAS CANNOT BE AVOIDED MUCH LONGER.
THE BOOK PROVIDED INTERESTING, INFORMATIVE, WORTHWHILE, READING
PERHAPS THIS BOOK WILL ENCOURAGE SOME OF THOSE "SHEEPLE" TO THINK

Dough V.   R-1481

EACH READING BRINGS MORE. VERY, VERY, VALUABLE!

Neo-Tech Advantage #61
APHRODISIACS — NEGATIVE AND POSITIVE

Casual sex, mysticism, neocheating, dishonesty, deceptive manipulation, compulsive gambling, hard and soft drugs, tobacco, caffeine, excessive alcohol, sugar, and prayer are long-term, negative aphrodisiacs that undermine self-esteem, romantic love, and psychuous pleasures. Also, folklore aphrodisiacs such as Spanish fly, yohimbine, ginseng root, and others have no long-term or physiological aphrodisiac value. The only effective aphrodisiacs are a desirable sexual partner, physical fitness, and the psychological/philosophical conditions of Neo-Tech that allow psychuous pleasures to flourish.

Neo-Tech Advantage #62
ROMANTIC LOVE, FREEDOM, AND THE DTC TECHNIQUE

Some people try to get involved too quickly in deep romantic relationships. The possible penalties of pressing for deep involvement too quickly include losing a potential romantic-love partner or unnecessarily wasting an irreplaceable portion of one's life by locking into an unsatisfactory relationship.

Many initial approaches to romantic love are possible: Some start hot and flaming, others start cool and conservatively. But the way a romantic relationship starts is usually unimportant because romantic love evolves through the exchange of mutually beneficial values. Therefore, any initial, honest approach is good and normally does not determine the outcome. ...What determines the success of a relationship is the creation and growth of mutually beneficial values.

By applying Neo-Tech/Psychuous Concepts, a person increases his or her *Life-Lifting Capacity*.* With that capacity, a person can lift a potential, romantic-love partner to new experiences and growth...to levels at which romantic love can move forward through mutual growth. By increasing one's own Life-Lifting Capacity, that person increases his or her skills for developing romantic relationships capable of generating psychuous pleasures and abiding happiness.

Paradoxically, only those partners who are free and independent can make honest, long-range commitments to build abiding romantic relationships. Partners involved in romantic relationships can and should avoid authority-backed commitments to the future. The only commitment between

---

*Life-Lifting Capacity does **not** mean changing or remolding another individual to suit one's own desires. Life-Lifting Capacity means providing an environment that helps other people discover and fulfill their **own** unrealized capacities and potential.

D. R.   R-402

HAVE READ NEO-TECH I & II.
MOST ENLIGHTNING & AWAKENING.
SAD INDEED THIS INFO. WAS
NOT AVAILABLE 100 YRS. AGO.
WOULDN'T IT BE A BEAUTIFUL
WORLD.

J.H.   C-1010

Thanks for all you've done and are doing for the entire world! I feel as if we are truly entering the greatest Renaissance yet! May it continue for infinity. You guys and gals are worth your weight in gold! Keep up the earth-shattering work!

Teremaru M.   R-2238,   NEW ZEALAND

I loved and greatly enjoyed the Neo-Tech package. It made me fully aware of the truth about neo-cheaters that existed, and defined what true, productive work is. The knowledge in the Neo-Tech package fills a hole in my life I didn't realise I had. There are many areas of life which only the Neo-tech package recognizes and acknowledges and relays this information to those who desire the truth. Thankyou for allowing me to be one

romantic-love partners necessary for success is a commitment to honesty and growth.

If a relationship grows out of honest free-choice, the values accumulate naturally. The relationship then increasingly forms a self-chosen permanence. If growth continues, the relationship can gain unbreakable strength and permanence. If growth stops, the relationship can benevolently end with most of the accumulated values retained by each partner. As a result, each partner will have expanded his and her capacity for future relationships. In addition, the benevolent termination of a value-oriented relationship can (if the partners so choose) remains open to possible changes that would allow resumption of growth and the relationship.

Since no one does or can know everything, everyone will at times make errors in his or her personal life. A person is particularly susceptible to errors in the initial stages of a relationship because of limited knowledge and experience about the new situation. Certain errors, if unrecognized or left uncorrected, can unnecessarily end a potentially good romantic-love relationship. With explicit knowledge of the Neo-Tech/Psychuous concepts, the possibilities of such errors are sharply reduced. And when errors do occur, they are usually quickly corrected by applying the Neo-Tech/Psychuous concepts.

The need for compromise in a love relationship is a value-diminishing, guilt-generating myth promoted by altruists, egalitarians, theologians, and other neocheaters. With the Neo-Tech/Psychuous concepts as a guide, conflicts between partners can be resolved without either partner's best interests being compromised, diminished, or sacrificed.

Romantic love never occurs automatically or by chance. Life values are earned through hard, honest efforts. That means constant, conscious efforts orchestrated in full accord with reality. As with all important values, romantic love and psychuous pleasures demand thought, effort, and time to develop. The positive values generated are proportional to the rational thought and honest effort invested. ...Romantic love, as any important personal value, is attained through the DTC technique: Discipline, Thought, and then Control. [Re: Concept 94, in Neo-Tech Reference Encyclopedia].

Neo-Tech Advantage #63
ROMANTIC-LOVE STANDARDS
Actions based on standards of other people or "authorities" stifle self-discovery and block the personal and intellectual growth necessary for romantic love and psychuous pleasures. Within romantic love, no action or behavior needs the approval or sanction of anyone beyond the partners themselves. Couples can and should experience any and all nondestructive sexual and nonsexual experiences they mutually desire.

Gary C. C-123

Dear Mr. Flint,

Thank-you, and all the other people involved in the Neo-Tech Discovery. It is, "without a doubt," the greatest discovery of mankind.

Before I obtained Neo-Tech, I listened to the advice of a Neocheat. This advice almost ruined my life. Since obtaining, and applying Neo-Tech, I've never felt more confident, relaxed, and capable to move forward, in spite of the <u>huge</u> set-back I've experienced.

I look forward to tommorrow with anticipation, and to a future of Biological Immortality; and the fall of Mysticism!

Chris R. C-124

Dear Sir,
   I have read the Neo-Tech Information package and found it a tremendous value. I am shedding the burden of the neocheaters and beginning to realize my potential.

As one develops intellectual and emotional character, that person's standards for romantic love rise. But rising standards cause a decline in the percentage of potential partners that could satisfy a romantic relationship. Partly offsetting that percentage decline, however, is personal growth, which increases the opportunities to contact higher-quality, potential partners.

Romantic love cannot survive a continually widening disparity of personal growth and character development between partners. For that widening disparity will eventually undermine any romantic-love relationship. A widening disparity between partners eventually generates reactions of inadequacy, jealousy, possessiveness, even envy in the less developed partner — and resentment, dissatisfaction, or disinterest in the more developed partner. Romantic-love relationships, however, can grow and flourish even if wide differences exist in creative or other abilities between partners. The key is growth: Disparity itself is not important if it does not widen — if both partners are creating and sharing growth. [Re: Concept 95, Neo-Tech Reference Encyclopedia]. Also, romantic-love relationships can flourish even with great differences in personalities. ...Growing values and attraction in romantic love arise from character growth and development, not from personality traits.

Neo-Tech Advantage #64
THREE SEGMENTS OF ROMANTIC LOVE
A romantic-love relationship has three segments:
1. Fundamental Basis
2. Man-Woman Relationship
3. Future Potential

Those three segments are identified below:

SEGMENT # 1

Fundamental Basis

The Fundamental Basis is the starting point of all relationships. That starting point is the similarity of both partners' views of life and their underlying philosophical premises. Without that base of philosophical harmony, no solid ground for mutual development of a value-oriented, romantic-love relationship would exist.

Forming and building a fundamental base is not a process of creating, but one of discovering mutual values, ideas, and thoughts already held. This segment of romantic love is usually the fastest, easiest aspect of the relationship to identify and establish. But discovering the infinite depth and full nature of one's partner is an exciting, life-long, unfolding process. Most of the fundamental, philosophical links between two people can usually be

Craig M.   R-738

I am very excited and stimulated by this excellent work. Your outlook has solidified and given a wonderful focus to many vague thoughts that I have had for some time. Thank you for bringing this wonderful manuscript to the world. May the Neo-Tech man and women soon control the planet.

Joseph S.   R-2137, CANADA

A powerful, selectively worded collection of knowledge that cannot be disputed. Powerful is the knowledge and well being of ones self that these readings give me. I have not ever read or heard of a collection of information that so clearly defines the laws of human nature. Thank you.

Lim K.   R-2018, SINGAPORE

It is a fantastic piece of work that has been thoroughly researched, analysed, and presented.

Rodney V.   R-638, CANADA

NEO-TECH IS THE TYPE OF BOOK I'D LIKE TO THOROUGHLY MEMORIZE. EVERY WORD HAS MEANING.

recognized early in the relationship. Unfortunately, one's fundamental basis is relatively easy to fake. Faking one's fundamental self to attract a love partner, however, is a disastrous error that will eventually be paid for in lost love, lost time, reduced self-esteem, diminished happiness, and a dimmed future, especially for the one doing the faking.

SEGMENT #2

Man-Woman Relationship

In order to establish a growing, long-range relationship, each partner must understand the ideas that the other holds about man-woman relationships. In order for both partners to work effectively toward creating a relationship, they must first identify the basis and nature of their own relationship. The Neo-Tech/Psychuous concepts identify the basis for man-woman relationships designed to yield growth, psychuous pleasures, and happiness.

SEGMENT #3

Future Potential

A romantic-love relationship moves forward with motivation and anticipation through a vision of future values, benefits, and happiness. The potential of a love relationship is a function of:

　　　　a. The nature of the relationship.
　　　　b. Each partner's rate and direction of evolvement
　　　　　　or development.
　　　　c. The amount of rational thought and effort each
　　　　　　partner keeps putting into the relationship.

Neo-Tech Advantage #65
TWO TYPES OF ROMANTIC-LOVE RELATIONSHIPS

Two types of romantic-love relationships exist:

Type A
Working Jointly Toward Major Experiences and Goals

One partner works through the other more creative or active partner in climbing to increasing levels of accomplishment. Both partners share the rewards according to the values that each contribute. The more productive, creative, efficient, one partner becomes, the greater are the benefits and growth opportunities for the other partner. In turn, that partner then grows to become increasingly valuable to the other partner. Each partner benefits greatly from such a combined working/growing relationship. And such a relationship is especially advantageous when major differences in

Norma K.   R-2328

I consider Neo-Tech as one of the most profoundly effective books I have ever read. It is not so much the information that is presented, but the way it is presented, that has a tremendously lasting effect. Dr. Wallace's deep conviction permeates through the entire volumes of Neo-Tech. His utterly uncompromising reasoning, immensely through investigative discipline, and courage to speak what is true to him evoked in me the same qualities that had been awaiting to come forth. These qualities have evolved in me ever since, and now, four months later, they have become an integral part of who I am.

There is no need to agree with Dr. Wallace. Neo-Tech still works. It makes one stand on his feet, and on his feet alone. It makes one think on his own, and only on his own. It makes one question all that he thought he knew, and brings clarity so that he can distinguish between mere believing and authentic knowing.

I genuinely thank him for his contribution he "makes" in my life.

Bob S.   R-3677

Dear Dr. Wallace;

Neo-Tech made me realize how the Mystics and Neo-Cheaters take their toll on our lives and eat up our earnings. Neo-Tech has me on the move. I now have a savings and will have enough to start a business soon.

productivity, creativity, or energy exist between partners. (A difference in productivity does not imply a difference in personal character.) In such a joint-working relationship, even wide differences in productivity and creativity do not threaten the relationship, so long as growing values are being exchanged between the partners.

A joint-working relationship has the outstanding advantage not only of the partners sharing much larger portions of their lives, but of the partners living their lives more intensely together. ...They are living integrally together before, during, and after work, everyday.

Type B
Working Separately Toward Major Experiences and Goals

Each partner can pursue independent routes toward separate careers or goals. Each partner can benefit from such a relationship by the cross-sharing of experiences, emotions, and rewards of their separate experiences and accomplishments. The separate-working relationship need be neither threatening nor competitive for either partner, but rather can be a continuous source of pleasures and enrichment not available to either partner alone.

Both A and B type relationships offer unlimited opportunities for personal growth and happiness. In such value-producing relationships, each partner knows either implicitly or explicitly that intimacy, pleasures, and happiness in a relationship arise from sharing personal growth, not from possessing or owning one another.

Neo-Tech Advantage #66
INDIVIDUAL UNIQUENESS AND PERSONAL WORTH

People are *not* equal in value or worth. Only in the rights to their own lives and property are people equal. Those and only those rights are inalienable for all human beings. By nature, no one has an automatic or natural right to anything else in life. Moreover, beyond the equality of individual or property rights, nothing is, can, or should be equal between human beings. Profound differences exist among people in their self-made qualities such as character development, earned skills, self-worth, extrinsic worth, aspects of intelligence, self-esteem, life-lifting capacity, psychuous-pleasures capacity.

The "average individual" does not exist. Each individual is unique. Average characteristics are a statistical tool that cannot be applied to *any* individual. So many variables are involved in an individual's character, physical structure, and psychological makeup that no individual can possibly be an average person. Moreover, no average psychology or life style exists.

Gary B. C-305

When I picked up my friends NEO-TECH book I thought to myself this is to good to be true, I have never read anything like this ever! This is great!!!

Then when I finally got mine in the mail I was so excited I couldn't put it down, everyone should have a copy of this book and if that were the case, Communication with other people could be great, not to mention everything else that could establish between people. Life doesn't have to be as complicated as people think it does.

Lou B. R-6095

Neo-Tech was very enjoyable and informative. It was a pleasure to read facts instead of fiction. I have touched on some ideals which encompass the basis for Neo-Tech while reading other philosophies and disciplines. They only skimmed the surface. Neo-Tech is presented in such a clear manner that it enabled me to conceptualize the whole picture. Every truth is summed up for easy reference.

I am looking foward to receiving more literature about Neo-Tech. It's important to identify the Neo cheaters that surround us all and beat them with a better game plan. This can only be done by learning and understanding Neo-Tech and intergrating Neo-Tech into my lifestyle.

In fact, all *rational* psychologies have a "random-walk" capacity for delivering happiness. That means that every rational, productive individual has the same capacity for earning abiding happiness regardless of intelligence, psychology, or job status. Abiding happiness is possible to the extent that a person rejects mysticism in utilizing the mind to think rationally and in exerting the effort to live fully.

Each adult stands uniquely separate and alone on his or her honesty, character, and earned worth. In dealing with anyone in a relationship (especially a romantic relationship), a person's honesty, character, and self-earned values count above all else. And earned values always determine one's self-esteem and happiness despite the constant efforts by politicians, media journalists, cartoonists, social "intellectuals" and other neocheaters to use nonearned characteristics such as face, skin, sex, age, race, nationality, or family background to praise, pay off, judge, or condemn people. Constant exposure to the anti-individualistic myths pushed by professional mystics and neocheaters diminish one's ability to honestly judge character and earned worth. Recognition of an individual's earned worth is the cornerstone of justice and essential for romantic love and psychuous pleasures.

People who choose mystical lives and destructive "careers" (such as politicians, theologians, and criminals) experience continuously decreasing self-esteems along with diminishing capacities for happiness and pleasures. Every person does, however, have the capacity to change personally by rejecting all forms of mysticism to become an honest, strong, productive individual able to achieve growing prosperity, abiding happiness, and psychuous pleasures.

Neo-Tech Advantage #67
CAPACITY TO CHANGE

People are capable of change...of changing their lives, character, attitudes, views, and actions. To be real, however, such changes must occur through one's own choices motivated by one's own desires and self-interest. Basic changes can never be successfully imposed on anyone, not even by a person's love partner. Changes accomplished by force, threat, coercion, or pressure are not genuine changes, but are pretenses or changes in external appearance designed to deceive, relieve pressures, or to avoid threatened consequences. Such feigned changes are never positive and always lead to harmful consequences.

Positive changes always require honest, self-directed efforts. Through ongoing character development, a person can become triggered to integrate new information quickly. That integration can cause significant, rapid changes in attitudes. If a person is unable or unwilling to act on valid new

E.G.P. R-3864

Words sufficient to describe the resultant benefits evidenced today because of the understanding gleaned from these writings escape me.

For nearly fifty years I have sought confirmation and reassurance that what I believed was true. Neo Tech has provided not only that confirmation and reassurance but also the means of overcoming the fear to practice this belief.

I am currently deep in the bowels of Neo Tech II and grow more day by day. Business and family understanding improve hourly, excitement and expectation are my nourishment and best of all I Love ME!

VIVA LA PRODUCER OF VALUES.

Ian H. R-2746, ENGLAND

AMAZING, FANTASTIC.
A REAL EYE OPENER.
I HAVE GOOD EYE SITE,
BUT I THINK I HAVE BEEN
WALKING BLIND.

information, then efforts directed toward changing that person will fail. That does not mean untriggered persons cannot eventually change. But, if they do, the change will be by their own choice and pace.

Avoiding Disguised Mystics

Integrated awareness is needed to identify and avoid partners whose lives are dominated by mysticism, especially disguised mysticism. Two types of mystics exist: (1) Mystics who project their problems and disorders onto others. Such mystics are often characterized by their paranoid use of non sequiturs to blame others for their own problems. (2) Closet mystics who inwardly hurt themselves by undermining values that enter their lives. Ironically, such mystics are often characterized by cluttered closets that reflect the hidden disorder they create in their personal lives. A disorderly closet may indicate a mystically dominated personal life that drains the lives of others.

Both types of mystics create problems where none exist. Both are incompatible with romantic love. And either will eventually destroy any value-based relationship. Yet, any type of mysticism can be overcome with Neo-Tech to yield competent lives filled with growing prosperity, happiness, and romantic-love.

Neo-Tech Advantage #68
1. FINDING ROMANTIC PARTNERS
2. BYPASSING SHYNESS

Finding the right partner with whom to experience psychuous pleasures and romantic love is one of life's most important responsibilities. Opportunities to discover a potential, life-long romantic partner exist everywhere. But unplanned approaches diminish one's chances of securing the best possible romantic-love partner. [Re: Table 35, Neo-Tech Reference Encyclopedia]

Every lonely person should remember that meeting a suitable partner to build abiding love and happiness needs only one connection, one meeting, one social function, one planned effort...and any time could be that one time. Until a person finds that right romantic partner, he or she should never stop searching for that person with whom to share and build values, love, and happiness. To give up searching would be to give up on life itself. And finding that one person makes all efforts worthwhile.

When one bemoans the unhappiness or falseness of guests at social gatherings that person is often projecting his or her own feelings of unhappiness or falseness onto people who may not be that way at all. But by looking past one's own mystical complaints, a person can usually generate self-benefiting values from most social circumstances, even if the people encountered hold values and life styles different from one's own.

Jerry C.   R-1928

This literature is a breath of life. No, this literature is the whole purpose of life. I went to Catholic school for 12 years & the last 4 years I couldn't swallow that BULL SHIT. That was 14 years ago. This is the best thing I have ever read, & the philosophy just doesn't sit on the shelf after done reading it. My only son will read it when old enough to understand

THANKX, DR. WALLACE, YOU ARE A

GENIUS!

Garth F.   J462

"Drop a pebble in the puddle" and watch the circles grow!

Neo Tech is such a powerful "Pebble" and the World the "puddle" that no wonder the circles grow. They will eventually and inevitably return from the edge to the center and back and forth until the Neo Tech advantages will prevail.

Still, a person must be selective to protect one's time. One must not let valuable, irreplaceable segments of life be consumed by those who waste time, retard personal growth, or work against one's best interests. But when unavoidably cast into a situation with undesirable people, a person alert with Neo-Tech knowledge can usually salvage valuable new insights. Whenever possible, however, a person should promptly exit from situations that waste time.

Bypassing Shyness

Feelings of social incompetence are generally unfounded. Such feelings are often caused by falsely negative views about one's self or mystical views about others. When a person becomes aware of and scraps those false views, the feelings of social incompetence diminish and often vanish.

An effective way to bypass shyness, nervousness, and feelings of social incompetence is by *intense listening* with full-focus awareness on the speaker. Not only does such attention elicit friendly reactions from the speaker to the listener, but intense listening increases the listener's ability to communicate and articulate. Intense listening is also a valuable tool to evaluate potential partners for romantic love.

Possibilities for contacting potential, romantic-love partners increase proportionately with the number of approaches made toward potential partners. Many opportunities for discovering romantic-love partners are lost by people who fear what others may think of them for trying to "pick up" people to whom they are attracted. Even more opportunities are lost through inaction caused by fear of rejection.

In finding the best romantic-love partner, a person must be free and forward in approaching potential partners. That includes all approaches from a self-introduction to a bold pickup by either the man or the woman. Through fear of rejection, many people lose valuable opportunities to discover romantic partners within whom the supreme values of psychuous pleasures and romantic love reside. That fear of contacting others dissipates on realizing the nature of rejections: Most rejections stem simply from unavailability. And many other rejections arise from inadequacies within the person doing the rejecting. Such rejections are not personal rebuffs, but actually serve as valuable sorting processes that allow the quick elimination of unpromising prospects with a minimum loss of time.

Relying on Natural Beauty

Those who rely on natural beauty or physical attractiveness to control love situations are generally unsuitable for romantic love. For usually they ignored the efforts and disciplines needed to develop capacities to receive or deliver romantic love and psychuous pleasures [Re: Concept 90, Neo-Tech Reference Encyclopedia]. Those who respond to one's initial, natural approach often

C.Z.   R-3866, NIGERIA

"---- Very attractive, stimulating and useful --- and not only from the linguistic point of view. Its purpose is much broader; it helps to creat a real human being, a highly civilised person.

It has injected me with confidence, and courage, and instructed me to develop the art of self-control, and free from Neo-cheaters, Mysticism, and External Authorities.

Throughout the months which it has occupied, not one minute do I regret. In fact, I would be surprised if anyone could receive so much profit for so little.

I for one, have joined my inner forces with I & O publishing company towards the achievement of her goals. This I have started by spreading the good news of Neo-Tech discovery through verbal advertisement to friends.

I should like to send my congratulations to Dr. Wallace for the Neo-Tech discovery and his entire staff working for the unending activities of I & O publishing company.

Remember to include me in your mailing list.

Wilbur V.   R-8000

Initially The Concept of Neo-Tech Was Somewhat Dubious, In That It Was 180° Opposite To Anything I Had Been Taught or Had Practiced However I Had Always Felt There Were Discrepancies To these Teachings

After Reading Neo-Tech I - V, And After Much Rereading & Study, I Have Come to The Conclusion This Is The Answer To Most of The World's Problems. I Definitely Intend to Further Improve My Life By Using Neo-Tech To Guide My Future Decisions.

I Want To Express My Gratitude To All the Individuals, Who Have Contributed In The Developement Of The Neo-Tech Way of Life

W. V.

make the best prospects for romantic partners. For that reason, a person must freely express his or her unique, natural self from the start in order for the selection process to work effectively in uncovering the best potential romantic-love partners.

Many people erroneously think that seeking potential romantic partners at social functions designed for that purpose (e.g., singles dances, clubs, introduction services, Parents Without Partners) is somehow degrading. But the opposite is true. People who value themselves and their happiness will resist mystically acting on such false feelings. Instead, they will place a high priority on those activities that will improve their chances of discovering the best-possible, life-long, romantic-love partner. The value of romantic love is far too important for leaving to random chance. Instead, a person must put the discovering of a life-long partner under one's direct control. One must exert organized, rational efforts to find the love partner with whom the greatest values can be exchanged. That direct-action approach contrasts with the mystical approach of those who count on random chance, a white knight, or someone else to deliver the values of love and happiness to them. ...To gain and keep a value as great as romantic love requires direct, constant, conscious effort.

Why Everyone Is Not Handsome

Most animals evolve to near their perfect physical appearance. But conscious beings do not because those without natural beauty can choose to work harder to develop their character and competence to higher levels. Thus, some people with less natural beauty work harder to develop superior characters. They do that to compete better in attracting mates for psychuous pleasures and reproduction. By contrast, those endowed with natural beauty lack the same competitive pressures to work harder to develop character and competence. Thus, because certain people without natural beauty make themselves more competitive, they remain well represented throughout the evolutionary stream. They even tend to raise to the top in power and intellectual attractiveness. That is why (1) naturally beautiful people can be found among the less evolved and (2) unhandsome people can be found among the highest levels of evolvement. Thus, unlike other animals, nature's drive for physical perfectness is not a controlling evolutionary force in man. For man-controlled, intelligent actions can outcompete nature-controlled, physical appearances not only for reproduction and survival, but for prosperity, happiness, and romantic love.

Leveraged-Knowledge Advantage #69
SHYNESS — CAUSES AND CURES

Shyness reduces contact and chances with potential romantic-love partners. But shyness is easily overcome once the problem is identified. [Re: Table 36, Neo-Tech Reference Encyclopedia identifies five types of shyness and lists ways to reduce or eliminate each type.] In addition, the constant

Pieire T.   F-109, FRANCE

Bravo and my most ardent compliments to Neo Tech. It is the most powerful book I know of to this day. This is comforting to my deepest conviction and will permit me to realize my dreams and go forward to a promising future. Continue to go forward by giant steps. Again thank you and my heart goes with you.

Sandra H.   R-1049

I enjoyed the Neo-Tech information package tremendously. I only wish I could have learned all that I have through Neo Tech years ago; it would have enabled me to prevent a lot of unnecessary mistakes.

But since I have read Neo-Tech I have been able to greatly increase my productivity and self-esteem.

I was raised as a catholic and was made to feel guilty about everything, especially sex and even happiness itself, and now for the first time I am truly happy and guilt free about being so.

It is amazing how I can spot the good from the bad, the productive from the parasites when I couldn't do so before.

misunderstanding of a uniquely different individual may cause that person to withdraw and become a loner. That aloneness may create an erroneous image that such a person is shy or a bore when neither is true.

A major step toward eliminating shyness is the acceptance of one's own self. To do that, one must realize that no "model" person exists with whom anyone needs to emulate or identify with in order to be healthy, happy, or successful [Re: Concept 96, Neo-Tech Reference Encyclopedia]. ...A person bypasses shyness by being one's own self in guiltlessly doing what he or she rationally desires, regardless of what others may say or think.

A shy person is seldom a bore. A bore is a person who is uninteresting, dull, or uncomfortable to another person. A person is not a bore to himself, but is a bore to another person. Often being a bore to a particular person is merely the result of that particular person's reactions. Such reactions depend on individual values and standards. Someone, therefore, can be boring to certain people, but exciting to others. For example, Aristotle, Leonardo da Vinci, Einstein, John D. Rockefeller, Henry Ford, and Thomas Edison while being very exciting to each other, probably would have bored or, more accurately, threatened the profoundly dishonest, pseudo self-esteems of Jesus, Mao, Stalin, Hitler, Ralph Nader, Albert Schwietzer, Charles Manson. Conversely, people who habitually project distorted (mystical) "realities" will by nature bore active, productive individuals.

Leveraged-Knowledge Advantage #70
EQUALITY OF MEN AND WOMEN
DIVISION OF LABOR CONCEPT

The human mind is neuter. Men and women have equal capacity for intellectual development, character development, integral honesty, self-esteem, physical fitness, psychuous pleasures, romantic love, and abiding happiness. But physiological differences as well as psychological differences exist between men and women. Those differences must be recognized in order to function effectively — to function as a human male or female is intended to function — to function as an honest, rational, human being. [Re: Table 37, Neo-Tech Reference Encyclopedia, illustrates the important physical and psychological differences between men and women.] Those differences cannot be considered good or bad, better or worse, or by any other label. They are just differences in their natures. But the differences are real. Thus, those differences must be recognized and dealt with as reality.

The feminist movement ignores or rejects the psychological differences and often even ignores the physiological differences between man and woman. That evasion of reality is reflected by the feminists' irrational, destructive demands for government-enforced "equality".

***

David H.   R-3582

The Neo-Tech Discovery is probably the most fantastic book I have read to this date in my life. And at the age of 36 I have read quite a few of the self help, positive thinking books with very little results. I have learned so much and can't wait to get the Neo-tech Encyclopedia, and other works from I & O. Upon each reading I gain more and more knowledge. Neo-tech will definitely have a very positive, honest, and financial change in my life

Edward R.   R-7059

Is Neo-Tech true? Is it for real? All one has to do is to read the entire information package, then read any newspaper, listen to any sermon or political speech. That should provide proof enough for anyone.

The often misunderstood division-of-labor concept is central to all beneficial relationships, ranging from individual man-woman romantic relationship to the mutually beneficial employer-employee relationship involving thousands of people. Next to their attacks on individual rights through the use of government force, the most harmful neocheating manipulations by feminists are their attacks on the voluntary division-of-labor concept. Some feminists advocate eliminating that division-of-labor concept from man-woman relationships. They demand, for example, that all jobs, chores, and activities be shared equally. Those feminists and other neocheating egalitarians want to use government force to reduce all value producers to the same level as value destroying mystics and neocheaters.

Almost everyone else desires and happily uses the division of labor to his great advantage. Indeed, the most fair, efficient way to exchange values for desired values is through division of labor. Even the traditional trade in which the man earns money while the woman makes an efficient home and living atmosphere is a valid, proper trade that can greatly benefit each, if each mutually agrees to and desires such a trade.

For what reason would a feminist or anyone else attack two people who agree to what they want to do with their own personal selves and lives? One reason is that such feminists are neocheaters using the tool of guilt to undermine values in order to usurp power and values earned by others. But, romantic-love partners responding to feminist demands for equality of actions (rather than for each partner offering the other his or her separately developed values), eventually eliminate happiness from their relationships. For equality of actions push love partners toward inefficient, restricted petty relationships in which mutual growth fades and love dies.

Women functioning in any of the following three categories can achieve psychuous pleasures, romantic love, and abiding happiness:

1. Self-sufficient, career or commercially productive* women have the greatest potential for experiencing the full-range of psychuous pleasures and romantic love.

2. Genuinely productive housewives or mothers who contribute significantly to increasing the commercial productivity of their husbands and the value potentials of their children can also experience growing psychuous pleasures and romantic love. But they must always keep growing toward their intellectual and productive capacities.

3. Women actively seeking growth by becoming knowledgeable or proficient in artistic, cultural, or recreational areas (such as art, music, literature, dance, sports) can experience growing romantic relationships. But such relationships will not continue to grow unless the woman passes the amateur stage to eventually become commercially productive and self-sufficient in that or another area.

---

*Commercially productive means being economically self-sufficient by producing more tradeable values in the competitive, free market than one consumes.

Dennis R.Z.   C-120

Dear I.O Publishing:

Over the past year or so I have read Neo-Tech and Neo Tech discovery. The information presented was just what I was looking for, of which I had been in years of search to obtain. It is concise, mind-broadening, and has done a great deal to change my life, forever. Simply it has given me values to live by, shown me what the proverbial cheaters are, and how to beat them. Most of all, it leads you to a confidant, productive, successful life. Currently I am a College graduate student in a Ph.D program. When I enter the job market, in Geology, this information will be invaluable, or "price less." It will also be a big plus factor when I eventually have a wife & family. Anyone who wants to live a happy, fulfilling productive life should read this. It is a must.

Gary J.C.   R-7076

Dear Dr. Wallace,

To say Neo-Tech is a fantastic benefit to mankind, is an <u>understatement</u>! Eight months ago, not having grasped the concepts of Neo-Tech, I entered into a partnership with a Neo-cheater. This partnership <u>almost</u> wiped me out! If not for Neo-Tech I-V, the loss that I would have suffered, (career and financial), would have been <u>unbearable</u>. As a result of applying the Neo-Tech concepts, I have "turned the tables" on this clown. Now he faces his just reward; Ruin!

For the first-time, in a long-time, I look forward to tomorrow. Life is beautiful, and full of opportunity. Biological immortality will be the greatest of human achievements. For me, it will be; A dream come true!

In most societies, more men than women are commercially productive. More men than women, therefore, have the potential for experiencing psychuous pleasures and growing romantic-love relationships. That disparity works against the happiness of *both* men and women. Thus, both men and women benefit as more and more females enter the romantic-love marketplace by becoming commercially productive, independent human beings.

The worst aspect of the feminist movement and other so-called "rights" movements is their advocating legislated government force or coercion to violate individual and property rights of others. All professional mystics and neocheating leaders require force or deception to survive by parasitically filling their needs. And those needs are usually disguised as "noble" ends. But no matter how noble sounding the end, it can *never* justify the means of force against any individual. The initiation of force against any individual for any reason is categorically wrong, immoral, and eventually hurts the rational well-being of everyone.

Government policies and laws backed by force have always been the major instrument for denying women their individual rights. So what about those legions of feminists advocating that same, legislated government force to achieve women "rights" by violating rights of others? They diminish everyone's rights and well being. Such use of government force was vigorously promoted even by early feminists such as Dr. Elizabeth Blackwell (1821-1910) who was responsible for tough, anti-prostitution laws that only increased government use of force to oppress both men and women. Moreover, Blackwell's guilt-laden, anti-sex, anti-masturbation writings were subsequently promoted by the Catholic church. Her writings led to the heavy masturbation guilt that still hangs over most women...a guilt that has deprived countless millions of women of healthy sexual development.

Leveraged-Knowledge Advantage #71
"CAREER" HOUSEWIFE AND HAVING CHILDREN
VERSUS
ACHIEVING "GREATNESS"

Most "career" housewives experience diminishing sexual pleasures and happiness. That occurs because they limit their personal growth by letting their intellectual and productivity potentials remain under challenged in being full-time housewives. To experience psychuous pleasures and abiding happiness, a person must fulfill his or her potentials. That means becoming independent — materially, intellectually, and emotionally. Today, such independence usually evolves from productive jobs or careers. And today, with the many domestic labor-saving conveniences, a housewife "career" is generally too unchallenging to provide the self-esteem, independence, and

Francis C.   F-116, FRANCE

For me Neo-Tech is for humanity the most profitable and fantastic discovery of the century. After studying Neo-Tech I can now identify neocheaters around me therefore eliminate them. Because of Neo-Tech the world will one day be rid of mysticism and neocheating. For people to be prosperous it is imperative that companies are managed by leaders who are non altruistic, applying the principles of capitalism, and concerned about long term development

Bill B.   R-2468

I have never witnessed a more complete expert capsuling and careful expression of words. Every item and concept written should have value to me now as well as the future.

growth needed to experience the full range of happiness available from life. But, exceptions exist in which being a housewife is a challenging life-time management profession delivering full self-esteem, happiness, and romantic love. Historical examples are the wives of the American pioneers and frontiersmen. Examples today include the partner-wives of super-productive entrepreneurs, businessmen, farmers, scientists, and other hard-driving producers.

Having children before achieving financial independence or even having children at all is an error for many romantic-love partners. Children can shrink the potential for career success, romantic happiness, and psychuous pleasures of both partners for two decades or more. Often the birth of children means the end of growth and happiness for the couple. And the parents' loss of growth and happiness can damage the well-being of their innocent child or children. Often when personal growth is ended by the burden of children, the parents' view of the future shifts to a downhill direction. Their lives then begin shrinking toward aging and death. But if parents fail their responsibility to properly raise their children into productive independent adults, those children become the victims of their parents' moral default. As with any uncorrected moral default, those parents responsible will suffer damaging consequences to their self-esteems and happiness.

Neo-Tech oriented couples would not have children until they were in a financial and maturity position to conceive a child as a net-happiness asset, rather than a draining task. Such couples almost always have greater capacities to love both life and their children than those who thoughtlessly or prematurely have children to "secure" the marriage, to meet the expectations of others, or other unhealthy reasons.

Romantic love and psychuous pleasures can still be achieved for couples who have children if they fully meet their responsibilities to both their children and to themselves. With children, the goal of building happiness and romantic love becomes more difficult and challenging. But if successful, a romantic relationship with the uniquely valuable experience of children can be even more rewarding than a romantic-love relationship without children. With children, increasing romantic happiness can be accomplished *only* after accepting a nonmartyr, full-responsibility role in preparing one's children for productive, independent lives. At the same time, one must always hold the romantic-love relationship, not the children, as the primary value.

In any case, having and raising children is a unique, profound life experience. And children can develop characters that yield major, long-range values to their parents, especially as the years go by. ...Well-evolved children can yield magnificent values, almost beyond imagination. Rationally bearing and raising Neo-Tech oriented children can yield a bonanza of values available from no other life experience.

Sam Y.   R-1689

One of the most interesting and valuable books that I have read. A major contribution to the concepts of individual rights. A moral and intellectual guide to a positive and productive life

Scot R.   R-221

Beyond ANYthing I ever expected To See iN PriNt.

Earl K.   C-120, SOLOMAN ISLANDS

Dear Sir,

Neo-Tech

My search for the right knowledge has been rewarded. Neo-Tech is fantastic. It beats all the mystical, pseudo sages that had cheated mankind throughout the ages. Neo-Tech will breed a new Pacific Man.

Financially secure, emotionally mature couples can genuinely desire the unique, value-generating experience of having children. Thus, they can rationally choose to bear and raise children without sacrificing or diminishing their careers, romantic love, or long-range happiness.

But raising children means continually yanking the parents out of their stimulating adult world back into the limited world of the child...a world that the parents outgrew and left behind long ago. The necessity to continually return to and live in a child's world must be accepted and is often not a pleasant or growth-enhancing experience. In addition, raising children diminishes the privacy available to the couple, which, if not recognized and properly organized, can rapidly diminish the romantic-love relationship to everyone's loss, including the children's.

But again, raising competent children oriented around Neo-Tech can be rewarding beyond any other life experience, except romantic love.

If the market for technology and research were free from government interference, genetically controlled, flaw-free babies would probably be routine in a decade or less. Moreover, externally produced babies could forever free women from the incapacitation, pain, physical damage, and life-threatening dangers of childbirth. That technology could also reduce childhood diseases and eliminate birth defects. Externally produced, genetically controlled babies would also allow selection of sex and certain characteristics that would provide the maximum advantages to their children.

But the key traits can develop only through the volitional choices of each living, conscious child. For example, personality, character, and integrity are traits that evolve from choices to be honest or dishonest, nonmystical or mystical, responsible or irresponsible, a value producer or a value destroyer.

* * *

Except to one's own self and dependent children, no one owes duties to *anyone* (including one's spouse, siblings, or parents) or to anything (including society, the government, the church, or to any other "higher" cause). The prime moral duty is to develop one's own potential to achieve abiding happiness through rational actions. Beyond that, however, a person's *only* other moral duty is to support and develop one's own children into honest, nonmystical, self-sufficient adults. That duty includes teaching children to objectively identify facts in full context and to live competently by rejecting all forms of mysticism, dishonesty, and neocheating.

Parents must, above all, teach their children to identify and avoid the disease of mysticism and its gaggle of neocheaters. Those children are then free to develop into independent, self-sufficient adults capable of achieving unlimited prosperity, psychuous pleasures, and abiding happiness.

Sharie A.   R-8009

Neo-tech . . . . — —

Neotech has become my life and part of everyone's life whom has come in contact with me.

My conversations are based upon Neo-tech

Neo-tech should be taught to every living; breathing; reasoning Men, Women, Child etc.

Neo-tech . . . . . . — — is life

Scott W.   C-1012

    The values I'm generating daily (made possible by Neo-Tech) are forever surprising and always life enhancing. My life is new, like I've just opened my eyes and in front of me are encyclopedias full of objective knowledge never before experienced. I'm able to filter out and reject the negatives and see what is real for prosperity and great happiness. This I place incalculable value upon.

Properly caring for and rearing children to honest, self-sufficient, competent, independent adults is the sole moral responsibility and duty of the parents. That duty is assumed from the parent's chosen act of procreation, for which the children are not responsible. Thus, parents have no right to place future claims or obligations on their children. Likewise, after children develop into self-sustaining, independent beings, all moral responsibilities and obligatory duties end for the parents.

***

Compared to men, few women have directly achieved greatness in the major areas of human accomplishment (e.g., arts, sciences, philosophy, music, business, industry, medicine, law). Those differences in achievement are not due to inherent or biological differences between men and women, but rather such differences are due to (1) women being more involved in the restricting tasks of raising children, and (2) the cultural, legal, mystical, and neocheating oppression of women that has occurred throughout most of recorded history [Re: Tables 38-39, Neo-Tech Reference Encyclopedia].

Few men attained greatness in any area of human achievement during the 1000-year Dark Ages during which the church oppressed everyone's intellectual and productive capacities. Likewise, few women have achieved greatness during their cultural dark ages that existed throughout most of recorded history. In recent years, however, radical changes have occurred to eliminate most differences in oppression between men and women. Those changes have occurred through the relentless, rational pressures of business and free enterprise, not through coercions of government, the feminists, or the non sequiturs of neocheating theologians, journalists, professors, and politicians.

Today, women in the Western World have essentially the same freedom and opportunity as men to develop their commercial values in most areas of human activity. But many women are by choice not exercising their new freedoms and opportunities. Thus, many women are failing to exploit their potentials for financial prosperity, psychuous pleasures, growing romantic love, and abiding happiness.

Divorced men and widowers are generally more desired or sought after by the opposite sex than are divorced women and widows. Aside from population statistics that somewhat favor men, no intrinsic or natural reason for that difference in desirability exists. The main difference is that, compared to women, men generally are and remain more productive in their jobs and careers and thus have more values and life to offer. By contrast, man-dominated housewives living as toys, pets, or servants generally have indulged themselves with mysticism instead of developing their characters, abilities, and talents. Thus, they have less values and life to offer.

Mark L.   R-6927

Neo-Tech has totally changed my life around for the better. When I received the Neo-Tech information package I was in a very depressed state of mind. I had recently separated from my wife and was laid-off from my job. Now, because of Neo-Tech, my wife and I have had a very happy and successful reconciliation and I have started a promising new job. Thank you very much for the Neo-Tech discovery Dr. Wallace.

Sincerely

Tony P.   R-3680

NZ $
Cost; $139-77 incl. bankdraft + postage
Benefit; $3,100+ 1st value delivered against neocheaters
— loss prevented —
2,250 % Return in 12 months
Scores a (10)

On the other hand, men and women of equivalent character and value development would have equal worth and desirability as value-oriented, romantic-love partners.

Neo-Tech Advantage #72
POTENTIAL OF WOMEN FROM 1300 BC THROUGH TODAY

Women hold great potential for gaining economic and cultural power in the Western world. But their potential is undermined by politicians, feminists, and other value destroyers who use the government to force their egalitarian equalities on others. Indeed, to survive without producing competitive values *for others*, professional neocheaters and mystics must use force, deception, and mysticism to usurp their destructive livelihoods *from others*. And physically weaker women are the easiest targets for their destructions. Thus, professional mystics and neocheaters more easily subject women to injustices and abuses to usurp power and values*. For that reason, throughout recorded history, women have suffered greater oppression than have men as illustrated below:

OPPRESSION OF WOMEN SINCE 1300 BC

Ancient Greece
1300 B.C.-450 B.C.

Homeric women (1300 B.C.-1100 B.C.) were relatively free and exercised considerable influence over men. But all women were subjected to double standards — legal and sexual.

Enlightened Greece
450 B.C.-27 B.C.

Courtesans held the highest positions of individual rights and personal respect available to women. Wives held the lowest position and were considered as house-keepers with few if any rights.

High-class prostitutes or courtesans were held superior to virtuous women and wives.

Roman Empire
27 B.C.-385 A.D.

With increased economic freedom, the drive for individual freedom brought new rights and respect for women. Oppression by mystics and conservatives decreased. Double standards diminished.

Drive for women's liberation and equality. As today, Roman feminists who advocated use of government controls and force to accomplish their ends failed in the long run by establishing the conditions for the increased oppression of women.

---

*After first oppressing women, men are then easier to oppress.

Andrew C. R-2724, AUSTRALIA

I anticipate that within three years, I will be financially independent. When I am 25, I will be a millionaire. Through reading Neo-Tech I realise that in order to create a powerful business, my business must be operated so that it is value producing and profit oriented.

To enhance my own happiness I would like to see a world eliminated of mysticism, and one that fully recognises the achievements of productive individuals

William D.   C-1013

Dear Mr. Flint:

Please add my name to your long list of satisfied buyers of Neo-Tech I-V. There is little I can say that has not been said by many others about the dawning of awareness and evolutionary growth in understanding afforded by the Neo-Tech Discovery.

I never was one to smile much. I was serious in my efforts to make mysticism work for me. Now, however, when dealing with Neocheaters I find myself smiling at them as I listen to their prattle. They recognise my knowing smile and "cut the crap" without my saying much of anything. It always works best with the master Neocheaters, thus, making them the easiest to stop. The poor deluded mystics require a word or two. However, with those little fish I usually just write them off as nothing to be concerned about.

My income has increased 50% since receiving Neo-Tech I-V three months ago but the greatest benefit has been the salvaging of my self esteem. I was ready to promote and market a "success system" that I believed in which was a mixture of logic and mysticism (as most of them are). However, when I realized the dishonesty involved I scrapped the program rather than profit financially from promoting something that would harm others. Instead, I turned to the marketing of a simple product that provides real value and found the financial success that had eluded me for almost three decades of effort.

Decline of the Roman Empire
100 A.D.-385 A.D.

The spreading altruistic influence of Christianity began stripping women of their individual rights and subjecting them to new, heavy oppressions while leading the civilized Western world toward asceticism and anti-sexual attitudes.

Christianity plunged Rome into asceticism, causing massive destruction and suffering. Women lost almost all rights with rising Christian power. ...Today, ominous parallels are developing with rising fundamentalist, born-again, anti-porn/anti-abortion movements.

Rise of Christianity
385 A.D.-1000 A.D.

The western world sank into the Dark Ages as women were pushed to their lowest position in recorded history. They had no individual or legal rights. The Church questioned if women were even human. The Catholic Church considered women as wasteful property who could be killed, beaten, tortured, ravished or forced into slavery with impunity by theologians and "devout" noblemen.

Catholic bishops argued that women did not have mortal souls and that women were pieces of wasteful property. The Catholic church sanctioned wife-beating. Killing a woman was not a very serious offense. Noblemen had the natural "right" to ravish any peasant woman.

Pre-Renaissance
1000-1300

The rise of courtly love and the de-emphasis of the Catholic Church began elevating women to emotional partners more equal to men. Respect and admiration for women increased with increased economic activity. But women still had few individual or legal rights. Extreme double standards were still practiced.

A new man-woman relationship developed that was previously unknown to Western civilization. Women gained respect and admiration. Courtly love elevated women from child-bearers and lust-satisfiers to more equal partners with men.

The Church vs. the Renaissance
1300-1500

The Church fought viciously to stop the rising new concepts of romantic love, happy man-woman relationships, and pleasurable sex. Pope Innocent VIII started the inquisitions and witch trials. Millions of innocent women were killed, tortured, and burned to death by the Catholic Church. But the growing enlightenment of the Renaissance with spreading economic freedoms began

John E. C-110, NIGERIA

   I have just concluded reading your Neo-Tech I-V and I am exuberantly thrilled and lucky to be one of those that belong to the electronic age of Neo-Tech. After reading the information packages, I have come to the conclusion that what will save mankind from the consequences of third world war and jet age incurable diseases is already around the corner — Neo-Tech. Very many thanks to Dr. Wallace and his team.
   Congratulations and please keep on the good work for posterities sake. You can count on my support in every way possible.

Ron F.B.   R-2934,   AUSTRALIA

I'm greateful for the many changes in my life already due to the piercing logic and "Crap Cutting" effect of the Neo-Tech Information.

Rohan N.   R-4911,   AUSTRALIA

Life is far more pleasurable when viewed from such a clear perspective of honesty and guiltlessness. Everyone should experience Neo-Tech in order to pursue happy, prosperous lives.
Thankyou Dr Wallace.

liberating the human mind and reason from the dark, brutal mysticism of Christian theology.

Renaissance noblemen equated women to beauty and good. The Catholic church fought back by promoting the "evils" of women and witchcraft. They advocated hanging "evil" women by their thumbs, twisting ropes around their heads, pushing needles under their nails, and pouring boiling oil on their feet in the "devout hope" of forcing confessions of their "wickedness". The Catholic church then proceeded to burn to death tens of thousands of innocent women.

The Puritans
1500-1700

With increasing economic activity, the Puritans rejected the Church's hatred of women, sex, and happiness. They accepted the normality of sex, pleasure, and happiness. Women's rights greatly improved under Puritanism. Women could divorce. They gained property and inheritance rights. Marriage became a civil contract.

The Age of Reason
1700-1800

Men respected women for their minds and intellectual development. People involved in business began scrapping the gloom and hatred of Christianity and its idea that women were evil. But women were still held as subservient to men.

The rationalists rejected the malevolence of Christianity. But women were often considered as ornaments, toys, or nitwits.

Victorianism
1800-1900

Slobbering sensitivity became the ideal. Men sought shy, virginal women. The togetherness concept developed. Glorification of "pure" women was a pretext for a desperate last attempt by neocheating conservatives and the Church to subjugate women as servants of men. A great increase in double standards occurred under the guise of "moral" standards. Women lost considerable individual freedom.

Men grew shy and sought "pure", virginal-type women. Women were "glorified" and idealized, but this was only a new pretext for the continued subjugation of women by men. The U. S. Surgeon General, Dr. William Hammond, issued the warning that decent women should not feel the slightest pleasure during sexual intercourse. Many doctors considered sexual desire in women to be pathological. But women began revolting against their "purified" and "glorified" status.

Jerry H. C-201

It's about time y'all put out NEO-THINK. You've had us all excited since the "Big Bang" weekend y'all had back in June of this year. At any rate, I'm looking forward to "Inside I & O - Money/Power/Romantic-Love Packages" which you advertised for $148.00; I'm sure it must be great stuff but the title is a little clumsy. Now, don't get pissed, y'all do some great advertising and are damn good at calling a spade a spade. I especially like the part "flipping off all those tradationalists" 'cause I've been doing that for years, them scamps! And whoever wrote the 14 Neo-Tech/Neothink Approaches leaves me in suspense 'cause #14. says,"The incredible Power-F'ing nuggets". I understand Power but F'ing is a bit unclear. However, the "right now, damn it!" part was great, I knew right away I wasn't reading any ole time 'Ligion Baptist Sunday School Quarterly. The part about the Jungle Bitch was fascinating. Sort of reminds me of an ole dyke Opera Director I used to have, she's probably still smoking her pipe, kicking ass and taking names.

Rashimi P. R-1434

I use to stay up all night, in disappointment and depression. I still stay up all night but only in anticipation.

Hezekiah M. R-1940

Neo-Tech II gave me a renewed confidence in myself and ability to make decisions that were for my benefit. I recommend Neo tech for all achievers. Everyday I re-read the Advance Concepts and try to apply them

The Decline of Religion and Victorianism via the Rise of Capitalism and the Emancipation of Women
1850-1900

Capitalistic economics undermined the oppressive customs of the past and broke the unjust, feudal hierarchy of the social classes. Capitalism crippled the influence of the Church. Capitalism created the atmosphere and pressure for female suffrage, individual rights, divorce reform, and equal legal and economic rights. Victorianism was a desperate delaying action against increasing honesty, individuality, justice, earned equality, and rising economic freedoms.

With the rise of capitalism, women gained significant economic rights for the first time since the anti-Christian, pagan Roman Empire. Capitalism broke the stifling, unjust religious/feudal-class patterns. A new optimism and cheerful happiness rose among the middle class. Capitalistic economics greatly accelerated the collapse of hypocritical snobbishness, racism, artificial social ties, and oppressive religious and social customs. The rigid Victorian home was threatened by increasing economic freedom for females, divorce reforms, and free-choice love. Victorianism was a last-stand action by the conservatives and the church against the inevitable, liberating changes caused by capitalism and a prosperous, industrial civilization.

The Emergence of 20th Century Romantic Love
1900-1960

Flourishing commerce among individuals, especially in America, discarded the anti-sexual, Victorian-Christian ethics. Double standards diminished with more equal educational, economic, legal, and sexual rights for women. Birth control and abortion rights were promoted. Capitalism liberated women and minorities by valuing all individuals according to their objective worth rather than to their sex, beliefs, social status, or race.

Women increasingly become equal to men in romantic relationships. Love patterns of all societies were drawn to the free and honest capitalistic style of Western love, which combined sexuality, affectionate friendship, productive work, and family functions...all into a single, equal-partner relationship. The modern, capitalist-generated, sexual revolution demolished most of the Christian-Victorian patterns of anti-sexual, patriarchal oppressiveness.

Modern Romantic Love
1960-Present

The sexual revolution broke the last vestiges of inequalities between men and women. But today, renewed oppression of individual rights has begun to rise ominously with the feminist and religious movements against pornography

Charles T.   C-1014

Dear Dr. Flint & Staff

I have had the NEO-TECH I-V information package now for about five months. It has been a very interesting and exciting time as I have based my attitude and thinking around Aristotelian values and Neo-Tech guidance. The advantages accumulate very quickly! The self confidence, the clarity of thought, the ability to make value decisions based on what is good for the business or what is good for me. The most amazing thing is how easy and obvious it all is now and how ridiculous have some of the decisions I have made in the past been, due to a totally bemused and confused thinking process based on mysticism, religion and what other people think.

I have just received three further copies of the Neo-Tech I-V information package that I am going to give to new business partners who I think will benefit most from the amazing discoveries within. Having recently acquired a 30% shareholding in their Computer and Software company I feel that it is of the highest priority that any decisions they have to make whilst I am not around are based on the right kind of objective, value producing thinking as promoted by Neo-Tech.

I am fortunate indeed, that I had the opportunity to read and understand the Neo-Tech concepts. My ignorance has been lifted and I feel the power of the concepts growing within me every day. I also note with some satisfaction that my business, my finances, and my self esteem is growing commensurate with the application of my new knowledge. Finally the happiness within my own family unit, my wife and 13 year old son, is now as intense and wonderful as it has ever been. All this good fortune, and I don't feel the slightest bit guilty! Producers of the world Unite!

Mark C.   C-105

I ordered Neo-Tech in late 1982, or sometime in '83. After reading the first few concepts I put the book away in disgust. This year I reopened the book. I am glad that I did. The conflict in my thinking is over. We must deal with the reality that is, and not with speculations about what might be, based upon feelings. Reality exists, that is all. The idea of biological immortality is both fascinating and exciting. I want to live forever and experience continually expanding psychous pleasure and growth.

and abortion. Those movements are inspired by neocheating authorities seeking unearned values and power. Still, the majority of women have not fully exercised their new freedoms and rights. Many neocheating feminist leaders seek unearned gains through government coercion and force. And that force will boomerang to increasingly subjugate the rights of all women...and men.*

Individual freedom that naturally evolves from capitalism made modern romantic love and the liberation of women possible. For, the capitalistic free market put values on individuals according to their objective worth rather than their sex, social status, or race. Women can now be fully independent. But having gained the freedom for equality, many women fear that equality might be too risky or challenging, or require too much independence or effort, or cost them the chance for love. Such women often buy "security" and "love" at the price of remaining unequal, unfulfilled, unhappy all their adult lives.

Today, men and women have essentially the same educational and economic opportunities. But many women in developed societies have no careers beyond the home. Thus, they deny their basic human need to develop competence and self-sufficiency. That need for competence and independence is usually fulfilled by pursuing productive work or challenging careers.

Future Romantic Love

Two approaches to life are open: (1) The neocheater's approach of using force-backed government or deceit-based religion to drain values from others, or (2) the producer's approach of using integrated honesty and free markets to deliver values wanted by others. That second approach obviates force, coercion, fraud in allowing all men and women equally to pursue prosperity, romantic love, and abiding happiness.

Despite feminist claims, nothing today prevents women from realizing their potentials. The battle is not for women's rights, minority rights, black rights — the battle is and always has been for *individual* rights. When individual rights are fully protected, then everyone's rights are protected.

---

* Women who usurp feminist-inspired, unearned values are heading back toward dependence...toward being taken care of and eventually subjugated by men. In essence, the feminist movement is designed to coerce productive people into taking care of protesting women. The inevitable results are opposite the goals of freedom declared by feminist neocheaters. And those same ploys are destructively used by politicians to usurp "freedom" for blacks and other minorities. Indeed, the more unearned values usurped by the neocheating feminists and politicians, the more their recipient clients move toward dependence and subjugation. ...All neocheaters who consciously transfer values from the earned to the unearned are black-hat neocheaters who harm everyone, especially those dupes they claim to help.

David C.   R-5440

As was mentioned in the instruction manual, upon opening the pages of Neo-Tech, I found myself on a journy from which I would never return. In reading just the first few chapters my first thought was to burn the books! but I have always had an open mind and soon found that I couldn't put them down. I have always sought the truth througout my life and I thought I knew the truth. You see I was a self proclaimed theoleogen and well studied on the subject, I thought that nothing could ever shake my faith. I truly believed in my way as truth. But many undeniable truths I found in the pages of Neo-Teck. At first my whole world felt around me I had never before felt such fear, anger, and confusion. Many times I had to put the books down, I could not handle any more. For days I walked around dazed. But I couldn't keep away from them long, they seamed to hold a strang aluring power I couldn't resist. And the more I read the brighter the light became. A ray of hope and desire I had never felt in my 33 years began to well up inside me. Hope for a future that most of man-kind dared not even dream about. A desire to pursue all my ambitions and to reach out beyond my wildest imaginations. I feel in me a strenght and power I had never felt. This alone scares me at times and those around me as well. For the first time in my life I have begun to stand up for my own rights and with much success I might add.

Most feminists diminish the potential for all women by trying to usurp unearned economic or money gains through government force or coercion in violating the rights of others. Such tactics are morally wrong and destructive to all individuals...and in the long run succeed only in giving government more power to oppress everyone — especially women. While stridently expressing goals of liberation and freedom, most feminist policies deny freedom of choice, voluntary division of labor, and open competition. Those policies reveal a fear of freedom, competition, and self-responsibility. Such dishonest, double-speak contradictions of demanding freedom while actually attacking freedom via government force is also common in "liberation" or "rights" movements of various Black, consumer, and environmental groups: Such groups demand benefits and "freedoms" via government force while reducing their own and everyone else's freedom.

Government laws backed by force have always been the mechanism that eventually oppressed women [Re: Section Four, Neo-Tech Reference Encyclopedia]. The genuine liberation of women occurred during those rare, historic periods during which the reason and logic of individual freedom gained influence over the dishonesty and mysticism of government and religious oppression. Those liberating periods were the Golden Age of Greece, The Renaissance, and the greatest, most profoundly moral period of all: the free-enterprise phase of the Industrial Revolution. In free-enterprise capitalism, the influences of reason, honesty, effort, productivity, and voluntary individual choice count for everything, while the influences of mysticism, dishonesty, racism, social status, and the use of force are dismissed as nothing. ...The causal relationship of reason and capitalism to freedom and prosperity for women is clear.

In attempting to establish credibility, feminists promote and publicize certain "famous" women of history as heroines. Some of those women were honest, value producers who contributed to human well-being. But most of those feminist "heroines" were demagogues and neocheaters who agitated for more government force to make individuals conform to their wishes or demands. In their promotion of "great women", most feminists hypocritically ignore one of the greatest benefactors to human life and champions of individual rights. That person was a woman. She was one of the most profound thinkers and writers, male or female, of all time. She was a world-famous novelist and the most important philosopher since Aristotle. Her name: Ayn Rand.

Why do most feminists ignore Ayn Rand? Because she intellectually refuted their concepts of mysticism, initiatory force, and government coercion to achieve ends. More important, she clearly identified the immorality of such approaches, thus repudiating the core of most feminist movements and methods. Also, Ayn Rand identified that the only proper moral issue is individual rights...not women's rights, black rights, or any other such "rights" or causes. For such causes are largely designed to support

Mark A.   C-1015

Dear Mr. Flint,
    Thank you for enlightening me on Neo-Tech. Personally, I have been studing authors on goal achievement & financial success for years. My wife who is a chiropractor, & I are what you might refer to as top acheivers. Although see hasn't read Neo-Tech yet she said she will, based on the change & growth she has seen in me since my study of Neo-Tech. It is truly a compliment in the highest regard!
    I cannot discount the benefits I've gained from people & things like Earl Nightengale, Dennis Waitley, EST, Norman Vincient Peal, Dale Carnegie, David Schwartz, William Nickerson, Robert Allen, Rich Devos, & yes even Robert Schuller. However I now feel these entities were only 1st grade so to speak. They now need to graduate. Graduate to Neo-Tech. Neo-Tech is by far the most mind expanding material I've ever read. The above names don't even come close.
    Neo-Tech in my experience is like the knockout punch a fighter receives, the acceleration of a rocket or shuttle launch, the force of a 1000 car freight train, or the mutual state of ecstasy 1/2 second before orgasm!

David B.   C-99

Dear sir/madam,
    Thankyou for the Neo-tech package. it has changed my life in more ways than one. It paid for itself in 6 weeks - I stopped smoking after reading Neo.Tech.

    THE WORLD WILL BE FREE

neocheaters. The feminists' rejection of Ayn Rand not only underscores their intellectual dishonesty, but demonstrates that their movement is not interested in individual rights. Instead, they are interested in usurping power, values, and advantages through the spurious, neocheating gimmick of women's rights. Because of their disregard for individual rights in their demands for government coercion or force, feminist movements bring, in the long run, only further government oppression of women. Indeed, that oppression is already reoccurring with, for example, the anti-abortion and anti-pornography movements.

And finally, most feminists stridently attack women's greatest benefactor and liberator — free-enterprise capitalism. Furthermore, many feminists actually support the prime causes for oppression of women — government and religion. In fact, some feminists remain active members of the most virulently anti-women, patriarchal organization ever contrived by man — the Catholic Church. Such feminists work against the well-being of all women and all individuals.

Neo-Tech Advantage #73
THE NATURE OF EMOTIONS AND SELF-RESPONSIBILITY

The Nature of Emotions

1. Emotions are neither good nor bad and are not subject to moral judgments, no matter how irrational or "bad sounding" they may seem. ...Only actions can be judged as good or bad, moral or immoral.

2. All emotions, no matter how irrational or how deeply repressed, are a real part of a person and need to be recognized, acknowledged, and guiltlessly accepted.

3. Each repressed, negative emotion becomes an integral part of a person's mind. Each repressed emotion subconsciously exerts a continuous negative effect on that person's thinking and emotional processes. That negative effect remains forever, unless the emotion (often an emotion from childhood) is identified and rationally re-examined through the mature adult mind.

4. The identifying and releasing of any repressed emotion through a non-mystical mind is a healthy, rewarding experience. [Re: Concept 104, Neo-Tech Reference Encyclopedia].

Self-Responsibility/Mouth Responsibility

Each individual is solely responsible for his or her own actions. That includes being responsible for what goes in and out of one's mouth. **Mouth Responsibility: the self-responsibility for the food, drink, drugs, smoke, genitalia that go into one's mouth and the words that come out.**

Daniel B. J-127

Ayn Rand hinted at a complete presentation of her philosophy in fully detailed form. I have read most of her works, I think she would be proud of your Neotech approach to fighting mysticism. As far as I know she never completed a detailed presentation of her philosophy; at first reading of Neotech I thought, my god Ayn Rand must still be alive!!, it's is so much her way of comming at things.

Mike K. C-106

I AM 16 YRS OLD, + LIVE IN A RELIGIOUS-INFESTED REGION OF THE SOUTHEAST. EVER SINCE I CAN REMEMBER, I WAS GIVEN A FREE(?) CHOICE ABOUT WHAT TO BELIEVE. (e.g. Christianity, Catholicism, Judaism etc., but not Atheism). GIVEN MY "FREE" CHOICE, I CHOSE A LITTLE-KNOWN, RELIGIOUS ORGANIZATION IN CALIFORNIA, BY THE NAME OF ASTARA.
THEN, ONE DAY, SOMETHING BIG HAPPENED. A LARGE, BROWN PACKAGE ARRIVED IN MY MAILBOX. IT WAS NEO-TECH I-V.
I MUST SAY, NEO-TECH REALLY SHOOK ME UP. BUT ONLY RECENTLY, AFTER HAVING NEO-TECH FOR NINE MONTHS HAVE I DISCOVERED MY MISTAKE. I WAS USING CLEVER RATIONALIZATIONS TO REMOVE THE AUTHORITIES OF MYSTICISM (AS DEFINED IN NEO-TECH), AND REPLACING THEM WITH THE AUTHORITY OF NEO-TECH. THE PROBLEM WAS & STILL IS, TO A CERTAIN EXTENT, THAT I'M AFRAID TO GO IT ALONE. I NEED TO FOLLOW SOMETHING INSTEAD OF BEING INDEPENDENT.
SINCE I HAVE DISCOVERED MY MISTAKE, I HAVE RUN INTO SOME KANTIAN PHILOSOPHY. THE CONFLICT BETWEEN KANT & NEO-TECH PROMPTED ME TO RE-EVALUATE MY LIFE & SURROUNDINGS. I NOW HAVE FOUR ABSOLUTES THAT I LIVE BY, (NOT AUTHOR-ITATIVELY) 1) I WANT TO LIVE -(LIFE ENHANCING OR DIMINISHING?)
2) I WANT TO EXCEL -(EXCELLENCE, CAN I EXCEL?)
3) I WANT ONLY TRUTH -(TRUE OR CAMOUFLAGED UNTRUTHS?)
4) I WANT HAPPINESS (HAPPINESS, CAN I ACHIEVE IT?)
THUS, I HAVE MY LETH METHOD WITH WHICH I EVALUATE EVERYTHING NOW.

Internal mysticism ruins people's lives through (1) allowing irrational, destructive ingestion of sugar, alcohol, or drugs into their mouths and (2) allowing irrational, destructive words to egress from their mouths. Everyone alone must personally battle to overcome internal mysticism in order to live prosperously and happily. Self-responsibility can not be transferred to anyone. For that reason, most therapies by psychologists and psychiatrists are invalid. Moreover, such therapies are often practiced by neocheaters usurping a livelihood by manipulating mysticism in others.

Almost all psychological problems arise from internal mysticism. Such problems are overcome only by each individual's continual, conscious choice to be honest rather than mystical. Each person must decide to self-determine the future or to surrender that responsibility to external "authorities" (including psychologists). That surrender is to ask others to do the impossible — to solve one's own problems and deliver happiness.

Fighting and rejecting mysticism within one's own self is the greatest, most important of all battles. And the most ironic, tragic loser of that battle was Ayn Rand. For she developed and harnessed the greatest mind to battle mysticism since Aristotle. Yet, she could never collect her full rewards, because she lost the battle to personal mysticism on several fronts. The most irrational, emotion-driven mysticism was her nurtured rationalization for smoking. The consequence of that mystical indulgence? ...Smoking killed her.

Having an external "authority" (e.g. a God, a drug, a cigarette, a psychologist) to provide "easy-way", "no-struggle" answers only avoids self-responsibility and feeds one's own mysticism. That in turn weakens the individual's competence and motivation to solve his or her own problems. That is why most therapies are long-range failures. Only individuals themselves can have sufficient motivation and self-knowledge to successfully overcome internal mysticism and solve life's problems. Only individuals themselves can put sufficient energy and knowledge into the efforts needed to become competent, prosperous, and happy. No mystical or outside source can provide those values.

Neo-Tech Advantage #74
NATURAL HIGHS

Strongly positive experiences such as major achievements, aerobic exercises, endorphin-producing runs, great music, art, literature, drama, and romantic love stimulate natural highs. The ultimate high, however, comes from feeling one's own self in control — being in control of life, living free of mysticism, living honestly, rationally, productively. In that non-mystical state, a person acutely feels the integrated physical and psychological process of living. He or she experiences the impact of living fully, in competent control of one's own self, destiny, and reality.

That clarity and control of self, life, and reality produces a physical and emotional high. That high evolves from an acute awareness of living in reality...of being in control. Such highs are far more exhilarating than those

Ken & Dee C.   C-1

A LABOR OF KNOWLEDGE, LOVE, AND VALUES. ALL ENCOMPASSING IN ITS' PERSPECTIVE. A TRUE WORK OF ART. ARISTOTLE, RAND, PEIKOFF AND WALLACE. THEIR IDEALS WILL LIVE FOREVER. FINALLY, ROOM FOR THE INDIVIDUAL, DEVOID OF EXTERNAL INFLUENCE.

Billie H.   J-64

I am 53 years of age and just come alive! To say the least the revelation is astonishing.

I have just completed reading through Dr. Wallace' Neo-tech discovery and, like many before me, it has been a rude awakening within the real world. Its effect on my life has been profound indeed.

Meredith A.   R-3002

I AM NOW READING THE JULY 1986 EDITION OF NEO-TECH AND CAN SEE MORE CLEARLY EACH DAY HOW I HAVE BEEN INFLUENCED BY MYSTICISM. ALSO THAT THERE HAVE BEEN TIMES WHEN I WAS A NEO-CHEATER. FOR AS LONG AS I CAN REMEMBER, I HAVE FELT GUILTY (ALMOST FOR BEING BORN) ALSO THERE WERE FEELINGS OF LOW SELF ESTEEM AND RESENTMENT.

I HAVE LOOKED AND LOOKED FOR THE MEANING OF LIFE.

NOW I AM EXPERIENCING A RELEASE FROM MYSTICM AND LOOKING AT LONG RANGE GOALS.

achieved through reality avoiding, artificial stimuli such as drugs, alcohol, religious or mystical experiences, manipulating others, ruling others, killing others. Those dishonest, control-seeking experiences are achieved through force or neocheating rather than through the honest production of values.

The most intense, reality high is psychuous pleasures. Reality highs, however, can be consistently experienced in almost any phase of one's life to produce continuous waves of pleasure and happiness. Most people have at times experienced brief or partial glimpses of those natural highs. Such experiences live vividly in nearly everyone's memory. On analysis, one will discover that those experiences occurred when a person was most free of mysticism — most free to be his or her own self — most free to function according to his or her biological nature. Moreover, everyone who has developed a rational, productive life style has the capacity for experiencing natural highs with increasing frequency. Those highs can eventually blend into a near continuous state of happiness marked by extra-intense moments of psychuous pleasures.

The Neo-Tech/Psychuous concepts deal with relationships between people. But those concepts also deal with the relationship of one's own self relative to reality, self-esteem, and self-awareness. Only through developing a nonmystical, integrated relationship with one's own body, mind, and objective reality can a person fully experience the prosperity, pleasures, and happiness available from life.

Natural highs involve the release of physical and emotional tensions while being fully aware of the mind and body. The sensation is that of "letting go" as the body tensions release and the emotional pleasures are guiltlessly felt. Those natural, euphoric experiences are contrasted to the destructive, tension-breaking actions of taking drugs, getting drunk, food gorging. Such artificial or mystical highs always leave hangovers and unhappiness along with damaged minds and bodies. [Re: Table 41, Neo-Tech Reference Encyclopedia].

Natural highs can also release chronic muscular tensions manifested in taut necks, shallow breathing, stiffly pulled up shoulders, tense buttocks, and uptightness in general. In fact, neck stiffness is an indicator of locked-in conflicts caused by mysticism.

Releasing such tensions also improves one's physical grace and coordination. The release of those tensions restore the natural, cat-like gracefulness of body motions as muscles begin working together in their intended, fluid, integrated manner. Also, the release of those chronic tensions and the deepening of breathing permit clearer, more effective thinking.

Certain exercises are also effective in both releasing chronic muscle tensions and improving one's breathing. [Re: Book Analysis 71, Neo-Tech Reference Encyclopedia]. Also, self-hypnosis can relax and/or release certain physical tensions. Hypnosis bypasses the conscious mind by putting orders

Steve & Mimi F.   R-2626

The Neo-Tech Discovery is the most interesting, informative and mind-opening book I have ever read. Each chance I get I try to read and understand a little more. I'm so excited about this new/true way of thinking -- I read it aloud to my husband and we discuss so many topics now. It was much easier for him because he basically thinks Neo-Tech already. Now we have so much more to discuss (not argue) together. We find each other great companions -- thanks to Neo-Tech.

Nicholas G.   R-2233, AUSTRALIA

Dear Sir/Madam
I thank you for supplying me with your valuable and thorough work. So few items sent away for return the money spent yet for the price of two weeks car fuel I have the foundations of a rental outfit for life.

JVL RP-101   Mexico

I want you and your organization receive my sincere congratulations for the integrations of de valuable knowledge of Neo-Tech Information Package. I consider that knowledge of vital importance for a near happy and successful business in the entire universe.

I meet Neo-Tech knowledge throughout a friend who has the books already. I became very interested in those books, but I did not expecting the enormeous changes in my personality after I took some of the advantages. I was involved in so many mystic activities. I am medical Dr. by profession but I am not graduated yet. I am working out of my profession in some interesting projects.

directly into a nonresisting, noncritical subconscious mind. [Re: Appendix C, Neo-Tech Reference Encyclopedia]. Effective hypnosis techniques are easy to master, but can be damaging to the subconscious mind when hypnosis is used carelessly or with improper dehypnosis. Moreover, hypnosis is usually used mystically, is generally unnecessary, and is not recommended.

Tension-releasing not only lets one relax and feel pleasures, but projects a freedom to others that helps them relax and share the pleasures.

Neo-Tech Advantage #75
JOY AND HAPPINESS

The emotions of pleasure, joy, well-being, and happiness have interrelating features. But each is a separate experience with unique characteristics and requirements. For example, one can be happy without experiencing pleasure, and one can experience temporary pleasure without being happy. Joy is a self-induced, here-and-now emotion that arises from pleasure, well-being, and happiness. Enjoyment is also induced by taking the time to consciously reflect upon the emotional rewards of pleasure, well-being, and happiness. To fully experience enjoyment, one must reject unearned guilt foisted on him or her by mystics and neocheaters. [Re: Table 42, Neo-Tech Reference Encyclopedia]. When a Neo-Tech oriented person earns happiness, he or she can then make a conscious choice to guiltlessly enjoy that happiness.

Neo-Tech Advantage #76
PHILOSOPHY FOR
ROMANTIC LOVE

Glib, shallow philosophies about love and sex based on selflessness, altruism, or slogans are easily conjured up by mystics and neocheaters. To some people, Leo Buscaglia's love-all philosophies may sound poetic, beautiful, comfortable, and easy to accept. But those pseudo philosophies are generally rigged from non sequiturs and then promulgated as the truth by glib psychologists, social "experts", religious "authorities", egalitarian writers, mountebanks, and other neocheaters who have never experienced integrated, value-oriented romantic love. Thus, their books and words work to diminish everyone's love and happiness.

Many books about love and sex are also based on spurious, altruistic philosophies that sound "good" on the surface and promise happiness through a system of destructively selfless, sacrificial acts. But altruism is a power-usurping tool contrived by neocheaters for contradicting reality, subverting the nature of human beings, and laying false guilt on everyone. Such glibly spurious, altruistic philosophies contradict the positive, valuable goals ostensibly presented in those books. Most authors never realize that an explicit, rational philosophy is necessary to form a consistent basis for their writings, especially when dealing with human relationships and love.

If philosophy is ignored or used inconsistently by the authors, the value of their work is diminished. Without a conscious philosophical position, no consistent principles are available to guide a person's work, life, or love

Dan G. RP-100

TO: THE NEO-TECH RESEARCH & WRITING CENTER
FROM: AN OWNER OF THE NEO-TECH MANUSCRIPT

AMAZING! THIS IS THE ONLY WORD TO DESCRIBE DR. WALLACE'S DISCOVERY.
WHAT IS IT THAT MAKES ALL HUMAN BEINGS SO GULLIBLE WHEN IT COMES
TO LIVING THEIR SHORT AND TEDIOUS LIVES? YEARS AGO, IT WOULD NEVER HAVE
EVEN OCCURED TO ME THAT THERE WAS EVEN A PURPOSE TO LIVING. LIFE WAS
INCREDULOUS, A BIG JOKE, A PASTIME BETWEEN BIRTH AND DEATH. RELIGION
SOON CAME ALONG AND BANG...I HAD FOUND, OR SO I THOUGHT, THE MISSING
INGREDIENT TO LIFE, A HIGHER BEING TO SERVE. WOW!...THIS WAS GREAT.
NOBODY COULD TOUCH ME BECAUSE I WAS DOING GOD'S WORK!? THEN HOWEVER,
SLOWLY BUT SURELY, I WAS DOING MORE OF HIS WORK, THEN MORE, AND THEN
MORE. HEY...STOP! THIS WASN'T FUN! WHAT ABOUT ME? THE ONLY PERSON THAT
GOT SATISFACTION FROM WHAT I WAS DOING WAS THE PERSON TELLING ME TO DO IT.
LIFE REALLY WAS A JOKE! WHO NEEDED GOD ANYWAY?
THEN SUDDENLY..."NEO-TECH" ENTERED THE SCENE. WHO WAS THIS DR. WALLACE?
WAS HE A RELIGIOUS LEADER PROMOTING A NEW GOD?...NO! WAS HE A POLITICIAN
WITH A QUICK TONGUE?...NO! HE WAS A MERE MAN WITH A STARTLING REVELATION
FOR THE ENTIRE WORLD! OOPS...DID I SAY MERE MAN? WITH NO HIGHER BEINGS
TO COMPARE TO, HOW COULD MANKIND BE DESCRIBED AS MERE HUMANS? FOR WHAT
HE REVEALED TO ME, HE WAS NOW A GREAT MAN! A GREAT BUSINESSMAN!
THANK YOU DR. WALLACE & THANK YOU I&O FOR PUBLISHING HIS WORK.
NOW LOOK AT WHAT HAS EVOLVED... THE NEO-TECH/NEOTHINK SYSTEM. DOES
MARK HAMILTON & I&O HAVE ANY LIMITATIONS? OF COURSE NOT! I AM IN AWE AT
WHAT I HAVE JUST LISTENED TO. BOY...WHAT A SYSTEM!!! MY LIFE HAS JUST
CHANGED! LIMITATIONS HAVE GONE. NOBODY CAN TELL ME WHAT I CAN OR CAN NOT
DO ANYMORE.
A SMALL BUSINESS THAT I WANTED TO CREATE, NOW SEEMS QUITE CREDIBLE AND
NO LONGER OUT OF REACH. BUT FOR NOW, BIOLOGICAL IMMORTALITY IS MY MAIN
CONCERN AS I DO NOT WISH TO DIE, EVEN IF IT IS AS A RICH MAN. NOTHING
MEANS MORE TO ME NOW THAN LIFE. THIS HOWEVER CAN ONLY BE DONE ONE WAY,
BY BREAKING DOWN THE WORLDS BELIEF IN GODS AND GOVERNMENTS. HOW?
WELL YOU ALREADY KNOW THE ANSWER...WITH "NEO-TECH!!!"

Manley T.   J-35

It has truely changed my life. I believe it is the only answer, and the only chance for human life to survive.

relationship. By contrast, every Neo-Tech/Psychuous concept is rooted in a consistent philosophy that integrates reality with the physical, psychological, and intellectual nature of human beings.

Consciously or subconsciously, all people make philosophical choices that determine the course of their lives. Two fundamental philosophical choices exist for all human beings: (1) a reality oriented, pro-life choice (Aristotelian), or (2) a mystically oriented, anti-life choice (Platonistic). The future of all humans and all societies are determined by those two philosophical choices. Aristotelian choices allow a person to experience success, prosperity, romantic love, psychuous pleasures, long-range happiness. Platonistic choices lead to a rationalized life that eventually produces failure, anxiety, destructiveness, boredom, unhappiness [Re: Table 43, Neo-Tech Reference Encyclopedia illustrates the results of those two choices throughout history while listing the social and personal consequences of choosing an Aristotelian vs. a Platonistic approach to life].

All philosophical concepts fall into one of two camps:
1. Platonistic-based, altruistic collectivism based on death-oriented dishonesty and laziness.
2. Aristotelian-based, free-enterprise individualism based on life-oriented honesty and effort.

All religions and most political concepts fall into the Platonistic camp. All Neo-Tech/Psychuous concepts are firmly grounded in the Aristotelian camp [Re: Table 44, Neo-Tech Reference Encyclopedia].

Neo-Tech Advantage #77
ARISTOTLE FOR THE LIVING AND THE FUTURE VS. PLATO FOR THE DEAD AND THE PAST

Philosophy determines the course of each individual's life [Re: Concept 107, Neo-Tech Reference Encyclopedia]. The diametrically opposite choices between Aristotelian philosophy and Platonistic philosophy profoundly affect every individual and society. [Re: Tables 43 and 44, Neo-Tech Reference Encyclopedia]. Aristotelian philosophy is the intellectual basis of Neo-Tech. Platonistic philosophy is the intellectual basis of every irrational, destructive religious and political system promoted in the past 2300 years. Indeed, Platonism is the philosophical foundation of mysticism, altruism, sacrifice, egalitarianism, existentialism, religion, dictatorships, theism, socialism, democracy, communism, fascism, evangelism and every other rule of force, coercion, and fraud. Except for free-enterprise capitalism, all political systems including democracy (a tyranny by the majority) require deception and force to exist. Thus, all those political and religious systems are immoral and harmful to human beings. Only free-enterprise capitalism is:
1. based entirely on voluntary free choice,
2. consistent with the nature of conscious beings and, thus is beneficial to all conscious beings,
3. moral and just: Offers freedom to everyone. Rejects all mysticism, racism, initiatory force, and fraud.

Ronald A.   R-4876

Dear Sirs,

I cannot put in words how much I have benefitted with Neo-Tech from a personal and financial point of view. After approximately 1 month of reading (only 1 time), a great surge of confidence and achievement has come over me. After going over the Neo-Tech II benefits, I recieved a top position at a large firm, and I have restored a strong sense of pride in myself and my abilities, I plan to continue moving up the corporate ladder and Neo-Tech will insure my ascendency. In addition, I would be more than proud to strive for biological immortality for myself and my loved ones.
Thank you for this remarkable work.

Platonism is also the basis of all public educational systems. Government-run schools today are inept at educating children because they embrace the ideas of John Dewey, a Platonist existentialist who replaced objective concepts with subjective concepts in education. (Dewey's contemporaries, William James and Sidney Hook, promoted similar but more cautiously disguised, existentialistic ideas.) Using dishonest non sequiturs, Dewey's philosophy dismisses as socially irrelevant the pedagogical teaching of fundamental knowledge such as reading, writing, mathematics, and science.

Dewey's philosophy promotes the mystical concept that children can be "educated" by allowing them to randomly pursue their own whims. The students' whims are considered socially relevant to the here-and-now and thus are deemed as the basis of education. The "teacher", therefore, merely follows wherever the child's feelings may lead (rather than the teacher providing the child with objective knowledge via systematic input of objective facts and information). With an existential action approach, Dewey deems the mind as the creator of "reality". Thus, in one mystical stroke, he negates both the integrating human mind and objective reality.

Although deceptively stating the opposite, Karl Marx's dialectical materialism is the same "reality creating" approach to action as Dewey's approach. Hitler's approach is also the same as Dewey's "willed realities" and "created logics". That "reality-creating" approach is the essence of mysticism. For it relieves the mind of the basic human responsibility of identifying and then logically dealing with objective reality. As a pragmatic existential neocheater, Dewey scraps logic, knowledge, and reason in favor of whims and feelings. He deems such whims and feelings as the primary guide to human knowledge, education, and action. ...Designed from dishonesty and laziness, Dewey's destructive "educational" approach is the center piece of public education today.

Plato provided the tools for rationalizing an "intellectual" basis for *any* false or specious approach, including Dewey's approach. Platonistic philosophy can "justify" *any* irrational or unjust means to "noble" ends or "higher" causes. That same philosophy provides the tools for rationalizing the two primary character faults of conscious human beings — dishonesty and laziness.

Aristotle, on the other hand, provides the tools that every person needs to develop the knowledge necessary for guiding his or her life to unlimited prosperity, psychuous pleasures, and abiding happiness. Aristotelian philosophy provides the tools for meeting the needs of the human organism for optimum survival and maximum happiness. Successful use of those tools requires integrated honesty and rational efforts.

The following chart illustrates how a civilization might have advanced if an Aristotelian rather than a Platonistic philosophy had dominated for the past 2300 years. This chart shows how free-enterprise capitalism would have eliminated mysticism, parasitism, religion, collectivism, altruism, and

Barry C.   C-1017

Dear I & O Publishing,

    Neo-tech is the best thing to happen in my life. After reading the Neo-tech I-V it has really opened my eyes. I no longer feel the guilt that the mystics and Neo-cheats have thrust on me over the years. The bonds of slavery to these people have been broken.

    After reading Neo-tech and having time to reflect on all the principles in the volumes it is the only logical way people can live and survive by being prosperous and happy.

    I have read many self help books some of which were by some religious mystics who use faith and positive thinking as their principles which never worked for me and now I realize how they were draining me of values and made me feel guilty about being productive and selfish, but no longer.

    I am now looking forward to a long and prosperous life with the help of Neo-tech. I read from the Neo-tech volumes everyday and figure ways to use the advantages daily.

force-backed governments with the subsequent elimination of neocheating, wars, crime, disease, poverty, and death itself. Some of the estimates made in the chart include steam engines and trains in operation at the birth of Christ (who in a free-enterprise society might have matured into an energetic, happy, value-producing carpenter or contractor rather than a lazy, immature, destructive mystic), mass produced cars available in 50 A.D., commercial airlines in operation by 60 A.D., crime and fraud eliminated (not by government police but by individual self-defense and private protection services, private courts, and computerized ostracism) by 65 A.D., nuclear power by 70 A.D., man on the moon by 80 A.D., cancer cured by 90 A.D., biological immortality by 120 A.D., immortal conscious individuals master of all known nature by 2000 A.D.

AN ARISTOTELIAN COURSE OF HISTORY

Assume that an objective, Aristotelian-based philosophy rather than a mystical, Platonistic-based philosophy had dominated the Western World since the Golden Age of Greece:

500 B.C.	Heracleitus (540 B.C.-480 B.C.)
450 B.C.	Socrates (470 B.C.-399 B.C.)
400 B.C.	Plato (427 B.C.-348 B.C.).
350 B.C.	Aristotle (384 B.C.-322 B.C.).
200 B.C.	America discovered.
100 B.C.	Free-enterprise capitalism established around the world. Free markets flourishing. All forms of mysticism and neocheating identified, discredited, and rejected. All government taxation and nonprofit spending programs abolished. All forms of initiatory force are morally condemned. Wars become obsolete and vanish. Arts, sciences, technology explode in totally free markets. Competition rules. Romantic love flourishes.
0 B.C.	All traces of mysticism, altruism, and collectivism are gone. Poverty essentially eliminated. The individual is the supreme value. Out of necessity, Christ develops into a happy, literate, productive individual rather than a joyless, hallucinating, paranoid mystic. Trains and steamships are major forms of transportation.
20 A.D.	Electrical power developed, camera developed.
40 A.D.	Internal-combustion engine developed.
50 A.D.	Cars in mass production. Airplane developed.

Dominic P. C-107

Six weeks ago I received Neo-Tech I-V. You can probably imagine my shock and consternation on discovering that I have been a mystic these past 35 years. Not only been a mystic myself but also surrounded by them — together with a few neocheats too!

The last six weeks haven't been easy. Bloody hard in fact. Disentangling myself from family and "friends". I have absented myself from a number of odious "duties", and of course the flack has really come in my direction.

Avoiding other people's mysticism has been (relatively) straight forward, though. It's countering my own mysticism that's taking up most of my energies, it really goes deep.

Gary R.   C-1018

I am surrounded daily by people who are believers in the mystics, politicians, and religious leaders and would like to see the spread of the Neo-tech principles for my good, their good, and the good of all mankind.

I strongly believe in I & O's major goal of Biological Immortality. In order for this to happen we must be freed from the bonds of mystics, Neo-cheats, politicians and government force and coersion. I am starting with my own life, to live prosperously and happily and would like to help to spread the advantages of Neo-tech in whatever way I can.

60 A.D.	Commercial airlines flourishing. Computer developed.
65 A.D.	Crime and fraud become unprofitable, obsolete, and essentially eliminated by computerized ostracism.
70 A.D.	Nuclear power developed.
80 A.D.	Man on the moon.
90 A.D.	Cancer and most other diseases eliminated.
100 A.D.	Man on Mars and heading for other planets.
110 A.D.	Need for sleep eliminated.
120 A.D.	Human biological immortality developed.
140 A.D.	Human prosperity and happiness are universal.
200 A.D.	Worldwide, commercial, biological immortality achieved. All diseases eliminated. Man colonizing, mining, and commercializing the moon, asteroids, and Mars. Commercial shuttle flights (passenger and freight) to space-station colonies. ...Achieve access to the interstellar computer.
1200 A.D.	Energy technology advanced to where sufficient energy can be generated for traveling to other earth-like planets in outer space. Science, knowledge, and fulfillment advanced to the point at which no economic or scientific incentive exists for communicating with the billions of other, outer-space civilizations.
2000 A.D.	Immortal conscious beings in a Neo-Tech, free-enterprise society are master of all known nature. People and goods are transported at the speed of light via electronic transfer. Most goods manufactured via nano technology with the electronic control of atoms and molecules. New knowledge is expanding at near the speed of light.
Five Billion A.D.	Burnout death of our sun imminent. Colonization and migration (via electronic transfer) to inhabitable planets and man-made habitats in other solar systems underway. Human consciousness has conquered nature. New knowledge continues to expand at near the speed of light. Individual consciousnesses privately create and control entire universes for the well-being and happiness of everyone. (Reference: "We, the Creators of Heavens and Earths", F. R. Wallace, I & O, 1986.)

Ellen O.   C-57

My life is changing very much since following Neo-Tech concepts. I can now spot manipulators a mile off and feel that my children have also benifited from my changed attitudes.

David D.   J-32

I have been wrestling with the God concept for many years. Now that I have read the Neo-Tech information package, my wrestling match is over.

Tracy H.   R-3658

Neo-Tech claims to be much. It is all that it claims to be, and more. In style, Neo-Tech is accessible to the unsophisticated producer, but it also gives ample opportunity for rejection by those prone to find any excuse to ignore meaning. The Neo-Tech message cannot simply be read, it must be acheived. Read for content, apply what you learn, and a life of guilt-free happiness <u>will</u> be yours. I know; for such is mine.

Neo-Tech Advantage #78
HUMOR VS. SENSE OF LIFE: A TEST FOR HUMOR

Spontaneous humor is a highly individualized characteristic that reflects a person's sense of life. Humor can also identify a person's psychology and philosophy [Re: Table 46, Neo-Tech Reference Encyclopedia].

Humor is a product of lateral or horizontal thinking [Re: Concept 143, Neo-Tech Reference Encyclopedia]. Through horizontal thinking, a new and unexpected way to look at something is developed. That surprise contrast between the conventional, expected view and the new, unexpected view is the essence of humor. The nature of that newly created view reflects the sense of life of both those who create and those who respond to that particular humor.

The spontaneous response to humor is normally a quick, accurate indicator of that person's sense of life (e.g., benevolent or malevolent). Even when they try, few people can conceal or successfully fake their response to humor. Thus, identification of a person's sense of life through humor is often quite reliable. Understanding the nature of humor helps identify one's own sense of life as well as that of other people [Re: Table 46, Neo-Tech Reference Encyclopedia]. Also, a compatibility of humor is one of the most enjoyable aspects of a friendship or a romantic-love relationship.

Neo-Tech Advantage #79
TABOOS AND LAWS AGAINST VOLUNTARY SEX ACTS

Deep-rooted taboos subconsciously affect nonsexual as well as sexual relationships between people. For example, fear of incest taboos can inhibit or even prevent an affectionate, rewarding father-daughter relationship. Subconscious incest taboos and fears can also block or limit communication between parents and their children concerning sex education and open discussion of sexual matters. Taboos can likewise inhibit nonsexual friendships and prevent loving, familial affections from reaching their full potential.

Objective examination reveals that most negative views of taboos are themselves irrational or mystical. Even negative views of the strongest taboos such as bestiality and incest are sometimes unfounded. But violating or performing any taboo can also stem from an unhealthy, neurotic, psychotic, or a criminal base.

Forcible rape and adult-child sexual relations are not just taboos, but are criminal acts. For, they involve the violation of individual rights by force or coercion. A child lacks the experience, knowledge, as well as the emotional and physical independence to make valid free-choice, sexual-relation decisions. Such a child, can easily be forced or coerced into sexual acts by his or her natural dependency on the adult for survival. Indeed, adult incest with a child is equivalent to rape in violating that child's individual rights and well-being. Thus, when a child is involved, incest is a crime exceeded in seriousness only by injurious assault, rape, and murder. ...Carrying out any

Eric S. C-1027

Dear John,

Upon my arrival in Las Vegas I did not know what to expect from this organization known as Neo-Tech. I was very apprehensive about what I was about to undertake, must less commit too. I came to realize later on during the day that I was not alone in my thinking of this Neo-Tech stuff.

I purchased the original Neo-Tech manuscript some months ago and read a little about the neo-cheating of cardplayers. However I looked upon it as just another book on how to win in Las Vegas. I then received in the mail the invitation to the Neo-Tech Summit and I began to immediately bone up on the subject matter, as all procrastinators do. I found myself beginning to get interested in this stuff called Neo-Tech, I received a much needed attitude adjustment.

As I read further into this new concept I became aware that this is the lifestyle and alliance that I was looking for, if it could only be true. I approached the conference with the same positive attitude that I use in my employment as a consulting engineer in the nuclear industry.

I took my seat in the conference hall at the hotel and looked around me, on my right was a gentleman from Japan, and on my left was a gentleman from Finland. I thought to myself that maybe I was a little out of place, however as the day went on and I had a chance to talk with these gentlemen and others, I felt more at ease.

I met a few of the many people that attended the summit. I wished I had more time to spend with the attendees, but my schedule would not permit it.

Matt H. C-1028

As a recipient of the original Neo-Tech, and now Neo-Tech/Neothink, I just wanted to write to express my feelings regarding the latter. Coming from I & O, I expected an interesting production but nothing like the scope of the Grand Event. This clearly was a massive undertaking for a worthy cause. I naturally plan to take advantage of every opportunity now made clear in your program.

With Neo-Tech I saw the building blocks for social change and thought how nice it would be if it could be implemented. Now I see the grand panorama unfolding worldwide. I definitely want to be a part of it.

Thank you for any information you can provide.

taboo, sex act, or any action for that matter becomes criminal when (and only when) the action harms, diminishes, or endangers an individual's rights or life by force, fraud, or coercion.*

But mutually agreed-on violation of other taboos can be from a healthy or "good-for-me" base. For example, most of today's vanishing taboos such as premarital sex, oral sex, enactment of fantasies, and the satisfying of fetishes are often (but not always) performed from a healthy base [Re: Concepts 111 and 112, Neo-Tech Reference Encyclopedia]. Violating other taboos such as adultery can be injurious when involving deception or dishonesty. Also plural marriages are generally (but not always) too difficult or demanding to be healthy, even if honest. The taboos such as homosexuality and bestiality are generally violated from psychologically harmful, neurotic bases (but not always, as when performed by adolescents motivated by curiosity).

Committing incest usually evolves from a neurotic or a psychotic base, but again not always. Incest between consenting *adults*, for example, is theoretically possible from a healthy base. Despite government laws,** nothing in the nature of voluntary, *adult-adult* incest is inherently wrong or harmful in the act itself. But conception among close blood relatives can activate undesirable, genetically recessive traits. Thus, the special problem of bearing defective children must be considered by closely related couples. The decision to bear children, however, always remains the right of the couple. But if they choose to bear children, they must be willing and able to assume full responsibility to provide for and raise to independent adulthood any children they bear.

The inherent non-wrongness of adult-adult incest is most obvious in the case of adult orphans who unknown to each other are brother and sister and who by chance meet. They could quite naturally fall in love, have sex, marry, and have children without knowledge of their blood relationship. Incest in that case obviously can be from a healthy basis. Furthermore, even known incestuous relationships between consenting *adults* are not necessarily

---

*But the highly emotional, serious-crime nature of child-adult sex has given government neocheaters a bonanza of causes célèbres for increasing their usurpation of power. As a result, individual rights are further transgressed. From such government over reactions, many innocent people are unjustly harassed, accused, even jailed. Consider, for example, the rash of witch hunts against child day-care centers a few years ago during which nearly everyone charged or prosecuted was innocent. ...Those politically ambitious, neocheating prosecutors simply swaggered away with arrogant impunity from their ruin and waste. Without a qualm, they never gave a backward glance at the ruined businesses, broken lives, and psychologically damaged children they needlessly caused.

**About half the states prohibit marriage of first cousins. All states prohibit marriage of blood relationships closer than first cousins.

Micheal M.   C-100

I am writing to express my gratitude for the many useful concepts and ideas imparted in Neo-Tech.

I have lost 30 pounds, kicked the sugar and nicotine addictions and am still attempting to integrate most of the concepts into my life.

In darkness my eyes have been opened to a world of manipulating "Neo-Cheaters" and a world of willing victims who seek but never find the way to all truth. Great minds and many lives are wasted in the intellectual suicide of mysticism....

N.W.P.   C-116

What an uplift. All my previous thirty eight years of consciousness could be likened to seeing our world through a mist. Thank you Dr Wallace for rolling away the mist.

unhealthy or neurotic (although today they often are). Throughout recorded history, incestuous marriages, especially among the ruling classes, were accepted as normal and widely practiced in many cultures.

No sexual act between consenting adults can objectively be illegal, even if the acts are physically or psychologically harmful to the consenting individuals (such as chronic homosexuality and injurious masochism or sadism). Only acts of force, fraud, or coercion that violate the individual rights of nonconsenting people* can be objectively illegal. Such criminal acts include forcible rape, adult/child sexual relationships, nonconsenting sadism, and any other acts that are physically or fraudulently forced on unwilling or unknowing victims.

Some of the more irrational government laws that violate individual rights are those dealing with sex. They range from the government sanctioning murder (e.g., some states allow the husband to kill with impunity the lover of his wife) to restricting the way one makes love to a consenting partner (e.g., in some states, couples can go to jail for oral sex).

Neo-Tech Advantage #80
INITIATORY FORCE — THE PRIME EVIL

Force, coercion, threat of force, or fraud** *initiated* against any individual for any reason by any individual, groups of individuals, societies, or governments is morally wrong. That is the only categorical moral statement possible. That statement must, by its nature, be the categorical, irreducible, and fundamental standard for all conscious beings, always, everywhere. That statement is the moral axiom upon which every Neo-Tech/Psychuous Concept rests. The initiation of force and fraud among conscious beings is not only the basic moral wrong and evil, but is the primary tool used by all professional mystics and neocheaters to survive through value destruction.

No exceptions to the immorality of initiatory force exist. No matter how "noble" the ends, they *never* justify the means of initiating force, fraud, or coercion against any individual. Any government or activity that depends on or uses initiatory force, threat of force, or coercion is immoral and harmful. Therefore, *all* taxation backed by force, *all* conscription backed by force, and all laws that regulate or control by force or coercion are immoral.

---

*Nonconsenting people always include children. For they are unable to give valid or informed sexual consent because (1) they have gained neither the knowledge nor experience to assume the responsibilities for the physical and psychological consequences of sexual actions, and (2) they are dependent on adults for survival thus can be easily coerced or lured into consenting to harmful acts. An extremely harmful form of unjust, human manipulation is the parent-child incestuous relationship. Such a parent not only manipulates the child's lack of knowledge, but uses the child's survival dependence on the parent to criminally coerce that child into physically or psychologically destructive actions.

**Fraud is an indirect form of initiatory force that deceptively or dishonestly deprives a person of his life or property. All religions and governments operate and survive on fraud.

Mike A.   C-1019

Dear Sirs:

I first recieved my Neo-Tech package in the middle of December. I became immediately engrossed in the reading and finished in about 2 weeks.

Since then, my life has changed considerably. I have doubled my income, my grades have gone from about a 2.5 to a 4.0, my marriage has been rekindled and I have quit drugs completely. All of these changes took place in less than a month!

Before Neo-Tech, I was lazy and irresponsible. I was a classic neocheat, trying every type of mystical means to gain an edge because I lacked the energy and integrity needed to do things the right way.

Now, things are different. I get up early every morning, excersise, eat a full breakfast and attack my day with energy + vitality. I accomplish more in one day than I used to in a week, and I still have more free time to enjoy with my wife than I

The *only* laws that are objectively just and moral are those that protect the life and property rights of individuals from initiatory force and fraud. All other laws that regulate people's lives or property are morally wrong, contrary to human nature, and harmful to everyone. Such immoral laws include those that restrict or prohibit drugs, alcohol, prostitution, abortion (of the fetus at any age), or any form of censorship or restriction of voluntary sexual activity. All such laws are morally wrong because they use threats or force against individuals.

While all governments have the power, none ever have the moral right to initiate force or coercion against any individual. The only beneficial and moral laws are those designed to protect the life and property rights of individuals from initiatory force, the threat of force, and fraud. In turn, the only moral use of force is for self-defense: That is for protection of oneself, property, or country from force *initiated* by other individuals or governments. ...Self-defense by any means, including force, is not only a basic moral right, but a moral duty.

No government has ever helped an individual produce more values or greater happiness than that individual could have produced without government. Governments differ only in the degree they harm people. In fact, except for protecting individual rights, no valid reason for government exists. Indeed, the entire concept of government is invalid, mystical, neurotic, sick. Government is nothing more than a mystical, big-lie hoax perpetuated by neocheaters through non sequiturs and the manipulation of mysticism.

Government is *not* the equivalent of one's country. Governments are based on invalid mystical notions that have no basis in reality; countries are objectively real entities of defined territories. A person can love his or her country, but properly despise the government that constantly harms and drains everyone within its realm of usurped power.

Neo-Tech Advantage #81
OPPRESSION AND FREEDOM — PAST AND FUTURE

The following chart demonstrates the trend of human oppression over the past 3300 years. That oppression is directly related to the extent that governments and religion exert force and fraud against individuals. The most oppressive, unhappy period of history was the Dark Ages when religious power controlled the political system and could with impunity use unlimited force against individuals. By contrast, human happiness and well-being increased markedly during those periods when honesty and business reduced government and religious power. Also, as shown in the following chart, the government and church always oppressed women more than men. Indeed, governments and churches have always been controlled by neocheaters who manipulate the mystical concept of altruistic sacrifice to gain power. And, historically, those male neocheaters have always found physically weaker, more mystically dependent women their first and easiest target to bully into submission.

In exercising their unearned power, male mystics and neocheaters gained added leverage by encouraging all men to bully physically weaker women. And they especially bilked "silly" women into following mystical stupidities

Dennis J.   R-7050

Seldom during ones lifetime does a revelation of this sort come about. In fact you might as well say several lifetimes. Truly a great work worthy of much praise. Its amazeing how the neo-cheaters have controled us for over 3000 years. They say every "dog has its day", well they have had theirs now its our turn. I think it goes without saying that we should be able to do more in 50 years than they did in 3000.

Roy W.   C-122

Dear I&O, and Dr. Wallace
 I lost my business and my life's savings to neocheaters — was about ready to throw in the towel. After reading Neo-Tech I'm starting over at age 62. — With Neo-Tech knowledge I'm going to make it and enjoy life.

such as astrology and religion. But with the rise of nonmystical, free-market economies, women have become increasingly productive, more independent, less mystical, thus less oppressed. And recently, for the first time in history, freedom for men and women has become nearly equal. But with today's reviving interest in the stupidities of mysticism and religion, more women are choosing to slip back into mystical lives controlled by others.

FREEDOM/OPPRESSION LEVEL
+6=Maximum Freedom to -6=Maximum Oppression

Period	Men	Women
Ancient Greece 1300 B.C. — 450 B.C.	0	-1
Enlightened Greece 450 B.C. — 27 B.C.	0	-3
Roman Empire 27 B.C. — 385 A.D.	+1	-1
Christianity Established 200 A.D. — 385 A.D.	-2	-4
Rise of Christian Power (the unhappiest period in history) 385 A.D. — 1000 A.D.	-5	-6
Romantic Love Challenges Christianity 1000 — 1300	-2	-4
Renaissance Weakens Christianity 1300 — 1500	0	-1
Church Fights Back with Witch Trials and Inquisitions 1300 — 1500	-4	-6
The Puritans 1500 — 1700	+1	0
Age of Reason 1700 — 1800	+1	-1
Early Victorianism 1800 — 1850	+1	-4
Rise of Capitalism 1850 — 1900	+2	0
Rise of Romantic Love 1900 — 1960	+3	+1
Sexual Liberation 1960 — 1980	+3	+2.5
Rise of Mystical Stupidities: Evangelism via television and astrology via President Aquarius. 1980 — Present	+2.5	+1.5

Nathen W. R-7058

I'm a financial planner - 57 years old. A dramatic change has taken place during this past year. Growth in areas of: Economics (income), spiritual, physically and mentally have helped me to grow romantically!!

My income has gone from $50,000-yr to over $200,000-yr and growing. My life is "prospering" gracefully in all areas mentioned above.

I see no conceivable limits and I intend to put together relationships and businesses (plural) that will continue to grow excellently. The next 20 years will be the most productive years of my life. Romantically, I share love as never before. Can't wait to continue my studying.

Danial   C-1020

Dear John,

I have been studying NEO-TECH for the past year. NEO-TECH came to me as a gift from my mother to help me understand gambling, but as I have read through the entire NEO-TECH DISCOVERY Manuscript (now on my third time) I found a more profound application for the material. The manuscript provided me with real life answers, based upon truth and reality to questions I have had for years.

One struggle was with the God concept. Since my youth I have been involved with Catholicism, Lutheranism, Born again Christianity, and various other religions and have found no solid foundation for my beliefs. After the initial charismatic adrenalin rush and the feeling of acceptance passed, I was again searching.

NEO-TECH has offered me concepts that feel right to me. NEO-TECH has given me the opportunity to un-program myself so I can lead a happy and prosperous life. This un-programming is an ongoing and sometimes difficult process, since most of my life has been spent among mystical and unproductive individuals.

Note: The long-term, general trend throughout history has been away from mysticism, poverty, stupidity, oppression, misery...and toward honesty, prosperity, intelligence, freedom, happiness.

Today, the various political-religious hucksters, neocheating academia, mystical feminists, and many journalists and political cartoonists are climbing over each other to attack and undermine individual rights, business, and value producers around the world [Re: Table 51, Neo-Tech Reference Encyclopedia]. Since business and its value producers strengthen individual rights, the attacks on business and producers are actually attacks on individual rights. Such attacks are designed to control the value producers for exploitation by neocheaters.

The worldwide trend of increasingly accepting mysticism and violence can culminate in either a government sponsored nuclear holocaust or a worldwide, terror-controlled government. Either course would end our current civilization. With a continued rise of worldwide mysticism, either (1) a nuclear holocaust would occur, or (2) a Leninist-style or Khomeini-style government would enslave or slaughter the best of individuals — the most valiant, independent, productive individuals. That enslavement and slaughter of the good, the happy, the best among us would drag humanity back into the Dark Ages...perhaps for centuries.

In a world of escalating mysticism and neocheating, what will stop this destructive trend? Neo-Tech followed by Neothink® will not only stop but will reverse the trend effectively, decisively. Indeed, Neo-Tech has already begun to check the trend. Nothing can stop the current, worldwide Neo-Tech wave from breaking across all continents to wipe out mysticism and its gaggles of neocheaters.

The alternative to all gloomy scenarios caused by mystics and neocheaters is Neo-Tech-driven competition — a competitive revolution led by honest, productive working people. That competition will render all professional mystics and neocheaters impotent, uncompetitive, unable to manipulate the producers, unable to survive. Neo-Tech-led competition will bring a forever prospering, happy business world [Re: Table 51, Neo-Tech Reference Encyclopedia].

In a Neo-Tech political, social, and business environment, an unstoppable surge in human happiness, well-being, productivity, and romantic love will occur. Against Neo-Tech, all professional mystics and neocheaters will appear as silly clowns and impotent wimps. They will be left unable to oppress, hurt, kill, or sponsor their plundering aggressions and wars. In addition, the completely free business and competitive technological atmosphere of Neo-Tech would create an economic boom with such an exhilarating climate for creativity, achievement, and the arts that the worldwide standard of living and happiness would soar. Poverty and famine would vanish. Most diseases including cancer and AIDS would quickly be eliminated. ...Human biological immortality would soon become commercially available, probably within a decade [Re: Concept 145, Neo-Tech Reference Encyclopedia].

Dear Dr Wallace

Leslie C. C-96

The Neo-Tech Discovery really does seem to work, & coming from me that is saying something, me who has read so many books on positive thinking, psychology, philosophy & related subjects.

I have been meaning to write a letter to you for some time but I decided to wait until receiving "RAPID POWER & WEALTH" because some of the things I have to say I am not exactly proud of & I cannot be sure of your response.

There is good news & bad news that I have for you & even though we live thousands of miles apart & may never meet, I hope you will want to try & understand somethings about me, & I hope also you will want to give me a chance to explain a little about myself & of how the Neo-Tech discovery has helped me to change in ways I used to only dream of.

The bad news is that I have discovered that I have been cheating myself. My family, my friends, people who I work with, I have been cheating them & not even realizing it. I have been living the life of a mystic & hating almost every moment of it. I used to search for perfection without thinking of or considering other people as separate individuals, as though individual life did not exist, only life in general; & yet I was more concerned for the general people than even for myself so my own identity was like swallowed up & lost all meaning.

More bad news is that I have not studied the Neo-Tech Discovery as much as I should have. I have only concentrated on a very small percentage of the concepts; not quite sure of what I was reading, not quite convinced, not quite able to fully accept what the Neo-Tech Discovery was teaching me.

continued next page

Neo-Tech Advantage #82
A CONSTITUTION FOR PROSPERITY, PSYCHUOUS PLEASURES, AND ROMANTIC LOVE

At no time in history have the ideas, influences, doctrines, platforms, or actions of any political or religious system ever yielded a *net* benefit to productive human beings. No such system has ever increased the long-range prosperity, well-being, and happiness of anyone.* Indeed, individuals and civilizations thrive to the extent that religious and government power is diminished. The anti-force platform of the Capitalist Party of the United States first appeared nearly two decades ago in BARRONS financial weekly. [Re: Table 52, of Neo-Tech Reference Encyclopedia]. That platform represents the only political structure that functions without force, fraud, or coercion and, thus, is compatible with the biological needs and well-being of all human beings. All other political systems depend on force, fraud, or coercion. Thus, all such systems have always harmed everyone throughout the ages.

Only the unique, anti-force nature of business allows people to fully use their minds and exercise their individual rights to live prosperously and happily. The question of having no government in a Neo-Tech business society versus having a limited government in areas of national defense, the courts, and police protection is meaningless so long as the moral principle of no initiatory force or fraud is observed. Within a Neo-Tech business society, a company called "government" or competing companies would deliver a needed, integrated package of services only to those who voluntarily paid for such services. Without power to initiate force or the threat of force required to collect taxes, governments would function only to the extent their citizens or clients found their services valuable enough to voluntarily purchase.

If the citizens were unwilling to purchase certain government services, those services would simply go out of business or be replaced by more efficient services that enough people thought valuable enough to buy. In a Neo-Tech society, government would by necessity be a competitive, profit-oriented service and protection business. In some areas, possibly several competing businesses, organizations, or companies might offer the same services in competing for citizens as customers.

---

*But different political systems can vary greatly in their *relative* destructiveness. Western-world democracies, for example, are much less oppressive and destructive than are the terror-totalitarian systems of Russia, Red China, Nazi Germany, Cuba. Left-wing or right-wing, all totalitarian governments use the same institutions of power, force, and terror. That is why when a right-wing dictatorship falls, a left-wing dictatorship can so quickly seize and use the instruments of force already in place. Without much effort, the new government can continue usurping power and values as did the previous government, but with ever greater force and terror.

The good news is that I have got very positive results, better even than I had dreamt of. It is eight months now since I received the "Neo-Tech I-V Information Package" & at the time I was looking for something magical, some instant solution to my problems, what I did not realise though is that things do actually take time to happen & to develop, & that it is sometimes necessary to be patient while waiting for the better opportunities to present themselves before making a move.

The best thing that has ever happened to me has happened in these past 8 months. I have found a girl-friend someone who seems to have most of the things that I lack, the very person I have been searching for. Our relationship is still young but it seems really promising & I have never met a person quite like this girl who has such extraordinary insight into my personality yet she is more than 6 years younger than me. We are like almost total opposites in so many things, (we do both share a love for water though), I'm sure I have never loved anyone so much!

There are more good things I could speak of but at the moment they seem to pale against what I have just said so I would like to reserve further comments for future letters.

Thanks for this magnificent work it might well be the best I have ever read, it is certainly one of the most practical & it stands the test of time.

The Neo-Tech Discovery is helping me more & more even though I am probably only making use of a dozen or so concepts. I am beginning to understand how to make use of the concepts in my everyday life gradually integrating some of the other concepts & recognizing situations for what they are & thus often being in a position to make subtle gains over the unaware Neo-cheaters!

By the way my wages have increased by an average £35 a week since receiving the Information Package so that's good too!

Voluntarily supported governments and voluntarily supported businesses would really be equivalent entities subject to the same free-market dynamics based on values. A nonforce government could be called Government, Government Company, or any other name. Likewise, that entity would be subject to the same economic disciplines of profits, losses, growth, competition, and bankruptcy as any competing business. In other words, in a Neo-Tech society, governments would have the same nature and disciplines as any free-enterprise business. And they would be subject to the same competitive influences and disciplines to improve quality and value.

The transition from a force-dependent government to a nonforce government could cause some temporary dislocations, such as cutting welfare, stopping transfer-payment "services", and selling government property to pay off and close out Social Security claims. But those problems would be minor and transitory compared to the flood of permanent, major benefits that would immediately assert themselves. For example, a nonforce government would mean no taxes, no controls or regulations, no government corruption, no neocheaters, no wars, and a spectacularly prosperous, happy society.

Neo-Tech Advantage #83
DISMISSING 3000 YEARS OF MYSTICISM
for a lifetime of
PERSONAL POWER, PROSPERITY, AND HAPPINESS

The purpose of each individual human life is to prosper and live happily. Anyone can achieve that prosperity and happiness when free of force, fraud, or coercion by others.

The Individual-Rights Amendment to the United States Constitution as featured several years ago on page one of the *National Review* forbids initiatory force, threat of force, or fraud by any individual, group of individuals, or government. No other law or rule is needed for a moral, rational society.

Forbidding initiatory force and coercion is the only political law compatible with the prosperity and happiness of human beings. Thus, the Individual-Rights Amendment evolves directly into a Neo-Tech constitution that leaves everyone with the conditions for prosperity and happiness. No other constitution or laws are valid or needed.

The Neo-Tech Constitution stated below obsoletes the constitutions of all nations:

THE NEO-TECH CONSTITUTION
Preamble

The purpose of human life is to prosper and live happily. The function of society is to protect those conditions that let all individuals achieve prosperity and happiness. Those conditions can be delivered by a constitution that prohibits the use of initiatory force or coercion by any person, group, or government against any individual:

Robert H. R-5027

Neo-tech was just the motivation + guiding light I needed! I shook all old ideas and what a difference!

Within 6 mos. I quit my job and started another immediatly at a 40% increase in salary as second-in-command. I also ventured into the stock market with five picks — all five are up at least 20% — one is up 55%!

I am presently setting groundwork for a comedy club which has no competition for 30 sq. miles.

I have control over my life now and find it mind-boggling how easy it is to win big in all phases of life.

The ability to "see-through" people has given me an unmeasurable advantage in negotiations.

Robert G. R-7057

After careful review of Neo-Tech principles, I believe these principles will prepare the informed for comfortable survival into the twenty-first century.

The Constitution

Article 1: No person, group of persons, or government may initiate force, threat of force, or fraud against any individual's self or property.

Article 2: Force may be morally and legally used only in defense against those who violate Article 1.

Article 3: No exception shall ever exist to Articles 1 & 2.

The Neo-Tech Constitution rests on six axioms:
1. Values exist only relative to life.
2. Whatever benefits a living organism is a value to that organism. Whatever harms a living organism is a disvalue to that organism.
3. The basic value against which all values are measured is the conscious individual.
4. Morals relate only to conscious individuals.
5. Immoral actions arise from individuals purposely harming others through force, fraud, deception, coercion or from attacking and destroying values.
6. Moral actions arise from individuals purposely benefiting others by profitably producing values for them.

How would the Neo-Tech Constitution be enforced? Through (1) self-defense force and (2) organized ostracism, which is much more effective than any form of force.

Background for The Neo-Tech Constitution

The purpose of human life is to prosper happily. By integrating the human mind with reality, people can prosper happily by making themselves increasingly valuable to others. But what keeps most people from doing that — from fulfilling their own nature? What has kept most people throughout history from experiencing the prosperity and happiness that they are fully qualified to experience?...The answer lies in three words: **Force, Mysticism, Neocheating**:

Force

Force is the instrument used to expropriate values earned by others: Directly or indirectly, all initiated force supports laziness and incompetence at the expense of productivity and ability. Criminals, mystics, neocheaters, governments, and religions use force, threat of force, or fraud to drain life, values, and happiness from the producers and society. But those who live by force or fraud live in discord with reality. They offer nothing to others except diminished happiness and lost values.

Professional mystics and neocheaters depend on force or deception to survive. But, the producer of values never needs to initiate force or use deception to prosper.

John M. C-301

My second reading is with deeper thought and open-mindedness. The first reading triggered many shocking thoughts some which had the initial impact of provoking anger at seeing many of my beliefs being attacked and logically destroyed before my eyes.

Throughout life I have been a producer but deeply religious (mystical). The Neo-Tech works are moving me toward a 180° change. A very difficult change to implement into my life at age 45. But paradoxically I feel a sense of relief and ease taking place psychologically. I know it will take some time to totally assimilate Neo-Tech logic into my day to day and long range thinking.

Martin L R-4069, AUSTRALIA

I have been looking for something like NEO-TECH since I was about 14. I found out religion has nothing to offer but guilt and government is a parasite. Without NEO-TECH life didn't seem much until I read it, it showed me life can be a lot more fulfilling and rewarding without parasites, religious time wasters etc, hindering me. Before NEO-TECH religion use to scare shit out of me but now I laugh. Thanks Dr WALLACE, you are a neat MATE.

Once productive individuals identify the nature of initiatory force, they will reject its use as criminal and harmful under *any* conditions. From that point on, the value producers can guiltlessly collect their earned prosperity and happiness. And all who have lived by force and coercion will find they can no longer live by usurping values. Instead, they too will have to produce marketable values for others.

Mysticism

Mysticism is defined as: 1. Any attempt to use the mind as a "reality" creating device rather than a reality integrating organism. 2. Any attempt to recreate or alter reality through dishonesty, feelings, non sequiturs, or rationalizations. 3. Any attempt to ignore, evade, contradict, or fake reality. 4. The creation of problems where none exist.

Mysticism is the tool used by neocheaters to manipulate or hide the force, fraud, or coercion used to usurp values from others. Mysticism is used to create illusionary standards, project undeserved guilt, and beguile individuals into surrendering their earned power, values, and happiness.

Neocheating

Neocheating is defined as: Any intentional use of mysticism to create false realities and illusions in order to extract values or power from others.

Neocheating is the technique for usurping values, money, power by using mysticism to manipulate others.

Neocheating is the essential technique politicians and clergymen use to gain power, money, and pseudo self-esteem from others.

The Nature of Mysticism Used by Neocheaters

Mysticism is an evasion of reality that is never supported by honesty or objective reality. Mysticism harms human beings in four ways:

1. Cripples the mental processes required to accurately understand reality. That understanding is necessary to make decisions competently and to solve problems effectively.

2. Diminishes everyone inflicted with mysticism, the stupidity disease, by draining one's intelligence, efficacy, and ability to live competitively.

3. Blocks the long-range thinking integrations needed to prosper continuously, love romantically, and live happily.

4. Subjects individuals increasingly to the control of professional mystics and neocheaters.

Mysticism is arbitrary, has no link to reality, and is based on nothing. Thus, it is nothing. Yet, by manipulating rationalizations, non sequiturs, aphorisms, parables, superstitions, modern art, poetry, songs, rock music,

David C. R-4030, CANADA

Shortly after starting to read the Neo-Tech books I started to take better control of my life in a much more dominant fashion. Instead of accepting the Neo-cheaters way of controling my life I turned the tables and realized who they are and what they represent., and now I use their own idiosyncrasies against them. I recommend this book and other works of this nature to anyone who wishes to get a better focus on what life can be like when you wish to be in control of your time and life management.

Keep up the good work Neo-Tech.

D. B. C-210

Dear Sir,

Your work is an outstanding achievement in logical scrutiny and is to be highly commended. I have just completed reading I-V. Probably the most important thing I've read since (and here it comes again) the works of Ayn Rand.

Thomas W. C-52

Having been raised a Roman Catholic I never had even thought of questioning my religion. As a matter of fact, I never talked about it with other people, I just took it for granted that that was the way it was. My background in computer science has trained me to think rationally and logically but I never thought to apply it to my own life.

chants, slogans, newspeak, quotes, or facts out of context, a mystic or neocheater can create illusions to seemingly justify almost any harmful action. Such "justifications" are essential for the pillaging of producers when no justification is possible.

Mysticism and neocheating have been used for 2000 years to create illusions that "external authorities" protect the lives of individuals, can solve problems for others, and can provide livings for non-producers. But, in reality, all such "authorities" are merely neocheaters using deception, force, or coercion to extract their livings from the value producers. Indeed, those neocheaters are the fountainhead of human-imposed suffering.

Mysticism and neocheating are the main causes of pain and failure among human beings. Mysticism and neocheating are anti-life...death-oriented. The core of all mystics and neocheaters is dishonesty and laziness. Their entire task is to beguile value producers into supporting them.

The Morality of Mystics and Neocheaters

Morality is defined as: Conscious actions that purposely benefit people and society are moral. Conscious actions that purposely harm people and society are immoral. Thus, value destroyers such as mystics, neocheaters, and their agents of force, coercion, and deception are immoral. For, they purposely harm others and society by choosing to usurp values from others rather than produce values for others. By contrast, value producers are moral. For, they purposely benefit others and society by choosing to produce more values for others than they consume.

Mystics violate morality: They purposely harm both their own and every other person's life. They are destructive, silly, immature, childish. By choosing to evade reality, they undermine their ability to identify reality, to think clearly, to produce values, to live happily, to compete honestly — to survive. As a result, they increasingly transfer responsibilities for their failures onto others. They routinely lay blame or guilt on others for their own problems.*

Neocheaters violate morality: They purposely expand their harm by orchestrating mystical illusions to plunder society. Moreover, they design their illusions to make themselves appear as innocent benefactors and their victims appear as the guilty malefactors. But the opposite is true: The neocheaters are the guilty malefactors; their victims are usually the innocent producers. Yet, as long as most people allow themselves to accept those

---

* Everyone must fight mysticism both from within and from without. Those who quit fighting let mysticism take over their lives. Those who surrender or stop struggling against mysticism become a part of the unhappy, dishonest, quasi-dead world of mystics and neocheaters. That world feeds entirely on the destruction of values.

Randy L.   R-4942

Upon reading Neo-Tech one must surely realize that many of the 144 advanced concepts hit directly home. Towards ones Biological envolvement as honestly as it can get. Then by continuing to read all the reference material. Slowly but surely your strength will begin to build. One begins to pursue and see things quite differently. Short and long range goals will develop for each person who reads and rereads Neo-tech material. I for one, will continue to reread all I can on a regular basis as to firmly plant the advanced concepts. I also firmly support Frank Wallace John Flint and all the other fine workers at I&O Publishing I in there pursuit of man's only ultimate goal. I wish to ~~encourage all new and potential readers~~ of Neo-tech to keep an open mind. Take your time and devulge these wonderous concepts. Then begin your new journey to Life itself!

Sincerly KIBI member

mystical inversions of honesty, the neocheaters will keep pillaging them and society. As a result, such neocheaters always harm society by draining prosperity and happiness from everyone.

Agents of Force violate morality: They purposely harm others by expropriating values through force or threat of force. Moreover, by choosing to expropriate rather than earn values, agents of force destroy their own lives by demolishing their competence, self-esteem, and happiness.

* * *

Nonmystics are moral: They accept the responsibility to think and act for themselves in order to produce objective values for others. With a loyalty to honesty, they act in accord with objective reality. They are mature, evolved people who strive to integrate their words and actions with honesty and reality, regardless of anyone's opinions, dictates, wishes, or emotions. As a result, nonmystics always benefit others and society.

Rejecting Losers

Mystics, neocheaters, and agents of force are losers. They are immature, unevolved people with self-arrested character development. They function through dishonesty and deception. For those reasons, they must depend on the producer for survival. But, they resent and envy the producer in knowing that they cannot experience his or her competence and happiness, no matter how much they extract from others. Mystics and neocheaters live unhappy, shrinking lives. Living through huckstered faith enforced by deception or force, they steadily lose respect for honesty, happiness, and the purpose to live. They increasingly move toward death. And they want everyone else to die with them. ...Thus, anyone can benefit by immediately rejecting losers such as mystics, neocheaters, and agents of force.

Free Choice

All people must continually choose between dishonesty or honesty, between laziness or effort, between accepting or rejecting mysticism from both within and without. Accepting mysticism means evading honesty and denying reality in favor of feelings, wishes, or external "authorities". And those consistently choosing mysticism become dependent on others or "authorities" to think for them, to lead them, to neocheat for them. But rejecting mysticism upholds honesty, builds competence, and enhances life for everyone.

Four Facts

1. No one can give another person self-worth or happiness. Yet anyone can achieve those two prime values by (a) producing more values for others than consumed by oneself; and (b) rejecting all mystics, neocheaters, and their schemes to usurp values from others.
2. Loyalty to honesty and rationality must replace mysticism in order to harness one's natural power. By remaining loyal to honesty and rationality,

Keith T.   R 344

Dear Dr. Wallace:

The information provided in Neo-Tech II-V has clarified for me the seeming contradiction of steadily increasing numbers of people professing love and concern for society, coinciding with the accelerating decrease in our productivity and quality of life. I, like many others, have had a vague sense of wrongness about the way our country is headed, without a clear understanding of the "cause and effect" involved.

Thank you for the values I have received from your work. I salute your efforts to make this information available to those who can still reason for themselves despite the best efforts of the Neo-cheaters.

a person can (a) disarm mysticism, (b) render neocheaters impotent, and (c) create the conditions that allow personal prosperity and happiness to flourish.

3. People who resist mysticism from within and reject neocheating from without will rapidly gain prosperity and happiness. But all others who remain foundering in the seas of mysticism and neocheating will become uncompetitive.

4. If everyone were a mystic, human life would end. If everyone were a value destroyer, an agent of force, a neocheater, human life would end. But if everyone were an honest value producer, human life and happiness would flourish beyond all imagination.

The Intertwining Dependency of Force and Mysticism

Mysticism destroys from within; force destroys from without. Yet, both mysticism and force are unnatural and disposable. Neither are rooted in reality or have any inherent power. Still, all unearned power and expropriated values depend on mystical illusions backed by force, fraud, or coercion. Nonproducers, mystics, and neocheaters need those illusions to beguile, flimflam, or force values from others. But once that intertwining dependency of mysticism and force is unraveled, the rationalizations crumble and illusions vanish. ...Without their illusions, mystics and neocheaters are powerless.

When producers of values understand that intertwining dependency of force and mysticism, they will stop supporting every mystic and neocheater who lives off the efforts of others. Those mystics and neocheaters will then be powerless. Their only means of survival will be to produce rather than usurp values. Once they become producers, their self-esteems and competencies will rise. And then, they too can evolve into self-responsible human beings who *earn* their prosperity and happiness.

Abolishing Initiatory Force by Ending Mysticism

The Neo-Tech Constitution forbids initiatory force or fraud with no exceptions. Without force or fraud, mysticism and thus neocheaters become impotent. Without mysticism, force becomes ineffective for extracting values from others. The axioms of the Neo-Tech Constitution are real and cannot be contradicted. They are based on human nature. By contrast, all mystical illusions are capricious and contradictory. They are based on nothing. And that nothingness is why force, fraud, or coercion are required to make others accept the dishonest illusions of mystics and neocheaters. Thus, by forbidding force, fraud, and coercion, the Neo-Tech Constitution vanquishes all mystics and neocheaters.

Policies for Ending Mysticism and Neocheating

Most people unknowingly let mysticism have disastrous effects on their lives and society. As throughout history, people unnecessarily accept the

Alberto G.   R-2097, SOUTH AFRICA

Neo-Tech is certainly helping me realize what life is all about, and what life is meant to be about, I am talking about objective values, happines, and the way in which to live ones life fully.
I have awoken to the fact that we do not need people to run our life

Richard Mc.   R-2028

THANK YOU DR. WALLACE.
THANK YOU I+O PUBLISHING CO.
MY LIFE IS MINE NOW THANKS TO NEO-TECH. I AM LOOKING FORWARD TO ALL THAT LAYS AHEAD.

Elijah C.   R-2133, CANADA

The price you ask is small indeed for delivering so great a value. Thank you so very much for the most comprehensive and valuable information I have ever received.

dishonesties of mysticism in allowing neocheaters to pillage them materially and spiritually. But, once the mystical illusions are identified and the neocheating hoaxes are rejected, all mystics and neocheaters will be powerless because they have no reality-based, earned power. Rejecting mysticism and its dishonesty means rejecting neocheaters and their agents of force. That rejection requires a policy of never knowingly giving values to or doing business with those who live by force, fraud, coercion, or deception. Such people include:

1. Politicians.
2. Clergymen.
3. Agents of force who extort values from individuals, businesses, and society.
4. Bureaucrats and "authorities" who impede the value producer.
5. Academe, journalists, cartoonists, and media people who distort facts and undermine objective values to sustain pseudo self-esteems and invalid careers.
6. Quisling business executives and professionals who neocheat and destroy within their own businesses and professions.
7. All other mystics and neocheaters who expropriate values while diminishing the prosperity and happiness of others.

With wide-spread rejection of mysticism and neocheaters, violations of individual rights become unacceptable, pillaging becomes impractical, and waging war becomes impossible. ...All people will then be free to live prosperously and happily forever.

Implementing the Neo-Tech Constitution

Individuals can implement the Neo-Tech Constitution by never voting, except to cast write-in ballots for and only for "The Neo-Tech Constitution" in every election, everywhere on earth. The Neo-Tech Constitution fully meets the responsibility of any government to its citizens. The sole purpose of The Neo-Tech Constitution is to protect individual rights through the abolition of *all* initiatory force.

The Neo-Tech Constitution not only provides impenetrable armor for individual rights, but embodies the principles of prosperous living. People one by one will recognize the consummate advantages of The Neo-Tech Constitution. Then, with increasing momentum, those people will reject mysticism and neocheating in order to avoid being left behind, unable to compete for power, prosperity, and romantic love among the rising army of Neo-Tech value producers.

Neo-Tech Advantage #84
PROTECTING CHILDREN
from
MYSTICS AND NEOCHEATERS

What if people existed who purchased healthy, well-formed children and professionally mutilated their young bodies to create monsters splendid for laughing at? What if their formula were:

Girard C. R-1730

Thank you.
It is something to be reread at different
times in one's continued life. I look forward
to many years now of productive life in the
guiltless spirit which has been awakened.
Success in your endeavors at the Institute

Anthony M. R-513

Very enlightening work! It has clarified many mysteries and confirmed some of my darkest suspicions about the ways of the world.

Culbreath W. C-84

I am understanding more about the Neo-Tech concepts all the time and have
advantageously used them in several instances to thwart and prevent cheaters
from harming and taking advantage of me.

LONG LIVE NEO-TECH!

> "Take a child two or three years old, put him in a porcelain vase, more or less grotesque, which is made without top or bottom, to allow egress for the head and feet. During the day the vase is set upright, and at night is laid down to allow the child to sleep. The child thickens without growing taller, filling up with his compressed flesh and distorted bones the reliefs in the vase. This development in a bottle continues many years. After a certain time it becomes irreparable. When they consider that this is accomplished, and the monster made, they brake the vase. The child comes out — and, behold, there is a man in the shape of a mug!
>
> "This is convenient; by ordering your dwarf betimes you are able to have it of any shape you wish."
>
> Victor Hugo
> *The Man Who Laughs*

Impossible? No one could be that evil? ...During the 17th century, organized bands of Gypsies called comprachicos (from comprapequeños, the Spanish word for child buyers) developed the profession of creating human monsters from children for the jaded amusement of master neocheaters and professional mystics of Europe — the royalty of government and church.

Did that period represent the height of evil toward children? Not at all. Today, comprachicos exist en mass around the world. And they are committing even greater crimes in creating less startling but more seriously mutilated children than their 17th century counterparts. Yet, their mutilations are more easily ignored or even accepted by the public:

Who are the modern-day comprachicos? And what forms are their mutilations? One group specializes in deforming the outer body while permanently damaging the internal organs. They produce adults incapable of experiencing happy, healthy, romantic lives. Those modern-day comprachicos habituate, for example, ice-cream parlors. In great numbers, those comprachicos gorge children with macro doses of the most widely destructive of all addictive drugs — sugar. An addictive sedative, sugar exhibits profound, long-range toxicity toward the human body and its organs. Sugar gradually and irreversibly damages the metabolic system and internal organs while bloating the body into unwholesome, grotesque shapes.

Those who are producing unhappy, sugar-addicted children by permanently mutilating their bodies while damaging their organs are committing crimes much more destructive than most child-molestation and child-abuse crimes. Moreover, those modern-day comprachicos are more culpable than their 17th century counterparts. The original comprachicos kept their children relatively healthy to achieve better market prices. They did not damage the children's metabolism or internal organs. Also, those 17th century comprachicos mutilated other people's children for money. But, the modern-day comprachicos mutilate their own children for nothing more

J.P.   C-1021

Dear Mr Flint,

For the past thow years, I have spent a small fortune on books which are <u>supposed</u> to give me power in money, Love, happines and many other benefits. All total tripe.

However when I heard about the neo tech discovery I felt very curious as it somehow appealed to me more than anything else at that time. When I recieved the neo tech information, I dived into the first few pages, and then carried on for the next couple of hours. I wasn't shocked but ashamed of myself. Mysticism was everything I used to be. I could not believe how accurate the truth was about myself.

I mainly bought the information for finacial gain, but that subject just didn't appeal to me as much as the neocheating and mysticism.

than rationalizing their own overweight or self-esteem problems in defaulting to destructive mysticism*.

Can anything worse be done to children? Yes, something worse is being done everyday to millions of children: By nature, a child's mind is honest, innocent, and struggling to understand reality. What happens during the most vulnerable, formative period in developing a child's thinking, competence, knowledge, honesty, integrity? Most parents and other adults traumatize and cripple that child's tender mind with heavy doses of mystical dishonesties. They do that by force-feeding the innocent child constant doses of blatantly dishonest religious or altruistic myths about spirits, God, Santa Claus. Such dishonesties are the antithesis of knowledge, truth, and justice. And such repetitive blows to the child's newly developing mind and character can inflict deep, permanent damage. Those dishonesties often induce the first unnatural steps toward becoming an unhappy mystic or a destructive neocheater. ...Nothing healthy is reflected in the innocent, truth-seeking child being intellectually devastated by such irrational dishonesties as religious myths and Santa Claus.

But even more severe crimes against children occur on a grand scale in most public schools and universities today. The perpetrators are the majority of educators and philosophers of this world. They implement those anti-educational ideas advanced at the turn of the century by master comprachicos, John Dewey. Thus, such educators methodically destroy the efficacy of the child's mind. By the millions, eager, knowledge-seeking children turn into lethargic airheads unable to achieve honest prosperity and genuine happiness.

Moreover, those comprachicos supported by government and religions schools are busily training millions of children to live dishonestly — to live not by producing values for others but by cleverly usurping values from others. Indeed, they are training children to become mystics and neocheaters. For, those modern-day comprachicos must always continue to generate mystics and neocheaters in order to perpetuate the big-lie hoaxes of mysticism.

Who will protect innocent children from those crimes? Neo-Tech can and will eventually protect all children from such crimes. And every Neo-Tech reader can help protect children by publicly identifying those modern-day comprachicos who carry out their mind/body mutilations in full view of a silently accepting public. The Neo-Tech reader can openly identify the damage being done to innocent children, particularly those children trapped within the public education system.

---

*Go to the beach. Look at the couples over 30. How many still look healthy, trim, attractive? Maybe 5%, probably less. ...Most adults surrender life by surrendering to mysticism. Indeed, they often mutilate and destroy each other's bodies and happiness. They directly or indirectly encourage or cajole their spouses into destroying their trim, beautiful bodies. Such insecure people actually want their spouses to grow fat and unattractive. Why? With an unattractive spouse, a person no longer needs to exert the care, thought, and effort required to prevent losing an attractive spouse in the competitive arena of romantic love.

David J.   R-2141, AUSTRALIA

NOT HAVING READ ALL OF NEOTECH I-V AS YET IT IS TOO SOON TO TELL OF ALL THE ADVANTAGES I WILL GAIN FROM THE KNOWLEDGE, BUT I HAVE BEEN ABLE TO OBTAIN A 40% INCREASE IN MY SALARY BY USING NEOTECH SO FAR

Jim R. C-118

Dr. Wallace,

Thank you for Neo-Tech! I canot understand how anyone who has the ability to reason and understand could posibily hold on to mysticism.

Martin K. C-1022

I have a new power. Thanks to a marvelous book.

Yours sincerely

All children are born innocent and filled with unlimited potential for productive, happy lives. To protect them from today's comprachicos, I & O Publishing Company is designing Neo-Tech packages for grade-school and high-school children. Comments are wanted from all Neo-Tech owners about protecting children from mystics and neocheaters. I & O needs Neo-Tech oriented individuals to work on this project. Please send correspondence and ideas concerning "Neo-Tech for Children" to Ken Clark, P. O. Box 19358, Las Vegas, NV 89132.

Neo-Tech Advantage #85
REJECTING MYSTICS AND NEOCHEATERS

Neo-Tech owners will have the opportunity to acquire a Protection Kit from the Neo-Tech Center. The kit provides many specific, real-life examples that show how Neo-Tech jettisons all mystics and neocheaters. For example, the following letter illustrates an attack by neocheaters and how Neo-Tech effectively dismisses such neocheaters:

Mr. Paul L. Douglas, Attorney General
Department of Justice, State Capitol
Lincoln, Nebraska 68509

Dear Mr. Douglas:

Important to your future is understanding the enclosed letter from Mr. Thomas P. Vlahoulis of your Consumer Protection Division. As Nebraska's Attorney General, you are responsible for actions of that Division and its use of taxpayers' money.

Please carefully read that letter, for it is under your name: Does Mr. Vlahoulis, you, or anyone in your Department of Justice have a single, concrete complaint about the Neo-Tech Research and Writing Center or any of our publications? If so, we request that you immediately inform us. For, we want to know exactly what the complaint is and who is making it. We insist on our basic right of knowing and facing our accuser so we may respond fully.

And very important, Mr. Douglas, why exactly is your Department of Justice gratuitously intruding into a publishing company with an inquisition directed at its writers and sources? What exactly is Mr. Vlahoulis implying or presuming, and on what basis? And what is the idea of his threatening us while remaining secretive in vaguely implying that the inquisition arises from "information forwarded by a concerned citizen". If someone has a complaint, then out with it so we can respond. Indeed, has Mr. Vlahoulis or anyone in that Division ever received even a single complaint? And what about the thousands of happy Nebraskans who have benefited from our work over the past sixteen years? Indeed, many of those individuals have responded with written testimonials. Just who is complaining and why? Or is Mr. Vlahoulis merely acting on someone's specious attack on values?

If no complaint based on fact exists, then I submit that Mr. Vlahoulis is consuming taxpayers' money in creating jobs by conjuring up problems

Nick N. C-72

It's amazing to me how the mystical concepts have integrated into my conscousness over the years. No wonder, what with all the programming going on all about us. When I first read the material through it was actually painful. I had to take a few days "rest" from it and then get back to it again. The second time through was very positive.

Obrizi O. C-119, NIGERIA

<u>Testimony</u> ON NEO TECH

THE WAY TO BETTER LIFE

AFTER Reading through my NEO TECH Discovery I found that to be honest is the only way to Property. Because NEO TECH itself is talks only of honesty and Honesty alone can lead you to Social Contacts that from Affairs, Bussiness Dealings, Job Careers, Finance Investments, Personal Relationships, art and Pleasure.

Talmadge B. R-2990

Thank you so much! My mind is free of all the guilt and hangups I was subject to for 50 years.

where none exist while sapping valuable time from innocent producers. If that be the case, is not your Department committing a double-edged fraud under the aegis of "consumer protection"?

What would the citizens of Nebraska think about spending their tax money on harassing value-producing writers in the name of "consumer protection"? What would Woodson Howe, editor of the Omaha World-Herald, or Tom White, editor of the Lincoln Star, say about your arbitrary threats aimed at a publisher of ideas? ...Ideas that will collapse mysticism to benefit everyone except the neocheaters.

Through the philosophically oriented books and articles developed by the Neo-Tech Research and Writing Center, we have delivered objective, long-range values to over a million appreciative individuals in all 50 states and over 130 countries. Still professional mystics and neocheaters who are threatened by Neo-Tech always attack it, often vehemently, often imploring government authorities to stop our publishing activities. But, as they sooner or latter discover, such attacks always backfire. For, we utilize all their attacks to our benefit. Indeed, their attacks directly enhance our business objectives of exposing mysticism to abolish neocheaters. Moreover, their attacks are published and marketed in our Neo-Tech Protection Kit. That kit allows honest, productive people to specifically identify and then forever dismiss those mystics and neocheaters who foment dishonest attacks on value producers.

We are resolutely principled and never knowingly yield to actions that are wrong or unfair, no matter what the cost. Indeed, over the long-range we build strength through a loyalty to honesty. And that means standing up to and publicly exposing neocheaters wherever we encounter them.

In addition to the definition of neocheaters on the second page of our enclosed statement of principles, I ask you to read the third page concerning our policies toward neocheaters. That policy includes never knowingly doing business, regardless of dollar losses, with those who live by force, threats, or fraud. The philosophical underpinnings of that policy evolve from Frank R. Wallace's enclosed, national-award-winning article on the bicameral mind: "Consciousness, The End of Authority".

Also, enclosed are samples of testimonials from Neo-Tech owners. As you can see in the inset on the second page, various mystics and neocheaters fear Neo-Tech so much that they stridently threaten us, even with physical harm. Some have physically threatened our writers and two have tried to carry out their threats. That is one reason we shield and protect our writers. Additionally, all our sales literature openly displays a printed warning requesting neocheaters, mystics, and non-productive value destroyers not to buy anything from us. Moreover, we will not knowingly do business with them. We reject their orders, return their money, and never want their business.

But above all, we as everyone in America are protected by the First Amendment. And we as everyone in America can freely publish our ideas without anyone's permission or license no matter what authorities, mystics,

Tere T.   C-68

Dear Dr Wallace & Co,
In reading Neo-tech I & II it has evidently changed my systematic way of thinking before reading these fabulous books written by brilliant minds. I never knew those Mystics and Neocheaters that usurp values by unknowing innocent people, leaving a path of misery. But through the eyes of a Neotech person I see the world in a different perspective. I am now learning to rehabilitate my follow suit attitude, and in time I will acheive guilt free unlimited goals, happiness and psychuous pleasures.

Jim O.   R-364

Dear Dr. Wallace,

I've just finished a study of Neo-Tech info package; fire-works, fire-works, fire-works on every page. It's not so important that I enjoyed it; but I learned something, and have already gotten results — simply by learning that I don't have to take all the garbage. I've been accepting these years. By all means keep my name on your mailing list.

or neocheaters may object, including those in government and religion, including you, your Department of Justice, and Mr. Vlahoulis.

That raises the question of why I spent the time identifying the nature of Mr. Vlahoulis' actions. Am I allowing something anti-productive to drain my time needed to produce values for others? I think not. For I am a publisher whose single, long-range responsibility is to develop and publish those identifications that will reveal and eventually eliminate dishonest mystics and destructive neocheaters, in and out of religion and government.

Being both a writer and a publisher, such time is never wasted as reflected by Murial Spark, author of "Loitering With Intent":

"Everything happens to the writer. Time is always redeemed, nothing is lost, and wonders never cease."

In other words, every such effort generates material for future publications. Those publications are dedicated to identifying and rejecting mystics and neocheaters with their 2000-year hoax used to pillage the value producer. For once free of mystics and neocheaters, society will be free of parasites and wars. Then all people will be free to earn full prosperity, personal happiness, and romantic love.

And now a most important note. A personal note offered in goodwill to you, Mr. Douglas: I ask you to take the following step that will bring you and the public great benefits, now and in the future: Although we do not sell Neo-Tech to mystics, neocheaters, politicians, the clergy, most lawyers, certain academe, and others listed in our policy statement, we invite you to leave politics, acquire Neo-Tech knowledge, and join in the ascent of man and woman to guiltless prosperity, happiness, and love.

If you arrange to leave politics to produce marketable values for others, I could arrange for you to acquire Neo-Tech as we have occasionally arranged for other nonqualifiers desiring to abandon their mysticism and neocheating in order to pursue a happy, productive life. So please let me know if you are interested in this new direction. For, we can help you. With Neo-Tech, you can be infinitely happier than working toward the next election.

Sincerely,

John Flint

John Flint
Director of RIBI

Note: Several months after receiving this letter and failing to take its advice, Attorney General Paul L. Douglas was impeached and later indicted for perjury and obstruction of justice.

Neo-Tech Advantage #86
POWER, PLATO, ARISTOTLE, AND NEO-TECH
A 2500 YEAR-OLD RIDDLE SOLVED

For 2500 years, citizens from ancient Greece to modern America have sought to understand and judge those holding or seeking power. The higher,

Robin P.   C-81

I previously considered myself to be a fairly honest person. However, after reading I-V I came to the realization as to how short I really was of the target. Certainly for my own benefit I've been able to rid myself of ingestation of most alcohol and other socially pressured drug use as well as riding myself of guilt resultant, rationalized deception and minor crime. I'm currently feeling much better about myself.

Like many others who have written to you and thanked you for your works, so shall I. The insight given, affirmation of my beliefs provided, and overall genuine value to my life has been astounding! Perhaps someday I can have the added benefit of truly understanding how such concepts have evaded "Discovery" for so long.

Richard B.   C-103

Dear Doctor Wallace —

My son, Richard, and I, have read discussed, + debated Neotech I-V with great interest. As the elder, a yankee of conventional New England education and predjudices, the study was a long overdue awakening to the facts of Life - so to speak. My son found the revelations stunning + concise — We have been greatly enlightened — Your writing is great

Peter H.

Why has it taken the human race so long to come up with all this?!

more powerful the authority, the more attention focuses on trying to judge that authority. In fact, attention expands geometrically on ascending the power scale to the president of the United States (or to the Pope). Yet, a consistent, reliable standard for judging power and authority has until now remained a riddle.

That riddle is solved by applying two metaphors: (1) Knowing the material world around us requires understanding the smallest atomic units. And (2) knowing the cosmos above us requires understanding its primordial origins. Now apply those two points to authority and power: (1) Knowing authority around us requires understanding the smallest authoritarian units. And (2) knowing the power above us requires understanding its philosophical origins.

Understanding the Smallest Unit of Authority

Understanding authority begins by traveling far from the great concentrations of government authority — traveling away from the eastern megalopolis, west to the small desert city in Nevada. By putting a microscope on that oasis of population, one can focus beneath its few, simple layers of authority. One can focus beneath the mayor, past the city council and paid government employees down to an unpaid, appointed planning commission. And finally, one can reduce that commission's microcosm of authority down to its most mundane exercise of authority — the granting or denying of a minor zoning variance to a lone, uninfluential individual with a modest home needing a second bedroom for his mother.

That property owner duly completed the proper forms, submitted blueprints, paid the filing fees, and presented the facts to the planning commission. He explained why variance was necessary not only to better the property, but to preserve one of the largest elm trees in the city. The owner detailed how alternative plans without the variance would neither be practical nor best serve the neighborhood. In addition, a professional urban planner (hired by the commission) found no problems or objections to the variance. He also concurred that well over half the homes in the neighborhood already had structures built in greater variance to the zoning ordinance than the minor variance requested.

Moreover, unlike the surrounding structures, the proposed structure was designed to beautify both the owner's home and the neighborhood. In addition, that would be done entirely at the owner's expense while providing local employment. And most important, a two-week notice posted on the property, an advertised notice in the local newspaper, and written notices mailed to 57 homes surrounding the proposed property improvement brought not a single objection. In short, everyone logically concerned supported the variance.

On concluding the hearing, the members seemed ready to approve this minor, routine variance. But then spoke a younger commissioner, a stocky, flush-faced government environmentalist living in a wealthy neighborhood atop a hill, far from the property owner. He turned enough to observe

C. D.   R-2027, AUSTRALIA

I will never find enough words to thank you for releasing me from mysticism. Although there are yet loose ends to be shaken free, every day rids me of another and puts me closer to previously unimagined freedom. Have been searching all my life for something like this. I just can't believe it. Will read again. Eagerly anticipate receiving complete library and Neo Think information.
Thankyou

Phillip S.   R-2180

In a world of socialism and altruistic ideas it is extremely refreshing to know that their are still people with the foresight and intelligence to fully comprehend and understand the full implications of freedom and free enterprise.

Bravo.

the property owner from the corners of his eyes. Then with twitching jowls, he stated that the property owner's needs and desires meant nothing in his considering the variance. He then cited three ambiguous, ordinance clauses with arbitrary interpretations — impossible interpretations that no home owner could ever satisfy. ...He chose the exercise of power for the sake of gaining unearned power by destroying the creation of values.

In prompt rebuttal, spoke an older commissioner, a trim, leather-faced workingman living in the same modest neighborhood as the property owner. He pointed out that no objective reason to deny the variance existed, especially after everyone in the neighborhood and all others who could possibly be concerned approved. ...He chose the creation of values over the exercise of power.

To fully understand the profound difference between those two commissioners, one must know that they are appointed by politically elected officials and meet four hours each month without pay. If they receive no pay, what do they receive? They receive political power and civic recognition with little expenditure of time and effort. Thus, the motivation for such people entering the world of government authority varies between political enhancement and civic enhancement. From those beginnings, from that political atom, emerge two types of people: One desiring to gain power and a political future by destroying values. The other desiring to enhance the civic needs of the community and its citizens by protecting values. ...The first type gains authoritarian power by destroying values of others; the second type resists authoritarian power by protecting values of others. The first type consists of bad-intentioned, destructive mystics and neocheaters. The second type consists of well-intentioned, but misguided value producers.

Understanding the Philosophical Origins of Power

The first type knowingly or unknowingly orients around Plato's philosophy — a subjective, mystical-based philosophy. The extent a person adopts Plato's views is the extent that he or she holds that:

    1. Standards for morals and ethics are products of changeable opinions rather than products of objective reality.
    2. Power is to be used as an end in itself to determine who through their "wisdom" (through their feelings, whims, wishes, "intuition") should rule or control others.
    3. Facts, honesty, and logic are relative.
    4. Principle does not matter: ends justify the means.

By nature, Plato nourishes not only all despots and dictators, but politicians and bureaucrats at all levels of government. Plato justifies the striving for power at the expense of the rights and needs of individuals. Plato provides the rationalization for all laziness and dishonesty — for all subjective, unjust non sequiturs and actions used to usurp power and values from others. According to Plato, the rights and needs of individuals are secondary to any external "authority's" desire to usurp values and power.

Rodney J. S.   R-2987

> Finally free from most of the guilt-producing nonsense learned during my life. I also feel more self-confident and sleep better realizing my true worth.
>
> I now know how to evaluate relationships with other people in any area of my life.

E.L.B.   R-6057

Wow, Neo Tech is guilt free. It's taught me to say no without feeling guilty. I no longer feel I must go hundreds of extra miles to satisfy someone else. My only duties are to be morally good to myself and others and propagate virtue. Besides if you can't help yourself you can't help your loved ones.

It's good realizing that I'm a genuinely kind person without feeling I must prove it.

Roy J.   R-1451

Mind boggling - has helped me with mysticism as I was a Baptist preacher for over 20 yrs. Has freed me from most guilt allowing me to experience greater peace of mind. Keep up the great work.

Indeed, Plato assigns virtue to sacrificing individual rights and needs to *any* arbitrary "higher cause", "higher power", or external "authority". ...Thus, Plato is the philosophical father of mysticism and neocheating.

The second type knowingly or unknowingly orients around Aristotle's philosophy — an objective, reality-based philosophy. The extent that a person adopts Aristotle's view is the extent he or she holds that:

    1. Standards for morals and ethics are products of objective reality rather than products of changeable opinions.
    2. The well-being of society is enhanced to the extent that individuals are free to produce objective values for themselves and others.
    3. Facts, honesty, and logic are absolute.
    4. Principle matters: ends do not justify the means.

By nature, Aristotle nourishes all value producers. The Aristotelian-oriented person has a loyalty to honesty above all else. That person avoids acting on whims, feelings, or wishes. But rather, that person strives to identify and integrate contextual facts in order to act in a rationally consistent manner that generates maximum values for everyone. Thus, Aristotle is the philosophical father of business and Neo-Tech.

Making Judgments

While most people outwardly exhibit mixtures of Platonistic and Aristotelian views, everyone holds a dominant view of life that is either Platonistic or Aristotelian. Once the Platonistic and Aristotelian views are understood, the dominant view of most individuals becomes evident. With that understanding, one can detect the philosophical core of anyone seeking or holding government power — from the president of the United States to a planning commissioner of a small desert town.

Now, after 2500 years, an objective standard exists to judge power and authority: Who should hold government power over one's life, property, and freedom? A person with Plato's view or a person with Aristotle's view? The answer is...neither.

The Neo-Tech View

All forms of external power or authority undermine the productive, self-responsible nature of human beings. Thus, all such authority is eventually harmful to everyone. No person, group, or government has the right to deny *or* grant permission for individuals to use their own earned property in ways not infringing on the life or property rights of other individuals.

Note: After sending this report to members of the city council, the property owner proceeded to build the room without permission or interference from the "authorities".

Neo-Tech Advantage #87
FREEDOM, RESPONSIBILITY, AND PROSPERITY

Mystic-free individuals who think and act with full-context integrations can easily retake power usurped by the mystics and neocheaters. And a

Gisela M.   R-3992

Like so many Neo-Tech owners, I was completly overwhelmed, realized however, that I had found the answer to life. After 55 years of living, there was always that sence, something is missing. Love, honesty and hard work seemed not anough for a happy life. Getting free of mysticism and guilt, is the missing link. To be able to identify Neo-cheaters so easely and clearly is great. Every time I read the Neo-Tech manuscript again, I learn more. Neo-Tech's new technology is the best news, I can give to my family. Thank you gentlemen.

John F.   R-4981

NEO-TECH works! Within one week after studying the NEO-TECH books, I began to apply the knowledge I obtained from Doctor Wallace. I began to conduct my business in a manner which corresponded with the NEO-TECH philosophy.

And the exciting truth is MY SALES DOUBLED! MY PROFITS DOUBLED! AND I WORKED FEWER HOURS THAN BEFORE TO MAKE TWICE AS MUCH MONEY!

The NEO-TECH books are magnificent!

Thank you for creating them.

mystic-free, Neo-Tech person can always outcompete those hampered with mysticism in personal and business endeavors. To consistently act in the *rational* interest of self, others, and society requires mystical-free thinking and actions in concert with fully integrated honesty...which is Neo-Tech.

With Neo-Tech, people can free themselves of the life-stunting oppression imposed by external "authorities". Once free, Neo-Tech people become totally responsible for their own actions and, thus, gain full control of their own lives and well-beings. Only with that responsibility and control can individuals be of maximum value to others in producing values. But that idea of freedom and responsibility contradicts the premises of both conservatives and "liberals". All such advocates of government control claim that individuals must in various ways be controlled by force or coercion to keep them from hurting themselves and others. And that is the greatest of all myths promoted since Plato.

That great myth begins by omitting the adjective *rational* from the words *self-interest*. Such an omission allows one to falsely imply that free individuals will normally pursue *irrational* "self-interests" such as fraud, theft, assault, rape, murder if not controlled by government force or regulations. Irrational actions are always destructive to a person's self-interest, thus, are contrary to human nature. Irrationality, by nature, *never* works to the well-being of anyone. The human organism, as any living organism, if unfettered and free, works by nature toward the long-range *best* interest of everyone.

Similarly, every cell and organ in one's body freely functions toward its own well-being in order to deliver maximum benefits to the entire body. Cells and organs do not sacrifice themselves to other cells and organs. If they did, the entire body would die. Likewise, individuals free to function toward their own rational, nonsacrificial self-interests will achieve maximum prosperity for themselves, others, and society. If they allow themselves to be sacrificed, everyone loses except the neocheaters promoting sacrifice of others to their "cause".

Free, unsacrificed individuals provide the maximum benefits to others and society. But that is not the reason why government force and coercion against individuals by nonproductive mystics and neocheaters is morally wrong. Independent of the practical benefits, the principle stands: Each individual has the inalienable right to his or her own mind, body, and earned property regardless of those benefits that naturally accrue to others and society. No one can ever rightfully own or morally take any portion of another individual's life or earned property.

Freedom and property can be taken from an individual in only one of two ways: (1) by his or her consent (moral), (2) by initiatory force, threat of force, coercion, or fraud (immoral). All governments throughout history have immorally usurped individual freedom and property from their

Keith P.   R-3572

Neo Tech I through V has been in my hands since February 1986, the excellent Neo Tech Library since July 1986. I have embarked upon a great journey since those dates and one that has yet to unfold fully, I'm pleased to say!

On my first reading, one of the negative testimonials struck me as interesting, but not for the reason which the writer intended it! : 'You must walk alone forever without rest'. In a way, that seems to me what biological immortality is about. Any honest producer would want to walk, to work, to produce, forever without resting or retirement. The only thing which doesn't gell is the 'alone' part. Honest producers will never be alone and Neo Tech will bind them together into an unstoppable force; it is doing it now in fact.

Neo Tech is helping me greatly in my daily life. It is almost as if I have found a switch in my mind which, when turned on, shines a brilliant white spotlight onto neo-cheaters and their methods, leaving them nowhere to hide. Whereas before I would have let people like that confuse me with their tactics, I can now confound them with pure unanswerable rationality. It gives me a great thrill to experience the feeling of finally starting to learn how to use my grey matter properly. Before Neo Tech I often felt alone and afraid, more trusting of others than myself; now I feel able to handle my own life and my own problems, using logic and rationality.

Recently a friend came to see me. We had lost regular contact when I had found Neo Tech and rejected mysticism. He still stuck to his own ways, but expressed a desire to find out about Neo Tech. We had a meal together at a restaurant, during which I would not discuss Neo Tech: 'you've got to see it for yourself' I told him. We returned home and over a cup of rose hip tea I let him look at Neo Tech II. Somehow he turned straight to advantage 29 and began to read about mysticism. That was a subject close to his heart but not described in the way in which he was used to! So great was his shock that he spilt his tea over the volume, and quickly handed it back to me claiming that it was too deep for him. He spoke no more about it. That taught me a lot, and made me realise just how powerful Neo Tech can be to a confirmed mystic - and how threatening!

I'm glad that I've got Neo Tech, and look forward to going on to greater things with what I have learnt so far from it, and with what I shall learn in the future. I'm excited at the prospect of getting my hands on Neothink, when it becomes available. The journey, and the adventure, continues!

James D.   R-7052

Dr. Wallace's insights are profound. The time has arrived for Truth to prevail and the unhealthy ways of the Neocheaters to be discarded.

citizens by initiatory force or the threat of force. And that theft is always done under the Platonistic rationalization of serving some common "good" or "higher" cause.* All governments today initiate force or threats of force to deprive their citizens of their property, prosperity, freedom, happiness. ...While everyone has the right to use self-defense force, no one or no government has the right to initiate force or threats of force against anyone under any circumstances.

Why do certain people such as politicians, thieves, theologians, social intellectuals, certain media people, professors, and other mystics and neocheaters seek to live by force, fraud, deception, or coercion? Why do they seek to live by usurping values from others rather than to live by producing values for others? One discovers the answer by stripping the layers of rationalization from such people. Beneath those layers is a lack of maturity and self-esteem, a lack of self-responsibility and independence**, a lack of honesty and effort. For they made a secret choice to be dishonest, lazy, and dependent on others for survival — a secret choice to avoid the constant, focused effort needed to produce values desired by others.

Also, neocheaters and other value destroyers hold various degrees of envious fear and hatred toward the producer. After stripping away the various rationalizations from those value destroyers, the same core — no matter how skillfully hidden — will always manifest itself. That core is laziness...a default against the constant hard effort needed to competitively produce values that benefit others.

Self-responsibility, rationality, and effort are necessary for human well-being and happiness. To live as designed by nature, people must produce tradeable values (goods or services) that others desire and will voluntarily buy.*** By contrast, laziness is the character core of mystics, neocheaters, politicians and all other value destroyers. Consider, for example, essentially all politicians are lazy, despite their often cleverly staged, look-like-work flurries. Those flurries of "work" are really nothing more than flurries of anti-productive machinations or ego-boosting power ploys. Such destructive

---

*For the individual, no higher good or cause than that individual person can logically exist in this universe. For that individual, what could possibly be more important than his or her own one-and-only life? Nothing can, could, or should be more important. Indeed, without the conscious life of individual beings, existence itself would have no value or meaning.

**The alternative to independence is dependence. And dependence on a producer can be sustained only through (1) the producer's permission or (2) force, threats, deception, or coercion executed by professional mystics or neocheaters.

***How many free, honest, productive people would voluntarily buy the "services" of a politician, a bureaucrat, a theologian, a dictator, or a social "intellectual"?

Mark G.   R-1427

Dear Dr. Wallace,

Since acquiring Neo Tech and upon reading every single word of the entire package my life has taken on new meaning. A sense of worth and a true understanding of what life is all about, will guide me through my remaining years. At 40 years of age, I thought I was destined to a life of insignificance, but because of you that condition has changed.

Today my life is moving in a forward direction seeking the new and the challenging. Never again looking back and trying to change what cannot be changed. Using past experiences only for the benefit of better living today and I am confident that today's better living will bring more tomorrow.

machinations are the daily routines of dictators, prime ministers, and presidents as so starkly revealed by Nixon in the Watergate tapes and in the personal accounts of neocheating politicians as Stalin, Hitler, Churchill, FDR, JFK, LBJ. They are all soul mates concealing their mutual secret of laziness and living off the productive efforts of others.

Most professional mystics and neocheaters are "liberal" oriented.* To live off the producers, those modern "liberals" must promote the false notion that human needs are human rights. They must promote their non-sequitur emotional hoax that being "compassionate" means forcing the value producer to fill their parasitical needs.

Gaining unearned values is the foremost concern of all "liberals". Yet, they constantly project the opposite that they are concerned mainly about "higher values" and "compassion" for others. But all their countless images are shams. For, all professional mystics and neocheaters are interested only in unearned power so they can go through life living off the values produced by others.

Since professional mystics, neocheaters, and other value destroyers are not self-sufficient, they must spend their lives in a deceptive, resentful struggle designed to extract their material and emotional needs from the producer. Even those nonproducers who have inherited wealth are psychologically dependent on the producer. Those wealthy nonproducers must attack or undermine the producer to elevate their own weak egos and to camouflage their nonproductivity.

Because of their parasitical nature, "liberals" are generally much more destructive than conservatives. For, conservatives are often worthwhile but misguided productive people who live pragmatically — without consistent principles. ...But also, some of the most clever neocheaters adopt conservative, free-enterprise images to bilk the producer by gaining his or her enthusiastic support.

Conservatives generally promote material and economic freedom. But they want government to control morality and ideas. Most "liberals", on the other hand, appear to promote freedom of ideas such as free press, academic freedom, no censorship, freedom in the arts. But ultimately that freedom is granted only to those who support their usurpations. For, to survive, "liberals" need governments to usurp money and values earned by the producers; while "middle of the roaders" favor various mixtures of government control over individual minds, morals, bodies, and property.

Only Neo-Tech people reject all usurpations and forced controls over

---

*"Liberal" is placed in quotes because those who are called liberals today are the opposite of the past, classical liberals who represented anti-force, pro-individual ideas. Modern "liberals" do not have good intentions. They are anti-individual, anti-intellectual, pro government-force reactionaries who have dishonestly usurped the label of "liberal" to create illusions of respectability and validity. Yet, they are nothing more than dishonest, immature people with criminal minds who survive by stealing power and values from the value producer.

David H. R-4015, New Zealand

In my first 30 years of life, I created just enough values and applied just enough effort to convince family and work mates that I was competent, however, in relation to a very incompetent society.

In the depressing moments of more objective self examination I was painfully aware that life was daily becoming unattractive and the future rather hopeless. Alcohol protected me from looking too deeply at the possible outcome to the way I was living.

Until Neo-Tech. Neo-Tech united many concepts, that I had a vague awareness of, into a logical concise and surprisingly obvious text. No longer was there a need to avoid reality. No longer did I require alcohol - and haven't since.

I gained, as I read, an exciting realization that anything I would contemplate for the future was possible if I continued to develop and integrate the realizations of the reality around me. A reality, the objective reality, of what actually is. A reality that sadly few are aware of.

Neo-Tech has opened my perception of what is required for a creative, innovative, challenging life.

My friends, with the exception of one, have reacted rather negatively to the obvious change of direction my life has taken. It has made them uncomfortable, my energy seems to be threatening, they would prefer me to remain in the "old mold".

One friend asked "what's wrong with you, you use to be a humanist, now you don't accept anyone." Comments like this are strengthening. I will integrate the values I'm discovering, and the results, perpetuate a growing desire for further personal development.

John A. R-289

'Gives meaning to the word 'life.' NEO-TECH got me to start thinking again, not for just a short time, but as something that is as natural as breathing.

individuals. For Neo-Tech people are oriented around individual rights, not fake human rights. Both conservatives and "liberals", on the other hand, are oriented around government power in the two areas they consider most effective for controlling others: (1)controlling the mind and moral realms for the conservatives, (2) controlling the body and material realms for the "liberals". ...But Neo-Tech people want to control no one. They have no need or desire to control the spiritual or material realm of anyone. They recognize everyone's sovereign right to both realms.

**

The link between big business and laissez-faire capitalism is largely a myth originating from Karl Marx's anti-intellectual canards in his book *Das Kapital*. Consider that laissez faire is a French phrase meaning, "to let do", or "to let people do as they choose". Thus, laissez-faire capitalism means neither pro big business nor anti big business, but means simply individual freedom. Yet, today, most chief executives of large stagnated businesses are anti laissez-faire. Indeed, many entrenched CEOs support fascist concepts of big government. For such concepts utilize force-backed government regulations needed to protect their jobs and businesses from more competent, harder-working entrepreneurs and foreign competitors.

Laissez-faire capitalism simply means no government control over individuals or their property — a Neo-Tech atmosphere. Within such an atmosphere, individuals are free to create and build businesses, including big businesses, even monopolistic big businesses. Within that laissez-faire atmosphere, government would have no power to support big businesses or protect monopolies (e.g., many banking, utility, and communication companies are monopolies protected by government force). Without government protection or assistance, big businesses and monopolies could exist and grow only by continually delivering better values than anyone else. Whenever any monopoly failed to deliver maximum values, the free-market dynamics in the absence of all government controls would cause that monopoly either to deliver better values or yield to others delivering greater values. ...Market dynamics free of government controls will sooner or later always collapse uncompetitive or harmful businesses, monopolies, or cartels.

Companies, businesses, industries, and monopolies are not detached entities, but are comprised of individuals who function through individual thoughts and actions. All business entities are the property and extension of individual human beings. Thus, businesses possess the same inalienable rights of free action and ownership of earned values as individuals. Also, individuals and their honest businesses exert power only through peaceful voluntary free choices, not through force, coercion, or deception as do all neocheaters in or out of government.

Iona L.   C-1023

Dear Dr Flint: ———

I have finished reading the manuscripts Neo Teck I—II and Neo Teck II, and will read them again. Much study will be required.

I whole-heartedly agree with the info related in these books. I am only very sorry I didn't "jump in" sooner!

I am 70 years old and very interested in Biological Immortality. I hope to live another 20 years and will strive to be as actual and vital as possible.

I read Ayn Rand many years ago and fully agreed with her concepts. She was right on target!

How did humanity get so far from Reality? Or have we ever approached it? The concept of God has been a very negative factor. Can we overcome that concept? Or negate the influence of Governments?

What a wonderful world it could be!

Most government agencies ultimately exist through force, coercion, or deception, not through the peaceful, voluntary, free choices of business. Thus, such agencies that depend on threats and force have no moral right to exist. Those agencies are in reality coercive engines of "legitimatized" antisocial actions such as:
1. grand theft via force-backed taxes and inflation,
2. destructive oppression via regulation and controls,
3. mass murder via waging wars and sponsoring terror.

Governments are colossal mystical frauds that usurp power and values by force-backed laws and regulations. And those usurpations are used to further violate individual and property rights. Such destructive processes keep building and feeding on themselves. ...All value producers would benefit greatly without such governments.

Today, upper management of big-business is increasingly controlled by altruistic, neocheating "businessmen" who apologize for the business they now control, but never built* [Re: Neo-Tech IV]. Those altruistic "businessmen" are usually fascist oriented. For they use government force to shield their businesses from competition. Indeed, they promote anti-capitalistic legislation, regulations, and controls. The unspoken policies of those executives are to gain government favors and to encourage

---

*Essentially every big business was originally created and built by an honest, heroically productive individual such as E. I. du Pont, Henry Ford, Andrew Carnegie, Thomas Edison, John D. Rockefeller, Harvey Firestone, and other industrial geniuses. Such men are the true benefactors of all working class people, of all value producers, of all society and civilization. For they all had the same moral objectives of benefiting their customers, workers, managers, and investors by delivering spectacular values to society at ever lower costs. Those creative, productive individuals contrast sharply with destructive, media-made "heroes" such as the Naders, Kennedys, "Tip" O'Neill's, and other such bad-intentioned nonproducers who survive by attacking and harming value producers, their products, their businesses.

While never honestly acknowledging those who produce great wealth and values, the "liberal" or neocheating journalists and writers often praise the wealthy, nonproductive scions of past industrial heroes. Neocheaters especially praise those immature, nonbusiness-like "philanthropists" who dissipate inherited wealth such as Henry Ford III and Nelson Rockefeller. The "liberal" media also attack nearly every major value created by outstanding businessmen, scientists, and industrialists. For example, under such guises as ecology, consumerism, or "compassion", the "liberal" media attack, often with rabid envy, the greatest, most heroic values created by conscious beings. Such outstanding values attacked include the automobile, the computer, the drug industry, the petroleum and mining industries, and America's magnificent food processing and distribution systems. At the same

(footnote continued on next page)

Mathew J.   C-128

I realized that I haven't expressed how I felt during my stay. My experience at I&O was a breath of fresh air. I really felt happy and alive. The difference between the atmosphere and sense of life at I&O and the sense of life at home and at school is phenomenal. The people who are rational and alive are drawn to the exciting life at I&O. It gets lonely out here among the dead and dying. I look forward to working with you and the other people at I&O.

Sincerely,

P.S. How do you manage to contain your excitement and happiness? I often feel so happy and excited that I could explode. Is this what it feels like to be a tornado in a bottle?

government-forced regulations that block more competent competitors and superior-value imports. Such executives realize that, without government interference, the free-market competition would eventually eliminate their jobs and their poorly run businesses that they have drained through harmful government-approved, socially oriented "business" policies.

Government-corporate collusions inflate prices, lower quality, block competition, and are the antithesis of free enterprise. Indeed, the greatest enemies of free enterprise are not the socialists or "liberals", but are those business leaders who collude with government to consolidate their power without having to earn that power in a competitive, free-enterprise atmosphere.**

Perhaps the most evil collusions occur between neocheating executives of large companies and government bureaucrats in promoting envy-motivated antitrust laws. Those immoral laws are designed to penalize the most competitive companies and productive businessmen. But soon, the growing number of Neo-Tech executives will rid the corporate world of those government-colluding executives who neocheated their way to unearned power through force-backed laws, regulations, and controls. [Re: Mark Hamilton's *White-Collar Hoax* published by I & O.]

Neo-Tech Advantage #88
NEO-TECHING BUSINESS

Neo-Tech IV reveals the malevolent destruction of altruism as opposed to the benevolent productivity of business. Neo-Tech IV also demonstrates how neocheating executives are today undermining many great corporations. They can often hide their destructive drain of assets for many years by continually shifting long-range efforts into increasingly shorter-range pay-offs that keep profits growing while concealing the eventual, dead-end quality of such profits.

If altruistic chief executives are taking over major corporations and causing their long-range demise, who then is left to stop the neocheaters'

(footnote continued from the previous page)
time, the "liberal" media are quick to praise progressively meaner values such as the car pool, the bicycle, the abacus, folk medicine, hand-made goods, growing one's own food. They promote those kinds of unheroic, mean values under good-sounding non sequiturs as returning to basic "values", returning to hand-made quality, returning to nature.

**An example of a big-business, conservative publication that effectively works against free-enterprise and Neo-Tech principles is "The Wall Street Journal". Its editorial policy is pragmatic (not based on principles) and often advocates the use of government industrial policies, controls, regulations to "help" those big businesses controlled by incompetent government colluders. Such an editorial policy is basically fascist. For their editorials often favor collusion of big businesses with force-backed government.

Luc S.   R-4411

After 3 years of study in philosophy, and personal growth and maturity, (I will be 20 soon) I now accept NT for REASONS. At first I thought if I had read Marx first then I would have believed in that instead. So at first I was literally indoctrinated by your words, but now I have experienced & lived NT & accept it not on faith but through reason & logic. I feel this is very important for everyone young & impressionable like I was, to realize.

Thank you sincerely for launching my great life!

James S.   R-5865

It is so simple that a child can understand and so intellectually advanced that no scholar from any field could successfully argue against it.

As far as I am personally concerned it is just fabulous psychology. Yes psychology.

To make it short, my wife was very ill. Her doctors said her next step was a mental institution. I started her reading Neo Tech. Today, just a few months later she is greatly improved and now looking forward & making plans to go into her own business.

continued consumption of business? Who will lead the way to a society in which mysticism and the resulting neocheating are eliminated? Who will uphold the productive individual as the highest value? Who will lead the way to a society in which prosperity, happiness, and biological immortality will reign supreme among all human beings?

The answer is today's growing army of value producers who are becoming knowledgeable about Neo-Tech. For such people hold all the power that exists as identified in the Epilogue in Neo-Tech IV. That Epilogue is from a report titled, "The Fundamental Principle that Determines the Long-Range Common Stock Value of a Corporation". And that report points the way for creating great, long-range wealth within any productive corporation. One key requirement is to establish an Industrial-Philosophy Department responsible for making all major actions consistent with the principles of fully integrated honesty (Neo-Tech). ...Neo-Teching business policies injects explosive vitality and dramatic profitability into any company, large or small.

Neo-Teching the World of Mystics and Neocheaters

Neo-Tech exposes the mystics' and neocheaters' world of big lies. Neo-Tech reveals the exact opposite to what most people have been led to believe by mystics and neocheaters. For example, how many people realize that:

1. The media-labeled, 19th century "robber barons", such as the transcontinental railroad builder Jay Gould, were heroic value producers who enormously benefited the working class and society — infinitely more so than all the politicians, clergymen, and Nobel peace laureates who ever lived, combined.

2. Despite Charles Dicken's burning intentions to depict the contrary in his Christmas Story, the most honest, moral, productive, and deeply happy character is Ebenezer Scrooge. That is until the mystics and neocheaters guilt-tripped him into becoming a maudlin altruist who as a result would eventually ruin his business and ironically destroy the well-being of those who had attacked him.

3. The political/religious/media axis have built the highest reverence and respect for some of the bloodiest, most morally perverted, but most brilliant succession of neocheaters in the history — the popes and cardinals. And with bizarre irony, all of those men, by competitive necessity, were and are closet atheists. In fact, the entire upper hierarchy of the most powerful religion (or of any powerful religion or other neocheating organization) would have to be secret atheists in order to be aware, competent, and competitive enough to achieve their power.

On knowing the nature of neocheating, one fact becomes compellingly obvious: To successfully impose such an ingenious, big-lie, 2000-year hoax continuously on millions of confused, mystical-accepting victims, all popes and cardinals would have to be sharp-thinking atheists. For any Catholic believing their own mystical, mind-crippling propaganda and God concept

Michael B. R-6471

For the first time in my adult life I am beginning to feel purpose and pleasure from everything I do. I've always felt a desire to be fully honest in everything I do, but now with neotech I realize the worth and need to be so. In the past I always felt alone when I was honest. Now I am better able to realize that there are others of us out there in Neo-tech. I can now "read" the mystics and neocheaters and am beginning to keep them from controlling my life and property. I look forward to each day as I become more integrated with Neo-Tech.

would be (1) too benighted to outmaneuver the fierce competition vying for power, and (2) too unaware and incompetent to orchestrate such a mighty hoax. Thus, all popes, cardinals, and probably most bishops would have to be atheists to be aware enough for attaining their positions of power. Also, theists would be too naive, unaware, and uncompetitive to perpetuate for centuries such a cleverly integrated mystical hoax. ...Only those who saw through their own promulgated mysticism would be aware and competent enough to beat out the fierce competition for attaining the positions of power occupied by popes and cardinals.

4. Only a small percentage of university professors and academe today are intellectuals. Most are anti-intellectual mystics or neocheaters. An intellectual by definition is one who engages the full rational, honest, productive use of the mind.

Great intellectuals exist in every major area of productive human activity. Genuine intellectuals are those businessmen, industrialists, scientists, engineers, artists, musicians, laborers, and educators who advance their profession by using their minds honestly in working hard through rational actions. A rational, hard-driving, successful mining engineer, for example, is highly intellectual in mining, but may not be highly intellectual in English literature. At the same time, a university professor of English literature is probably not highly intellectual in mining. Indeed, he may be incompetent to function intellectually in any area of business. Perhaps he is even incompetent in English, especially if he or she is the low-effort, laid-back, pipe-smoking tenured professor living off taxpayers while using non sequiturs to attack hard-working producers and their values.

The only difference between intellectualism in the business world versus intellectuals in the academic world is that performance in business is much easier to measure and thus more difficult to fake. That is why the academic world accumulates such a high percentage of lazy charlatans and pseudo-intellectuals compared to the business world. Those charlatans and pseudo-intellectuals usually cannot survive in the business world. For they are too lazy and dishonest. But they can fake lifelong careers in the academic world. And as long as mysticism and altruism dominate philosophical thought, such pseudo-intellectual neocheaters will proliferate throughout the academic world.

5. The many pseudo ecologists and self-appointed "consumer advocates" today are not interested in protecting the environment or human beings. Deceptively hidden behind their neocheating non sequiturs and destructive work is a contempt for human life and happiness. They use ecology and consumerism as tools of demagoguery, often with the goal to cripple and eventually eliminate the benefits of technology, industry, and free enterprise. As a result, many valid ecological problems are obscured, confused, and remain unsolved. Moreover, the long-range destructiveness of such neocheaters is surfacing in many areas. For example, consider Rachel Carson's thirty-year-old book, "Silent Spring": Its specious charges and

S.B.   C-1024

Dear Dr Wallace,

I have had the Neo-Tech manuscripts for many months now, and I can genuinely say that my whole outlook on life has been changed.

I know now that I can no longer be satisfied with a mediocre salary, or personal possessions and relationships. Neo-Tech helped me to decide many things, I know now that I am heading in the right direction.

My religious views were totally over-turned and I could not believe how strong your case was on this point!

Your most important revalation of course was Neo-Teck V, and I am eagerly awaiting the follow-up literature promised in the Neo-Tech II manuscript.

Yours faithfully,

Felix E.   C-101,   NIGERIA

Dear John Flint,
   Having read the Neo-Tech I-V, and having assimilated all its concepts, I have the supreme self-confidence in describing the work as an intellectual fact aiming at the emancipation of humanity from illusionary waves into axiomatic realities of modern life for the achievement of self-creativity and mastery. I equate the reading of Neo-Tech I-V as being born again and a must for all ambitious beings who want to free themselves from the shackles of external authorities. Neo-Tech treatment of bicameral mind is highly thought-provoking.

unscientific conclusions caused the banning of DDT, which in turn caused a resurgence of malaria in Asia and Sri Lanka at the eventual cost of perhaps a million lives — lives of human beings, not birds or fish. Yet, people will never find those facts among the neocheating academe and media.

With government banning of DDT and other pesticides, the mosquito and insect populations burgeoned along with a proportional rise in "ecologist" caused famine and disease such as malaria and encephalitis. In addition, those irrational bannings have decimated trees and crops in the United States and around the world. The banning of DDT has also lowered the world standard of living by billions of dollars per year in crop losses and expenses. That, in turn, significantly increased third-world inflation, hunger, suffering, famine, and death. All that human death, destruction, and suffering starting from the handiwork of just one "ecologist" needing to feel good by boosting her pseudo self-esteem with dishonest non sequiturs. [For more details on the banning of DDT, see footnote on page 271.]

An even more destructive breed of neocheaters exist who methodically decrease the living standards for everyone. That breed includes self-appointed, "consumerist-advocate" demagogues epitomized by Ralph Nader and his raiders [Re: R.De Toledano's book, "Hit & Run", Arlington House]. In the long run, their destruction surpasses that of even the murderous bannings of DDT and cyclamates (see page 273). For the real targets of those "consumer advocates" are the value producers from which come all life-enhancing values. Moreover, the pervasively destructive work of Nader sets up the psychological conditions for unjust attacks on great value-producing companies such as Union Carbide:

A few years ago, a great benevolent company, Union Carbide, was excoriated and threatened with extermination by the neocheating media and politicians for a tragic *accident* in India for which the Indian Government itself was responsible: The Indian politicians arbitrarily and irrationally forced Union Carbide to hire incompetent, distrustful nationals who were unable to perform even basic security-control operations. That forced interference by government neocheaters left Union Carbide unable to properly protect its business from sabotage by envious, anti-business value destroyers. That sabotage at Union Carbide *for which the Indian government was responsible* left 2500 dead — the worst industrial "accident" in history.

But that tragic loss of life was minuscule when compared to the routine, purposeful slaughter by political neocheaters. To the "liberal" media, the murder of 2500 people by their Marxist soulmates would hardly be newsworthy — too common, too minor, too routine, not really that bad.

Such examples starkly contrast the good of business people to the evil of political or government neocheaters. The loss of life from the worst industrial *accident* in history is little more than a casual day's slaughter for totalitarian neocheaters. For example, at the same time that Union Carbide was being excoriated by the dishonest media for sabotage that was not even their fault, little or no media outrage was expressed toward Marxist value destroyers who

Daniel S.   R-1972

Two things — ① I can't believe how naive I've been all my life, and ② I now can't imagine going through life any other way than this, with my eyes opened.

An absolutely incredible discovery, that is right under anybody's nose. Anybody that cares to think about it!

B. K.   R-14

I found the information packages
to be excellent, especially Neo-Tech
III and V. They made clear why
people can be controlled through
their bicameral minds and that
the ultimate goal is biological
immortality. Neo-Tech, taken as
a whole, has helped me understand
how I have been cheated and
deceived in all areas of my life.
Neo-Tech has been a new awakening
for me, a new birth and a new life.
Dr. Wallace has put together the
information necessary for mankind
to shape his future and ultimate
destiny: conquering the cosmos.
Neo-Tech is not just an information
package but the blueprint for man's
destiny

were *purposely* murdering and starving in Ethiopia millions of innocent men, women, and children they considered politically troublesome. Instead, the media were going through news-twisting contortions and telethon spectaculars in trying to falsely show the cause of the coldly calculated mass murder was a drought rather than their soulmate Marxist-Leninist politicians. They were mass murdering so they could feel good, feel important, feel some unearned power.

Neo-Tech Advantage #89
PROTECTION FROM GOVERNMENT DESTRUCTION

People build. Governments destroy. Who really needs governments? Productive individuals always suffer a net loss from mystically conceived, force-backed governments. Such governments diminish everyone's values, earnings, life. They survive by always expanding their unearned power. And they expand that power by increasingly transferring the earnings and property of the producer to the nonproducer by force, threats, coercion, fraud. Thus, governments and politicians, by nature, can offer only life diminishment as they continually increase their force-backed demands on the value producer. At the same time, they aggressively finagle respect and adulation for their destructions through non sequiturs and fake altruistic catchwords such as "compassion", "the heart", "humanitarian", "human rights". But never do they mention the only valid point — individual rights.

To psychologically survive, politicians must garner praise for their usurping values from others without producing values themselves. They use the handy, God-like, "goodness" gimmicks of altruism to make their destructive actions seem "good", "compassionate" and "humane" while hiding the criminality of their destructions. Such is the nature of political neocheaters and their media, academic, and religious collaborators. For that reason, effective business people who exist by producing values for others have no desire, time, or reason to diminish their lives by becoming politicians or other neocheaters who exist by usurping values from others.

All political, religious, academe, and media neocheaters today are destroying personal property, wealth, and freedom through (1) their escalating usurpations from value producers and (2) their dishonest, power-enhancing "social" programs. Without Neo-Tech to stop them, neocheaters would eventually dissipate all productive wealth and individual freedom, causing a worldwide economic collapse with an enormous loss of human life, well-being, and happiness. [Re: Table 53, Neo-Tech Reference Encyclopedia shows how to protect property and happiness from government destruction.]

The need to protect oneself from neocheaters reveals another destructive effect of mysticism: Government neocheaters usurp values for themselves and their parasitical soulmates. As the neocheaters attack and usurp those values, the most productive citizens are drained of investment capital, creative energy, individual freedom, and precious time. Those producers must increasingly struggle to protect themselves, their loved ones, their property,

Dan R.   R-1570

99.9% RIGHT STUFF

Volker J.   R-531

DEAR IO AND DR. WALLACE

READING NEOTECH I-V PUT A LOT OF THINGS TOGETHER FOR ME. IT WAS LIKE SHINING A LIGHT IN THE DARK, IT REVEALED MANY THINGS ABOUT THE CONDITIONS AROUND ME. I'M A PERSON WHO DOES A BIT OF READING NOW AND THEN, I ABOUT BROKE MY BRAIN THE FIRST DAY I GOT YOUR MATERIAL I READ FOR ABOUT 12 HOURS I WAS SO EXCITED. I READ THE INSTRUCTION AND FOLLOWING THEM I READ IT ALL IN 2½ DAYS. THEN I WALKED AROUND IN A DAZE FOR SEVERAL MORE DAYS, AMAZED AT WHAT I SAW AROUND ME.

Bob D.   R-519

Your writings are very Educational and most Powerful in all aspects of life. They are worth many times over what they cost. I am very much satisfied ———

and their means of production from the ravages of government value destroyers. More and more valuable time, capital, and effort are consumed not only in following government regulations but in studying, paying attention to, and speculating in nonproductive asset protectors, tax shelters, inflation hedges as gold and silver. Many go broke through such speculations, especially those who act mystically. For example, the backbone of the libertarian movement was broken by self-mysticism — by those acting on emotions and wishful thinking, in hopes of acquiring effortless wealth through leveraged gold and silver speculations.

With such speculations come the sick emotions that accompany disaster-oriented speculations. Those emotions include hoping for economic collapse, crop devastation, mass destruction, war, or other major disasters in order to have those speculations "pay-off". ...Holding gold and hoping for disaster is an unhappy way to live.

Also, people increasingly lose concentration on their productive work as they follow their speculations. Producers become unproductive speculators as they increasingly look for easy wealth through speculation rather than through producing values with honest thought and hard work. But in a Neo-Tech society free of neocheaters and destructive governments, all that time, energy, and capital would be channeled into uses that benefit the individual and society: Producers would spend more of their time and energy on producing values for others rather than on having to protect themselves from government value destroyers.

Governments are nothing more than groups of people. Most are nonproductive people, some are value destroyers who exist by usurping values from productive people to the harm of everyone. Some honest, valuable people do work in the government, especially in the postal, park, library, scientific, technical, military, intelligence, and other similar areas. But all governments are controlled by neocheating politicians, lawyers, and bureaucrats living off the producer. Behind all their rhetoric about "service to society" and "working for higher causes" is their need to survive by usurping values earned by others.

Power usurped through government force gives neocheating politicians illusions of control over reality. They use those rationalized illusions to build pseudo self-esteems needed for psychological survival. Their need for unearned power grows from a base of laziness, immaturity, a lack of self-responsibility, and a desire for an easy route to "accomplishment" and "control".

By contrast, self-sufficient producers such as successful business people earn genuine self-esteem through their own thoughts and efforts. They have no need for unearned power or usurped values. They have no desire to forcibly control the lives of others. That is why genuine value producers are seldom, if ever, interested in politics. ...Productive business people are too busy being creative and productive to waste their precious time on unhappy, destructive politics.

Earning major values along with long-range happiness requires an independent aloneness. Neocheaters, nonproducers, value destroyers, and politicians dread that aloneness. The glib politician, being psychologically

Scott W.   R-5285

The motivation and individual power gained from Neo-Tech has become an integral part of my life. The valuable tools allowed consistent positive action for growth. The depression, the personal habits, and lack of esteem have all been replaced by real happiness and optimal health. The advantages Neo-Tech allowed brought fantastic control and freedom which lead to the prosperity I've always sought. This remarkable work holds my acclaim and seems essential for all. Finally individuals have the logical truth to obtain a really great future.

Sincerely,

and materially dependent on others for survival, has a desperate need to be among people, to buy their favor, and to become increasingly involved in their lives by escalating his control over them. The worst situation for the neocheater or politician is to be left alone, especially to be left alone to survive by his or her own efforts. By contrast, the value producer usually has no desire to get involved with the "public" lest his or her valuable time will be wasted.

Perhaps the cruelest of government neocheaters are (1) those William Proxmires whose hypocritical golden-fleece gimmicks serve as publicity grabbing, non sequitur decoys to expand, not decrease, government harm and spending, and (2) those Claude Peppers whose actions pass under the specious humanitarian banner of protecting the elderly. Instead, their neocheating actions eventually debilitate the well-being, happiness, and earned savings of all honest hard-working people, especially elderly people.

Most elderly people no longer have growing assets or competitive earning power. A large percentage of them have worked hard and honestly throughout their lives only to have government policies drive them into an inescapable corner of dependency and inflation. They are further lured into the government dependency trap by economic cycles that offer relative relief from inflation only to be devastated by the next inflation wave and a failing social-security system.

Government manipulations through taxation and inflation diminish the well-being and happiness of everyone. But those destructive manipulations especially debilitate elderly people dependent on the government for survival. For all governments subtly push their dependent elderly citizens toward unhappiness, suffering, early death.

Most elderly people deliver themselves into that dependency trap by believing that government is a benevolent, positive force that will somehow benefit them in the present and help them in the future. The opposite is true. By nature, no one can ever look to any government for net benefits. Indeed, the essence of government is value destruction from which long-range benefits and values can never flow. Thus, one must avoid government dependency and contact to protect his or her well-being and happiness.

The unhappiness trap shuts when a person becomes dependent on government for well-being. Once the trap is shut, that person's life turns downward with declining self-esteem, well-being, and happiness.* To avoid that trap, a person must recognize that government is by nature a destructive, life-negating force that should be avoided in every possible way.

---

*Innocence is what traps most honest, productive people. Believing that most people are basically good and honest (which is true), productive people cannot grasp or imagine the dishonest nature of governments. They can not grasp the immature, evil nature of neocheating politicians, high-ranking bureaucrats, and their agents of force who exist through camouflaged value destructions.

Zack G.   C-1025

Gentlemen:

Thank you for helping me to overcome the mystical beliefs that I have struggled with for many years. I recall as a child realizing there was no Santa Claus, Easter Bunny, or Tooth Fairy, and now can rationalize denial of religion, governments, and other authorties that attempt to intimidate.

You have opened my eyes to many concepts that continue to spark new ideas.

Rex S.   R-46

As a young man I realized there was a hidden knowledge, an answer that would bring perspective to lifes many complex problems. For over 50 years U have searched and only Neo-Tech has given promise of a clear and definitive answer; further study should brighten the light.

A person should never believe in, count on, or become dependent on any aspect of government for his or her present or future well-being. The only way to retain growing prosperity and happiness is to remain independent, self-sufficient, and commercially productive, *especially as one grows older*.*

For younger people, the best asset for future prosperity and the best protection against government, mystics, and neocheaters is fully integrated honesty — or Neo-Tech. For, Neo-Tech is the development of personal honesty, integrity, and the ability to perceive reality accurately in order to produce values for others. Thus, the most valuable gift given to children and adults is Neo-Tech knowledge. For that is the knowledge to accurately perceive reality, to reject mysticism and neocheating, to develop personal honesty and integrity, to competitively produce tradeable values desired by others.

Conservative, libertarian, and most anarchist political movements offer no long-term protection from government or other forms of value-destroying neocheating and mysticism. In fact, such political movements eventually add to the destruction of values. For even those movements are pragmatic and not based on fully integrated honesty. Thus, they only serve to tear down one destructive, mystical system while providing a starting point for an even more destructive, mystical system as happened in Russia, Nazi Germany, Cuba, Iran, Nicaragua.

Similar shifting forms of mysticism are happening in the United States. Such examples include those *anti-government* movements orchestrated to undermine rational efforts for self-protection. One specific example is the combined effort of "liberal" demagogues and mystical libertarians to undercut any effective self-defense system against the murderous Marxist-Leninist value destroyers. One such highly rational, heroic effort to protect United-States citizens from nuclear destruction is the SDI or the "Star-Wars" defense system. ...But, in any case, the only certain self-defense protection from government, domestic and foreign, is to collapse the hoax of mysticism in order to eliminate all its symbiotic, value-destroying neocheaters.

Neo-Tech Advantage #90
GOVERNMENT DEATH MACHINES AND
THE ULTIMATE BATTLE

All current governments depend on coercion and force. Thus, they all are destructive to human life, productivity, prosperity, and happiness. The destructiveness of the United States government is implemented mainly through force-backed bureaucracies such as the IRS, FDA, INS, EPA, HEW, FTC, SEC, FCC, OSHA.

Consider, for example, the Food and Drug Administration (FDA): That bureaucracy has been responsible for the premature death of many thousands

---

*Useless old age is neither natural nor inevitable for anyone, despite constant government inducement to become aged, retired, useless, and dependent on neocheating politicians for survival [Re: Concept 114, New-Tech Reference Encyclopedia].

Robert C.   R-2421

I'M AMAZED AT WHAT I HAVE LEARNED FROM YOUR MANUSCRIPT. MY DESIRE TO CONTROL MY LIFE IS A PRIORITY. ELIMINATING THE CHEATERS HAS BEEN GREATLY REWARDING. YOUR RESEARCH IS, IN MY OPINION, THE MOST IMPORTANT PROJECT ON THE PLANET. IT IS SAD SO MANY PEOPLE WILL NOT UNDERSTAND.

William S.   R-2443

"You shall know the truth and the truth shall set you free" — the church says it but neo-tech did it!

58 years of guilt about sex and money GONE!

Married 36 years — nine children — now enjoying and deliting in sex with NO GUILT.

Started business in basement 21 years ago + built it into a 5 million manufacturing corp. — 90 employees inside — 1400 sales reps outside — now for the first time really proud and guiltless of my success!

I am now the man that I always wanted to be!

John N.   R-1203

Great stuff — I've written before. Am concluding my third reading. New inspirations, new insights! Planning a book. My life has changed. Able to look at life with a more discerning eye hence, greater enjoyment and happiness. Opportunities abound.

of people through its arbitrary, forced banning of such life-saving, free-choice discoveries as the cyclamate artificial sweetener. (The FDA would also like to ban life-saving saccharin and aspartame.) Cyclamates effectively replaced the deadly poison of sugar to reduce caloric intake, obesity ailments, diabetes, heart-attack deaths for millions of people. ...All that value destruction to satisfy some value-destroying bureaucrat's need to feel important, to feel unearned power.

Also, the arbitrary banning of life-saving products such as DDT, other pesticides, herbicides, and food preservatives has caused death and suffering on massive scales.* In addition, FDA regulations on drug research and marketing retard or prevent the development of many life-benefiting, life-saving drugs, medicines, and devices while increasing research and development costs to prohibitive levels. The drug industry, for example, would certainly have developed effective cancer cures years ago if the industry were free from all regulations and controls. Such freedom would allow competitive companies to openly pursue the huge profit potential in discovering and marketing effective cures for cancer, AIDS, and other diseases.

Even more important, FDA regulations block the required risk taking, incentive, and business freedom required for rapid development of human biological immortality. Indeed, the requirements for development of commercial biological immortality are freedom from both mysticism and government controls in a free-enterprise market environment [Re: See Neo-Tech V].

The blocking of human progress along with mass suffering and death are the natural results of government force. And government agencies are

---

*The government-forced end to DDT alone is responsible for perhaps a million or more malaria deaths in southeast Asia and the Indian subcontinent, especially Sri Lanka. The use of DDT in Sri Lanka reduced the number of malaria cases to seventeen. DDT was then banned because of Rachel Carson's book "Silent Spring". Five years later, the number of cases of malaria in Sri Lanka alone soared to over a million [Re: J. Maddox, "The Doomsday Syndrome", McGraw-Hill]. Moreover, forced banning of DDT, other pesticides, herbicides and chemical preservatives is decreasing food productivity while increasing production costs, poverty and suffering.

That irrational banning of valuable agriculture chemicals and food preservatives also causes greater food scarcity in famine areas to greatly increase worldwide malnutrition and starvation. The massive suffering and death in the name of protecting the environment or "doing-good" by government bureaucracies is documented in Grayson and Shepard's book, "The Disaster Lobby", Follett Publishing Company. That book also demonstrates how advancing industrial and business technology free of government interference steadily (1) protects human life, (2) improves the environment — water, air, land — for human habitation, and (3) integrated honestly solves ecological problems.

Charles T. R-6234, U.K.

I have found great benifit and value from your publications. From the first pages of the NT Discovery that I started reading nearly a year ago, to your Lifetime Value Nov.3rd publication received just a few days ago (and paid for a day later) I have never been so sure of myself, so effective in my business and so secure in the knowledge that there is no reason for my success to end. Business is booming my wife is blooming and my son (14) is reading the discovery!

I consider myself very fortunate indeed to have found your advertisement and obtained the incredible values of the Neo Tech Discovery. I have given copies of the Discovery to three of my senior employees and I find it amusing and exciting to observe the changes in their attitude and the new committment that has effected them and their work, producing positive results both for them and for the company.

My personal life has never been better! My 18 year romance with my wife has been rejuvenated and strengthened and my son will become a producer because after reading Discovery he will understand why it is so important that he create values. We will teach him right from wrong with such a clarity that has not been possible prior to Neo Tech.

Well this is all I have time for just now, I hope you have found this an interesting read, for I am sure you have some incredidible letters to absorb from people who like me have found a new, exciting direction in life, free from the encumberences of mystical notions, neocheaters and time wasters, politics and misguided religious zealots.

THANKS!
Yours sincerely,

Colman F.   R-829

Thanks to the Neo Tech discovery, my life is truly free from limitations — many of which I was previously unaware of. I need never look back with guilt, and, more importantly, regret - ever again in the future. You have my sincere gratitude and support.

the instruments of such force. The gun-toting automatons of the IRS, INS, FDA, EPA, FTC are prime instruments of force. Their essences are always destructive and their intentions are *never* good. Such agencies costing billions of dollars each year serve only to harm productive individuals and society. Indeed, those life-depriving agencies are subtle death machines that are directly and indirectly responsible for more suffering and deaths than all wars of history. (All wars are also government sponsored.) Throughout history most governments with their use of force, fraud, and coercion begin as "legalized" protection rackets and always end as destructive engines of crime and death. Such governments operate under the rationalizations of protection, altruism, the social "good", and "higher" causes.*

Agencies such as the FDA and EPA often carry out their destruction through dishonest assertions. They assert, for example, that DDT, cyclamates, aerosols might be "bad" for the ecology, cause cancer, or disturb the atmosphere. Then they expand their power with a job-creating bureaucracy to control or ban such substances. Usually those agencies hide their dishonesties with non sequitur "facts". They often manufacture unscientific data developed from spurious research to "prove", for example, that use of cyclamates might cause cancer in humans: Research on feeding megadoses of cyclamate diet sweetener to rats indicated that humans could experience bladder irritation or even tumors if they drank the equivalent of 700 bottles of diet soft drinks per day over an extended period of time. When, in fact, that amount of water alone (to say nothing of the immediately fatal amounts of sugar in 700 bottles of non-diet soda) would fatally break down the kidneys in human beings.

Still, the FDA used those non-sequitur, rat-feeding data to assert that cyclamates can be cancer-producing in human beings. The FDA then demanded that the producers prove that cyclamates do not produce cancer. Since a negative cannot be proven, the government neocheaters subsequently used its dishonest, non-sequitur data to ban the sale of cyclamates without any scientific evidence of harm to a single human being. At the same time, those neocheaters purposely ignored the wide ranging beneficial, life-saving effects of that artificial sweetener.

The FDA, EPA, or any other government agency never honestly attempts to prove their assertions. Rather, those agencies demand that the producers disprove their assertions. Their demands to disprove assertions or accusations contradict all concepts of objective law and justice. Indeed, to demand proof of a negative undermines all honesty by shifting the burden of proof away from the source making accusations (the neocheaters) to their victims (the producers).

---

*As the frauds of altruism and "higher causes" are identified and rejected by the value producers, the neocheaters will lose their unearned power. Once the producers identify and reject mysticism, all fraud-based religion and force-backed governments with their evil-intentioned administrators will become powerless.

Richard G.   R-5747

Before Neo-Tech, I thought I was scarred for life from Catholic schools and a Catholic upbringing. Years after I rejected God and the Church, I remained altruistic. I couldn't be content until I'd sacrificed everything — a real Francis of Assisi. I remained altruistic and I also remained feeling dissatisfied and short-changed in life. The most frustrating part was I didn't know why.

Now, after Neo-Tech, I know why.

You've got something big here. Thanks for letting me in on it.

Rob R.   R-1494

Keep up the good work! The Information package is of great value to me. Made a 180° turn in my thinking and I'm very happy for it.

Without the burden-of-proof standard, government and religious neocheaters avoid the responsibility to prove their assertions and accusations. Without the burden-of-proof standard, neocheaters are not accountable to honesty. Then anything goes. For, honesty and dishonesty are treated as equals. And that arbitrary standard is exactly what all professional mystics and neocheaters need to survive.

Theists use that same arbitrary, anti-intellectual standard in asserting the existence of God. Unable to back their assertions with proof, they expect nonbelievers to prove that God does not exist. But that proving-a-negative ploy is intellectually untenable and undermines the protector of all honesty, which is: **the burden of proof always rests on the one making an assertion or accusation.**

***

To exist, government bureaucracies must be destructive. For, by nature, they can produce nothing. Also, to grow, such bureaucracies must usurp power by destroying values. For they cannot earn power by producing values. Moreover, value destruction requires little competence or effort. Thus, by necessity, value destruction is the modus operandi of most government bureaucracies and agencies — the most virulent being the IRS, FDA, INS, EPA, OSHA. To conceal their destructions, they masterfully use non-sequitur facts and mystical ploys to justify their attacks on producers and usurpation of values from everyone. But, for the first time in 2000 years, their fake empires are about to be collapsed and eliminated by Neo-Tech. [Re: November-3rd Trap]

Often, only a trained scientist familiar with the scientific method can identify the neocheater's dishonest use of facts and information. Without Neo-Tech, most people have no way to discern the dishonesty of neocheaters. And without Neo-Tech, most people must simply accept the neocheater's usurpation of values.

The most invasively destructive of all bureaucracies is the Internal Revenue Service (IRS). No one in that organization, from top to bottom, has the right to carry out in any way his or her immoral activities [Re: Concept 25, Neo-Tech Reference Encyclopedia]. All their actions are directed toward destruction — toward threats and force to usurp the earnings and property of producers. Those confiscated earnings are then dissipated by the neocheating politicians and bureaucrats as they strive to expand their power by continually expanding government. ...Neo-Tech will end all their destructions.[Re: November-3rd Trap]

By usurping property and earnings from productive individuals and redistributing them to nonproductive individuals, politicians glorify themselves as "humanitarian benefactors". Those neocheating politicians and powercrats can perpetuate their destructive machinations only by continually draining the producers. All that will soon end. [Re: The November-3rd Trap]

Neo-Tech Advantage #91
SUICIDE OPTION
In addition to the false guilt laid on value producers by the mystics and neocheaters, a subtle psychological block inhibits many producers from

Patrick J. W. JFE-315

On my first reading I became so enthralled by the Neo Tech transcripts that I began skipping the letters.
On the second reading I read all the letters and quotes. In fact I read some more than once. Its amazing how one can relate to the same experiences and emotions of many other people, male or female, before and especially after reading Neo-Tech. I-V.

It is easy to read Neo-Tech II especially after reading the translations of Aristotles' Ethics. However it is difficult to admit one has been duped for over forty years, but the honesty of Neo-Tech and the letters helped me face the true facts. Thank you all.

I thought I lived an exciting happy life but now I am so excited and happy, as never before with undreamed of goals ahead especially Human Biological Immortality. Once again.

Thank you all very much indeed

Jeremias P. CB-106

Dear Mr. Flint,
    Neo Tech is the "Bible" of prosperity and happiness in life. Before reading the <u>Neo Tech I-V Manuscripts</u> my life was dominated by neocheaters, mystics, and the God concept. Neo Tech has opened my eyes and freed me from the grip of the mystics and recognize the Neocheaters.

experiencing their earned happiness. That block is the subconscious fear that sometime in life one must lose his or her happiness...that someday one must endure terminal suffering and pain.

Even without biological immortality, that notion is not valid. A terminal loss of happiness never has to be endured. So long as a productive person has some degree of freedom and choice, that person can always maintain and expand happiness. If circumstances totally beyond one's control forever eliminate all possibilities of maintaining and expanding happiness (e.g., a no-escape situation from a terror-totalitarian torture death or the final stages of a painful, terminal illness), the individual has the right and option to avoid a terminal existence of unhappiness and pain. That right and option is suicide.

Suicide can be a valid, rational choice when suffering a high-pain terminal illness or when in an absolutely-no-escape, slavery/torture/death situation. But more important is the psychological impact of realizing that life never needs to become *permanently* unhappy, for one always has that final, guiltless option of suicide.

Suicide is every individual's personal right and final option. By fully and guiltlessly realizing that suicide is always available, a person is freer to live more fully in traveling an open-ended journey toward ever-expanding happiness. By accepting the concept of the suicide option, one *never* needs to fear the permanent loss of happiness.

The suicide option should *never* be misconstrued as an escape or option when life is difficult, or seems hopeless, or even when one seems to lose everything, including one's invaluable, irreplaceable romantic-love partner. With consistent rational choices, a person can always experience increasing happiness again, no matter how difficult or painful the immediate situation seems. The *only* two situations in which suicide is a rational option for the productive individual are (1) a no-hope, high-suffering, terminal-illness situation, and (2) an absolutely no-escape, no-hope slavery/torture/death situation.*

Ironically, suicide is also the only viable, rational option for those irredeemably evil neocheaters who murder others for their "causes", livelihoods, and power (e.g., all murderous dictators and terrorists as Castro, Idi Amin, Gorbachev, Qaddafi, Pol Pot, Yasir Arafat, Ariel Sharon, Abu Nidal, Menachen Begin, Sinn Fein leaders, Khomeini).

Neo-Tech Advantage #92
ANTI-OBSCENITY LAWS, CENSORSHIP, AND THE SUPREME COURT

Despite the sexual errors projected by the "Playboy" philosophy that can lead to impotence and frigidity (see Neo-Tech Advantage #19), the Playboy Corporation made important contributions to both individual and

---

*An absolutely no-hope slavery situation could exist only after all escape, resistance, and guerrilla warfare options were irrevocably exhausted (if that is possible).

Billy H.   R-378

I have just completed reading the information package on your neo-tech discovery and feel overwhelmed with the simplicity of life, as opposed to the tread-mill I've been on for about the past forty years.

I feel wide awake and alive for the first time. I'm 53 years of age, and feel like the dawn of my life has just arrived. Your works will be read again and still again until I fully understand its entire content to reap full benefits. The practical way you sum up the nature and needs of humanity is the only logical way that we could ever (can ever) have healthy, productive life styles and high, self-esteem.

In the past I've been as guilty as anyone else in accepting mysticism and external-authority, all the while not fully accepting the reasons given for those causes, or necessarily believing in them, but going along thinking it the socially acceptable thing to do.

Those days are no more, thanks to you.

I'm middle class, have been productive all my adult life, have raised 4 children who are productive, still have the same wife of 36 years, have a good job, and finally starting to pull ahead financially. I'm also still supporting a lot of non-producers and their "Hyper Causes".

I already have embarked on my journey to recognize the neocheaters, and feel strongly that never again will I be cheated out of the earnings of my productiveness. Neither will I personally ever neocheat except neocheaters.

sexual freedom [Re: Concept 37, Neo-Tech Reference Encyclopedia]. "Playboy's" contributions come not only through its open, guiltless views of pleasure and sex expressed in its magazine, but also through the Playboy Foundation and its monthly magazine feature, The Playboy Forum. That feature provides constant public exposure to the ongoing government-neocheating ploy of usurping power through oppression of private sexual activities and other victimless "crimes".

Perusing any issue of the Forum starkly reveals that even in this sexually-liberated era, individuals all over the United States are being arrested, harassed, humiliated, injured, tried, fined, and sent to jail for private, consenting sexual acts. The following list provides several examples of sexual oppression as taken from a randomly selected, six-page Forum feature in "Playboy" magazine:

* Couple out camping privately engage in oral sex in a secluded area of the woods. Both arrested by Texas Sheriff for sodomy. Both faced jail sentences of 2-15 years for their private, harmless love act.
* Four young people arrested for private nude bathing. Sheriff refused to let them dress and forced them to travel nude to the courthouse for arrest.
* In Sheboygan, Wisconsin, a couple was fined $100 each for engaging in sexual intercourse while not being married.
* In Machias, Maine, a man was fined $35 plus court costs for engaging in sexual intercourse while not being married.
* Man released by a California Supreme Court order after serving five years of a *life* sentence for indecent exposure.
* A 1600 member organization of the Catholic Priest Association asked a Catholic bishop who defended birth-control pills to resign because of his "monstrous views". The Catholic organization declared that the bishop failed to "show the purity of Catholic doctrine", and failed to "rise above the murk and filth of modern man's sex life".
* A Canadian man charged with rape and gross indecency admitted at his trial that he had performed cunnilingus and intercourse with a consenting woman. Before the jury retired, 68-year-old Judge Campbell Grant said of cunnilingus, "Well, can you think of a more grossly indecent act?...Frankly, gentlemen, I had to get the dictionary to know what it was about. I venture to say that most of you are the same." He went on to declare that "a dirty, filthy practice such as this that is resorted to by no one but sexual perverts is surely an infringement of the criminal code." The jury found the accused not guilty of rape, but guilty of gross indecency. He was sentenced to three years in the penitentiary.

A book published by the Playboy Press, "Sex American Style", cites many government laws that can and do jail innocent people for harmless,

Sylvia S. J-166, AUSTRALIA

truly fascinating; I started reading the Instructions at lunch-time, had a quick look at the last chapters of volume I, and then skipped here and there through volume II, and it was all I could do to put it down until I could resume it later on that evening. When I did settle down to study it properly, at about 6-30 p.m., <u>eight hours</u> fled by, and I would have still been reading if my eyes hadn't been burning! I staggered off to bed at about 3 a.m. with my mind full of new insights, and more knowledge about who <u>I</u> am than I have ever acquired at one sitting.

Again, I can't wait to get stuck into volume II <u>again</u>! It's like taking a handful of pep-pills! I must confess that some of the concepts are almost scary, and I'm not sure that I agree with all of them in total. I'm not even sure that I even want to be the kind of "Neo-Tech" person that Dr. Wallace describes. But that, in <u>my eyes, only</u> goes to show how much fear and self-denigration have been bred into me over the 50 years of my life. It is said that "you can't teach an old dog new tricks," (one of the many ancient catch-phrases that most of us have accepted as "true", which Dr. Wallace warns against), but he has just taught me to think of myself as a human being, who <u>can</u> and <u>will</u> be taught a few new tricks, and to stop identifying myself as that "old dog". Hell, I don't even <u>like</u> dogs!

I was interested to find out whether I was suffering from "Growth Death", convinced that I <u>was</u>, but was most pleasantly surprised, on going through the check-list of Growth-Death indicators, to find that I am positively flourishing in the Growth department. Then I had a go at the sentence-completion techniques, very interesting indeed. I never dreamed I had so many repressed emotions! It was like a voyage of discovery, reading over my completions to those sentences. I was almost asleep when I did those, but the answers I got awakened me up again. I was too tired to think up "dishonest" completions, and really did put down the first thing that my mind came up with.

continued next page

mutually consenting sex acts. That book includes articles by Hugh M. Hefner; "The Legal Enforcement of Morality" and "Tyranny Under the Law".

Three decades ago, comic Lenny Bruce, despite his existentialistic errors that eventually killed him, made a major contribution toward breaking the oppressive religious/government grip of sexual-oppression laws and censorship. To stop his defiance of "moral" authority, the government directly abetted the death of Lenny Bruce.

Hustler magazine, however disgusting, also played an important, front-trench role in buffeting the forces of sexual oppression and censorship. The government/religious axis in their failing trial designed to jail Hustler's founder and publisher, Larry Flynt, inspired the assassination meant to kill or cripple him: As he walked before the courthouse in Atlanta, Georgia, bullets severed his spinal cord, paralyzing him for life.

Over a decade ago, a nude-streaking fad broke across the United States. That fad was a timely, counter-response to the oppressive Supreme-Court anti-obscenity decision a year earlier. The motives for streaking and the effects on the streakers' self-esteem were probably unhealthy in most cases. But such overt, widespread flouting of sexual authoritarianism helped undermine the enforcement of oppressive censorship and anti-obscenity laws. Nude streaking broke the anti-obscenity momentum that was ominously building in the United States from that Supreme-Court decision. But the anti-obscenity forces of religious/political neocheaters are now trying to reassert their oppressive powers granted to them by the conservative justices of the United States Supreme Court.

The United States Supreme Court was meant to function as a principled, philosophical body designed to protect individual rights.* But recent decisions on obscenity and pornography have been void of principle in ignoring the concept of individual rights. An earlier Supreme Court (Memoires vs. Massachusetts) stated the following criterion for pornography: "A book cannot be proscribed unless it is found to be utterly without redeeming social value." That criterion ignored the principles of individual rights and property rights while opening the way for people to be jailed on the basis of some other person's judgment of the "social" merit of their work.

Seven years later, the Supreme-Court Miller vs. California case negated

---

*Throughout the checkered history of the United States Supreme Court, one finds many disgraceful exceptions to its role as a principled body for protecting individual rights. Early in this century, for example, the United States Supreme Court favored explicit censorship by removing films from the protection of the First Amendment (free speech). The court then decreed that since films were made for profit, they did not deserve constitutional protection. In their decision, the justices conveniently ignored the fact that books and newspapers were also made for profit.

I have always admired people who controlled their emotions, and have always thought less of myself for being unable, at times, to keep mine in check. But Dr. Wallace, in one simple sentence: "Emotions are neither good nor bad," has caused me to see the whole emotional side of myself in a completely new light. That really amazes me is that I had never seen the <u>simplicity</u> of that concept, even by accident, in all these years. It is just like being separated from almost the whole of self-understanding by a wall of thinnest tissue-paper for years, and then suddenly realising that the wall is there, and is the only obstacle to all I have been seeking. More than that, on the other side of that wall are riches not only of self-understanding, but of hundreds of other kinds which I am only now about to discover. The wall has dissolved, in a few minutes of those <u>fateful</u> 8 hours between Sept. 26th & 27th, 1984, and <u>I'm about to live my life</u> among the riches it has concealed.

Years ago, I read Ayn Rand's "The Fountainhead", "Atlas Shrugged", and "The Virtue of Selfishness", which contains some essays by Nathaniel Branden if I remember correctly. Rand's philosophy of Rational Self-Interest had quite a profound effect on my ways of thinking, which I suppose must have influenced more of my subsequent activity than I realised. But, having been made aware of an alternative to the lifestyle of guilt, altruism, irrational values, etc., which is thrust upon most of us before we have learnt to think for ourselves, I was no more able to use it than a sheep could use a knitting-machine. I wasn't even as integrated with myself as the sheep: I wasn't even using the wool on my own back, as it were, until someone came and shore it off. I was consistently being shorn of <u>everything</u>, by people I really had no time for, and instead of cooling me down, it was getting me increasingly over-heated. And <u>still</u> I couldn't find the key to applying what I had learnt during my adult years. Now I think I have found it, in Neo-Tech. It is simply that Dr. Wallace has explored much further, and explained his findings in much greater depth, than those audacious and brave pioneers of Rational Self-Interest, and coupled it with the exposure and analysis of Neocheating.

continued next page

individual rights in determining the following criteria to *criminally* convict for victimless pornography: "(a) whether the average person applying contemporary community standards would find that the work, taken as a whole, appeals to the prurient interest...(b) whether the work depicts or describes, in a patently offensive way, sexual conduct specifically defined by the applicable state law, and (c) whether the work, taken as a whole, lacks serious literary, artistic, political, or scientific value."

That Supreme Court ruling left the individual unprotected and at the mercy of any judge, prosecutor, police force, or community. Any of those forces can now attack, prosecute, and jail an individual under arbitrary standards such as (1) contemporary community standards, or (2) "offensive" as defined by a state law, or (3) if the work lacks serious literary, artistic, political, or scientific value. In other words, anyone who disagrees with the arbitrary standards of the empowered authorities (judge, police, community leaders) can potentially be jailed through current anti-obscenity laws. Such nonobjective law is a major step toward censorship, which is the precursor to totalitarianism.

The above Supreme Court majority opinion, which abridges individual rights, was written by the conservative Chief Justice and supported by the other four conservative justices in a 5 to 4 decision. Only Justice Douglas identified the issue of individual rights in his brilliant dissenting opinion:

"The idea that the First Amendment permits punishment for ideas that are 'offensive' to the particular judge or jury sitting in judgment is astounding. No greater leveler of speech or literature has ever been designed. To give the power to the censor, as we do today, is to make a sharp and radical break with the traditions of a free society. The First Amendment was not fashioned as a vehicle for dispensing tranquilizers to the people. Its prime function was to keep debate open to 'offensive' as well as to 'staid' people. The tendency throughout history has been to subdue the individual and to exalt the power of government. The use of the standard 'offensive' gives authority to government that cuts the very vitals out of the First Amendment. As is intimated by the Court's opinion, the materials before us may be garbage, but so is much of what is said in political campaigns, in the daily press, on TV or over the radio. By reason of the First Amendment — and solely because of it — speakers and publishers have not been threatened or subdued because their thoughts and ideas may be 'offensive' to some."

The conservative Chief Justice and his conservative associates on the Supreme Court shifted from the principle of protecting individual rights to an arbitrary, undefinable standard of "social good". Hitler, Stalin, and Mao also subjugated individual rights to their standards of "social good". Those arbitrary standards eventually included killing tens of millions of their own citizens for the "social good".

I always suspected that all those "Positive Thinking," "Transactional Analysis," "Pulling Your Own Strings" books were lacking in something: now I know they are lacking in practically everything, at least everything that I was searching for. Thank you, Dr. Wallace.

Stephen E. R-2083, ENGLAND

THIS IS ONE WAR THAT THE GOOD, HONEST AND INNOCENT CHILDREN OF THE WORLD MUST WIN. I KNOW THAT I AM PREPARED TO FIGHT!

I WISH LONG LIFE, PEACE, HAPPINESS, AND MENTAL AND PHYSICAL PROSPERITY TO DR WALLACE AND HIS 'NEO-TECH' COLLABORATORS

Eric D. C-93

John Flint/
Dr Wallace:
Just a quick note of appreciation for the Neo-Tech information package. It has been worth every cent and more. It has clarified many of my own thoughts and made me acutely aware of the fallacies that most people labor under. Even those productive people whom I have always looked to with respect seem unaware of the tactics of Neo-cheating politicians and the detrimental effects their Altruistic preaching has. The effects of Neo-Tech can't be felt too soon.

Neo-Tech Advantage #93
1. FAILURE-TO-JUDGE SYNDROME,
2. ERRORS IN JUDGMENT, AND
3. SEGMENTED JUDGMENT

A central theme of today's existentialist culture is "do not judge others". The neocheating media, social "intellectuals", and theologians continually tout, both implicitly and explicitly, the themes "do not judge others", "there are no absolute morals, no rights or wrongs", "everything is relative". Neocheaters have strong motivations for sowing themes of nonknowing and nonjudgment. Their livelihoods depend on keeping others from knowing and judging the parasitism and destruction inflicted by professional mystics and neocheaters onto society. The continuous campaign to repress moral judgment depends largely on the specious non sequitur of pointing to various erroneous judgments and then implying that such errors are inherent in all judgments. Therefore, they dishonestly conclude that all moral judgments are wrong, unfair, or harmful. From that conclusion, they compound their dishonesty by further concluding that moral judgments should never be made. Moreover, armed with specious egalitarian slogans or Biblical parables, those neocheaters, especially media journalists, malign or castigate those who have the courage and confidence to make honest moral judgments about value destroyers. While, at the same time, those same neocheaters constantly make viciously dishonest moral judgments about their enemies — the value producers.

How are valid moral judgments made? Such judgments are made by using the biological nature and well-being of the conscious organism as the moral standard. With that objective standard, all human actions can be consistently and validly judged by acquiring adequate facts and knowledge:

1. Only volitional actions involving conscious choices can be morally judged. All other actions are amoral.

2. A volitional action is moral, for example, if the action is beneficial to the conscious organism. Likewise, a volitional action is immoral if the action is harmful to the conscious organism. Or more simply, *if a volitional action is rationally "good for me", it is moral; or if a volitional action is irrationally "bad for me", it is immoral.*

3. The ability and willingness to make moral judgments are necessary to make sound decisions and function effectively. The more important the personal or business decision, the more important is the need to make accurate moral judgments. In turn, such judgments are crucial for making the correct decisions needed for abiding prosperity, long-range happiness, and romantic love.

Since making moral judgments is necessary for quality survival, a person must be aware of the possible traps and errors in making such judgments. Some of the traps and errors are those that the nonjudgment advocates take out of context to support their harangues that moral judgments should be avoided.

Three common judgment traps or errors are listed below:

1. Erroneous or inadequate information to make a valid or accurate judgment: This is the most obvious and common cause of judgment errors. Everyone is subject to this error. But that does *not* preclude certainty over moral issues and judgments. The central argument of the

John N CB-102, Nigeria

Since I got my Neotech Information Package, I can't stop thanking you for this brilliant work.

A day cannot go by without my grasping & integration of the entire concept of Neotech discovery.

Despite other better changes I have experienced, I now realize that the cause of my absolute poverty is due to my support for mysticism, this motivated me to resign my job with them for positive changes.

Furthermore I have recognized my consciousness as the only valid authority to guide my life and actions. I must obtain all books & works put out by I & O Publishing Company

Gordon C.   R-1908

After over 70 years on this planet its amazing how one changes their thinking after studying Neo-Tech. How could the world be so stupid for so long.

nonjudgment neocheaters is that since no one can know everything or be error free, no one can be certain about anything, especially moral issues.* That argument is false. A person can be absolutely certain if given sufficient facts and context to validly measure against the axioms of objective reality. For example, questions of omniscience (knowing everything) and infallibility (being totally free of errors) do not enter into one's certainty of the axiomatic fact that two plus two equals four. The certainty of that fact is independent of anyone's thoughts or opinions or of any culture, society, or time in history. And that fact also holds true with certainty in other worlds and other universes. Indeed, that fact would hold true if no conscious life ever existed anywhere.**

In the normal context, therefore, anyone can be absolutely certain about the judgment and knowledge that two plus two equals four without fear of error or contradiction. Likewise, without being omniscient or infallible, a person can be absolutely certain that one will not be struck by a car while

---

*The certainty issue is a popular non-sequitur gimmick among mystics and anti-judgment neocheaters. They assert (often with ironic certainty) that since man cannot be certain about anything, he cannot know anything. If that were so, which it is not, then all judgments and reason itself would be invalid. But professional mystics and neocheaters must constantly promote the false notions that reason is impotent and moral judgments are invalid. ...They must obfuscate reason and judgment to keep their own destructions from being recognized and judged by themselves and others.

**Certain out-of-context, non-sequitur anomalies are used by neocheaters and mystics to falsely invalidate axiomatic facts such as two plus two equals four. They point to the mixing of two quarts of water with two quarts of alcohol, which yields a mixture of less than four quarts. But that occurs because of certain, known intermolecular-bonding forces between water and alcohol. Such physical-bonding facts have nothing more to do with mathematical facts than if one tosses two parts of sodium metal into two parts of water to produce a fiery explosion and a caustic mess that does not equal four. But, ironically, both of those reactions can be precisely predicted and understood because of the exact, absolute nature of mathematics. ...Or the neocheaters and mystics point to various examples of relativistic, noneuclidean mathematics or quantum mechanics that seem to contradict standard mathematics or physics. Such illusionary contradictions arise only because those facts have nothing to do with standard mathematics or physics. Yet, those facts are dishonestly used out of context to create false illusions of contradiction.

Gary G.   R-337

FORTUNATELY FOR ME, ALMOST ALL MY LIFE I'VE BEEN HONESTLY HAPPY. AFTER READING NEO-TECH II I KNOW WHY. I'VE BEEN PRODUCTIVE, HONEST, AND REALISTIC, AN ATHEIST, AND ENJOYED ALL THE PLEASURES OF RESPONSIBLE SEX. IN RECENT YEARS I'VE GROWN TO DESPISE GOVERNMENT.

Louis G.   R-1498

Your book has straightened me to live a better life and to stay away from people that have been using me and my family. I am already getting ahead financially and I am excited as I have never been before. I know what paths to take from now on. Thank you.

Dorothy S.   R-1759

I have read Neo-Tech and found it to be very exciting. I will no longer be manipulated by others because I now have a new way of thinking and evaluating conversations and situations. Thank you, Dr. Wallace, and I hope for your continued success.

Sincerely,

riding in an airplane at 30,000 feet. A neocheater might try to invalidate that certainty by positing the non sequitur that someone could smuggle a mini car aboard, unveil it, drive down the aisle, and strike someone.

With neocheaters and their non sequiturs dismissed, one can know with certainty the facts of objective reality on which abiding prosperity, happiness, and romantic love are based as identified by Neo-Tech. For, those facts of objective reality have always existed throughout the universe and will forever exist with certainty. And that certainty exists independent of consciousness and without requiring omniscience or infallibility by anyone. The function of human consciousness is not to "create" various realities, which is mysticism, but to identify and integrate the one and only reality as it resides anchored in existence. Identifying objective reality is the survival mechanism of conscious beings. For those identifications are the basis of all rational judgments, beneficial actions, and rational successes.

Since no one is omniscient or infallible, everyone is subject to specific errors. But that vulnerability to errors has no bearing on knowing objective reality or being able to make moral judgments with certainty. For example, with inadequate information and judgment errors, a person can temporarily choose the wrong romantic-love partner. But, at the same time, he or she can still know with certainty the objective standards needed for a valid romantic-love relationship. With that certainty, a person can more quickly recognize and correct such judgment errors. In other words, with adequate objective knowledge, a person can make moral judgments with certainty without being omniscient or infallible.

A person can confidently proceed through life knowing that moral and character judgment can be performed with certainty. But again, that person must be aware of those areas subject to error because of inaccurate or incomplete knowledge or information. By always keeping the mind open to new information and being prepared to correct errors, the damage of judgment errors is minimized. All errors cause some damage, if only to waste a person's time. By nature, one is always responsible for and must bear the consequences of his or her actions and errors, innocent or not.

2. Infatuation: This is a subtler and often a more dangerous judgment error, especially when it occurs without realizing the error. Infatuation is the focusing on a single attractive or desirable characteristic of another person and then considering the total person as that one positive attribute. Infatuation is not only an unfair burden placed on the person being judged, but can lead to long-range disillusionment and pain for the person making the erroneous judgment. The infatuation-judgment error is a common "true-love-turns-sour" theme so often used in movies, novels, and magazine fiction. Infatuation is also the judgment error that delivers undeserved adulation to charismatic politicians, evangelists, and other neocheaters.

Larry V. C-113

Neo-Tech has: 1) given me the courage to start my own business and double my income and 2) made me more relaxed in social settings, which, for some reason, has made me more attractive to the opposite sex.

I could write paragraphs on what you've done for me inside and out, but let me sum it up with "THANKS."

Steven H. R-6033

Have abandoned my belief in God, which prior to NEO-TECH would have been unthinkable. Am beginning to enjoy the benefits of self-responsibility, self determination, & rational thought. Realize now that biological immortality is both possible and desireable. Although it takes time for my goals to be realized I can forsee my future & prosperity. Man's greatest gift to himself and society — the honest, rational, productive individual.

3. **Reverse Infatuation**: This is perhaps the most subtle form of judgment error. Still, reverse infatuation is a common error that can cause losses of potential values and happiness. Reverse infatuation involves the focusing on a negative characteristic of an individual and then considering that total person as that one negative attribute. That judgment error can be blinding, depriving, and unjust in obscuring areas of earned values and worth in other individuals. Even minor reverse-infatuation puts unjust penalties on the person being judged. While valid criticisms about an individual should be identified and expressed when appropriate, the criticism should explicitly focus on those specific issues, not on the whole person. Reverse-infatuation is constantly used as a grossly unfair, dishonest technique by media people as well as by politicians, clergymen, and academics to discredit value producers and their products, businesses, and ideas.

***

THE SEGMENTED-JUDGMENT METHOD

Segmented judging is a method to decrease judgment errors. This method provides a more fair, accurate, and valuable way to judge individuals, especially those important to one's life. This method is particularly important for judging potential romantic-love partners.

Segmented judging consists of two essential parts: First, the recognition that people are many-faceted combinations of complex character traits — usually combinations consisting mainly of objectively positive traits with some (often hidden) negative traits.* And second, objective judgments require a breaking down of those various character traits into as many separate components as possible.

Once that breakdown is done, one can make more fair and accurate judgments by weighing specific positive traits against specific negative traits ("positive to me" values versus "negative to me" values**). The extent that

---

*Value destroyers such as politicians and religious leaders are less complex than a value producer. For, they have more narrow or limited, anti-life characteristics. Moreover, all neocheaters have essentially the same destructive character. They differ mainly in their dishonest styles and the deceptions they project in concealing their harmful actions.

**To the extent that personal "to-me" values contradict objective values is the extent that one is judging on erroneous philosophical or moral premises. Segmented judgment is thus not only helpful for judging others, but is helpful for judging one's own values.

Not all "to-me" values, however, can be measured against objective moral standards. Many "to-me" values are personal-preference values that have

(footnote continued on next page)

Terry P.   R-2245

Dear Friend,
    Since I read Neo-Tech my purposes in life became very clear. And I am very happy realizing them As a result, I have a great deal of confidence and "guts".
    (over)

I am sure that Neo-Tech will be regarded as a "Classic" in history because it honestly addresses the issues that are most important to the human individual.
    I am having a ball —

Tammy L.   R-1735

Since discovering Neo-Tech I've truly begun to realize my own potential to do whatever I really want to. I now have a better perspective on life and people. Now I know better what to believe in, what to know and what I still need to learn.

the positive values outweigh the negative values is the extent one makes a positive *moral judgment*. Similarly, the extent that "positive to me" values outweigh the "negative to me" disvalues is the extent one makes a positive *personal-value judgment*.

During a person's life, many of the personal "to me" values can change. But objective moral values are constant and *never* change.

The most useful and accurate method to judge a potential romantic-love partner (or any person) is on a segmented "value-scale" basis. One should not judge the whole of an individual on any specific aspect of his or her character, personality, actions, words, or behavior. Exclusively focusing on specific aspects of a person yields distorted, infatuation-type judgments. Instead, one should judge an individual by placing all the known characteristics and qualities of that person on either the "value to me" side or the "disvalue to me" side of the balance scale [Re: Table 58, Neo-Tech Reference Encyclopedia]. The person is then judged by the extent that the scale tips to the value side or to the disvalue side.

The evaluation of each person should always be kept open. In accumulating more experience or information about any person, the balance tilt can change. Growth, change, or deterioration of either the person doing the judging or the person being judged can cause the "value scale" to tilt more or less in one direction or even to switch to the other direction.

The "value to me" standard is the most reliable, valuable way for an individual to judge the personal value of another individual. The direction and extent the "value scale" tilts is influenced by the personal-value system of the individual making the judgment. For the value weights often depend on personal wants, goals, needs and thus will vary from individual to individual.

The same value scale can be used to measure the moral value of any individual. Unlike the subjective nature of many personal values, moral values are objective, definable, unchanging absolutes. [Re: Table 58, Neo-Tech Reference Encyclopedia]. ...*Personal values* are both objective and subjective, thus vary according to personal tastes and emotions. But *moral values* are objective and absolute, thus never vary.

(Footnote continued from previous page)
no bearing on moral issues. For example, differences in attraction to various physical or personality aspects of another person or preferences towards different careers, recreational activities, tastes, intellectual interests, and appreciation of art and music usually (but not always) have no moral implications. Many personal values are merely preferences and tastes that develop from past experiences, interests, and motivations that are not grounded in right or wrong issues, but arise from the uniqueness of the individual and his or her past experiences and development.

Ejesi E. CB-110, Nigeria

I have gone from one posture to another due to lack of self knowledge and belief in non-existent powers, drifted from one religion to another one secret society to another and I was gradually moving to the grave when Neo-Tech accosted and rescued me and today I live revived. Thank you.

Although, I have gone to train as Computer Operator/Programmer before the arrival of my Neo-Tech package, this has successfully kept me ahead of every other competitors. My performance marvels my fellow students and the lecturers. I have given up my former ambition of becoming a lawyer and subsequently a politician. I have no parasite friends again, no more bad habits because I want to live forever.

I believe Neo-Tech is the greatest piece of work in philosophy in this planet after Aristotle. It is a masterpiece indeed.

My fellow Africans need Neo-Tech more than all other peoples of the world and I wish to indicate here my willingness to assist the center in any way it thinks necessary in the efforts to achieve biological immortality.

I vote for you and your co-producers, you are a great bunch.

Cheers.

Neo-Tech Advantage #94
OBJECTIVE THINKING VS. EMOTIONAL THINKING

Positive emotions deliver pleasure and happiness. Negative emotions provide warnings that something is wrong. Thus, negative emotions and negative experiences should *not* be repressed* [Re: Concept 54, Neo-Tech Reference Encyclopedia]. Avoiding emotional repression involves consciously and guiltlessly feeling one's own emotions in order to know and control them. That honest, open dealing with emotions is necessary for (1) resisting harmful mystical actions, (2) building mental health, and most important, (3) experiencing psychuous pleasures, romantic love, and abiding happiness.

Also, openly knowing and experiencing one's own emotions are necessary to distinguish those emotions from the independent world of objective reality. That, in turn, is necessary to avoid unhealthy mystical actions. For basing judgments and conclusions on emotions rather than on reality causes harmful mystical actions. Such mystical actions, in turn, diminish the prosperity, well-being, and happiness of all human beings. If important judgments or actions are mystically based on emotions, then grave errors with harmful consequences will result.

A person can react to emotions in two ways: (1) The mystical, erroneous, harmful reaction that ranges from repressing emotions to overtly injecting emotions into the decision-making process. And (2), the nonmystical, beneficial reaction that recognizes and freely feels emotions, but then separates them from reality in order to make reasoned, logical judgments undistorted by emotions, whims, or feelings [Re: Table 59, Neo-Tech Reference Encyclopedia].

Because no one is infallible or omniscient, errors are always possible. But errors from honest, *objectively* based thinking are less frequent, less severe, and easier to correct than are errors from mystical, *emotionally* based thinking.

---

*Emotions never should be repressed, but at times emotions can and should be suppressed:

Suppression involves being fully conscious of the emotion, but because of the circumstances, the emotion is temporarily set aside for experiencing at a more appropriate time. Suppression is a useful, healthy method for avoiding harmful mystical reactions based on emotions.

Repression involves trying to deny an emotion by permanently forcing it out of the conscious mind. That act is a mystical distortion of reality, for emotions are a real, undeniable part of a person. By repressing an emotion out of the conscious mind, the emotion is pushed into the subconscious to remain buried. And accumulating buried, negative emotions can harm both one's psychological and intellectual well-being. For those festering, buried emotions can interfere with a person's ability to accurately perceive reality in making effective judgments and profitable decisions.

Abelardo S.   R346

NEO-TECH IS A VERY POWERFULL THINKING TOOL. TREMENDOUS POWER IS GETTING TO ME EVERYDAY AS I USE IT. IT HAS SAVED ME A LOT OF OTHERWISE WRONG DECISIONS SINCE READING NEO TECH I-II

P.S. My copy of the Neo-Tech I and II has given me a lot of information, which I have been using everyday since I have gone over the volumes. It has proved very valuable to me; it has gained for me more persuasive power as a practising attorney. If your company has other materials along the Neo-Tech discovery, I will be glad to order them if you let me know what they are.

Gerald W.   C-86

I hate dealing with "mail order" companies... . Not only did your company acknowledge, confirm, and provide me with a shipping schedule, my order was here today, the date it was to be mailed. Thank-you! It is a pleasure dealing with a company who does what they say they will do.

Neo-Tech Advantage #95
FOUR LEVELS OF COMMUNICATION

Four well-defined levels of communication exist. The appropriateness of each level depends on the circumstances as illustrated below:

LEVELS OF HUMAN COMMUNICATION

Level of Communication	Description
Impersonal/Automatic Exchange of familiar or automatic phrases (e.g., how are you, good morning)	Smooth, pleasant, cheerful, efficient, noninvolvement method of dealing with people.
Impersonal/Factual Reporting facts.	Efficient, noninvolvement method of transmitting information to people.
Impersonal/Personal Reporting or communicating one's own ideas, thoughts, and judgments.	Can range from completely impersonal to deeply personal.
Personal Communicating personal feelings and thoughts.	Personal to deeply personal. Communication requirement for romantic love. Most intensely experienced with an individual who is of great personal value to oneself.

Many books on sex, love, marriage, and personality development imply that impersonal communication is inferior or undesirable. They further imply that highly personal communication is a superior, more honest form of communication toward which everyone should strive. Such implications are false and out of context:

Openly revealing one's deep personal self to everyone diminishes self-esteem. That, in turn, militates against one's best interests and happiness. Nevertheless, many authors, gurus, and "therapists" advocate revealing one's personal and private self to all comers. Those "total-openness, let-it-all-hang-out" advocates are promoting an egalitarian recipe. That recipe calls for breaking everyone's ego by sharing all personal values and emotions with all comers. Such ego-breaking recipes are often well-disguised, downhill roads to impotence and unhappiness.

Those advocating ego-breaking, emotional egalitarianism usually do so under false labels of openness and honesty. But the opposite is true. Failure to discriminate with whom one shares his or her private personal feelings destroys the potential for experiencing a close, genuinely open, romantic-love relationship with another human being. Instead, an egalitarian "total openness" to everyone is a cheap giveaway of an individual's most precious

George M. R-750

Best book I have ever read. This is my 3rd complete reading of Neo-Tech II and it will not be my last. So far, I am using it in dealing with customers in my company. I fully support your research in biological immortality.

Trevor J. R-1475

MASTERPIECE OF RATIONAL THINKING

Much gratitude is due Dr. Wallace for the thoroughness, superb organization, and uncompromising objectivity which are the rule in his monumental work.

Edward R. R-732

After reading the concepts, it has become clear to me that the pages of Neo-Tech I-V hold the secrets of life — a happy, guilt-free, and perhaps eternal life on earth. I feel that everyone on this planet should read and follow these concepts. If this knowledge were acquired by every honest, productive person, in a very short time a world wide rebellion against all authorities would occur, bringing the freedom and happiness we all have a right to enjoy.

possession — one's own personal, private self. Nothing squelches romantic love more completely than a Leo Buscaglia's love-all, share-all egalitarian approach.

A person can and should be sincere and honest to everyone without sharing his or her private self or emotions with everyone. In fact, when a person does share his or her private self with everyone else, that person's sincerity and motives become questionable.

An objectively beneficial level of communication exists for every type of human relationship. [Re: Table 61, Neo-Tech Reference Encyclopedia]. Only within a romantic relationship in which the partners love and value each other in their private universe can the full range of physical and psychological sharing be experienced without diminishing self-esteem. Within the romantic relationship lies the full scope of psychuous pleasures: the combination of full-range sexuality with the freedom to fearlessly share any aspect of one's self...any thought, feeling, fantasy, emotion — good or bad, rational or irrational. Thus, a person can let go completely to share and guiltlessly experience any aspect of one's body, mind, emotion, imagination with his or her romantic-love partner.

Within a romantic-love relationship, one can freely share *any* aspect of one's self and life. But one need not share *every* aspect. A person always has the guiltless right to privacy to any area of his or her life, even within the closest, most open and honest romantic-love relationship. Total honesty does not require total revealing all of one's private self. Indeed, absolute and total sharing of one's self and psyche involves losing the most profound essence of privacy. That loss, in turn, diminishes the sense of "I" and one's self-esteem. Retaining the essence of personal privacy is not an act of repression, inhibition, dishonesty, or lack of openness, but is a self-respect preservation of an individual's inherent right to privacy.

To experience psychuous pleasures through romantic love requires genuine self-esteem (valuing of one's own self). Beyond the romantic-love relationship, self-esteem is diminished or even destroyed by indiscriminately sharing or by giving away one's personal, private self too cheaply. That loss of self-esteem can be especially severe (even leading to suicide) if one promiscuously gives away his or her private self just because socially-chic books, gurus, and media commentators falsely promulgate the need to be totally open with everyone. The most harmful of egalitarian neocheaters are the high visibility Leo Buscaglias who mystically promulgate the self-destructive, love-everyone concept. They imply that love, openness, and honesty are demonstrated by the giving of one's private self to all comers.

Valuing of one's private self does not mean holding back or manipulating communication in order to bargain for advantages. The sharing of oneself

Carson M. C-97, IRELAND

Dear Sirs,

I have studied all of the Neo-Tech II Manuscript, and I can accept it all. Neo-Tech is probably the greatest thing in the history of human evolution short of the development of consciousness.

I look forward to receiving <u>all</u> relevent information please, and co-operating <u>fully</u> with you. Let me help you in Northern Ireland, in Ireland, and in the United Kingdom. Neo-Tech could solve our otherwise intractable problems. We need the Salvation of Neo-Tech in Northern Ireland.

Kenneth S. C-107

On the first reading, I found that I could agree with many of the Neo-Tech concepts, but was not immediately aware of the interrelationships. On the second reading I was more aware of connecting links, then finally was convinced that there was a definite matrix to the Neo-Tech ideas.

Within a month, I have lost ten pounds, have almost completely stopped watching television (electronic news is a thing of the past to me) and have become intensely aware of Neo-Cheaters and Neo-Cheating in all aspects of life.

By using the Neo-Tech principles, I am studying the machinations of the stock market with new interest and insight.

is a personal choice and judgment. Such sharing with another person may occur quickly, even on initial contact if judgment responses trigger desires to move toward deeper personal or romantic possibilities. Chances should and must be taken on exploring potentially valuable relationships. Errors in judgment are often made. But minimum harm from such errors results so long as the individual is making his or her *own* conscious choices, using reason and reality rather than following the words of mystics, social "authorities", or gurus.

Surrendering one's independent judgment to mystics, social "authorities", or gurus and offering one's private self to all comers result in:

1. Diminished self-confidence and self-esteem.

2. Unproductive, unrewarding consumption of time: Such wasting of irreplaceable segments of one's life span continually diminishes the time needed to build a competent, productive life necessary for growing prosperity, romantic love, and abiding happiness.

3. Diminished personal desirability: Indiscriminate "openness and honesty" is often a boring imposition on those being gratuitously subjected to such personal openness.

4. And most important: After selflessly giving one's self to all comers, little if anything that is private, exciting, or precious is left to share exclusively with one's closest friend or romantic-love partner...little if anything is left to build that unique, priceless, private universe crucial to a romantic-love relationship.

Happiness exists as a private world within one's own self. That world expands into a mutually exclusive universe shared by two people involved in a psychuous-pleasure, romantic-love relationship. And that exclusive, private universe is a uniquely precious, emotional treasure. But that treasure can be forever lost by indiscriminately or promiscuously sharing oneself physically, psychologically, or spiritually with others.

That selfless giveaway and subsequent destruction of one's private inner world is exactly what the egalitarian advocates of "total openness" wish to accomplish. Only by negating everyone else's private values and self-esteem, can they justify their own prostituted inner world. Moreover, most of the "total-openness" egalitarians are neocheaters who depend on extracting their material and spiritual livelihoods from others. To do that, they first must dupe productive people with altruistic guilt. Then those neocheaters can psychologically pull the producers down to the level of nonproducers, free-loaders, mystics, and neocheaters through selfless egalitarianism.

D.H.J. C-50

Thank you, Dr. Wallace, for this work, which is enormous in scope and value - a great contribution to the advancement of mankind. It will help man's understanding of himself and his fellows.

Neo-Tech will, undoubtedly, change the world for the better by advancing man's thinking. It is about time that our politicians were exposed for the manipulators and neo-cheaters that they are!

You have been successful in cutting a swathe through the altruism, mysticism and nonsense to expose the bare truth and to get rid of the confusion. Now the fog is lifted, I can see and think more clearly.

Richard P. R-2801

THE MOST PRACTICAL CONCEPTS I'VE EVER COME ACROSS. SINCE READING NEO-TECH I HAVE STARTED TO FEEL A GREAT CONTROL OVER MY LIFE NOW. I'M SO EXCITED ABOUT NEO-TECH AND I KNOW I'LL NEVER BE THE SAME AGAIN.

Kevin M. C-53

NeoTech has opened my eyes about a lot of things. I see now how I've been cheated out of happiness and self esteem by others. I'm much more confident in myself. I wish everyone would read it; the world would be a much better place.

Once the producers are reduced to their level, the neocheaters can more easily usurp values from those producers.

By contrast, avoiding that self-giveaway trap leaves romantic love and abiding happiness open for any value producer.

Neo-Tech Advantage #96
COMMUNICATION IN ROMANTIC-LOVE RELATIONSHIPS

Crucial in a romantic love relationship is open communication, especially during negative emotional experiences. During stressful or negative experiences, deliberate reason-based (rather than automatic emotion-based) conclusions are needed to make fair, honest judgments [Re: Concept 127, Neo-Tech Reference Encyclopedia]. The ability to communicate honestly (without mysticism) during emotional stress is the hallmark of successful love partners.

The first step to reason-based communication between partners is to identify and separate the emotional aspects of the problem [Re: Concept 74 and Table 26, Neo-Tech Reference Encyclopedia]. For, knowing the difference between reason-based conclusions (business-like thinking) and emotion-based conclusions (mystical thinking) is the most important step in developing communication skills during negative situations in personal, love, and business relationships.

The ability to generate reason-based conclusions out of negative situations has powerfully beneficial effects on a person's well-being and happiness. Reasoned conclusions in emotional situations, for example, can prevent irrational actions that destroy business, financial, and romantic-love values. The habitual use of reason-based conclusions in emotional situations leads to more confident, honest, effective communication — especially in business and romantic-love situations.

The Judeo-Christian ethics instill fear in women about expressing sexual assertiveness. Those same ethics instill fear in men about expressing tender feelings and emotions. Such fears cause various degrees of emotional repression and diminished happiness in both men and women. The Neo-Tech/Psychuous concepts eliminate those pleasure-depriving fears by allowing free, guiltless communication about emotions, love, and sex between romantic-love partners.

A person can enter the future with either a reality-oriented philosophy that continually expands into personal wealth, happiness, and life...or with a mystical-oriented philosophy that continually shrinks into personal impoverishment, unhappiness, and death. Mystical or Platonistic-based philosophies and the resulting dishonest, altruistic ethics offer only negative, unhappy life styles. Neo-Tech/Psychuous or Aristotelian-based philosophies and the resulting honest, reality ethics offer positive, happy life-styles. ...Anyone can choose at anytime between either philosophy and life-style.

Bruce N. CB-101

It's hard to believe that a single publication could have such a major impact on how one looks at life and oneself. The affect on me has been remarkable. The highlight of my summer vacation was reading the Neo-Tech package. It's as if I had a total housecleaning of my mind, ridding myself of all the unnecessary garbage accumulated over my 45 years.

Neo-Tech was able to change my thinking processes. Now I'm more attentive to detail, with a greater interest in reading, listening and reducing commentary to its "real" meaning. .It's like having a dull blade sharpened; or a mind that was dulled by mysticism and neocheating to one sharpened with objective reality. The mist has been lifted from mysticism!

I have much to thank you for, and appreciate Dr. Wallace's exceptional works and your business concepts. Thanks to Neo-Tech, there is optimism and strength from within. It's nice to know that one can obtain this strength (power, prosperity, happiness, and romantic love) from honesty and anti-mysticism.

Fabian H.   R-1870

Excellent. Neo-Tech has uncovered puzzles that kept my life tangled w/ disappointments. Now I have become more decisive and confident about myself and the future

Rodney S.   R-3004

Neo-Tech is the Future. I'm just proud to be a part of it.

Neo-Tech Advantage #97
PRODUCTIVENESS AND HAPPINESS
VS. LAZINESS AND MISERY

Inseparable links exist between productive work, earned values, prosperity, psychuous pleasures, and happiness. Too many productive people live without experiencing their earned happiness or psychuous pleasures. That deprivation of happiness and psychuous pleasures is an unnecessary tragedy due to altruistic, mystical guilt inculcated into the producer by the neocheating value destroyers.

Psychuous pleasures and abiding happiness depend on psychological health, which in turn depends on productive work. Without productive work or preparations for such, psychological health is impossible. Moreover, psychuous pleasures and happiness act as the emotional incentives to constantly increase one's value and productivity.

Generally, the producer of values thrives on a fast-paced life in high-density environments (major exceptions are, for example, productive farmers, ranchers, miners). Nonproductive and destructive people, on the other hand, generally fear and enviously hate high-density, fast-paced, highly productive environments (such as New York City*).

Professional mystics and Marxist neocheaters destroyed countries such as Cuba, Cambodia, Iran, and Nicaragua. Such black-hat neocheaters work explicitly for the demise of modern, highly productive, highly technological societies.** They gain their power by pandering to the miserable, unproductive masses who desire to die by returning to a religious or statist fundamentalism falsely promising a simple, non-effort, "peaceful" existence — a prehistoric, unthinking, "animal-nature" past. Their ultimate dream is a mystical, non-effort, problem-free nirvana. But that dream contradicts

---

*Master black-hat neocheater, Fidel Castro, expressed the ultimate desire of all envious mystics, neocheaters, and other value destroyers in his publicly stated, personal desire to drop a nuclear bomb on New York City to destroy the greatest, most intense fountainhead of objective values known to mankind.

**The black-hat neocheaters' ultimate, envious dream is to destroy all fast-paced, high-tech, high-intensity life, especially as experienced in productive, free-market metropolitan areas. That dream was actually achieved by the terror-totalitarian government of Cambodia. To gain unrestricted power, the neocheating leader, Pol Pot, executed his destruction of urban life by a forced, death-march evacuation of the entire capital city of Phnom Penh. His totally destructive, murderous actions represented the highest attainment of egalitarian ideals and the natural end-result of all altruistic-based philosophies. For that reason, few objections or cries of outrage about such blatant, mass-murder were heard from the "liberal" media, soul-mate mystics, social "intellectuals", and other black-hat neocheaters.

Herne B.   F-117, FRANCE

At last, thanks to you the 2000 yrs of mysticism, deceit, unearned power will dissapear.

I can now detect Neo-cheaters and through Neo-Tech I can build values and I plan to start a business as a producer of values and money.

We know we are the strongest, we'll get them and we will soon live freely.

James C. R-1783

    I think your book is the best there is. You have opened my eyes to the things I never knew existed. I now understand things that were always a mystery to me. I know now I can control my own future and nothing can stop me from achieving my goals. I was shocked when I first read your book. I could not believe such things were true.
    Then I read your book a second time. I began looking at things differently. I then realized you are right. It is hard to understand how I could have been so blind. I know now who my enemies are and to defeat them. Neo-Tech has already saved me a lot of pain and money. It has paid for itself many times. Please let me know if there is any way I can help you achieve your goal of biological immortality or help you with your research. I know you don't accept donations.

life, nature, and reality as does all mysticism. Indeed, that no-effort, problem-free mysticism is the essence of death, dishonesty, and the destruction of values as opposed to the high-effort problem-solving essence of life, honesty, and the production of values.

Integrated links exist between productivity, self-interest, self-esteem, psychuous pleasures, and happiness [Re: Table 65, Neo-Tech Reference Encyclopedia]. Production of tradeable values is the integrating, growth force for all conscious beings. Production of values provides freedom, prosperity, psychuous pleasures, and abiding happiness.

Productivity and rational self-interest are not only essential to happiness, but are essential to life itself. For without productive self-interest, only consumptive altruism remains. What would a world of consumptive altruism mean? What if all people began living as selfless, unproductive consumers, temporarily surviving by sacrificing one another in consuming all the values created by the past producers. One can imagine what an unhappy, destructive world that would be. One can imagine the malevolence and meanness that would exist among those human beings as they cannibalized the final values and then one another. Soon after that, nearly everyone would be dead, even those with guns.

But what if all people began living as rationally selfish, productive individuals, all intent on producing maximum values for others in order to achieve maximum prosperity, psychuous pleasures, romantic love, and happiness for themselves and their loved ones. One can imagine what a benevolent, happy, exciting, thriving world that would be...a world free of mysticism and neocheaters...a world without guns...a world in which everyone forever increases his or her productivity, prosperity, and happiness.

Most productive individuals are of much greater value than their mystically diminished self-image* lets them realize. A truer self-image is sometimes unknowingly experienced when a productive individual goes, for example, to a performance in which a talented, attractive, famous

---

*The image of productive individuals is constantly denigrated by neocheating authors, media journalists, university professors, educators, theologians, politicians, and social "intellectuals". The productive middle class is projected in the ugly, inverted, false images of the Babbitts and Willie Lomans. The ultimate unjust irony lies with the destructive government bureaucrats and "professionals": They who never produce values, only consume or destroy them, coined and contemptuously use the term "working stiffs" in describing the self-sufficient, working middle class. Those "working stiffs" are the honest people who daily produce a flood of values for others, including those government bureaucrats. Indeed, those bureaucrats could not survive without those "working stiffs". But those "working stiffs would thrive without those bureaucrats and professional value destroyers.

Brian L. M. C-21

Dear Sir,

Your Neo-Tech II publication is certainly filled with many exciting concepts, linked by apparently unassailable logic. It is certainly the most thought-provoking and — in view of the possibilities arising from its practical application — stimulating work I have read. Some of the notions outlined in N-T III and V have left me in something of an intellectual whirl. However, I begin to suspect that such a reaction in me is due not so much to their novelty (for me) but largely to the fundamental differences between those notions and the ones which I have come into contact with earlier in life and which have lain unchallenged (and unprogressed) in my mind since then.

Donald R. R-2516

I am 50 yrs. of age, after three yrs. of mid-life crisis & a divorce. Neo-tech brought it altogether for me: The first time I feel I have the answers & I can finally define who I am, what I want in life, & where I want to. The most conflicting information I've ever acquired.

entertainer seems to be looking directly at that person and delivering the show just to him or her alone.* In those few moments, such people in the audience feel how good and worthy they really are in imagining that someone important as that star has finally recognized their worth. Most significantly, those productive individuals are every bit as good and worthy as they were imagining at that moment. During that brief "looking-at-me" experience, they are allowing themselves to feel, perhaps for the first time, the full worth that they really possess. They feel their worth by briefly discarding the years of unearned guilt foisted on them by the mystics, politicians, social "intellectuals", media commentators, and other neocheating altruists and egalitarians. Indeed, such productive people can and should experience the pleasure of feeling their full worth all the time. And now with Neo-Tech, they can forever free themselves of egalitarian altruism and its envious neocheaters to always feel their deserved worth and happiness.

The underlying cause of egalitarianism and envy is dishonesty and laziness.** Laziness means the abdication of self-responsibility. That abdication is the root cause of mysticism, envy, altruism, neocheating, and chronic unhappiness [Re: Concept 133, Neo-Tech Reference Encyclopedia]. Also, incompetence and lost potential arise from laziness and defaults of self-responsibility [Re: Concepts 133 and 134, Neo-Tech Reference Encyclopedia].

Mystics and neocheaters all have vested interests in attacking Neo-Tech, individualism, prosperity, and free-enterprise. The master neocheaters among the politicians, theologians, and social "intellectuals" live by attacking the producers and usurping their values. Through such attacks, those neocheaters create their needed illusions of personal power and self-worth. And they must continue attacking the producers, the values they produce, and individual rights to maintain their altruistic, collectivist illusions. For those fake illusions let them physically and psychologically live off of the value producers.

But being dependent on others for survival, nonproductive mystics and neocheaters are unable to earn the self-esteem and competence needed to achieve psychuous pleasures, romantic love, and abiding prosperity. Also,

---

*Good entertainers develop a technique during which they can look at large sections of the audience and simultaneously make many individuals feel that the entertainer is personally performing directly to each of them alone.

**The mechanism of laziness in both the mind and body is the yielding to actions of least effort. But conscious beings cannot prosper or be happy through actions of least effort. And unlike all other animals, conscious beings cannot survive by letting nature rule them. Conscious beings depend on volitional efforts and logically reasoned choices to survive. They must constantly choose to exert effort, think logically, and act beyond their feelings to prosper. They must exercise discipline, thought, and then control (the DTC technique) to succeed.

Joseph S.   C-32

Dear Neo Tech;

    I have just recently finished my second reading of the Neo-Tech Information packages. The first reading was a shock but after thinking about it for a while it all began to click together.

    I never really did beleive in the church but I was carrying a sense of guilt in me for not conforming to the "ways of society", you have now released that guilt.

Harry T.   R-1040

Since I have been aware of and have been using Neotech there has been a dramatic change in my life. It seems that things are happening for the good that in the past would have been mystical; but I no longer waste valuable time on prayer or other superstition, and am able to devote all my energy toward rational and beneficial conclusions. Thank you and Dr. Wallace for opening my eyes to reality.

Lelia G.   R-1350

I have already reversed the ageing process at age 72.

not having earned values, they hold no genuine power.

Productivity is the building block for prosperity, love, and happiness. The most common character and behavior traits associated with productive men and women are identified below:

CHARACTER AND BEHAVIOR TRAITS OF VALUE PRODUCERS

Character Traits

Honesty
Integrity
Consistency
Rationality
Perseverance
Individualism
Enthusiasm
Compassion
Passion

Behavior Traits

- Loyalty to honesty.
- Acts with honesty and fairness regardless of near-term consequences.
- Recognizes and pursues the values of honesty and integrity.
- Thinks rationally, logically, objectively.
- Focuses on reality.
- Observes in full context.
- Organizes self, life, and work toward profitable actions.
- Asks clear questions and listens carefully.
- Values time. Uses it efficiently and profitably.
- Anticipates achievement.
- Sets value-producing goals and strives to accomplish them.
- Tries to understand fully and contextually before judging.
- Shows passion, benevolence, and innocence toward life.
- Avoids mystical reactions.

Neo-Tech Advantage #98
GROWTH DEATH/PSYCHE DEATH AND ITS PREVENTION

Growth Death or Psyche Death are terms used to describe the tragedy of dying as a competently functioning conscious being while continuing to exist physically. That phenomenon unnecessarily occurs in a high percentage of people. Indeed, the disease of mysticism and Growth Death affects well over 99% of the world's living adult population [Re: Concept 89, Table 31, Neo-Tech Reference Encyclopedia]. Growth Death is a uniquely human phenomenon that involves the stagnation and death of the human psyche, often at an early age — even before the human body reaches physical maturity.

The human psyche embraces both the emotional and intellectual spheres of the mind. Contrary to popular myth, both spheres are inseparably linked and symbiotically function together. If one sphere grows, so does the other.

Richard M.   R-5300

After reading the manuscript I-V, it became apparent to me our existance is in danger unless everyone can be properly educated. Your work is the most valuable tool for life preservation ever written. The Neo Tech philosophy is the only way to live and prosper guiltlessly. My life is momentum with only truth and reality and nobody will ever change that again. The door is now open for gaining financial independence.

Utt N.   R-628

I have never enjoyed my life more than when Neothink allowed me to replace false values I had with real values, which in turn enabled the first positive production of my memory, and more importantly bridged the gap in my marriage. As a result, I was a productive partner and better parent. Fullfillment of positive, productive goals brings all else into focus.

If one sphere deteriorates so does the other. Most important, the human psyche has no age or capacity limitations on its growth.

Unlike the physical body, the human psyche has no growth limits. It never needs to stop growing. In fact, the continuous growth of the psyche is the process of conscious living. When that process stops, the individual ceases to function as a conscious being is designed to function. If a person's psyche is not growing, that person is living contrary to his or her nature. That person is dying. And if one's psyche is dying or dead, that person cannot experience abiding prosperity, love, or happiness.

PSYCHE GROWTH VS. PSYCHE DEATH

People generally display various mixtures of living and dead psyche characteristics. But the mixture is always tilted to one side or the other with the general direction usually moving unnecessarily toward death. With the following checklist, most people can determine whether their psyches are living or dying. A person with a dying psyche can reverse the trend and live again by using Neo-Tech to cure the disease of mysticism within one's own self.

CHECKLIST FOR SELF-MYSTICISM
Characteristics of a Dying or Dead Psyche

- [ ] Envious of others for their achievements, success, happiness, or material well-being. Resents heroes, value producers, and especially great business people and their productive accomplishments.

- [ ] Operates on subjective feelings or wishes involving short-range, pragmatic, and often dishonest approaches to problems and goals.

- [ ] Desires the destruction, distribution, or leveling of the wealth, happiness, and well-being earned by others.

- [ ] Holds anti-individualistic views.. Has egalitarian and collectivist desires to seize, destroy, and level values produced by others.

- [ ] Fears freedom and independence.

- [ ] Praises humble, selfless altruists. Attacks or maligns proud, productive achievers.

- [ ] Unhappy with life. Only interludes of short-term happiness. Represses the tragedy of death. Recoils at the possibility of biological immortality.

- [ ] Seeks government controls and laws that forcibly restrict and undermine individual freedom.

David M. J-222

After having read Neo-Tech, I find myself wanting more information from which to build. This knowledge has unlimited potential and I thirst for more.

As far back as I can remember, I have believed that the individual came first and foremost, but was unable to put all of my thoughts into the logical pattern as have your material and staff. Not only does this material effectively block the non-producers, but charts a course for continued and further development of the individual-self. I can think of no better way to help mankind than by helping yourself.

Your material has put light on subjects many of us have difficulty accepting in the dark. For in the dark lies ignorance. Only in the light can we find truth and honesty. Those who would profit from our ignorance are the one's who wish to keep us in the dark. Please keep the light lit. I have no desire to live in the dark any longer.

- [ ] Plagued with anxieties and self-doubts.

- [ ] Holds a cynical or malevolent view of life and people.

- [ ] Life is viewed as unhappy and people as inherently destructive, wicked, or sinful.

- [ ] Emotionally and physically experiences life with increasing unhappiness and lethargy.

- [ ] Accepts harmful, mystical concepts such as original sin and predestination.

- [ ] Orients around mystical premises and beliefs in God, statism, astrology, the occult.

- [ ] Orients around an altruistic, Platonistic philosophy that holds the sacrifice of the individual to "higher" causes as a virtue.

Characteristics of a Living or Growing Psyche

- [ ] Non-envious. Admires and encourages individual achievement in self and others.

- [ ] Operates on objective principles. Oriented toward long-range, value-producing goals.

- [ ] Produces tradeable values. Desires a life of achievements and happiness for self and others.

- [ ] Orients around rational self-interests. Independently fills own needs through production of tradeable values for others.

- [ ] Seeks freedom and independence.

- [ ] Admires and seeks productive achievers.

- [ ] Happy with life. Only interludes of short-term unhappiness. Recognizes the tragedy of death and hails the possibility of human biological immortality as the highest moral goal.

- [ ] Seeks freedom. Opposes all forms of initiatory force and oppression, especially government force and oppression of the individual.

- [ ] At ease and comfortable with self. Increasingly feels joyful life building within his or her physical and emotional self.

- [ ] Holds a benevolent view of life and people.

- [ ] Life is viewed as naturally happy, beautiful, exciting. People are viewed as inherently good.

Drew L. R-2999

The Neo-Tech I-V Package appears to be a meticulous, accurate, and well researched construction of effective material, which devastates the ploys of the Neo-Cheaters. I am Grateful for having this material, and to Dr. Wallace for sharing his ~~Revelat~~ revealations through his development of the Neo-Tech Science.

G.W.   C-1001, UNITED KINGDOM

Dear Mr Flint,
        I have recently recieved and read Neo-Tech I-V.
As a long time member and recruiter for the Church of Scientology who resigned from the church over policy five years back. Neo-Tech was a vital slap of reality which I have found most rewarding. Of course its difficult to dismiss a deep held bkbief in ones spiritual nature instantly, however ,the practical benefit of being a Scientology "Clear" is minimal, when compared with the real benefits I've achieved just from reading through the neo-tech discoveries. I know this neo tech viewpoint should stand me in good stead. The few dollars payed are nothing ,considering the many thousands I'd spent in the Church over many years. Neo tech was undoubtedlly the best purchase I've ever made, and I mean ever!

Does this mean that I'm standing on my head ? Well I want every scientologist to find out about Neo cheaters neo tech and Biological Immortality, these radical ideas ,with the lodgical approach must be the way ahead.

To me and I dont want to seem funny. its like meeting Mr Spock from Star Trek. asking him how Vulcans changed from savages to a lodgical and highly respected Race. I'm sure he'd say Dr Wallaces Neo tech !

I wish you every success. and as a free lance writer in the U.K. I'm at your service .

- [ ] Experiences life with increasing joy and intensity.

- [ ] Rejects mystical concepts such as original sin and predestination.

- [ ] Orients around honesty and objective reality.

- [ ] Orients around an Aristotelian/Neo-Tech philosophy that holds the individual as the supreme value in the universe.

To let one's psyche live or die is always a volitional choice made by each individual alone — a choice usually made early in life, often in childhood. The tragic, unnecessary surrender of the psyche to mysticism and Growth Death takes the subconscious form of:

"What's the use. Why struggle any more to understand reality or bear the pain and pressure of being honest? I am not going to live by my own mind because the effort and responsibilities are too great. I'll let others think for me. I'll let the authorities tell me what to believe and do. I want the easiest, safest way through life. Thus, I want to be a believer and to follow some 'wiser' authority or 'higher' good. I'll live by the thoughts and feelings of others."

From that point of surrender, the individual may become more knowledgeable, skillful, and proficient in specific areas, but his or her psyche will diminish as overall growth of the mind stops and turns downward toward death. At some future time, that individual could decide to countermand that subconscious surrender order and restart psyche growth. If not, the quality of his or her life will continuously decline, always controlled, always pushed or pulled one way or another by outside forces, by the influences of "others".

The "others" represent any higher "authority" that an individual lets control his or her thoughts, judgments, actions, life (rather than using one's own mind). Those "higher authorities" may be friends, relatives, politicians, social "intellectuals", neocheaters, university professors, the media, the church, the ruler, the Messiah, Allah, coke, cocaine, the Bible, the stars and planets, the state, "society"...anyone or anything outside the individual's own mind.

People default on the primary function of the human mind by allowing outside others ("authorities", neocheaters) to do their thinking and make their decisions. When people default on using their own minds, they lose control of their lives and begin dying as they become controlled by others.

By nature, control through others always contradicts an individual's long-range well-being. Thus, accepting such outside control always begins the process of growth death. For no one can experience growth, prosperity, and happiness while under control of others.

Brian N L   C-16

It took me many years to realise how much of my time/energy etc. were being "drained" by the seemingly sweet and reasonable requests from other people. I always felt virtuous about responding positively and energetically to these requests. At the same time, I was always vaguely aware that I was never quite getting around to doing the things that I most wanted to do. I also became increasingly aware of the fact that if I asked other people to help me, I frequently got polite refusals or excuses ("I'd love to be of help, but..." and so on). Alternatively, I got what I would describe as minimal effort or "grudging" help. I also noticed that, on the few occasions when other people did offer substantive help, they always managed to make me feel under a great psychological obligation to them. And they hardly ever failed to call in the debt, at some later stage, by requesting a larger favour from me!

So, when I got your Neo-Tech material, it rang a lot of bells and got me thinking much harder about the subtle ways in which people manipulate one another, and create dependency relationships — often without even realising it. It appealed to me to see this whole complex of phenomena reposed within a Total Theory of Cheating. So I am in broad agreement with most of what you say, and have already recommended Neo-Tech to certain friends.

I think that the general thrust of the Neo-Tech material might be strengthened by placing a bit more emphasis on <u>sanctimony</u> and <u>shaming</u> as being (related) modes of manipulation. The ploy takes such forms as "Surely you are not going to just sit back and ignore so-and-so?", or "You surely can't be thinking of doing <u>X</u> now?" The implication is that you are hard-hearted, insensitive, etc. unless you do something that the other person is urging upon you. (e.g. "You surely are not thinking of going off on holiday and leaving your poor old mother behind...") It is very easy to cave in under this sort of moral blackmail, and end up making our own lives more miserable.

R.E. H.   C-80

I received NEO-TECH I-V serval months ago and was quite surprised at the contents. It is very provoking, in that it reveals so many things most people find away of hiding from themselves in order to be like everyone else around them. I'm sure that the light you have shed on life as it is will continue to grow and as you pointed out in the manuscripts there is an awful lot of Neo-cheating going on from close friends to enemys and strangers.

The human mind is an adaptable, resilient organ having great self-healing powers. Helping or curing the mind seldom needs outside help. The powerful self-help nature of the mind is purposely ignored by the neocheaters dominating the psychology profession. The mind can suffer psychic or psychological damage. But if and when the individual chooses, that damage can almost always be reversed by attacking and eliminating the self-indulged mysticism that is usually causing the problem. That effective, self-help approach sharply contradicts the messy, usually harmful external "authority" approaches involving psychologists, psychiatrists, therapists. Such external "authority" approaches ignore the essence of both mental health (Neo-Tech: honesty and effort) and mental illness (mysticism: dishonesty and laziness). Thus, in the light of Neo-Tech, most but not all approaches by the psychology professions are invalid, harmful, and mostly practiced by neocheaters*.

Through honest thinking and sustained efforts, a person can self-heal and strengthen his or her mind. Through such self-healing, that person retakes control of life and reverses that mind atrophy caused by mysticism. On healing the mind, the future can once again promise boundless prosperity, growth, love, and happiness. One's psyche can then experience anew an exhilarating freedom and control over reality, perhaps for the first time since early childhood.

Most people have defaulted, at least partially, on the independent use of their minds. By abandoning any part of their minds to "others" (including the professionals manipulating psychology), they diminish their means to prosperity and happiness. Yet, through Neo-Tech, the potential is always available to rescue one's self from mysticism and its external "authorities". That self-rescue of one's own mind is needed to recover life and happiness.

Few people choose to resurrect themselves from Psyche Death and Growth Death.** Those who have surrendered their minds rationalize their deteriorating self and shrinking potential as a natural, biological aging process. Growth Death may be common, but is neither natural nor necessary. Furthermore, rebirth of a dying mind or psyche is not only possible but quite easy for anyone possessing Neo-Tech knowledge.

Neo-Tech leads the way to mental health by dumping the disease of mysticism from everyone's mind. ...And without mysticism to manipulate others, the neocheaters are powerless.

---

*Certain *cognitive* psychological approaches can be valid and at times valuable when used to gain specific knowledge that enhances one's competence and happiness.

**Recovery of independent thought is possible at almost any age through the nearly infinite self-healing powers of the human mind, especially when made mystic-free through Neo-Tech. For, Neo-Tech forever cures mysticism. Thus, Neo-Tech will put most of the psycho-labeled professions out of business.

Jesse C.   R-368

For the first time in my life my eyes have been opened. A great achievement

Joseph H.   R-242, CANADA

The most valuable information
I have ever received.
Thank you Dr. Wallace.

Rock S.   R-133

I feel it is the best investment I have ever made.

Mark G.   R-1455

VERY ENLIGHTENING.

Neo-Tech Advantage #99
THREE STEPS TO ACHIEVING COMMERCIAL BIOLOGICAL IMMORTALITY IN OUR LIFETIME
(Outlined and summarized from the Neothink article with same title.)

The elimination of mysticism is required for Biological Immortality. That will be accomplished in three steps:

STEP ONE

The first step in achieving Biological Immortality is defining its meaning: Biological Immortality means to live as flesh-and-blood human beings forever — not just an extended life, but to live mind, body, and spirit as one's own self for centuries, millennia, forever. The purpose of Biological Immortality is not to serve others, society, or mankind, but to preserve forever the most precious, important value in the universe — one's own integrated physical/conscious self to experience expanding prosperity, love, and happiness, forever.

STEP TWO

The second step in achieving Biological Immortality is dispelling the following six myths (the full article refutes each myth in detail):

1. Death is not final. False. Life after death exists. False. [See Momento Mori, page 133 in Neo-Tech V]
2. Everyone wants to live forever. False.
3. Living forever would deprive younger generations of opportunities. False.
4. People living forever would cause overpopulation. False
5. Living forever would be boring. False.
6. Achieving Biological Immortality presents technical, biological, medical, and scientific problems that are so complex and difficult that they could be unknowable or, at best, remain unsolvable for centuries. False.

STEP THREE

The third step in achieving Biological Immortality is understanding the requirements for achieving [A] personal prosperity, and [B] social prosperity with political freedom allows [C] commercial Biological Immortality. Achieving [A] and [B] is necessary to achieve [C]. The formula is [A] + [B] = [C]:

[A]=**Achieving Personal Power, Prosperity, Happiness:** Neo-Tech delivers honesty, power, love...page 4.

[B]=**Achieving a Free, Prosperous World:** Neo-Tech delivers freedom, business, prosperity...page 6.

[C]=**Achieving Biological Immortality in our Lifetime:** Neo-Tech delivers science, technology, immortality...page 9.

SUMMARY

Commercial Biological Immortality is achievable within our lifetime. But that achievement depends on the collapse of the 2000-year hoax of mysticism and the subsequent elimination of neocheating. The Neo-Tech Research and

Mark B. R-5861

When I purchased NEO-TECH in late 1986 I had no idea of the impact it would make on my life. I was shocked and confused after reading NEO-TECH the first time. To be honest I just refused to believe it. But over one year later I realized that my life was no better than before. I decided to read NEO-TECH a second time and after I finished it I realized how come I was not making any progress in life. Like so many other people I was depending on GOD to help me. I was a fool to believe that because a myth can not help anyone. The only GOD that I have now is myself. NEO-TECH has also **helped** me to realize that I owe the government nothing at all. Thanks to NEO-TECH I now look forward to the future like I never did before.

Marshall P.   R-1818

THANK YOU! SINCE I FIRST READ NEO-TECH JAN. 82 I HAVE MADE GREAT PROGRESS TOWARD HAPPINESS. IT HELPED ME TO UNDERSTAND WHY THE PARISITIC EXTERNAL AUTHORITIES ARE WHAT THEY ARE. IT MADE ME SEE HOW I WAS BEING USED, BY GOVERNMENT AND RELIGION, THROUGH UNEARNED GUILT, BASED ON THIER ALTRUISTIC AND MYSTIC PHILOSOPHIES I AM NOW REREADING NEO-TECH II, IT'S LIKE A BREATH OF CLEAN FRESH AIR, AND I CONTINUE TO ENJOY. I CAN NOW LIVE, LOVE, WORK AND PLAY GUILT-FREE; I NOW HAVE ALL THE TOOLS. THANKS AGAIN FOR YOUR ASSISTANCE IN MY SEARCH FOR THE TRUTH. SINCERELY MP

Writing Center will accomplish that achievement alone, without asking anyone to donate time or money, without anyone's support.

People must fully experience prosperity and happiness to value their one-and-only life with enough passion to motivate rapid, full-scale development of commercial Biological Immortality. Neo-Tech will trigger that full-scale development by freeing millions of productive individuals around the world from mysticism and neocheating. Once free, they will flourish naturally toward open-ended prosperity and happiness. They will flourish by (1) collapsing mysticism, (2) rejecting false guilt for living honestly and fully, and thus (3) rendering the neocheaters impotent. That, in turn, will unlock the needed motivation to develop commercial Biological Immortality rapidly — in a few years.

The entire purpose of Biological Immortality is to experience ever increasing happiness — to experience future realms of ever expanding prosperity, love, and happiness. Such unimaginable happiness is available to every conscious being living in a mystical-free world of forever evolving knowledge and adventure.

Other Biological-Immortality References
Neo-Tech III-V: (83), 133-136, 138, (139), 141, 150, 154
The Neo-Tech Discovery: ix, (57, 61, 197, 199, 211, 271), 321-323, 387-393

Neo-Tech Advantage #100
MALEFACTORS AND ENVY

Malefactor is a label that can be applied to all envious people. An envious person wants values destroyed. An envious person works to undermine individual and property rights, both of which are needed to achieve well-being and happiness. [How and why do people develop envy? How do they operate? See Table 68 in the Neo-Tech Reference Encyclopedia.]

Envy distorts and then consumes a person's view of life. Envy and laziness are prime evils (from a "not good for me" standard) that people let develop within themselves to their great personal harm and unhappiness. Laziness is a basic *cause*. Envy is a basic *effect*. Envy is the desire to destroy values created or earned by others...to destroy the good because of its goodness. Why? Because the objective good (rational human values) threatens to expose by contrast the envier's defaults. That, in turn, would wipe out the envier's pseudo self-esteem, which is needed for both psychological and physical survival (i.e., needed to prevent a mental breakdown or suicide).

Values earned by others make the envier feel unworthy and impotent. The good inherent in objective values reveals what the envier lacks. Such values reveal the human goodness that the envier has defaulted on. Such values leave the envier aware of his or her incompetence to live as a self-sufficient, independent, happy human being. The envier fears and hates such values.

Envy grows out of the defaults resulting from laziness and is a major destructive force in human relationships. In contrast to jealousy that is

J. L. R-2465, AUSTRALIA

Dear John Flint & Neo-Tech researchers,

I purchased these volumes I-V for my wife and ended up reading them myself. Words truly fail me. I am full of hope and confidence that your writings and research will spread. I am a very successful share trader and long term investor and very proud of my "rags to riches" success. I worked 12-15 hours a day, 6 days a week to find a method of trading & investing that's 100% mathematical & scientific.

Through hard, honest work, I have achieved many goals that I set myself. And, the more goals achieved, the more one wants to achieve.

Janet U.   C-30

Having been divorced for 1½ years, I wanted to be emotionally free from the seducer so that I could start looking for a nice husband. YOU HELPED ME TO DO IT. It's marvelous and I can't thank you enough. I can still be nice to the seducer, but he no longer has my emotions. I feel like a mother to him.

directed toward the *possession* of values, envy is directed toward the *destruction* of values. The desire to destroy the values, happiness, and pleasures earned by others is the essence of envy. Envious attacks against the producers and their values are woven throughout all the "good sounding" non sequiturs of media journalists, religious leaders, politicians, social "intellectuals", "consumerists", "ecologists", and other envious neocheaters.

Contrary to the misconception promoted by envy-oriented writers and journalists, envy is not analogous to jealousy. While both reduce happiness, their causes are opposites [Re: Concept 77, Neo-Tech Reference Encyclopedia]. Jealousy is rooted in valuing and coveting a value...because the value is good to the beholder. Envy is rooted in resenting and hating a value... because the value threatens to expose the dishonesty and failures of the envier. The jealous person is threatened by the loss of a value. The envious person is threatened by the presence of a value.

Enviers have always hidden, camouflaged, and distorted the meaning of envy. Enviers must not let their inferiority and dependence on the producers become known to themselves or others. For, if everyone understood the nature of envy, the professional mystics and neocheaters would lose their survival tools and rationalized self-esteems. And such losses would result in poverty, disgrace, even suicide — unless the envier chose to change — to prosper by becoming an honest producer of values.

Out of fear and resentment, enviers must attack values earned by others. At the same time, they must constantly usurp those values in order to survive. That contradictory life of enviers brings only increasing resentment, anxiety, incompetence, unhappiness.

Those free of envy have no way of knowing the malevolent nature of the envier. Thus, most value producers, because of their naive innocence, are relatively helpless in protecting themselves from envious value destroyers. ...Who are the envious value destroyers? They are identified in the chart on the next page. The issue is black and white: All people can be clearly classified as either envious or nonenvious [Re: Table 69, Neo-Tech Reference Encyclopedia]. From value-destroying bureaucrats right up to genocidal dictators, the survival of envious people depends on their victims never discovering the nature of envy. To accomplish that concealment*, destructive enviers must use one or more of the tactics shown in the chart on the next page.

---

*Over the centuries, concealing the nature of envy has been easy. For without Neo-Tech, most nonenvious individuals have no way to comprehend envy. In their innocence, envy-free productive people cannot emotionally or intellectually grasp the idea that people actually exist who want to destroy values because of the *goodness* represented by those values.

Jeff H.   R-5433

At the risk of seeming redundant, the Neo-Tech Discovery is truly amazing. I was at a low point in my life when I received the initial info package, and had never before purchased any kind of "self-help" product. I'm now grateful our paths crossed. Instead of a crutch or partial answer, the Neo-Tech Discovery transcends the "self-help" category by providing the logical foundation and perspective a person needs to deal with reality.

Neo-Tech is helping me get acquainted with someone I've ignored for a long, long time — myself! When I received N-T, I was 31, overweight, smoked, and had a lazy stagnant mind. As I read N-T, I became aware that it possesses a sense of "rightness." For me, this "rightness" is taking shape in the form of a logical integration of myself with reality. My mind has come alive again, and has begun to show me the power I have in myself. After reading N-T, I stopped smoking cold turkey. My only surprise was the ease with which this was accomplished. I have also instigated an exercise program and dietary changes, and the weight is coming off. I am now much more mentally alert than I have been in years, and I am gaining in physical energy almost daily.

My mental alertness has opened my eyes to the neo-cheating going on around me. I am now able to turn aside neo-cheaters, and am learning to use them for my own benefit. One neo-cheater that has been a thorn in my side for years — holding me back and getting me to do things for him — has begun to turn his attention to easier game now that I've made it difficult for him to get what he wants from me — unless I want it!

Neo-Tech has saved me from a premature death — both mental and physical. I see a bright future ahead in the Neo-Tech world. Thank you Dr. Wallace!

Jeffrey W.   R-2505

ABSOLUTELY INVALUABLE!

ENVY TACTICS

Tactics to Conceal Envy	Commonly Used By
Avoiding the word "envy"	Politicians, theologians, lawyers, "liberal" journalists, social "intellectuals", dictators
Distort and confuse the meaning of envy (e.g., falsely blending its meaning with jealousy)	Politicians, theologians, "liberal" journalists, social "intellectuals"
Deny the existence of envy	Politicians, theologians, "liberal" journalists
Invert the destructiveness of envy into a socially "good" action (e.g., the "good" of mass destructions that force everyone to the same level)	Egalitarians, "ecologists", social "intellectuals", lawyers, politicians, dictators
Claim that envy is inborn or is "forced" into people by the environment and, therefore, envious people are blameless. Society and inequality are to blame	Social "intellectuals", theologians, lawyers

Envy is a destructive character development resulting from:
1. volitional laziness and dishonesty, and
2. the choice to default on the self-responsibility to live by one's own mind and efforts.

The envier must depend on the minds and efforts of others to survive. Envy comes from within the self-made character of a person, not from society or the environment. Envious people, therefore, are responsible for their own envy, destructions, and harm to others. Enviers are the malefactors of civilization:

THE ENVIOUS MALEFACTORS OF CIVILIZATION

Who are the envious malefactors or value destroyers of civilization? They are identified below:

General Classes of
<u>Envious Malefactors</u>
Professional
Value Destroyers
Neocheaters
Parasites
Mystics

Robert H.   R-471

Dear Dr. Wallace,
  Your Neo-Tech I-V Packages represent the most awesome, electrifying, & enlightening collection of information I have ever been exposed to. (I am still a bit stunned by it all, several days after having completed Neo-Tech V.)

Joann A.   R-1474

With a background as a newspaper reporter, I found that the first 20 minutes of Neo-Tech II answered the five W's in this specific order: How, Who, What, When, and finally Why. My breakthrough was total and awesome! I had already read some of the books you summarized, had the counsel of three wise friends, but found that wisdom is of no value if buried deeply under a layer of religious brainwashing. Neo-Tech (the only <u>right</u> way to say "born again") has made it impossible for me ever to forget reality and truth again. I no longer spend precious time and scarce capital on garbage people. I'm going into a new field and will be starting my own business. Viva la Frank Wallace,

George M.   R-2015, AUSTRALIA

Very interesting. Caused me to stop and really <u>think</u>. Changed my outlook completely. I will always refer to it regularly.

Specific Classes of
Envious Malefactors
Dictators
Politicians
Theologians
Social "Intellectuals"
Criminals

High Percentage of Envious Malefactors Found in Specific "Occupations"

Law* (some exceptions)
Media journalism* (with some exceptions)
University professors* (with a few notable exceptions)
Mafia members (destructive but often not envious)
Theologians and politicians (incorrigible enviers)
Skid-row inhabitants (envious but often not destructive)
Unproductive scions of inherited wealth (envious destructive
    spenders and "public servants" such as Nelson A.
    Rockefeller, Ted Kennedy)
Social "intellectuals" (e.g., social "scientists" — their
    entire field is spurious and the antithesis of science)
Self-appointed professional feminists
Self-appointed professional environmentalists**
Self-appointed professional consumerists**
Self-appointed professional peace activists**

The value destroyers above are basically immature, anti-intellectual people who seek to deny or hide honesty. By contrast, most value producers are mature, intellectual people who seek only facts fully integrated with honesty.

---

*Envious malefactors or value destroyers are not inherent to these specific occupations. But a particularly high percentage of such malefactors populate these easy-to-fake professions. By contrast, envious malefactors rarely exist in productive hard-to-fake activities such as competitive, profit-making businesses.

**These professional, self-appointed types (e.g., the Nader type) are destructive enviers who use neocheating demagoguery to gain unearned power. Such neocheaters use non sequiturs to create falsely inverted "realities" of the "hero" consumer pitted against the "villain" producer. But those neocheaters always hurt both the consumer and the producer by promoting government controls and force. By contrast, those "villain" producers of values are and always have been the only real benefactors and heroes of mankind. Without those producers, no consumers would exist since no products or values to consume would exist. Indeed, without those producers, little, if any, human life would exist.

    No disparagement is meant toward the valuable efforts of consumer-aid organizations (e.g., Better Business Bureaus) that do not sanction, use, or depend on government force or the violation of individual rights. Also no disparagement is intended toward the few honest, professionally trained ecologists who actually deliver values by *objectively* studying the environment relative to improving the long-range prosperity and happiness for all value producers.

Porter J   C-14

I was recently reviewing my copy of your fantastic NEO-TECH and had to write and tell you how much its has changed my life. It has brought a whole new insight as to what life is all about. Your writing has uncovered for me whole new ways of looking at myself and at the NEO-CHEATERS. Boy there sure are a lot of them out there. Wish this was being taught in school so everyone could be exposed to what is really going on.

Lynn K.   R-2603

> Thank you for making clear the many concepts I found enlightening - especially the God-concept. I feel **free**. Also, after reading Neo-Tech, I was able to quit smoking marijuana which I've been trying to do for over a year. And I find I no longer enjoy drinking. I enjoy REALITY. I enjoy LIFE!!

John B.   C-115,   AUSTRALIA

The applications of Neo-Tech are everywhere!!! You are right.

The direction of my career has certainly changed and developed leaps and bounds since aquiring Neo-Tech knowledge. Everything now has high potential.

To all at Neo-Tech, I am grateful for sharing this knowledge.

Essentially all politicians and social "intellectuals" are immature value destroyers who survive by neocheating the value producer. Such people promote altruistic social "ideals" designed to harm and drain every value producer on this planet. Those immature value destroyers include not only politicians but a significant percentage of university professors, especially in the fields of social and political sciences, philosophy, psychology, education, law, religion, and a smaller percentage in all other fields. Their crusades for social "justice" are motivated by envy. And their attacks on values are neocheating ploys not only for plundering the producers but for hiding their own incompetence, laziness, and dishonesty. But the greatest evil of those academe is their irreparable mutilation of millions upon millions of young, developing minds.

Why are theologians also classified as neocheaters, malefactors, value destroyers, and parasites? What about the "good" that theologians do, such as help the poor? Indeed, their "good" is exactly that...good in quotes. Their "good" is usually specious and contrary to human well-being and happiness. For, their "good" is based on the altruistic sacrifice of the value producer with the theologians collecting both the praise and a middle-man's cut without producing any values.

Most theologian-type "good" depends on dishonest, guilt manipulations of the producer. Indeed, that "good" arises from their subtle, unjust denigrations of personal success, prosperity, and happiness. Furthermore, their "good" generally involves hypocritical, neocheating ploys designed for living with praise and "ease" without working to produce competitive values. In other words, theologians support themselves by promoting God-like altruistic schemes designed to usurp values earned by others while collecting unearned respect and power. ...That is the total purpose and livelihood of *all* theologians.

Neo-Tech Advantage #101
ENVIERS AND LAZINESS

Value destroyers such as demagogic "ecologists" and "consumerists", neocheating politicians and bureaucrats, evil dictators and ayatollahs usurp enough power to directly execute their envious destructions. They camouflage their envy by operating under non-sequitur banners of common "good", human rights, social "justice", "peace", and equality. ...They live by usurping power and values, by attacking and undermining the producers of those values.

But most other enviers lack the power and resources to directly destroy values. To satisfy their envy, they eagerly support the destructive causes promoted by those demagogic "consumerists", "environmentalists", theologians, politicians, social "intellectuals", and other neocheaters.

A person can cure his or her envy only by becoming a self-sufficient producer of competitive values to achieve genuine independence, competence, and self-esteem. If not cured, the malignancy of envy will keep growing, consuming that person in malevolent hatred toward self, all productive people, objective values, and life itself.

B.P. R-1868, South Africa

Neo-Tech is incredibly clear and coherent and I love every word of it. How can you bear living in a world with neocheaters?

I have kept a diary since 1977, trying to solve the riddle of god, and people's behavior. With Neo-Tech knowledge it hit me between the eyes: the god <u>concept.</u>

Thanks again for Neo-Tech. It's worth a lot more than you ask for it. And thanks for Neo-Tech III-V. I have much to learn.

I wish I & O Publishing Co. were in South Africa. I would like to discuss Neo-Tech with someone who knows it.

Thomas F.   R-607

I am overawed with this masterpiece. Finally a treatise on modern philosophy is complete with no loose ends, consistently logical, rational, and with examples illustrating all possible viewpoints.

D. Keven G. C-108

I feel that when it is truly perfected and accepted, that Neo-Tech will be the ultimate system for living an organized, powerful, full life. I also feel that everyone will be following the overall NeoTech system someday, it simply offers too much to refuse.

Expressed another way, growing envy destroys a person's potential to earn genuine prosperity, psychuous pleasures, and happiness. To break free from envy's grip, a person must first identify the envy. Next, that person must reduce the need for envy by becoming increasingly productive until competent enough to live by producing values desired by others. Then a metamorphosis occurs that changes envious fear of objective values to a passionate desire for objective values. On evolving into an independent, self-sufficient producer of values, envy fades as a new, exciting life emerges with growing prosperity, psychuous pleasures, and abiding happiness.

Producers of objective values have prosperity and happiness always open to them. But first they must break free from the unearned guilt foisted on them by the enviers who surrounded them. The producers must realize that they are the ones who hold the real power. And only they can guiltlessly collect genuine prosperity and happiness.

Neo-Tech sharply contrasts the effects of mysticism and envy against the production of values and self-esteem. [Re: Table 71, Neo-Tech Reference Encyclopedia]. One does not cross into the envy-free zone until that person becomes competent enough through consistent logical thinking, integrated honesty, and hard efforts to be self-sufficient by producing competitive values for others.

As previously identified, laziness and dishonesty are volitionally chosen, prime evils. People allow laziness and dishonesty to develop within themselves to their great personal harm. Laziness and dishonesty are the basic causes of mysticism, neocheating, and envy. Moreover, that default to laziness leads to Growth Death or Psyche Death (see Neo-Tech Advantage #98).

Laziness always involves mysticism undercutting the conscious mind. One must exert a constant, life-long effort to maintain a prosperous, happy, healthy life. By contrast, mental and physical laziness means defaulting on the key human attributes necessary for independent, self-survival and happiness.

Rationalizing laziness and envy requires dishonest inversions of facts and values. For example, certain social commentators disparage modern, labor-saving appliances as causing laziness. They lament that modern appliances bypass old-fashioned virtues of hard work. Their laments are misleading non sequiturs useful for neocheating. The facts are that labor-saving devices are created and put to best use by those who are the least lazy. For, such modern devices free people from low-productivity, mind-stifling routines to provide the time and opportunity to spend their lives in ever more productive, creative activities.

Criticisms of labor-saving devices usually originate from either neocheaters attacking values or from those yearning to return to bygone days. But those bygone days were when so much brute labor, time, and energy were needed just to survive that few if any demands were made to expand

Anthony J.   R-5722

By any reconing your organization has given the ordinary working person faith in the future of mankind.

Thanks to Dr. Frank Wallace my future is looking brighter and happier all the time. With his knowledge I hope to be able to square my income and achieve biological imorlality.

Alvin C.   C-88

Neo-TECH II Blow clean my 46 year old muck filled mind — I feel reborn -- at last - the pure, clean truth — When I started to read, I couldn't stop -- my mind had been crying out for the truth all my life — my days of being a victom are over — Saying thanks is not enough — how can I help?

conscious effort. Those criticizing modern labor-saving devices are generally seeking rationalizations to avoid the responsibility of living by sustained, conscious efforts. They prefer to exist without conscious effort — by rote — as people did during the Dark Ages. Those who criticize labor-saving devices are usually projecting their own mental laziness and lack of effort to live fully.

The logical use of the mind combined with consistent rational effort is required for human survival and prosperity. But, mental default for many is seductively tempting. A person simply adopts someone else's thinking, thus avoiding the responsibility of exerting one's own mental effort and honesty for independent survival and prosperity. Such "pleasantly easy" defaults against using one's own mind are traps that corrode self-sufficiency and lead to intellectual, psychological, and eventual physical dependence on others, especially "authorities".

Usually those "authorities" are neocheaters who dupe the defaulter into accepting their dishonest, destructive doctrines. ...Such neocheating "authorities" survive by promoting their mystical hoaxes and specious doctrines of altruistic self-sacrifice in order to control the defaulters and neocheat the producers.

Independent, logical thinking* does not preclude errors or wrong judgments. But only through habitual, independent, logical thinking does one become efficient in identifying and correcting errors. If a person defaults on that thinking effort, he or she must live increasingly through other people's thinking. That person then gradually loses the ability to recognize the errors in other people's thinking as well as to correct his or her own errors. Such a person eventually becomes incompetent to live independently. That person then becomes dependent on destructive, neocheating "authorities" to survive.

Essentially all willful destruction, all purposeful violence, all initiation of force against individuals and their property, all destructive philosophies can be reduced to a single, originating cause — mysticism originating from laziness and dishonesty. That laziness and dishonesty evolves from choosing not to exert the constant, rational efforts required to understand reality in order to make one's own independent decisions.* ...Laziness and dishonesty are the cause of evil; envy is the effect.

Neo-Tech Advantage #102
NEO-TECH VERSUS ALTRUISM

Attacks on free enterprise, producers, and objective values by envious altruists, powercrats, social "intellectuals", theologians, lawyers, academe, and other neocheaters are on the rise around the world. Before Neo-Tech,

---

*Effective, independent, logical thinking is not a function of intelligence, but is a function of self-responsibility, self-honesty, and self-effort.

Larry R.   R-1608

Just some quick notes:

Neo-Tech II is very enlightening. Often comforting. Often frightening, but such "growing pains" are very healthy.

After reading it, I was able to immediately prune unnecessary people, actions, etc, from my life.

I loved the invaluable section that summarized so many other books. It has saved me hours.

The juxtapositioning of work and love finally paints a clear picture of most of the world's problems. That is, the individual's problems. (I am not putting the neo-cheaters into the picture because they are obviously and readily seen to be the base for most of the problems. What I meant was, the love/work stuff helped those who see to see clearer. The cheaters work on those who rarely see at all.)

I loved the work/love stuff. I am using this new knowledge to overcome many old obstacles, while I forge ahead building a genuine solid base of self-esteem. (I am in graduate school now, and I particularly appreciated the Neo-Tech examples of the "hard working producer who shuts himself in a laboratory for two years for the good of mankind and personal economy reasons".)

I admire the integrity of the writer. Everything is crystal clear. And when hazy, stated so. (Concept 114 runs into some touchy ground, and the author readily admits it. Admirable.)

Otherwise, a wonderful book that did indeed change my life. It gave no plan for financial success, instead, it gave a plan for life success. Long term. I like that.

Patrick E.   F-103, FRANCE

I will simply say that Neo Tech must get known throughout the world, in all languages; among the people of all levels in the hope of eliminating mysticism forever

envious altruism was increasingly undermining the value producers. But today, Neo-Tech not only identifies the nature of envy, but also reveals how neocheaters use mystical altruism to attack and undermine the producers in order to usurp their power and values. Thus, just in time, at the crucial Nuclear-Decision Threshold (See Neo-Tech Advantage #31), Neo-Tech has become available to identify, counteract, and reverse the destructive trend of mysticism. Moreover, timely Neo-Tech also demonstrates how guiltless psychuous pleasures and happiness arise from rejecting all mystical dishonesties. And, finally, Neo-Tech renders powerless all neocheaters — all altruists, mystics, powercrats, parasites, and enviers.

Neo-Tech means the eventual demise of every politician, social "intellectual", theologian, and every other neocheating altruist and egalitarian who usurp values and power from the value producers. At the same time, almost anyone can achieve a prosperous, happy life with Neo-Tech, even those hapless mystics and neocheaters who have been exposed and rejected by the producers armed with Neo-Tech.

Without Neo-Tech, the legions of altruists, mystics, and powercrats would have eventually buried the producers and their values, causing a new dark age. But today, Neo-Tech knowledge is spreading around the world. That expanding Neo-Tech matrix is rendering impotent all mystics and neocheating altruists caught in its web. Yet, ironically, those foundering mystics and neocheaters can with Neo-Tech join the producers in experiencing genuine prosperity and happiness by rejecting their own mysticism and producing competitive values for others.

Neo-Tech Advantage #103
PLATO, ARISTOTLE, AND NEO-TECH

Those with Neo-Tech knowledge will gain powerful advantages in every competitive situation. For they fully understand the crippling, 2000-year hoax of Platonistic-based philosophies that today dominate most people's thoughts and actions. Thus, by removing that hoax, Neo-Tech leaves a person with profound competitive advantages over those without Neo-Tech.

Plato's philosophy provided the foundation for all subsequent philosophies involving mysticism, sacrifice, and the use of force to achieve "higher" goals. Plato's philosophy also provides the basic tools for rationalizing laziness [Re: Concept 108, Neo-Tech Reference Encyclopedia]. And because Plato's work is so profoundly and subtly anti-intellectual, his philosophy inflicted sweeping, anti-intellectual destructions on all subsequent civilizations and cultures to this day.

Indeed, Plato was one of the most original, creative thinkers of all time. His work was the first complete, fully integrated philosophical system recorded in writing. The depth and breadth of his system are awesome, matched and surpassed only by the philosophical writings of his student, Aristotle.

But much of Plato's credit, particularly the sounder aspects of his philosophical system, perhaps belongs to his teacher, Socrates.

David H. C-66

I am very happy about the Neo-Tech Package and consider the honesty and integrity of both Frank Wallace and his team, and the I/O. Comp. reflected in the really give-away price

Yours sincerely

Lois M. RP-103

July 15, 1988

It has been several months now since I first received my NT info. Oh, I remember my anticipation in awaiting the arrival of "some seemingly far-fetched business info" - being a conservative yet open-minded business person with a propensity for NEW knowledge. Little did I expect what I call "THE ETERNAL AWAKENING"...that I was about to experience.

NT allows one to see through the cheaters like lasers through butter with impeccable accuracy. I have found very far reaching implications for ALL humans.

Jerry L. R-6414

It crystallizes workable ideas with razor like precison. Expands

the mind beyond infinity. Will grow in a compounding fashion-

true freedom resides in it. Neo-Tech III is TREMENDOUS!!!

I am a Neo-Tech man with much to learn.

Unfortunately, Socrates never recorded in writing his ideas or philosophical system. No writings of Socrates are known to exist. And knowledge of his work was left to the mercy and plagiarism of Plato, who perhaps deleted crucial Aristotelian-like views that would have contradicted Plato's own views. Nevertheless, Socrates was probably the first man to develop a broadly integrated philosophical system.

Plato held enormous leverage with his great intellectual and creative abilities. Thus, profound philosophical errors would occur if he were tilted even slightly toward immaturity, dishonesty, mysticism, and neocheating. And that is what happened. Some of the most integrated aspects of Plato's philosophical system are in profound error. His errors involve the integration of dishonesties, mysticism, "higher purposes", the use of force, and the exercise of authoritarian power into a full-blown, ethical philosophical system of enormous deception and dishonesties.

Furthermore, the foundation of Plato's philosophy is not based on reality, but on mysticism. His philosophy does not recognize the life of the individual human being as the supreme value in the universe. Indeed, Plato is not a man to be respected. For he was an immature, dishonest conniver who wreaked death and destruction on this world for over 2000 years. He subordinated human beings to arbitrary "higher" powers and mystical "values". Yet, the tight inner logic and integrated completeness of his specious philosophy provided great staying power for his false ideas. Thus, his specious philosophy became the intellectual foundation of all subsequent specious philosophies, religions, and political systems.

Plato's philosophical system has been the greatest tragedy of our civilization. But at last, today, Neo-Tech is in the process of eliminating that tragedy.

By contrast, Aristotle was perhaps the greatest intellectual power in history. He built his philosophical system on objective, noncontradictory premises by placing objective reality as the only basis of honesty. Aristotle placed the individual conscious being as the supreme value in the universe. ...The philosophical roots of Neo-Tech lead to Aristotle.

Major competitive advantages accrue to those who use Neo-Tech knowledge to reject all mystical, Platonistic-based frauds.

Neo-Tech Advantage #104
DESTRUCTIVE POETRY VERSUS VALID ART

Can poetry be destructive? Can poetry undermine romantic love? Yes, most certainly. Some poetry (including song lyrics, especially certain rock lyrics), if taken seriously, can have powerful, mind-crippling effects that undermine a person's rational-thinking processes and prevent romantic-love relationships from developing. In addition, certain poetry can block personal growth and prevent prosperity and long-range happiness from developing.

Plato, whose philosophy has been utilized by the anti-intellectuals, mystics, and neocheaters for the past 2300 years, was ironically the first

Robert L. L.   C-209

Dear Mr. Flint,
I'm sorry for my delay in writing you. I feel that your Neo-tech will be a major contribution to the advancement of the human race. With the many ways Neo-cheaters have gained power. I find it increasingly hard to believe that we have come this far. I've always been sort of a prove it to me, just show me what I'm suppose to do man. But I found that religion fell a whole lot short of the forever present bill or need. I would like to see Neo-tech engulf the whole of it, and spread like ten coats of molasses. You bet I'm totally and one hundred percent for biological immortality. My only handicap at the present is the state of poverty that I have allowed the Neo-cheaters to push me into, but armed with this well need information I feel I now have a chance to at least a better effort and chance to win.

Johnny Mc.   R-258

pure, distilled logic, powerful reading. If enough people read and put even small parts of this book to work in their lives—it will save mankind.

to identify the harmful, anti-intellectual nature of poetry. Plato recognized that the sing-song, rhythmic nature of poetry set up automatic, hypnotic, nonthinking patterns that unconscious people used to pass on information which often sounded good or pleasant, but had little or no validity, accuracy, or objective meaning. In other words, through poetry, so-called knowledge or packages of "truth" could be handily acquired and passed on with little conscious effort, independent thinking, or regard to honesty. Poems and chants established dogmatic patterns that blocked new or more accurate ideas from developing.

Plato properly identified part of the problem with poetry, but his philosophical dishonesties prevented him from identifying the total problem. Poetry can be cast in what appears to be beautiful gems or nuggets of packaged "truth" and knowledge from "authorities". Those packaged "truths" are designed for consumption by quick, convenient gulps. That gulping of "truths" bypasses the analytical mental effort required to integrate information and assess its validity through one's own mind.

Determining the truth or validity of any information requires analytical integration of facts and information within a full, accurate context. But poetry and song lyrics effortlessly bypass the demanding thinking process needed to identify objective reality. In that way, poetry and lyrics subvert the effectiveness of the mind. Most poetry and lyrics, no matter how beautiful, right, and true they sound (that being their seductive nature) cannot be substituted for honesty or facts any more than good-sounding slogans or parables* can be substituted for honesty or facts. Furthermore, cleverly used poetry and lyrics can be powerfully effective tools for rationalizing laziness, dishonesty, injustice, mysticism, and neocheating.**

---

*A parable is a short, fictitious story usually used to illustrate a moral or religious principle. Almost all parables are specious rationalizations, non sequiturs, or false wisdom used out of intellectual weakness to conceal or evade facts and logic. Jesus taught almost entirely by parables, which underscores that his teachings were not only deceptive and false but that he was a man of stunted intellectual capacity. Indeed, Jesus was a relatively minor mystic during his life time. Not until nearly a century later did the professional mystics resurrect him as a handy symbol around which to rally their victims.

**Unintegrated music, especially rock music, breaks down the thought patterns of the brain. That breakdown provides a drug-like effect in blocking or avoiding the struggle, effort, and at times the pain required to think consciously. Such brain-blockage leaves one in a "pleasant", nonthinking stupor. With music constantly pounding on their eardrums, rock addicts effectively block all thinking efforts. That rhythmic pounding, in turn, keeps the anxieties of their incompetence buried within their non-thinking minds.

Oscar M. C-326

Neo Tech philosphy has turned my whole
life around. I have discontinued all
financial support of churces, politicians
and all charitable organizations
regardless of who they are. I beleive
I am entiteled to the fruits of my
own labor.

Sheila B. R-2034, ENGLAND

Has enhanced my understanding of my own behaviour and that of the people around me, and led to a greater freedom in experimenting with ambitious business plans. I am looking forward to going on experimenting for ever!

Most poetry if taken seriously (especially emotional or "beautiful" poetry that lacks an objective base), not only undermines a person's ability to make independent judgments but diminishes one's capacity to think objectively about crucial matters. That, in turn, decreases one's ability to achieve prosperity, psychuous pleasures, and long-range happiness. In other words, certain poetry or song lyrics taken as packaged truth will bypass the independent, in-context thinking processes required to make the integrations and decisions necessary to develop long-range prosperity, pleasures, and happiness.

Most poetry rests on specious or mystical foundations. But even poetry resting on objective, Aristotelian foundations is valid only for a specific context and is not valid for other contexts. If, for example, one or both partners in a love relationship rely on poetry by "authorities" to express "truth", the relationship in that particular area will be detached from reality — stunted by mysticism, unable to grow on sound premises in that area.

Poetry based on mysticism or even poetry based on a particular context of objective reality is almost always, by nature, nonexact or abstract. That nonexactness or abstraction can symbolize certain categories of reality, but poetic abstractions are not facts in themselves nor can they be substituted for independent, integrated thinking.

But valid art forms (e.g., music, fine art, literature, and even certain intellectually honest poetry) can be abstract expressions of objective values executed with skill and projected with a powerful sense of life. If the artist's abstract symbols reflect the observer's own values, then the particular art form delivers pleasure to the beholder.

If the art work (music, fine art, literature) symbolizes disvalues or threats to the beholder, then the art delivers dislike to the viewer.* Nonskilled or amateurish art may attempt to symbolize values to the beholder. But such art work is not emotionally felt if the style, craftsmanship, or abstraction is too unskilled, obscure, inaccurate, contradictory, or badly executed. In such cases, the viewer's reaction is nonrecognition, confusion, indifference, boredom, dislike, especially if combined with a negative sense of life. Those cases include most of the *subjective* "modern art" that has been foisted on the public by neocheaters as a ploy to further undermine life, attack values, and drain the producer through the arts.

But much more harmful is the mystics' and neocheaters' use of *objective* art forms to bilk the producer on a grand scale: The prime example in history is the brilliant coup by the Catholic church to save itself during the rise of honesty and logic that occurred during the Renaissance. The master neocheaters of the Catholic hierarchy recognized the starkly obvious values

---

*Art work (including certain poetry) that reflects negative values to the viewer can still be admired for style or craftsmanship if skillfully executed.

Mark G.   F-105, FRANCE

Reading Neo-Tech was one of the best thing that has ever happened to me. No work ever written before, brings such a staggering of basic conceptions of human behavior.

Henceforth everything can be explained and most of all controled. Especially our attitude towards governments, religions and death mostly. In a word not one aspect of life escapes the Neo-Tech's clear analysis, and each "sensitive point" historical, political, economical, psychological undergo a real adjustment to reality.

Today, after practicing the Neo Tech principles I can vouch for their astonishing efficacity. My life and that of those around me has experienced a real transformation that does not cease to grow more and more positive.

Nothing is more motivating and innovating than the Neo Tech propositions. Among others passionnate things, the possibility of never dying, at last guaranteed eternal life, and the application of a research program towards that goal is certainly one of the biggest event of the century

of the burgeoning, new art forms. They then captured those art values for exploitation by aggressively commissioning the most skilled artists to produce highly obvious values. The master neocheaters captured those values at first through architecture, the fine arts, and sculpture. Later they added music to their arsenal through the great classical composers. Governments and tyrants right up to Lenin, Hitler, and current neocheating rulers also seized that neocheating ploy. To gain easy credibility and to capture support through the emotions, they used the fine arts, literature, music, and even the most integrated art form — opera*.

Since the value of art can be sensed through emotions and requires no intellectual analysis, the public needs only to notice the obvious art and architectural values to erroneously link those values of the master artists to the master neocheaters presenting that art. Thus, the masses are deluded into seeing those obvious values of great art as also representing the values of the neocheating church or government. Subconsciously they conclude: "I can see, hear, and feel those architectural, art, and musical values. I know those values are real and valid. Thus, those values must also represent those who own and present this art — the church or government. Therefore, all that I do not comprehend about the church or government must be as good and valuable as the art that represents them."

Through that brilliant, but dishonest use of art as non sequiturs, the church and governments were able to survive the rise of honesty and logic during the Renaissance, the resulting industrial revolution, and then the rise of capitalism and free enterprise.

Regardless of their understandings or economic conditions, those great artists betrayed honesty by selling themselves to the dishonest intentions of the neocheaters in church and government. Those artists are culpable and responsible for giving a major boost in power and endurance to the evil machinations of especially the Catholic church and its neocheating leaders. Even Michelangelo must be held accountable. His great work in the widest context must be condemned as a net disvalue to human life for the dishonest role it played in supporting the immoral mystics and destructive neocheaters throughout the subsequent ages. Without selling out, he might have lost some immediate prosperity and fame. But if he had stayed honest to reality, his work would have risen to even greater beauty, value, and fame.

***

A major difference exists between the beholder's *view* of valid art versus one's *use* of poetry. Art represents an abstraction that symbolizes a value. The beholder merely contemplates a piece of art for the emotional pleasure

---

*Opera integrates the major art forms: music, romantic fiction, plot, performing arts, fine arts. Verdi's opera "Aida" is the first and only major art work that celebrates the heroic production of a major commercial and technological value — the opening of the Suez Canal. ..."Aida" is a distant precursor to Neo-Tech art.

Dr. Francisco G. C-215, ARGENTINA

See translation below

    Estoy deslumbrado y conmovido con lo que estoy leyendo y releyendo. Me parece un hallazgo sensacional. Es para mi como la llegada de Copérnico para el conocimiento científico.
    La coherencia de sus ideas y directrices básicas y las ilimitadas pautas de acción que sugiere, eran lo que necesitaba para reordenar mi vida a los 50 años, dándole un sentido acorde con su destino natural de prosperidad y felicidad.
    Como abogado tengo interés en el futuro Servicio de Protección Neo-Tech. El Neo-Tech ha venido a aclararme e ilustrarme en la búsqueda de la verdad la felicidad y la prosperidad, comprenderá que tengo muchísimo interés en Neo-Tech.
    Estoy conmovido, agradecido y entusiasmado. Por lo tanto espero comunicaciones de Uds.

    I am dizzy and trembling with what I am reading and rereading. I believe it is a sensational and most interesting find. For me it is as the coming of Copernicus's science of knowledge.
    The coherence of your ideas and the unlimited action guidelines that you suggest has been necessary to renew my 50 life years. It gives a sense according with the natural destiny of prosperity and happiness.
    As lawyer I have enormous interest to give my Legal Protection Services to Neo-Tech.
    When Neo-Tech clarified and illustrated my ideas about truth, happiness and prosperity, you can understand that I have very much interest in Neo-Tech.
    It is enormous the enthusiasm I received to read Neo-Tech. Neo-Tech is of profound contents.
    I am ecstatic, appreciative, and enthusiastic.
    Truly Yours.

George V. C-303

I HAVE RECENTLY RECEIVED NEO-TECH I & II. I AM VERY GLAD TO FIND THAT SOMEONE HAS FIGURED OUT WHAT "LIFE SHOULD BE ALL ABOUT".

it delivers in reflecting back or symbolizing that person's own values. Unlike poetry, the beholder normally does not use art abstraction to replace his or her own independent thinking for understanding reality or establishing facts.

Art is a crucial value for human beings. Art is a source of pleasure and psychological fuel that reflects and confirms one's deepest values through aesthetic symbols. Poetry, on the other hand, can harm a person's thinking process if that person accepts as concrete truth the inexact, out-of-context nature of poetic abstractions. When accepted as self-contained packages of "truth", song lyrics, parables, slogans, epigrams, cartoons, and "famous" quotes by "authorities" fall into the same harmful category as poetry [Re: Table 72, Neo-Tech Reference Encyclopedia].

Aristotelian-based poetry that is intellectually valid and certain song lyrics that are non mystical can be objectively valuable when viewed as symbols of one's own values and not as packages of "truth" to be swallowed whole, without integration. Still, the effect of poetry on most people is harmful because they allow the abstract symbols of poetry to enter their minds as unintegrated, unchallenged "truths" or as pre-packaged value systems ready for direct use. The problem is amplified because many poets, song lyricists, and political cartoonists proceed with dishonest, destructive intentions to mislead the reader. They want their work swallowed blindly as "truth" by their audiences, regardless of the validity or context of their work. Such work is neither art nor honest; it is neocheating.

If an individual is aware of the misleading nature of poetry, he or she can avoid its harmful effects and perhaps gain some reflective values from certain Aristotelian-based poetry. For example, the following poem, while not deeply intellectual, does aesthetically reflect the soul and character of heroic, innocent producers:

THE GOLDEN

They are the rare, the radiant men
The children of truth, the parents of ken.
Pain but strengthens them, pity intrudes.
Rebuking surprises them. Guilt eludes.

Deception disgusts and envy astounds.
Misfortune challenges. Malice confounds.
They are the open, the honorable,
The honest, the just, the vulnerable.

With no respect for the twisting of truth,
Faithfully wed to the promise of youth,
They are the pure, the benevolent,
The incorruptible few — the Innocent.

(Reprinted with permission from Darlene Bridge and Bridgeberg books)

George V. C-94

I have finally gotten around to writing this long-overdue letter. Please accept my humble apology for not having done so sooner, sometimes the realization of whats important and what is not takes time.

I wish first of all to express my thanks and gratitude for providing me with a philosophical infrastructure to follow. Also for the pleasures and the burdens it has added and taken away. In my case just having the text in plain sight on my desk or table top ready for reference provides me with inspiration.

I continue to be pleased with every new connection, integration and application of concepts and principles in the Neo-Tech 'Bible' that I make.

Even though I'm slow at understanding it's due more to laziness on my part than anything else. I clearly recognize the values to be gained and continue to strive at connection and application and eventually will

Poetical sing-song or hypnotically rhythmic meter are often found in the rhetoric of dictators, evangelists, politicians, theologians, mountebanks, social "intellectuals", media men, medicine men, psychotics, chanting shiites, and screaming terrorists. Consider how millions of normally rational Germans thrilled and responded to the poetical cadence and charisma of the consummate altruist neocheater, Adolph Hitler. The results: a reign of destruction with tens of millions of human beings slaughtered to let one man indulge his mysticism. All that slaughter was for nothing more than to help one neocheater fake a pseudo self-esteem in order to feel important. ...Twenty million dead so one man could *feel* important.

"So what!" cry the mystics as the lifetime efforts of a thousand productive, innocent individuals are blown to bits every day without a backward glance. So what if the troops roll across the country with military cadence and guns ablaze. So what if they level town after town, reducing to rubble and corpses all the values, beauty, and life that took generations of productive effort to build.

And that is all the chanting religious automatons or splendid Panzer divisions know how to do — to destroy in a moment, without a thought, all the values that producers labored for lifetimes to build. Chanting mobs or marching troops never glance back, never think for a moment of the death and destruction they leave behind. So what! the mystics and neocheaters cry. So what if it happens in Iran, Nazi Germany, Afghanistan, Cuba, Cambodia, or in our land. "I don't want to hear it! To hell with the lifetime efforts of productive individuals! ...Save the snail darter!"

By using specious nuggets of poetical "truth" and spell-binding slogans, malefactors, demagogues, and neocheaters such as Hitler, FDR, Nader, Khomeini, Jesus, Lincoln, Mao, Billy Graham, Pope Paul, Jerry Falwell, Castro, Kennedy, Martin Luther King Jr., Jim Jones could smoothly and quickly subvert the objective concepts of justice, good, and love (often while manipulating words to sound good, just, or loving) in order to promote their own rationalized schemes of "higher" causes. Such people use those poetic techniques to keep their rationalizations sounding valid. And their unthinking followers grab the beautiful nuggets of "truth"; they eagerly swallow the nuggets whole, without thought or challenge.

Modern Art

Below is a quotation from a forefather of modern art:

"Most people can today no longer expect to receive consolation from art. The refined, the rich, the distillers of quintessence (art critics) desire only the peculiar, the eccentric, the scandalous in today's art. And I myself, since the advent of cubism, have fed these fellows what they wanted, and satisfied these critics with all the ridiculous ideas that have passed through my head. "The less they understood them, the more they admired me. Through amusing myself with all these absurd farces, I became celebrated. But when I am alone, I do not have the effrontery to consider

Roy W.R. C-204, ENGLAND

   I have now completed my first reading of Neo-Tech 1 to 5 which has been the most enriching and enlightening experience of my life. It has fully opened my eyes to reality and given me a clear-thinking mind. I am now an atheist, and will always fight mysticism from within and without.

  Health and fitness has always been important to me, mainly to help slow down the aging process. Neo-Tech has certainly helped and corrected me there, especially regarding food and diet. I have slowed down on growing my own food (time wasting!) and stopped sugar and caffeine intake. I now have a copy of Dr. Atkins' Diet Revolution and Dr. Cooper's book, Aerobics. Already I feel much fitter, stronger and have much more energy. I feel youthful again! I am of couse very interested in achieving biological immortality.

  Although I am 67 I have been attending some business training courses with the intention of starting my own business. Reading Neo-Tech has <u>rapidly</u> increased my enthusiasm to start a business, and the Neo-Tech concepts will be my guidance and will greatly affect my future.

  I am proud and thrilled to be an owner of Neo-Tech and have just started my second reading.

 I am excitedly looking forward to all the years that lay ahead, thanks to you Dr. Wallace. My kindest regards and thanks to all your co-workers at the Neo-Tech Center.

Peter W.   R-459

Unbelievably detailed, well written, the only true source of valid life-improving information I have found. Truly well done.

Ed R.   R-1545

It helped me understand my wifes looking for another man after 7 years of marriage.

myself an artist at all, not in the grand old meaning of the word. Giotto, Titian, Rembrandt and Goya, they were great painters. I am only a public clown.

"I have understood my time and have exploited the imbecility, the vanity, the greed of my contemporaries. It is a bitter confession of mine — more painful than it may seem. But at least and at last it does have the merit of being honest."

Pablo Picasso, November, 1951
A master neocheater making an
honest statement.

To "appreciate" modern art, a person must figure out, interpret, or understand the "artist" and his meanings that "transcend reality". By contrast, all lasting classical art of great value is immediately recognized as a value by nearly everyone throughout all ages. Such art needs no interpretation or understanding of the artists. Such art represents beauty, values, and skill that are immediately recognized by the expert and the untrained layman alike. That is why the Catholic church acquired only classic art — art that needs no interpretation to understand and value. They were too shrewd to buy art needing interpretation.

Indeed, modern art seldom represents beauty, values, or skill. Moreover, the layman does not know what most modern "art" means, while the chic "expert" plays phoney games of interpreting the artist's meanings.

Today, the high prices of famous modern art works are supported by the tax-deduction system: Wealthy holders of such modern art can profit handsomely by donating purchased works to the major modern art museums. (e.g., The Museum of Modern Art in New York). In turn, such museums provide grossly inflated appraisal prices for tax deductions, while gaining the art works along with cash donations for those fake, tax-purpose appraisals. Thus, the wealthy "collectors" profit and modern-art museums perpetuate themselves through the tax system. When that neocheating scheme collapses, most modern art works will fall to their true market value and become essentially worthless.

The Law of the Arts

"For this seems, finally, to be the law of all the arts — the one essential prerequisite to the production of a great work of art is a great man. You cannot have the art without the man, and when you have the man you have the art. His time and his surroundings will color him; his art will not be at one time or place precisely what it might be at another; but in the end, the art is the man and at all times and in all countries is just as great as the man.

"Let us clear our minds, then, of the illusion that there is in any important sense such a thing as progress in the fine arts. We

John C.   R-676

OUTSTANDING. IDEAL SOURCE FOR IMPROVING PERSONAL GROWTH. I WAS TRULY AMAZED HOW ALL FACETS OF OF MY LIFE HAVE IMPROVED

Gary W. CB-105

Yes I am interested in RTSI. How productive a mind must become after a couple hundred years. Awesome thought!

A. S.   R-143

Does a masterful job of unmasking of countless thousands of years of theocratic and political control over the downtrodden masses. Finally a method whereby people can develop themselves to the fullest without depending on external "things".

may with a clear conscience judge every new work for what it appears in itself to be, asking of it that it be noble and beautiful and reasonable, not that it be novel or progressive. If it be great art it will always be novel enough, for there will be a great mind behind it, and no two great minds are alike. And if it be novel without being great, how shall we be the better off? There are enough forms of mediocre or evil art in the world already. Being no longer intimidated by the fetish of progress, when a thing calling itself a work of art seems to us hideous and degraded, indecent and insane, we shall have the courage to say so and shall not care to investigate it further."

Kenyon Cox
The American Academy of Arts
and Letters
December 13, 1912

Abstract Symbols — Real vs. Unreal

Real abstract symbols are accurate metaphors serving as powerful, shorthand communication that can deliver intense personalized values, especially in love relationships. On the other hand, unreal symbols are inaccurate metaphors or non sequiturs that misrepresent reality to undermine values in life and love. A person must differentiate between real and unreal symbols to flourish [Re: Table 73, Neo-Tech Reference Encyclopedia]. By making use of real symbols or metaphors, a person can experience new dimensions of life and romantic love. By recognizing and rejecting unreal symbols, a person preserves confident control over reality and, thus, over his or her own life, love relationships, and future.

Neo-Tech Advantage #105
SELF-AWARENESS VERSUS MYSTICAL AWARENESS

Developing accurate awareness of self and reality is the prime responsibility for all human beings. In fact, such awareness is a necessity to live prosperously and happily. That awareness is available to those who exert constant, rational thinking efforts toward understanding self, reality, and the relationship between the two. No one can deliver that awareness to another. Indeed, developing an accurate awareness of self and reality is one's major source of power throughout life.

Mystics struggle to avoid that constant, rational thinking effort needed to honestly and accurately assess one's self and reality. That understanding is the key element in being competent enough to prosper in a competitive world. But mystics seek anyone or anything promising to deliver prepackaged knowledge that lets them avoid the hard work required to develop their own knowledge and awareness. That is why mystics embrace such quackeries as astrology, graphology, biorhythms, fortune telling, graphoanalysis, most psychoanalysis, or any other flimflam that deludes them with a sense of gaining effortless knowledge, awareness, control. By accepting such

Bob M. R-4069

This month, I attend my high school class reunion, the 50th. If your publications had been available to me during high school age, my life would have been so much more rewarding.

Had Neo Tech been available to me early-on for constant reference, my approach to life and the world have been far different. But though the class reunion this month is my 50th, I am far from through with life. I intend to live without mysticism, with dead aim on reality; to provide and obtain value for value in all relationships; to be impervious to neocheating; to develop my abilities and intellect as much as possible; to be the best that I can be.

My best shots are yet to come! And Neo Tech is providing power and powder for those shots.

Charles A. R-4066, PAPA NEW GUINEA

Thank you Dr. Wallace for bringing me back to reality. I always thought there is "SOMEBODY" out there who is controlling my life. I use to go to church services every Sundays, pray and read my Bible when I feel depressed etc. Not anymore.

Now I can pick out the neocheaters from the producers in my working environment. Sometimes, I really detest the sight of them.

Thank you again Dr Wallace for sending me my "The Neo-Tech Discovery" package. It is the best ever literature I have read, that "REALLY CHANGE" my life. I hope to live to see the day when "NEO-TECH" overthrows the Bible and runs the world.

specious awarenesses conjured up by others, a person keeps drifting further from reality, becoming increasingly unaware, unhappy, and incompetent while rationalizing the opposite.

Acquiring awareness, competence, and happiness is a *self*-responsibility no one else can deliver. No one can deliver awareness and happiness to another person because no other person is in a position to:
1. know one's own integrated self.
2. think knowledgeably and contextually about one's own life.
3 control one's own actions.
4. integrate one's own nature with reality.

For anyone or any "authority" to have an integrated awareness of another person is impossible. No matter how complete or scientific looking (e.g., computer printouts of horoscopes or biorhythms), any such outside self-awareness analysis is invalid and mystical. And any seeming validity of such "self-awareness" packages is a specious illusion. Such illusions lead a person further away from an awareness of reality and deeper into the dumbness of mysticism — the disease that poisons all life and love.

Entirely different from such fake "awarenesses" through mysticism is the awareness arising from the mutual mirroring of character and personal qualities between self and a friend or romantic-love partner. Such mirroring genuinely enhances self-awareness, communication, and pleasure especially between romantic-love partners. That reflecting of a person's character and qualities is based on direct, intimate knowledge of that person. Such honest, valuable reflections differ profoundly from fake awareness packages mystically reflecting a person's character and qualities based on nothing.

As with happiness, self-awareness can not be given from one person to another. But by reflecting personal values, one can enhance another person's self-awareness in a similar way that one can enhance another person's happiness.

Neo-Tech Advantage #106
BEYOND UNDERSTANDING

Throughout the universe, much remains unknown. Yet, nothing tangible or conceptual is unknowable to the conscious mind. But with human emotions, certain specific feelings in a person can never be known or experienced by others. For all human emotions are products of individual characters based on unique finger-print combinations of physical and psychological natures. That means personal, unique experiences cannot be duplicated by others. Thus, any emotion in any individual person can never be exactly understood or fully known by any other person.

Recognizing one's inability to know certain emotional experiences in others is particularly useful in romantic-love relationships. Two important emotional experiences that cannot be cross-experienced or fully known between men and women are identified on the next page:

Jean Paul G.   F-110, FRANCE

Astonishing realistic synthesis of a "Tablet for success" for the present and the future. Neo Tech is an ensemble of prestigious, rigorous, coherent and undisputable methods.

Real stimulating feat that liberates the preconceived ideas, illusions and neurotic ideologies.

The Neo Tech Concepts really have a universal impact that is revitalizing and synergetic.

The best demonstration at work of the possibilities of the human mind to achieve happiness, integrated advantages and creative independence.

Finally Neo Tech is the spectacular success of "Pro-life principles" over all obstacles and obscurantisms, past and present.

Thank you for the lesson in humanism and the benefits I obtain from it every day.

1. The Penetrated versus The Penetrator
Experiences and Feelings

A man can never fully know the feelings, sensations, and emotions of a woman being penetrated during intercourse. Likewise, a woman can never fully know the feelings, sensations, and emotions of a man penetrating a woman. That eternal mystery of feelings further deepens between a man and a woman when they try to comprehend the feelings of orgasm in the other.

That eternal, unsolvable mystery between the sexes enhances the pleasure and excitement of a love relationship as each partner struggles to get closer to the other's feelings and experiences. But they can never close the gap. Never can the feelings of orgasm in one partner be known or felt by the other partner. And for romantic-love partners, that elusive mystery is delightfully maddening and eternally challenging. That unknown quality can forever keep the heterosexual* experience fresh, haunting, and mysterious. Men and women can only imagine the feelings and emotions in the other, always wondering yet never knowing how distant their imaginations are from reality.

2. Female-Nature Versus Male-Nature
Experiences and Feelings

A number of exclusive male or female emotions and experiences can never be fully experienced across sexual boundaries. Two examples are illustrated below:

<u>An Exclusive Female Experience:</u>

An implicit, constant physical threat toward women exists from essentially every man. That threat exists because the different physical and psychological natures of man and woman leave most men with the power literally to kill any woman at any time. Even smaller, weaker men could kill most bigger, stronger women in a bare-hand fight to the death. Thus, most women are perpetually at the physical mercy of men.

Under that threat, women often must silently take the degradation of being bullied or treated as sex objects as their earned qualities are ignored. No man can fully know that particular degradation because he has no way of duplicating the conditions which create that uniquely female situation. Even if the man were unjustly treated as a sex object, he would still have no way of knowing the woman's feelings. For unlike women, his different physiological, psychological, and social orientations do not leave him under a constant, implicit death threat.

---

*The homosexual experience of male-male or female-female intercourse cannot really simulate the exclusive male-female experience. Homosexuals fail to simulate heterosexual experiences not only because of the obvious physiological differences, but because of the profound psychological differences involved between the homosexual *act* and the heterosexual *act*. Even when the physical actions are the same (such as oral sex), the wide psychological differences between men and women preclude similarities in emotional experiences.

Richard P.   R-4536

    The clarity of Neo-Tech is as brilliant as any of the finest works that man has ever produced. The genius of Dr. Wallace is unarguable. The difficulty lies in the consumer of this jarring masterpiece. Despite nods of the head and audible agreement while reading, the integration process is slow, as old programmed thoughts and habits die kicking and screaming. However, die they must under the withering power of this great truth.

    Neo-Tech is the ultimate freedom, and the cost of such freedom is the initial pain of the psychological purge. However, never before (and I suppose never again) has that process been so worthwhile!

An Exclusive Male Experience:

A strong emotion felt by highly productive men is the desire for a peaceful core to counterbalance their aggressively assertive lives. That desire usually relates to a woman with whom such a man is free to retreat from his battle-field actions to experience peaceful love, tenderness, serenity. For only during that precious time is he free to fully expose and share his soul exclusively with another human being — his woman. During those moments, that woman becomes to him the supreme value in all the universe.

Ironically, the strongest, most productive, independent men have the greatest need and capacity to receive a woman's love, support, and tenderness. Tragically, however, many such men never recognize or admit, even to themselves, that supremely important emotional need and pleasure. Similarly, strong men often never admit to other emotional needs such as being free to cry when suffering great sadness or pain. ...A man crying has been erroneously viewed as a weakness or unmanly.

Many women are unaware of the need in productive men for a peaceful, private world containing a one-woman love. But women who understand that need hold a key for delivering powerful values and happiness to their men and to themselves. Understanding and filling the need for a peaceful core in aggressively productive men is among the most powerful of all binding ingredients in romantic-love relationships.

Aggressively productive women also have a need to periodically retreat into peace and serenity. Yet, that need does not comprise the same psychosexual emotions as within men because of the inherent psychological and physiological differences between men and women.

Neo-Tech Advantage #107
VALUE THEFT VS. VALUE EXCHANGE

Through the 2000-year history of altruistic-based cultures, most material achievements have been maligned and attacked by neocheating politicians, theologians, and other neocheating mystics and altruists.* The motive for

---

*Adolph Hitler was a consummate altruist. He scorned material values in his personal life. He was the personification of asceticism and sacrifice. He demanded the eventual sacrifice of all human beings and their values to his deemed "higher" cause of duty and obedience to society. He fed his weak ego and pseudo self-esteem with an ever increasing need for power and control over others by force. Similarly, people like Jesus, Mao, Pol Pot, Nader and other altruists ignore honesty, scorn material values, and survive on unearned power gained by neocheating deceptions or brute force. They need increasing control over others to support their weak egos. ...All such altruists gain their power by attacking values, harming or killing the innocent value producer, and usurping values earned by others.

Roland D.   F-113, FRANCE

At the first reading of Neo-Tech I had many reticences. At the time I nearly gave it up but certain concepts kept my interest so I decided to read it for a second time. I realised then that I had been controlled all my life and I was beginning to feel my conscience, that is to say my autonomy. I was starting to feel free. Today I have taken hold of my life conscious of my existence. I thank you for that. I am with you all the way.

Laurent B.   F-112, FRANCE

Really satisfied with Neo Tech. I want to let you know of the joy I experience at each reading. Because of Neo Tech I see life and people with optimism. When a problem arises I refer to Neo Tech and each time I find the non mystical, logical solution which I would never have thought of or even hoped to. Neo Tech is a key. The key to understanding the mechanism that guides man and society. The key to living in symbiosis with his environment and to decipher what one had never dare to face. Simply the key to happiness, with a long range view.

scorning human-produced values has always been to saddle the value producers with unearned guilt. Once saddled with guilt, value producers can more easily be manipulated, duped, and usurped out of their earned power and values. Indeed, to survive, professional neocheaters and mystics must constantly usurp material and psychological values from those producers.

The production of values for others is the single most important function of any person's life. Every person's survival and happiness as well as every facet of his or her physical, mental, and psychological well-being depends on the production of competitive values for others. If a person chooses not to produce sufficient values to survive, then that person must become parasitically dependent on the producers to survive by cajoling, neocheating, deception, or theft.

Thus, the producer (not the consumer*) is essential to human life and happiness. By contrast, nonproductive people are dependent on the producers to survive. And those nonproducers who neocheat to survive exist with deteriorating competence and mounting envy and unhappiness. That nonproducer's life soon terminates in Growth Death, then in emotional death, and finally in physical death.

A society that functions exclusively for the rational benefit of the individual has never existed.** A totally free, just, and rational society would by definition be a Neo-Tech society. Such a society would be a free-enterprise, nonforce government...a government and society that has yet to exist on planet Earth. The ethical essence of a Neo-Tech society is the holding of individual rights as supreme. Thus, *any* form of initiatory force, coercion, or fraud against any individual by any individual, group, society, or government is immoral and thus is ostracizable.

Any suggestion of force-free societies strikes fear into all neocheating politicians, demagogues, and mystics. Knowing they could not survive in a

---

*"Consumerism" is an invalid concept conjured up by self-appointed consumer advocates. They are backed by neocheating journalists, dishonest academe, self-appointed environmentalists, "liberal" politicians, socially chic "intellectuals", and fake business people, including most lawyers and many bankers. ...Indeed, the value producer, not the consumer, is the hero of all conscious life and of all civilizations throughout the universe.

**A society has no moral or logical reason to exist except to benefit the individual and protect his and her property rights. But a fully moral, logical society has never existed. For the producers have always been tricked into accepting and supporting value-destroying mystics and neocheaters posing as "authorities". And those "authorities" always use altruism to control value producers through false guilt. Thus, those producers work to support those very neocheaters who harm, pillage, and eventually destroy them, their loved ones, and everyone's happiness.

I WILL NEVER THIRST AGAIN NOW THAT I HAVE OBTAINED THE FOUNTAIN OF KNOWLEDGE: THE NEO-TECH DISCOVERY by Dr. F. WALLACE. HE HAS INTEGRATED ALL THE MODERN-DAY CONCEPTS, NEEDED FOR SURVIVAL IN OUR SOCIETY, IN ONE PRECISE MANUAL. NO ONE NEEDS TO DROWN IN THE SEA OF NEO-CHEATERS, WITH THIS KIT!

ONCE THE CONCEPTS HAVE CRYSTALLIZED, ONE CAN ONLY TAKE CONTROL AND MOVE ON WITH LIFE IN THE BEST POSSIBLE DIRECTION. A RESULTING HIGH SELF-ESTEEM WILL FOREVER STAND FIRMLY ON THE "NEO-TECH" FOUNDATION. MY GRATITUDE GOES OUT TO DR. WALLACE IN HELPING THE LITERATE WORLD IN SORTING OUT ITS GOALS WITH MUCH HARMONY!

nonforce, noncoerced, free-enterprise system, they desperately vilify the free, competitive values of such a society with out-of-context attacks designed to undercut values. For in a Neo-Tech society, mystics and neocheaters would quickly be identified and banished forever. ...On rejecting mystics and neocheaters, the value producers would be free to prosper guiltlessly and happily by benefiting others.

Prohibiting initiatory force, threats of force, and fraud is the only law in any Neo-Tech society. Highly effective enforcement of the individual-rights law by an integrated ostracizing system is much more punishing and effective than any police force or government jailing system. Thus, with that single, highly enforceable law, each individual would be solely responsible for his or her own actions, life, and well-being. The resulting free-choice interaction among free people would deliver maximum benefits to each individual and society. That, in turn, would greatly enhance every productive person's well-being and happiness. Then, to survive, the nonproductive mystics and neocheaters would quickly have to begin producing values for others instead of usurping values from others.

Most social interactions are reducible to individual interactions. Relationships involving value exchange occur, for example, in all valid business, friendship, and romantic-love relationships. The basic requirement for any valuable human relationship is the exchange of tangible values. But, nonproductive people often feign contempt toward competitive, tangible, and material values. For they are trying to conceal their defaults in failing to produce the competitive values needed to be self-sufficient and happy.

From the production of competitive values, all other values grow, including prosperity, self-esteem, psychological well-being, romantic love, and abiding happiness. Furthermore, competitive, tangible, and material values are important building blocks and binding ingredients of all conscious relationships, especially business, friendship, and romantic-love relationships. All nonproductive mystics and neocheaters desperately try to deny the crucial role of producing competitive values in living happily and in gaining romantic love. But only through the exchange of such values can personal relationships become fully integrated: From an exchange of tangible or material values, a far greater stability, intensity of love, and abiding happiness can develop than is possible from a relationship consisting only of abstract values.

Material or tangible values in a romantic-love relationship can also directly affect sexuality: Exchanges of tangible values can markedly increase sexual intensity and psychuous pleasure.

Still, abstract values are the crucial ingredient for initiating and establishing a friendship or a romantic-love relationship. However, tangible and material values *combined* with abstract values are the variables that cause psychuous pleasures and happiness to ignite and then grow constantly

Jeff C.   C-1011

MR. WALLACE:

I am writting to thank you for writting the "Advanced Concepts" and making the "Concepts" available to me.

The seventy dollar purchase I made in 1982 to obtain your writtings was the best investment I have ever made.

Before reading the "Concepts" I was the adolescent mystic man like most men living now and for the past 2000 years. After incorporating N.T. into my life — My Power is growing everyday, My Income is Constantly Increasing, I am Invincible in all my undertakings.

Neo-Tech has made my life GREAT, COLORFUL AND EXCITING.

I agree with you — GREAT DAYS ARE Coming — RENAISSANCE, ACHIEVEMENT, GIANT LEAPS IN PROGRESS FOR MAN!

I ADMIRE YOUR ACHIEVEMENT.

THANK YOU.

Frank W. R-532

Neo-Tech is a rude but welcomed awakening. Neo-Tech puts everything into proper perspective and erases the guilt feelings of the things I have been striving for, and the neocheaters who are trying to take them away.

I am a producer, an achiever and doer. I am resetting my goals along Neo-Tech lines. I have only begun to study it, but am enjoying every minute of the time invested.

[Re: Table 74, Neo-Tech Reference Encyclopedia]. Both love and deep friendship relationships require a base of abstract values to start. But the production of tangible and material values is necessary for moving a relationship into unlimited growth and high-gear happiness. A comparison of abstract values versus tangible values in friendship and love relationships is illustrated by the following chart:

ABSTRACT VALUES VERSUS TANGIBLE VALUES
(Delivered from one person to another person
in friendship or love relationships)

Abstract Values

Psychologically valuable reflections

Philosophically valuable reflections

Reflections of each other's values

Analytical feedback of thoughts and ideas

Mirroring of personal worth, values, and ideas

Tangible and Material Values

Practical contributions to increasing efficacy and productivity

Practical contributions to reducing or eliminating value-destroying and time-wasting problems and errors

Practical contributions to producing tangible and material values

Providing tangible and material values to the other in the relationship

Neo-Tech Advantage #108
VALUE EXCHANGE IN FRIENDSHIP AND ROMANTIC-LOVE RELATIONSHIPS

Without value-generating interactions, two people are of little direct value to each other — at least no more value that any two random people might be to each other. Valuable human relationships evolve when two people deliver objective values to one another. That exchange of values measures the value of a relationship.

Aside from the intrinsic value of human life that exists among all people, a person is not a value to others by merely existing. Instead, a person must deliver desired values to others to be a value. And a person must continue delivering values to be a continuing value. Moreover, one must continue

Paul W. R-2652

You have created a well defined and logical road map to a life of happiness and success. Any question which arises in a readers mind is anticipated and answered in a mind-opening manner. After reading much of the "self-help" materials on the market I must conclude that you HAVE the only complete, integrated system to help one reach their "highest and best use!" Congratulations to a mega producer!

Fernando C.   F-118, FRANCE

You have written the truth about man. Its a good thing the concepts were developped at the end of the 20th century if they had been brought up in any other centuries since man has learned to read in the time the mystics were in power they certainly would have made you dissapear.
If Neo Tech was a country it would a world power, we are the best that is our philosophy. You have the head office in the U.S.A. the most modern country in the world.
Here in France we are far away from all these concepts because the mystics and neocheaters are everywhere now
Thank you.

adding new values to existing values to experience value growth within one's self and within a relationship. Value growth is a self-created, pyramiding process that requires rational thought and constant effort to sustain. Such a growth process is the essence of human living. For value growth fills life's needs and delivers life's major rewards — abiding prosperity, romantic love, and happiness.

To fully experience life and sustain value growth requires continuous thought and effort. The need for value growth is not someone's philosophical theory or ethic. That need is an integral part of reality: Constant value growth is required for the conscious organism to function properly. A person makes a disastrous error by failing to put forth the rational thought and effort needed to produce growing, competitive values for others.

Tragically, most people choose to stop their growth early in life. Many stop soon after exerting the learning efforts to read and write. When they stop exerting that effort, they stop growing. The quality of their lives then declines until physical death. Without that growth, people cannot experience abiding prosperity, happiness, and psychuous pleasures.

Growth Death is a great, unnecessary tragedy. It never has to happen to anyone; it is imposed on no one. Growth Death occurs only when the victim chooses to avoid the rational thought and effort required to produce and deliver increasing net values to others. When Growth Death occurs, then all value-based friendship and love relationships stop growing and begin to die.

* * *

Both romantic-love relationships and friendships can involve deep psychological, philosophical, and communication interactions. But the distinguishing characteristic of a romantic-love relationship is its physical-sexual sharing that in turn offers physical and psychological intimacy unobtainable from any other human relationship. Those unique physical/psychological intimacies can lead to growing psychuous pleasures.

Friendship is a necessary ingredient of romantic love. Without friendship, no basis for romantic love exists.* A romantic-love relationship has all the ingredients of a value-oriented friendship plus the powerful ingredient of physical intimacy and sex. ...Friendship can be more personally intimate and involved than any other human relationship except romantic love.**

---

*Valuable, family-love relationships also develop from a base of friendship.
**A friendship or any human relationship changes irrevocably upon having sexual relations. But a sexual relationship is not synonymous with a romantic-love relationship. Still, a romantic-love relationship must by nature involve sex.

Wayne R.   R-6038

I found your work very enlightening. Dr. Wallace weaves an intricate and logical matrix of information into a working system of knowledge. So many philosophers and so called "great thinkers" have fed our minds with so much abstract and irrational nonsense — it's amazing that we even know which way is up! Dr. Wallace exposes neocheaters for what they are — LEECHES! Politicians always pretend to serve our best interests but they are out for personal gain. The Church wields tremendous power through the use of guilt over anything dealing with sex. The Church mauls and mutilates the minds of millions with their egalitarian philosophy It's a real shame that most people take the easy way out, they sit back and let politicians and priests do their thinking for them. Life involves growth + change not stagnation + neocheating (aka. death). Neo-Tech will solve the neocheating problem, It is a must for everyone. I am looking foward to the Neo Tech future. Thank you Dr. Wallace.

    W.R.

Lois M.   R-7095

The more I study and apply "Neo-Tech" it exposes the deceptions of mysticism, politicians, and neocheaters. They are like windows you can see right threw them. "Neo-tech" is the only way we can achieve guiltless profits, pleasures, happiness and biological immortatily in our life time

The value of friendships should neither be underestimated nor overestimated. A person can achieve unlimited psychuous pleasures and happiness through romantic love alone, without any close friend beyond one's love partner. Friendship alone, no matter how valuable or extensive, can never deliver the full spectrum of values and happiness available from a friendship-based romantic love.

Only two ingredients are needed for a complete, prosperous, happy life:
 (1) achieving self-sufficient independence through honest production of competitive values for others
 (2) achieving psychuous pleasures through romantic love.

In other words, a person needs only his or her productive work and a romantic-love partner to achieve a full-range, prosperous, happy life. But productive work is a basic requirement for achieving romantic love. In that sense, productive work is a cause and romantic love is an effect.

Productive work is the basic requirement for all human values. And romantic love and psychuous pleasures are the rewards for achieving those values. ...One cannot experience self-esteem, happiness, and romantic love without productive work. But one can experience self-esteem, happiness, and productive work without romantic love.

Friendship can offer great values and pleasurable experiences. Yet, friendships, even good friendships, can in certain cases drain valuable time needed for high levels of business, creativity, and achievement. In a demanding business or intensely creative work, a person with a valuable romantic-love partner can often reach higher levels of achievement and happiness with few or no other friends. Friendships, moreover, are subject to errors that can turn into liabilities which drain a person's productiveness, efficacy and, thus, happiness.

***

In the end, reality prevails over all life. The total experience of every person's life always moves toward justice as reality asserts itself: Productive, rational individuals increasingly gain prosperity, love, and happiness from life. Conversely, unproductive, irrational individuals increasingly lose prosperity, love, and happiness — no matter what the surface appearances.

Abstract values of a friendship are normally not negotiable for tangible and material values. Likewise, tangible and material values normally cannot be converted into abstract values. Occasional exceptions do exist. Exceptions occur mainly in romantic-love relationships because the intense physical/psychological interactions tend to pull abstract values and material

Michel C.   F-114, FRANCE

Extremely interesting information that must be read by the maximum of people and will bring to those who are looking for truth and real values an acknowledged guide.

A personal experience that one wants to yell it from the rooftop so that everyone will exploit their potential to the maximum and become aware of the neo-cheaters all around them. I am anxious to participate and make contact in France of people who have become conscious of the Neo-Tech concepts.

R.F. A.   R-3962

Dr. Wallace:

The individual has only one decision to make: To practice or not practice the tenets of the Neo-Tech Discovery. I now know precisely where I stand, thanks to you Dr. Wallace.

values closer together. At times, within a romantic-love relationship, those values can become interrelated. For example, emotional and sexual love provided by one partner can tangibly increase the creative, productive output of the other partner. Likewise, certain tangible values can amplify abstract values. For example, creative and productive accomplishments of one partner can increase the emotional love, sexual exhilaration, and psychuous pleasures of the other partner..

Generally, in a friendship or romantic love relationship, an exchange of abstract values (be they healthy, neurotic, or a mixture) is taken for granted and occurs naturally. In friendship relationships, much of the abstract value interchange consists of open, casual exchanges of ideas and suggestions — a type of easy two-way communication that often is mutually valuable. Indeed, such exchanges of ideas and suggestions occur in most good conversations between friends or lovers. Other abstract values exchanged between two people in a valid love or friendship relationship may include psychologically pleasing or enhancing reflections, consistent encouragement (especially during difficult times), mirroring various psychological values, understanding feedback of the other's thoughts or activities, and the exchange of practical ideas obtained from each person's unique, life experiences.

Sometimes abstract values from a friend or love partner can be beneficially integrated into one's personal life to increase awareness, productivity, and happiness. Generally, abstract values are offered freely, without the thought or expectation of material or tangible payment. In a love or a friendship relationship, no one needs to measure or weigh that natural interchange of abstract values. For that exchange is freely taken and given as a natural, pleasurable, expected part of any good relationship.

Thus, abstract values cannot be used to pay for material values. For material values must always be fairly traded. Material values represent irreplaceable segments of a person's life, effort, and time required to earn those values. Every productive human being needs to trade (not give away) his or her produced values in order to survive, grow, and be happy. If material and tangible values are not traded mutually and fairly,* then a portion of a person's life is sacrificed to another person at the expense of both people. As a result of that unfairness, both happiness and friendship decline. [See "Two Letters about Friendship and Love", pages 379-389; Neo-Tech Reference Encyclopedia.]

Those who misunderstand the nature of friendship or romantic love may try to use abstract values as payment for material values. In doing so, they

---

*Fairly traded, tangible values do not necessarily mean evenly traded, tangible values. Moreover, a highly competent, nonmystical housewife can contribute great tangible and material values to her husband's ability to work more effectively, thus, generate more values and income. For that, he fairly trades by providing his wife with tangible and material goods. By contrast, if either partner is, by choice, net destructive toward the other, nothing can then be fairly exchanged and the relationship should end. [Re: Concept 95, Neo-Tech Reference Encyclopedia]

Bob S.   R-3677

My first reading of NEO-TECH triggered many emotions. Unveiling politicians for the cheats that they are was compatable with my thinking but the attacks on religion, Christianity and Christ himself evoked anger.

Before reading NEO-TECH I would not have classified myself as a mystic. I am age 45 and have been in the insurance claim business for many years. I saw myself as a producer of values but also a person with a devout belief in Christ. I made generous contributions to the Church even when I really couldn't afford to.

I had the mystical philosophy of "spreading my bread on the waters and it would return to me many fold."

I honestly forced myself to read NEO-TECH completely and not throw it away. I am reading it now for a second time and periodically I re-read parts that relate to things going on in my life at that particular time.

There are changes going on in me. I have stopped contributions to mystics. I have discontinued going to church and don't feel any adverse psychological effect. My two children still believe in religion and attend church. They question me on my change. At this point I respond by evading the issue. I can't explain it clearly to them. They are age 17 and 12 and depend on me to take them to church.

The Logic of NEO-TECH is sound to me. NEO-TECH FOR CHILDREN IS A NECESSITY IF NEO-TECH GOALS ARE TO BE ACHEIVED. NEO-TECH for adults is a valuable contribution to happy successful living. Please keep me advised on new developments.

are exploiting their friendship or love relationships. Such people unjustly extract material values from others for the "privilege" of those others being in their presence. They unilaterally deem their abstract values as payment for tangible and material values. That kind of exploitation, aside from being unjust and parasitical, poisons the relationship.

More important, habitual trading of abstract values for material values diminishes a person's ability to produce and deliver material values. Such unfair trading leaves that person increasingly incompetent and dependent on others for material or tangible values. ...The potential for friendship, romantic love, and happiness is always the greatest among value producing men and women who fairly trade tangible and material values in all of their relationships.

Neo-Tech Advantage #109
UNDERSTANDING JUSTICE, GOOD, AND LOVE

Contrary to the pronouncements of most modern linguists and social "scientists", words and language are primarily tools of thinking, not of communication. To prevent clear thinking and detections by others, mystics and neocheaters must constantly attack and debase words and language. For their existences depend on obscuring, distorting, and concealing reality through fuzzy thinking of each victim. To accomplish that obfuscation, they (1) use words out of context, (2) twist and invert meanings of key words and concepts, and (3) dishonestly use rationalizations and non sequiturs. ...They develop their own newspeak without regard to honesty.

Honest intellectuals concerned about the decay of language know that twisting and misusing words corrode the tools of thinking. But that is only half the problem. Protecting honesty and language also involves *context*. Powerful thinking requires not only using consistent, exact definitions but also precise, accurate contexts for all words or concepts. To accurately define meanings *and* contexts of important words and concepts is not only central to precise communication, oral or written, but is the key to effective thinking and understanding reality.

By contrast, twisting meanings of key words and using concepts out of context are the primary techniques of many mystics and neocheaters, especially those in the media. For they exist by distorting or inverting language to deceive others. They invert the meanings of important words in order to rationalize their deceptions, destructions, thefts, use of force, and other irrational, immoral actions. And they do that often under inverted newspeak pretexts of justice, social good, human rights, and "higher" causes.

In seeking honesty and understanding of reality, one must be aware of *both* definition and context of key words. But neocheating "intellectuals",

Ronny S.   R-375

Neo Tech may well be the greatest discovery of this century. It explains exactly how mysticism works. However it may never achieve widespread knowledge or popularity because it seems to me that people actually <u>work</u> to avoid responsibility for their own lives, much harder than they would have to work to achieve happiness by using Neo Tech.

Partrick L.   F-119, FRANCE

Because of Neo Tech life makes sense again because I was beginning to doubt the qualities of honesty, sincerity, truth tenderness and love. You opened my eyes and for that I will be forever in your debt. I am still young and I will profit entirely of the information found in Neo Tech.
Thank you to Dr Wallace and all of you who work to make Neo Tech known in the world

in their need to conceal meanings, exert mighty efforts to distort and invert the meaning of crucial words such as:

Capitalism	Peace
Consumer	Producer
Ecology	Reality
Good	Rights
Justice	Selfishness
Love	Truth

Words can also represent concepts. The more basic the concept, the greater abstraction and integration is required to fully grasp that concept. The most difficult concepts to grasp in their full, accurate context are the most basic human concepts such as:

Good
Justice
Love

Throughout history, those three basic concepts have been used out of context or inverted in meaning by all neocheating mystics and politicians in their constant need to camouflage their destructive, parasitical existences. When neocheaters speak of justice, they are usually promoting unjust, destructive actions against the value producer, objective values, individual rights, private property, and the means to achieve happiness. When neocheaters speak of good — the common good or the "higher" good — they are usually promoting destructive altruism designed to usurp values earned by others. When neocheaters speak of love and brotherhood, they are usually promoting envious schemes to cripple competitive value producers.

To fully understand the basic concepts of justice, good, and love requires an accurate understanding of human nature relative to reality. That understanding requires integrations of the many specific concepts identified by Neo-Tech. To understand the concept of romantic love, for example, requires understanding the various Neo-Tech/Psychuous concepts needed to understand romantic love in full, accurate context. Because the concepts of *justice*, *good*, and *love* are inextricably linked, all three concepts are fully integrated throughout the Neo-Tech literature.

Neo-Tech Advantage #110
FACTS AND JUSTICE

In American cities, white neighborhoods are generally safer than black neighborhoods. Throughout history, men have reached greater heights in intellectual, aesthetic, and commercial achievements than have women. In general, Jews are more intelligent, productive, creative and, therefore, more potent in life and sex than people of other religions, nationalities, or

Einar F. C-102

Dear Mr. Flint,

I received my Neo-Tech manuals on January 31 with a great deal of enthusiasm and anticipation as to what I was about to read. As I began to read, however, I was shocked at what I was reading as it contradicted everything I had been brought up to believe. My first inclination was to put it all aside and dismiss it from my mind as so much rubbish.

I have always been an avid reader and have quite a library of books, mostly philosophical and religious. Your Neo-TEch material prompted me to read a book "Deceptions and Myths of the Bible" by Harold Graham, which had been in my library for a long time but one I had not yet read. Having read this book it opened my eyes to many things I had formerly believed and it persuaded me that I had been deceived all these years. It was then that I went back to the Neo-Tech manuals with a different perspective and understanding of what I was reading. Now I am enthused and eager to learn more.

I only wish that I had known of this forty years ago. What a difference it would have made in my life. At the age of sixty it is not easy to begin all over again and erase all that subconcious garbage which has been deposited in my mind, but I will try.

I have always been one to "think" about things but was always told that there are just some things one has to accept on "faith" and not to question. I accepted that but there was always that nagging feeling that something was not just right. Things just did not "add up". So I continued to read and to search and to think but no answers were forthcoming until I started to read Neo-Tech. NOW THINGS ARE BEGINNING TO ADD UP.

R.T.A. C-109, NORTH WALES

Dear Sir,

Thank you for enlightening me with the Neo-Tech Discovery. It is a truly discerning piece of work.

I find is has pulled together all the loose ends in one's thinking, giving a coherent, rational outlook on life.

To use a metaphor: the binoculars were blurred — now they are in focus — the view is now fine.

races.* Are those the words of a racist, a chauvinist, a Zionist zealot?

---

*Jews are generally more evolved, moral, productive, intelligent, creative, and potent than other groups of people mainly because the Jewish religion is less harmful than religions or mysticism practiced by other people. The Jewish religion itself is harmful and irrational as are all mystical religions and governments. But the Judeo ethics project less guilt toward value producers and less malevolence toward human values such as productive effort, sexual pleasures, creativity, self-sufficiency than do the much more virulent, envious ethics of Christianity (especially Roman Catholicism), Islam, and other religions. Also, the Jewish religion is more oriented around respect for self and less around respect for external "authority" such as government. In addition, the post-Renaissance Jewish god has been basically a god of justice as opposed to the Christian god of mercy. (Mercy is subjective and unjust — the opposite of justice.**) Jewish people, therefore, have been freer to live for their rational best interests. That allows them to more fully and guiltlessly develop their own creative and intellectual capacities to the maximum benefit of themselves, society, and civilization.

The state of Israel, despite its illegal origins, is comprised of individuals — mainly innocent individuals. And Israel today has perhaps the only moral foreign policy among all nations. That policy is based on the profound moral right to self-defense. In fact, a single-purpose foreign policy based entirely on self-defense is the only rational, moral foreign policy possible. For that alone, Israel must be recognized and morally supported.

But twentieth-century Zionism is a catastrophic, mystical/racist error that violates the individual and property rights of many Palestinians. The injustices and moral wrongs experienced by those Palestinians forcefully separated from their homes and properties were very real and condemnable (even though the Palestinians who suffered property losses were financially compensated by Israel). Yet, as justice asserts itself over the long-term, the Zionists will pay the price for their neocheating injustices. Still, today, most Jews are innocent. For, they are not responsible for that error and can never be held guilty by association or penalized for the actions of others. Likewise, the immorality of the Zionists can never be condoned, even though the magnitude of their immorality seems counterbalanced by the atrocities committed throughout history against the Jews. ...Those past atrocities against the Jews were mainly committed out of envy over their superior accomplishments, successes, competence, and happiness.

** Based on immutable, objective principles, justice is an end in itself. The idea behind all modern government "justice" systems is not justice at all, but is the subjective, arbitrary idea of mercy. For mercy nicely serves the

(Footnote continued on next page)

Ramon S.   R-7065

Of all the so-called truths that I have been exposed to, none has been as objectively real to me as has Neo-Tech.

I am so overwhelmingly pleased with Neo-Tech by virtue of the fact it has removed the mysticism and all the false notions that have permeated my entire life with confusion.

Neo-Tech has given me the light, self-confidence and esteem; direction and knowledge; energy and wisdom necessary to pursue objectively the goals that I have never dreamed possible to attain.

I have introduced Neo-Tech to my eldest son as well as to other members of my family. He and I have started our own business and with the help of Neo-Tech, great strides have been made on the road to success.

I would like to express how proud I am to have this Neo-Tech knowledge and philosophy, especially in view of all the rewarding benefits that I have enjoyed since first reading the discovery.

Thank you so much

Perhaps so if such statements were directed toward or used in judgment of particular individuals. But the statements are made in reference to objective, statistical facts that are real. When those statements are placed in the proper context of being generalized statistics that do *not* characterize any particular individual, they are then validly applicable to *generalized* situations.

If the data are accurate, then in-context inferences from those data are true and must be considered in order to make honest evaluations and correct decisions. Consider, for example, the provable statistic that in all major U.S. cities a significantly higher percentage of Blacks than Whites injure and murder people.* That is a statistical fact regardless of the reasons or so-called social causes. But to apply that statistical fact to any individual would be out-of-context, unjust, and wrong because such statistics can not be validly or honestly applied to any particular individual.

On the other hand, to ignore in-context facts is an evasion of reality and dishonest. Moreover, to evade facts is a dishonest evasion of reality that mystically conceals the knowledge required to deal accurately with reality in making effective decisions and judgments. For example, consider if a white or black person is concerned with physical safety for one's self, loved ones, and property: What if that person had the choice of living in equivalent housing in a predominantly black, depressed community or in a predominantly white, equally depressed community? Basing that choice on facts, that person would choose to live in the white community. Indeed, that

---

(Footnote continued from page 377)
neocheater's need to control others. How mercy only serves the neocheaters is most evident in the ideas behind jailing people: Imprisonment for rehabilitation, correction, or deterrent are mystical notions designed by neocheaters to arbitrarily exercise force over individuals. The only punishments that are moral (including execution for first-degree murder) are those based solely on justice to the victim. Mystics and neocheaters will always hide the concept of justice for it would leave them powerless, stripping them of their major aggression tool for controlling and usurping values from others. For example, with the concept of objective justice, all such victimless-crime and confiscatory-tax laws would be unenforceable because no individual had been previously injured by force, fraud, or coercion to which justice could be addressed. In fact, enforcing such subjective laws is the antithesis of justice in that such laws make problems where none exist in order to unjustly and criminally control others by force or threat of force.

*References: "Crime in the United States: Uniform Crime Report", issued annually by the FBI; "Crime and Race" M.E. Wolfgang and B. Cohen.

Dallas W.   R-1439

I found Neo-Tech to be a truly fascinating piece of literary work. The realization that I am my own Master, wholly & completely, was a new experience for me. To be free of guilt is one of the greatest benefits from Neo-Tech for me. I enjoy not caring what others think of me. As a business broker, I am constantly able to "read" people who are potential buyers & sellers. My sales have increased through the use of some of Neo-Tech's teachings.

You have shed the light on how truly harmful drugs, alcohol, & religion are to one's self. It is truly amazing to see how entrenched all three are in our society today. And I believe them to be great destroyers of one's self-esteem & ambition. Without self-esteem & ambition, one will wander through life with no direction & end up as a poor pawn only to be used by the Neocheaters.

I am amazed at what I see of the people that I come in contact with. People of varying degrees of drive, self-esteem, & ambition. Neo-Tech has given me the knowledge necessary to deal with people & to direct my actions toward them accordingly. Of biological immortality, I am very interested in the pursuit & realization of this goal.

In closing, I thank you for such a thought-provoking work.
Sincerely yours,

Marshall T.   R-1167

It brought it all together & gave a moral reason for believing & trusting that productivity is the key.

person would have made the correct decision without necessarily harboring any bigotry or without acting unjustly or harmfully toward any individual.

Likewise, from factual statistics, a much higher percentage of men than women accomplish major intellectual, artistic, and commercial achievements. Regardless of the causes or reasons, that statistical fact has been true throughout recorded history and is still true today. However, with the increased educational, social, economic, and financial freedoms now available to Western women, the percentage of women attaining high achievement has increased. But the increase is nowhere near the proportion of increased opportunities for women. Women in general, have not fully utilized their increased freedoms and opportunities. Still, to blindly apply that statistical fact to any individual women would be unjust, inaccurate, and out of context. But to ignore that statistical fact in its proper, generalized context would be a mystical evasion of reality that could result in serious errors in judgment and thinking needed for honest business and personal decisions.

Proper in-context generalizations based on accurate facts is necessary to accurately perceive reality, to know what is going on, and to make correct decisions. On the other hand, a person must never apply statistical data or generalizations to any specific individual. To do so would not only be unjust and dishonest, but would be inaccurate, misleading, and a mystical distortion of reality.

Conversely, applying individual characterizations to general groups of people would also be invalid, dishonest, misleading, unjust, and mystical. To most effectively use the Neo-Tech/Psychuous advantages, one must not only integrate thought with action, but must integrate both in-context generalized facts with in-context specific facts [Re: Table 77, Neo-Tech Reference Encyclopedia].

Neo-Tech Advantage #111
NEO-TECH — THE BENEFICENT SOLUTION TO RACISM

As with any feeling or emotion, an unacted-upon racist feeling is not subject to guilt or moral judgment. Mind crimes do not exist, except through the false-guilt ploys of political, religious, and "intellectual" neocheaters. Only when racist feelings are translated into harmful actions does racism become unjust, immoral, guilty. Destructive, government-implemented racism occurs in Zionist Israel and in apartheid South Africa. But much more destructive racism occurs in all Arab, Moslem, and black-African dictatorships as well as in many Asian countries such as the USSR and India. But, ironically, the freest countries practicing racism potentially present the most tragic dilemmas:

What is the remedy to Zionist racism that forcibly violates the individual rights of millions of Palestinians? The only moral position is to restore full individual rights to everyone, including the Palestinians. But that would seem

George H. C-111

Dear Dr. Wallace:

Neo-Tech has provided me with the missing pieces to the puzzle of why peoples, governments, societies & religions act the way they do.

Frankly, without using Neo-Tech as a guidebook, mankind will continue to wander in the fog of unconscious confusion & death.

In the course of my continuing search I found Neo-Tech & with it my findings were confirmed & the "Big Picture" emerged.

It is extremely valuable to have so much concentrated truth contained within these few publications and (as you well know I'm sure) to have access to even a portion of this information without Neo-Tech would require shelves of books (some of which might only have a few pages of useful information)!!

But, with Neo Tech, all your readers have the concentrated truth readily at hand for review & reference.

I can now go forward & look towards a productive, fulfilled life.

Thank you for a product of great & perpetual value.

G.H.

Frederic D. C-112, FRANCE

MONSIEUR

I read with a great interest the Fantastic Dr WALLACE's book.

Mr F. WALLACE wrote the most genial and useful book that had ever been written.

Thanks to this book I have now an ambition : create my own enterprise. This book completely destroys the power of such card-sharpers as politicians, religious, mystics or same close relatives.

It ends with tyranny, lies and oppression and takes everyone on a new lease of life, to the life we should have had if we hadn't be handled by what we can called "anti-human persons" that is to say those whose only dreams are dreams of mastery and depravity of the human race.

Dr WALLACE's book is the best cure we may bring to someone who is seeking for understanding "his" life.

No matter the criticism you may face, I'm sure you will begin because you are the great luck of Humanity.

to allow even greater violations of individual rights by permitting a much worse, Syrian-like dictatorship or a murderous, Iranian-like theocracy take over.

In principle, Israel's problem is similar to that of South Africa's. Both forcibly implement racist policies. But in South Africa, the problem today arises not from racism but from the fear that a much worse, murderous racism would take over. Most rational South Africans, both blacks and whites, fear that ending the current system would allow the worst form of neocheating and mysticism (murderous Marxist-Leninism) to take over and destroy whatever is good and worsen whatever is bad.

An unsolvable dilemma? Not at all. Instead, spectacularly beneficial solutions exist through Neo-Tech: By using Neo-Tech principles, people can explicitly and permanently eliminate initiatory force and fraud by anyone, group, or government. In other words, Neo-Tech effectively dismantles the mechanism for government to initiate force or fraud. A Neo-Tech based society has but a single law and responsibility — to protect the individual rights of everyone. [Re: Neo-Tech Advantage #82]

Neo-Tech is the solution to racism in South Africa, in Israel, as well as in all fascist, Marxist, and theocratic nations. For, Neo-Tech collapses force-backed power and laws (including all apartheid-type laws), leaving that society with the sole power and function to protect individual rights of everyone — black, white, Jew, Palestinian, business person, capitalist. Neo-Tech frees everyone from initiatory force and destructive oppression. Neo-Tech protects each person's individual and property rights from Marxist-Leninism destruction and all other forms of force and coercion.

In South Africa, Israel, and all totalitarian nations, Neo-Tech would free all victims of force-back racism and vanquish all laws backed by force. In turn, eliminating that mechanism for initiating force would dramatically strengthen self-defense for protecting the individual rights and property of everyone.

Thus, Neo-Tech would eliminate the threat of destruction that now awaits those in South Africa and Israel, especially the value producers and their property. For, Neo-Tech delivers a safe society of unprecedented prosperity and happiness reaching forever into the future. Thus, Neo-Tech is the freedom and inspiration for all people still living under force-backed, totalitarian governments. In one stroke, Neo-Tech would end those fears and threats by denuding the neocheaters and mystics of their power. For Neo-Tech dismantles their mechanisms of initiatory force and coercion. At the same time, Neo-Tech provides iron-clad protection to individual rights.

The choice is (1) a holocaust or (2) the dark ages, or (3) the sunlit world of Neo-Tech. With the rapidly accelerating, worldwide distribution of the Neo-Tech Discovery occurring today in all major languages, the choice will be Neo-Tech. No, nothing can stop Neo-Tech. Nothing can stop the demise of mysticism and all its symbiotic neocheaters.

Max L. R-3638, AUSTRALIA

Dear Sir,

Despite the fact that I was the owner of the Neo Tech Volumes I-V, including Neo Tech II, and the Rapid Power and Wealth, Nothing quite prepared me for the Neo Tech II Reference Encyclopedia.

My wife and I had stifled in a Catholic Closed Marriage situation for over 20 years.

I have now turned this situation into a Godless, Guiltless Open Marriage situation. My wife and I are constantly assailed with pleasures we never knew existed, or, if we did, believed the Christian "Shit about their sinfulness" and "evil". Our thanks forever.

Neo-Tech Advantage #112
VERTICAL THINKING, HORIZONTAL THINKING, AND DREAMING

Vertical thinking is thinking within the known boundaries of knowledge. Vertical thinking is *developmental* thinking that leads to fuller development of knowledge. Through vertical thinking, the depths and richness of life are developed. Many areas of life from business to romantic-love relationships have vast potentials for rewarding development through vertical thinking.

Horizontal thinking is thinking beyond the boundaries of known knowledge. Horizontal thinking is *creative* thinking that leads to new ideas, thoughts, experiences, humor*. Also, horizontal thinking yields new areas for vertical development. The combination of horizontal and vertical thinking leads to a never-ending progression of values, prosperity, and happiness. Vertical and horizontal thinking are uniquely human attributes that have no limits or bounds. Such consistent, honest thinking propels a person to never-ending prosperity, romantic love, happiness.

In a Neo-Tech society, all individuals are free to think and function to their fullest. Being free of mystics and neocheaters, individuals guiltlessly become responsible for their own lives, thinking, actions, well-being, and happiness.** Then, with vertical and horizontal thinking combined with rational action, success and romantic love evolve from an ever-upward spiral of prosperity and happiness.

[Re: The concept of vertical versus horizontal thinking originated from E. DeBono, *New Think*, Basic Books, N.Y.]

Dreaming — Thinking in Reverse

Dreaming is the thinking process in reverse: Dreaming is the mind's garbage-disposing process. Dreams help purge the mind of unintegrated clutter, mysticism, and meaningless non sequiturs absorbed while awake. Thus, contrary to the mystical notions of Freud, dreams have no meanings

---

*Effective humor is created through horizontal thinking on formulating surprising, unexpected ways to look at something. The swinging back and forth from the expected and conventional to the new and unexpected is the essence of humor [Re: Concept 109 in Neo-Tech Reference Encyclopedia].

**Except for the moral responsibility to one's dependent children, no one is morally responsible for anyone else's life, well-being, or happiness [Re: Concept 102, Neo-Tech Reference Encyclopedia]. Yet, throughout history, professional mystics and neocheaters have duped the value producer into believing that he or she is responsible for supporting them — the non-producers, the parasites, the value destroyers, the mystics, the neocheaters.

Dennis R.   C-29

Dear I&O

It has been about three months now since I have received the Neo-Tech information package (Vols I-V). I must say that it was some of the most interesting reading I have ever done. I have read Neo-Tech II three full times now and I have read some of the concepts many more times. I've considered myself an agnostic for a long time now but now I can honestly say that I am an atheist. Your concepts have indeed changed my life. I am more productive at work and at home and I have gained more respect from the management of the company that I work for. My self esteem has improved a lot. I can't thank you enough.

Andy G.   J-227

After understanding Neo-Tech I let go of all the guilt I placed on myself for giving religion up. I soon took 100% control over my life. Now I'm extremely happy + prosperous, my goals coincide with each other instead conflicting.

Mark M..   J-157

I have found Neo-Tech to be highly interesting and psychologicly motivating. The "Concepts" unveiled, have began to lead me into objectively looking at my life.

or connections to reality. And dream "analysis" is nothing more than feeding regurgitated clutter back into the mind. Plus, the more mysticism and non sequiturs that crowd the mind, the more frequent and nightmarish become the dreams as their therapeutic effects dwindle. If the mind becomes increasingly loaded with mystical notions, one's dreams grow less effective in protecting the mind. The mind then becomes unable to store, integrate, or function efficiently enough to let that person live as a happy, productive, conscious being.

Neo-Tech Advantage #113
UTOPIAS REJECTED
THE BEST PERIOD OF HISTORY — NOW

Left-wing, right-wing, conservative, and "liberal" views all stem from the same reactionary, Platonistic root. All are dependent on dishonest mysticism and all are philosophically entrenched in the neocheating ploys of sacrifice and altruism. All such altruistic philosophies are contrary to human nature and well-being. Social utopias extrapolated from any altruistic premise are by nature destructive and totalitarian. All such utopias depend on doomsday predictions*, sacrifice, force, coercion, and controls. With those conditions, the individual's best interests are always subjugated to the utopian "higher" causes. Thus, being continuously neocheated by utopian rulers, the individual is unable to effectively produce values for others and society.

By contrast, in a Neo-Tech society, the individual is free to function according to his or her biological nature in being a productive, competitive human being. The natural happiness and freedom in a Neo-Tech society starkly contrasts to social utopias. In such utopias, individuals are compelled to sacrifice their value-producing competence and efficacy to the altruistic, "higher" causes of utopian rulers. [Re: Table 79, Neo-Tech Reference Encyclopedia]. Only in a noncoercive, nonforce, Neo-Tech society are productive individuals free to function according to their nature in order to achieve maximum prosperity, psychuous pleasures, and happiness by delivering maximum values to society.

---

*Most of the past and present doomsayers (such as "God", Plato, Jesus, Thomas Malthus, Adolph Hitler, Paul Ehrlich, Julian Huxley, Paul Kurtz, Margaret Mead, Ralph Nader, Luther Evans, B.F. Skinner) use dishonest projections of free man destroying himself. But those projections are false non sequiturs used to promote the neocheaters' own value-extracting utopias. All such utopias are not only totalitarian by nature, but would be boring, static societies frozen *by force* around some predescribed "ideal". All such utopias would block the exciting, never-ending discoveries that naturally occur through advances in knowledge, technology, and art by productive individuals in a non-utopian, free society.

Bill M.   R-6784

Upon first reading Neo-Tech I-V something deep inside me knew much more than my neocheated and restrained consciousness would, previously, ever dare to admit.

Things have been happening so fast in my life the last few months that I have been unable to answer your letter until now. Please feel free to use any of my comments in previous correspondence to market Neo-Tech. I sincerely hope millions of victims become winners and that my comments can help encourage them to take the action necessary to do so.

Irma N.   C-1030

I must say from the first day I encountered the NEO-TECH materials, I was transformed. And at that, at first, not at all willingly. There were many difficult passages and ideas to swallow. But I persisted, perhaps because when I first began to understand the concept of "cheating", and the extraordinary effects such sinister weapons had upon ALL mortal life, in particular my own, I was actually GALVANIZED into motion. And what had begun happening in my MIND, had a most terrific effect on everybody I came into contact with---not excluding myself! (That contact has improved vastly!)

Carl H.   C-85

About a year ago, I purchased from I&O Publishing Co. Neo-Tech Manuscripts I-V (NT# 322DL). I have been thoroughly delighted with them. Since reading them, not only have I been able to see the deceptions used by Neo-cheaters in the government, clergy, and media; I have found power and control in my own life, as well as sky-rocketing self-confidence. Thank you for bringing these books into my life!

Although altruistic, anti-individualism is still growing throughout the world, today stands as the most exciting, enlightened period of all history. For the first time in history, Neo-Tech knowledge is available to collapse mysticism and replace every neocheating system with a free, prosperous, happy Neo-Tech society.* Productive individuals will then reign free and supreme to experience endlessly growing prosperity, romantic love, and abiding happiness.

Neo-Tech Advantage #114
HUMAN BIOLOGICAL IMMORTALITY
(Also see Neo-Tech V)

Animals live and die without choice, according to their environment and biological nature. That no-choice situation does not exist for human beings. Only human beings have the choice and power to control nature. All people can learn to continuously expand the value of their lives. They do that by increasingly developing knowledge and productivity to experience prosperity, love, and happiness. Likewise, all people can learn how to continuously extend their biological/psychological lives through Neo-Tech knowledge, technology, and business. Commercial biological immortality is the supreme moral achievement for conscious beings as their individual lives become increasingly valuable with increasing age, knowledge, and experience.

Life can be immortal. Today, for the first time, no one has to die — intellectually, psychologically, or physically. With current technology, free of mysticism and neocheating, commercial biological immortality for all conscious beings is possible in a decade or less by not one but by several different scientifically feasible routes. Indeed, biological immortality will be quickly accomplished when the current anti-life, mystical/neocheating cultures are collapsed by Neo-Tech. With that collapse, all the professional mystics and neocheaters will lose their power. In their place will rise a Neo-Tech/Neothink society in which the life of the individual is revered above all else as the supreme value in the universe. [Re: Concept 116, Table 51, Neo-Tech Reference Encyclopedia].

In a Neo-Tech/Neothink society, exact-replica growth of replacement body parts, including the entire body could be possible in less than ten years through already known biological techniques and future nanotechnologies. Today, however, the primary problem of achieving biological immortality is *not* medical or technical, but is philosophical. ...With Neo-Tech collapsing mysticism, conscious life can change from always terminal to forever eternal.

---

*In a Neo-Tech society, the *only* actions that are prohibited are the use of initiatory force, coercion, or fraud against any individual. That prohibition is upheld by ostracism as well as the right to use retaliatory, self-defense force or legal action against any initiator of force, coercion, or fraud.

Albert C. R-6082

My mother is very active in an Assemblies of God church. Neo-Tech was most successful in warding off her continuous attacks on me for not conforming to her willed realities. The realization of how mystics seperate context from fact has given me incredible insight into the way they operate.

Furthermore, concept #28 alone has given me an incredible power for living along with an awesome releose of guilt. For I now know that it is I who is in control of my life, and that I am the highest value in the universe.

It gives me great pleasure to know that I now have the tools to achieve financial prosperity, romantic love, and abiding happiness. Neo-Tech is a magnificent value.

Victor O. C-1025, Chile

I have read Neo-Tech and for me it is the most extraordinary and wonderful discovery, incomparable with anything else. To me, it is the best event of my life. Neo-Tech gave me back my freedom and independence. I have back my self-confidence and self-esteem.

Neo-Tech made me more strong to confront the reality of life. Now, I am free of the disgusting mysticism which made me lose 30 years of my precious life, and perhaps my entire life had I not found Neo-Tech in time to wake up.

Biological immortality could be achieved quickly in an unregulated, free-enterprise, Neo-Tech atmosphere. That atmosphere would boom commercial research seeking maximum profits from immortality developments and services. Biological immortality would have the widest market and maximum value of any commercial product or service possible to conscious beings. The enormous commercial and moral incentives to achieve human immortality remain unrecognized because of the prevailing, mystical, anti-life philosophies and the neocheating "authorities" whose control over value production prevent the motivation and freedom for producers to develop biological immortality.

An even more advanced technological development toward absolute human immortality would be the four-dimensional electronic transfer of the contents of the human mind. Such technology would include the transfer of one's consciousness and sense of one's self (I-ness) not only into other entities (e.g., to blank or tabula-rasa brains in cloned bodies), but into three-dimensional, holographic storage banks for future retrieval of identical mind content, consciousness, and sense of self to be used if the functioning brain were ever physically damaged or destroyed. That development would be verified by electronically reproducing the entire contents of a person's mind while the original mind was still functioning. That person would then have a dual (but gradually separating) sense of self (I-ness) in two or more entities or bodies simultaneously.

Absolute immortality accomplished by electronically creating a perfectly restorable conscious mind* and sense of self (I-ness) would have a profound psychological impact on every productive human being: Imagine the impact of planning one's own life for the next 300 years. Imagine the time that would be available to build accomplishments, careers, and interests. Imagine if one's life span were suddenly expanded to 300 years, 1000 years, 10,000 years. Imagine the value and respect placed on human lives that forever increased in value. ...Current technology indicates that such definitive, biological immortality would be both scientifically and technically possible in less than a decade in a free society that recognizes individual consciousness as the supreme value in the universe.

---

*No matter how advanced human technology may become or how free a social system may become, the need for and right of individual privacy will always remain. With the development of electronic recording and storing the contents of the human mind, technological safeguards would be developed to protect each individual's privacy to his or her own mind. Politically such safeguards could be assured only within the philosophical atmosphere of a Neo-Tech, free-individual system that holds the rights of each individual as supreme. Protected privacy would naturally follow immortality developments because a Neo-Tech ethic is required to develop commercial biological immortality in the first place.

Thomas M.   R-202

Neo-tech is the only way. I was never truly happy before. It has allowed me to start, for the first time to live a guilt-free life and free myself from the life diminishing forces of altruism, religion & marijuana. THANK YOU! I am spreading the word.

Angela C.   C-31

I am enjoying my Neo-Tech materials immensely. I haven't gotten through the whole thing yet, but my life is taking on more meaning and momentum than ever before. This is the SANEST stuff I've ever seen. I've thrown away all the bibles, philosophy books, "self-Help" manuals and never felt better in my life. Thank you for being there. I'm only 29 1/2 and am really glad I found this before too much more time had passed.

L.J.   R-4171

Gentlemen:
Truly a higher education, more useful than a B.A.

The Value of Life: Einstein and the Factory Worker

If Einstein — or just his brain — could have been kept functioning after his death, imagine the additional benefits that mind would have bestowed on society: Is not that the main motivation for and value of immortality? Is not that the moral purpose of biological immortality?

No, absolutely not. That is an altruistic view that stymies the effort, motivation, and moral mandate needed to develop commercial biological immortality within our generation.

The entire purpose, motivation, and goal of biological immortality is not so a brain can continue to serve some "higher" cause, but so the flesh-and-blood individual, Einstein or a productive factory worker, can continue to physically enjoy life and create happiness for his or her own self and loved ones by continually producing values for others. As a result (*not* a purpose), the immortal individual will increasingly benefit others and society as that person becomes increasingly knowledgeable, experienced, and efficient at producing values desired by others.

The value of Einstein's or anyone else's life is meaningful only to one's own flesh-and-blood life and living happiness, not to some society or "higher" cause.

Why Do So Many People *Not* Want to Live Forever? Because They Fail to Earn Guiltless Prosperity, Love, and, Happiness.

The more people let mysticism influence their lives, the more they become unknowledgeable, undermine values, grow lazy, lose happiness, dislike life. With increasing mysticism, they become increasingly incompetent to earn honest values, power, love, and happiness. In addition, the more people accept mysticism, the more neocheaters can manipulate them. And the more manipulated and less successful one becomes, the more painful and difficult life becomes until the idea of living forever becomes abhorrent, even terrifying. ...Only people who guiltlessly repel mysticism to earn independence as well as honest values, expanding power, and happy romance can love life enough to have a passion to live forever.

Unstoppable Neo-Tech

Mystics and neocheaters have perfected and perpetuated their hoax for the past 2000 years. But now, Neo-Tech is in full, forward motion. The Neo-Tech matrix is spreading. It is unstoppable, irreversible, and will collapse the entire, destructive hoax of mysticism. No mystic or neocheater can stop Neo-Tech from eliminating mysticism and its symbiotic neocheaters.

Happiness Forever

With life immortal and human beings free of mysticism, personal prosperity, love, happiness, and life itself could grow forever through productive work, romantic love, psychuous pleasures, and biological immortality. The moral purpose of all human life would then be met — happiness forever.

Trevor D.J.   C-205

The past several decades have borne witness to seemingly inumerable assaults on the dignity of the human spirit. Wherever one may turn, the fruits of this onslaught are appallingly evident. The total inversion of the concept of value, most strikingly manifested in the glorification of the anti-life, has left few in our society unscathed. To those resolute individuals who have refused to give place to this obscenity, the struggle has been at times exhausting, often bitter, yet always worth the heroic effort.

One of the most painful aspects to observe of this pervasive influence is the near stranglehold it has acquired on the performing arts. The supreme vehicles for the projection of life as it can and ought to be have been utilized to convey every conceivable life-draining image, every spirit-breaking philosophy; sometimes subliminally, sometimes with numbing directness. The sheer volume and intensity of these assaults on the good, the productive, and the efficacious can leave all but the most thoroughly grounded souls in a state of enervation and bewilderment. In the face of this tidal wave of malevolence, a few of those resolute individuals to whom I earlier alluded have chosen to stand defiantly.

Recently, I experienced the joy of witnessing a group of performers whose embrace of all that is life-affirming is total and pure. Their utter repudiation of the doctrine of the inherent depravity of man is reflected in their every creative effort. Working from their integrated philosophical foundation, these performers unceasingly projected images of values honored, of productive efforts rewarded, of virtues upheld. During the performances, I quickly noted the conspicuous absence of the feeling of malaise, the suspicions about the artists' true motivations, and the need to wrap my consciousness in a protective filter. With these draining influences eliminated, my energies were freed and I had the singular pleasure of opening myself to true kindred spirits and breathing deeply of the atmosphere of benevolence. Of course the performers evidenced passion; of course they exhibited commitment. These phenomena can be witnessed in the basest of endeavors. It is only when passion and commitment are fused with an integrated, life-affirming philosophical base that a performance can convey the true grandeur and potential of the human spirit.

...I direct you to NEO-TECH LIVE ARTS

Michael G.   R-2110, NEW ZEALAND

Neo-Tech is infact the best thing that has happened

APPENDICES
(A-C)

Negative Testimonials

BUT THESE ARE PEOPLE WHO FEAR OR FEEL THREATENED BY NEO-TECH

"Neo-Tech is the ultimate winning system. God will vent his wrath and anger on you." D.R., Canada; "I'm sure the devil loves you." L.N. IA; "Neo-Tech only satisfies the human desire for wealth and power. You out-maneuver God in order to gain riches." R.H., IA; "Neo-Tech people may die with both hands filled with thousand-dollar bills. But where are you? Why not write for a free Bible course from the Voice of Prophecy?"; "My cardiologist instructed me most emphatically that under no circumstances was I to become involved with Neo-Tech." W.W., CA; "Neo-Tech promotes outright individualism — a crime that should be punishable by death." R.M., CA; "You will gain greater and greater ability to manipulate the material world. I can only look to the ultimate source to stop you." P.P., WI; "It is my destiny to eliminate Neo-Tech...the forces of darkness which are supporting you will dissolve at my will." M.R., United Kingdom; "Do you really think you can find true happiness through such a material approach?" C.B., MD; "Neo-Tech shocked me, and I refuse to read it." C.S., UT; "Neo-Tech is undermining God-fearing people by benefiting one's animalistic self." Deacon A.B., TN; "You blatantly deny the spiritual in assuming humans as the ultimate creation." Ms. J.G., CA; "Man wallows in the lower-plane earth geared to materialism and ego." F.W., GA; "I purchased your original volumes (the ones bound in satanic or funeral black). I now have a copy of the Atheist bible." C.S., CA; "Sex, gold, and the pursuit of knowledge — keep it to yourself." W.F., CA; "You can't take the gains from Neo-Tech with you when you die."; "You have allowed the Devil to use you and deceive you. I do not doubt your Neo-Tech system is potent, Satan is quite capable of working miracles." R.S., CA; "I cannot accept anything as fact that is based solely on logic and nothing else." R.C., NV "Romantic love stinks! And only God gives riches. You must walk alone forever without rest." J.H.; "You are totally human centered and doomed to destruction." A.A., NJ; Neo-Tech puts man at the level of God. You give people power, prosperity, love — total control of one's life — as if they were the greatest things in life. You dismiss self-sacrifice in your haughty exaltation of the individual. Confess your sins, repent." C.G., GA; "Your publication teaches gaining advantages over others. May the Lord have mercy on your soul." Ms. J.B., TX; "Incredible that the most powerful discovery of earth is made by selfish Neo-Tech people." A.V., England; "Based on self-centered ideas to gain advantages and control over others. The immediate satisfaction and ego trip that accompanies Neo-Tech is so tempting." L.V., MA; "You believe that fallen man can help himself. Satan himself is the ruler and initiator of your program." M.B., Canada; "Holding such incredible power over others through Neo-Tech is quite obnoxious. 'Winning is all' is not bred into our British System from early childhood." Mrs. M.M., England; "Cranks and crackpots." H.B., The Objectivist Forum; "I am much in favor of mysticism and must reject Neo-Tech." T.c., CA; "A grave threat to mystical beliefs." B.D., NY

* * * * *

Sadly, the people above are those who need Neo-Tech the most. But, as the Neo-Tech world begins passing them by, many will eventually sweep away their mysticism in allowing themselves to finally understand and benefit greatly from Neo-Tech. And that will be a happy day for everyone.

ef/NT-VI/wwmcgt/unfortunates

APPENDIX A

UNBEATABLE PERSONAL, BUSINESS, AND FINANCIAL ADVANTAGES

by

Eliminating Mysticism and Neocheating

Unbeatable advantages are gained by rejecting mysticism and eliminating neocheating: Neo-Tech people are the antithesis of neocheaters. Master neocheaters usurp their way into positions of false power. They do that by using mysticism to attack, undermine, and destroy values without their victims realizing who the neocheaters are or what they are doing. But with Neo-Tech, one can quickly earn his or her way to power and prosperity by outcompeting others — by producing more effectively than those crippled by mysticism and neocheaters. With Neo-Tech, one knows exactly what mysticism is, who the neocheaters are, how they are draining the value producer, and how to render them powerless. ...Neo-Tech knowledge delivers unbeatable power and advantages.

Quelling the Mystics and Neocheaters

Most people live and die without ever discovering the existence of an innocent, exciting, brilliant world. That world is the clean, mystic-free world of Neo-Tech: a cheerful, crystal-clear world that generates unending values, prosperity, and happiness. In that world, Neo-Tech transforms the manipulations and dishonesties of the mystics and neocheaters into advantages for everyone.

Neo-Tech revitalizes crucial words corrupted by mystics and neocheaters. Dead words brought to life include honesty, power, prosperity, love. Through vitalization of the entire language, Neo-Tech reveals the futility of all mystical, mind-over-matter, positive-thinking approaches that lead to nothing. By collapsing the 2000-year hoax of mysticism, Neo-Tech eliminates the neocheater's survival tool. Through Neo-Techs incorruptible matrix of personal, business, and financial advantages, Neo-Tech quells all mystics and neocheaters while delivering that crystal-clear world of prosperity and happiness.

The Entelechy

Neo-Tech *is* the entelechy of prosperity and happiness. For Neo-Tech delivers unbeatable advantages in:

COMPETITIVE ACTIONS
BUSINESS DEALINGS
JOBS AND CAREERS
FINANCE AND INVESTMENTS
PERSONAL RELATIONSHIPS
ART AND PLEASURES

APPENDIX B

THE NEO-TECH MATRIX
for
ENDING MYSTICISM AND NEOCHEATING

The primary value of language lies not in being a tool of communication but in being the tool of thinking. Efficient, conscious thinking requires language words, metaphors, and analogs with consistent meanings. Indeed, the essence of consciousness is language since all ideas are formed by thinking through language. But professional mystics and neocheaters purposely alter meanings, concepts, and language to manipulate the minds of their victims. They accomplish their manipulations by confusing and mocking reality in conjuring up their own "truths" and "realities". For them, any "truth" and "reality" that accommodates their whims, wishes, desires, or hoax will do.

The very nature of unintegrated words and concepts leaves language vulnerable to manipulation by mystics and neocheaters. But a fully integrated matrix of the prime concepts would leave words and reality indivisible, thereby blocking corruption by mystics and neocheaters. ...Such a matrix of integrated honesty is invulnerable to attack and corruption because all its words are integrated into a single, indestructible gridlock.

Neo-Tech integrates the original 144 primary concepts into an indivisible web or matrix*. Such a matrix protects from distortion all words captured within its gridlock. Because all its concepts are inextricably integrated, the Neo-Tech matrix is invulnerable to attack or corruption by mystics and neocheaters.

The Neo-Tech matrix means the eventual end of all professional mystics and neocheaters. For their survival depends on Machiavelli-like "divide and rule", "confuse and control", and "distort and destroy" techniques. To survive, those mystics and neocheaters must constantly divide concepts, confuse language, and distort words in order to prevent their victims from thinking about and understanding what is happening. Indeed, those mystics and neocheaters survive by separating meaning from context. They use concepts out of context while distorting words to block clear, honest thinking. They are then able to forge an infinite variety of mind-created "realities". And through those fake, mind-created "realities", they conjure up all the rationalizations they need to live off the efforts of others.

---

*The original 144 primary concepts of Neo-Tech were first identified and developed by Frank R. Wallace in his original Neo-Tech Reference Encyclopedia. Wallace's concepts were then recognized as a gridlock matrix by Dr. Peter Meier at the Institute of Cognitive Infomatics, Wilen bei Sarren, Switzerland. That Neo-Tech matrix is now evolving into an array of Neothink matrices that will eventually envelop all societies to collapse the hoax of mysticism worldwide.

Using divide-confuse-distort tactics, professional mystics and neocheaters can subvert any meaning or concept to divine their own "truths" and "realities". They need their divined "truths" and "realities" to usurp values from others. But against the gridlocked Neo-Tech matrix, such subversions and confusions are impossible. Thus, against Neo-Tech, mystics and neocheaters are impotent and cannot survive without themselves becoming honest, self-supporting individuals.

The Web Effect

Integrated honesty and consistent effort assure the dominance of Neo-Tech over mystics and neocheaters. By nature, human beings want to live the most productive, happiest lives possible. But mysticism and neocheating are contrary to productivity and happiness. Thus, as Neo-Tech develops within each individual, a clearly integrated matrix or web called the X-factor arises. The X-factor is what pulls nature's survival trigger. Pulling that trigger causes a person to act in his or her rational best interest. And that means rejecting mysticism and neocheating. ...The X-factor will trigger that survival mechanism in any individual caught in the forthcoming Neo-Tech/Neothink web. For the Neothink web consists of 144 primary concepts more fully developed than Neo-Tech and integrated into an even more powerful, clearer, inescapable matrix.*

With the spreading Neo-Tech/Neothink matrix, the twin scourges of mysticism and neocheating will forever vanish from this planet.

APPENDIX C

THE NEO-TECH DISCOVERY

First Known Identification of Master Neocheaters
"If we go back to the beginnings of things, we shall always find that ignorance and fear created the gods; that imagination, rapture and deception embellished them; that weakness worships them; that custom spares them; and that tyranny favors them in order to profit from the blindness of men."
Baron d'Hobach
THE SYSTEM OF NATURE (1770)

First Known Identification of Governments as Mystical
"The state is the great fictitious entity by which everyone seeks to live at the expense of everyone else."
Frédéric Bastiat
1801 — 1850

First Known Identification of Prosperity and Happiness
via Vanquishing Mysticism
"Within our minds, we all fight the same life-and-death battle against mysticism. We all fight the same battle against living by internal feelings rather than by external reality. And we all must make the same choice to exert effort and think rationally in quelling mysticism. For every individual who fashions a successful, happy life has chosen effort over laziness...honesty over mysticism."

"All values — all prosperity, power, love, happiness, and eternal life arise from vanquishing mysticism:

John Flint
Late twentieth century

NEO-TECH REFERENCES

Primary Direct Reference
Neo-Tech Reference Encyclopedia

Primary Indirect References
The works of
Plato (immoral)
Aristotle (moral)
Immanuel Kant (evil)
Ayn Rand (moral)

Secondary Indirect References
The works of
The Bible (immoral)
Nathaniel Branden (mixed)
Leonard Piekoff (moral)

THE NEO-TECH DISCOVERY

(Primary Reference: The Neo-Tech Reference Encyclopedia)

LISTING OF THE 114 NEO-TECH ADVANTAGES

Preface	i
Introduction	iii
Definitions and Understandings	vii-xlvii
Table of Contents	li

Advantage#	Neo-Tech Advantage	Page#
1	The Nature of Man and Woman	1
2	Child of the Past	3
3	Carving One's Own Destiny	5
4	Dogma and Rules Eliminated	7
5	Good and Bad Actions	7
6	Abandoning The Neocheaters	13
7	Prosperity and Happiness Goals	15
8	Happiness Test	15
9	Rewards from Life	17
10	The Highest Cause	17
11	Self-Esteem and the Ultimate Reward	21
12	Unjust Criticism and Guilt	23
13	Sense of Life	27
14	Selfish vs. Selfless View	27
15	Avoiding Sacrifice	29
16	Retaining Happiness	29
17	Countering Altruistic Ethics	31
18	Benefits from Romantic-Love	31
19	Religious/"Playboy"/Psychuous Views	31
20	Requirements for Psychuous Pleasures	35
21	Psychuous vs. Sensuous	35
22	Psychuous Experiences	37
23	Psychuous Capacity	37
24	Other Books vs. Neo-Tech	37
25	Valuable Books	39
26	Harmful Books	41
27	Mysticism and Destruction	45
28	Who Created Existence	47
29	Techniques of Mysticism	47
30	Tools of Destruction	49
31	Astrology, UFO'S, and Other Myths	53
32	Existentialism and its Influence	63
33	Seventeen-Hundred-Years of Oppression	67

Advantage#	Neo-Tech Advantage	Page#
34	Aesthetic Pleasures	77
35	Value of Emotions	81
36	Emotions and Reality	83
37	Religious Condemnation of Emotions	83
38	Fear of Emotions	85
39	Emotions of Fear; Value of Fearlessness	85
40	Fear of Rejection; Risk Taking	87
41	Independent Judgment; Opinion of Others	87
42	Casual vs. Serious Sex	89
43	Multiple Partners and Values Systems	89
44	Relationship Errors	93
45	Achieving Psychuous Pleasures	95
46	Ending a Relationship	97
47	Handling Problems	97
48	Guiltless Freedom	101
49	Injustice of Jealousy	105
50	Poison Core of Jealousy	111
51	Unnecessary Aging	113
52	Parents as Scapegoats	115
53	Adolescent, Premarital, Nonmarital Love	117
54	Seduction: Casual, Serious, Mutual	119
55	Physical Beauty/Sexual Roles	123
56	Psychuous Pleasures	129
57	Natural Phenomena	129
58	Personal Appearance	131
59	Physical Fitness, Diet, Addictions	133
60	Alcohol, Drugs, Sugar, and Mysticism	137
61	Aphrodisiacs — Negative and Positive	143
62	Romantic Love and the DTC Technique	143
63	Romantic-Love Standards	145
64	Three Segments of Romantic Love	147
65	Two Types of Romantic Love	149
66	Individual Uniqueness; Personal Worth	151
67	Capacity to Change	153
68	Finding Partners and Bypassing Shyness	155
69	Shyness — Causes and Cures	159
70	Equality of Men and Women	161
71	Housewife, Children, "Greatness"	165
72	Potential of Women, 1300 BC thru Today	173
73	Nature of Emotions; Self-Responsibility	185
74	Natural Highs	187
75	Joy and Happiness	191
76	Philosophy for Romantic-Love	191
77	Aristotle vs. Plato	193
78	Humor and Sense of Life	201

Advantage#	Neo-Tech Advantage	Page#
79	Taboos vs. Voluntary Sex Acts	201
80	Initiatory Force — The Prime Evil	205
81	Oppression vs. Freedom	207
82	Constitution for Prosperity	213
83	Dismissing 3000 Years of Mysticism	215
84	Protecting Children from Mystics	227
85	Rejecting Mystics and Neocheaters	233
86	Power, Plato, Aristotle, and Neo-Tech	237
87	Freedom, Responsibility, and Prosperity	243
88	Neo-Tech in Business	255
89	Protection From Government	263
90	Government Death Machines	269
91	Suicide Option	275
92	Obscenity Laws and Censorship	277
93	Failure-To-Judge Syndrome	285
94	Objective Thinking vs. Emotional Thinking	295
95	Four Levels of Communication	297
96	Communication in Romantic Love	303
97	Productiveness and Happiness	305
98	Growth Death and Psyche Death	311
99	Three Steps to Biological Immortality	321
100	Malefactors and Envy	323
101	Envy and Laziness	331
102	Neo-Tech Versus Altruism	335
103	Plato, Aristotle, and Neo-Tech	337
104	Value of Art	339
105	Self-Awareness vs. Mystical "Awareness"	353
106	Beyond Understanding	355
107	Value Theft vs. Value Exchange	359
108	Value Exchange/Friendship/Romantic Love	365
109	Understanding Justice and Love	373
110	Facts and Justice	375
111	The Neo-Tech Solution to Racism	381
112	Vertical/Horizontal Think vs. Dreaming	385
113	The Best Period of History — Now	387
114	Human Biological Immortality	389
***	Happiness Forever	393
Those Fearing Neo-Tech		396
Appendix A	Unbeatable Advantages of Neo-Tech	397
Appendix B	Ending Mysticism and Neocheating	398
Appendix C	The Neo-Tech Discovery	400
	Why Neo-Tech Succeeds When All Else Fails	405
	Justice at Last	406
	Neothink, The Mind of The Future	407
	Original Neo-Tech I and II Manuscripts	425
	The Business of Neo-Tech	426

Guy R.   R-2649

Reading Neo-Tech was an enriching and invigorating experience--and motivated me to study Julian Jaynes' "The Origin of Consciousness in the Breakdown of the Bicameral Mind." I have thus been inspired to compose the enclosed chart depicting what I see as the three states of human consciousness.

Humanity has collectively evolved out of the unconsciousness of the bicameral mind. Yet, as individuals, we experience to varying degrees difficulty in maintaining the "crystal clear" state of consciousness.

As a result, each of us spends a portion of our time in a transitional state, characterized by a desire for the happiness, wealth and satisfaction of a fully conscious life, but lacking either the courage or the initiative to completely forsake the security of our bicameral past.

Most people waste the major portion of their lives floundering in the confusion and contradiction of the transitional state, with an occasional lapse into unconsciousness, and too few glorious encounters with truly conscious life. Some individuals lose consciousness so often as to be unable to participate effectively in even a transitional society. And a third group is comprised of the powerful, vibrant producers of objective values, those who rise above themselves day after day, self-motivating to create the riches of a fully conscious life.

I would enjoy hearing your response to this chart. I would also enjoy an in-depth discussion of your efforts toward biological immortality.

Sincerely,

BICAMERAL/UNCONSCIOUS	CONSCIOUS	TRANSITIONAL
1) Right/Left Brain Autonomy	1) Right/Left Brain Integration	1) Right/Left Brain Antagonism
2) No Self Concept	2) Self Esteem	2) Self Doubt
3) No Time Concept	3) Finite Time Concept (time is precious)	3) Infinite Time Concept (time is devalued)
4) Externally Motivated	4) Self-Motivated	4) Unmotivated
5) Subservient to External Authority	5) Authoritative	5) Resents Authority
6) Not Responsible	6) Responsible	6) Irresponsible
7) No Intellectual Pursuit; Slavish Obedience to Faith	7) Pursuit of Truth; Free, Independent Thinking	7) Pursuit of Illusion; Slavish Obedience to Dogmatic Belief Systems; Confusion; Contradiction
8) Powerless	8) Powerful	8) Power games; Userps Power From Others, or, is Victimized By Others
9) React	9) Act	9) Try
10) Hallucinations	10) Visions/Dreams	10) Hopes
11) No Honesty Concept	11) Honest	11) Dishonest/Guilty
12) Survival Values	12) Objective Values/Reality Based	12) Subjective Values/Existential
13) Habitual Survival Efforts; Productive of Survival Values	13) Productive	13) Non-Productive/Counter-Productive/Envious/Lazy
14) Biological Life/Dependence on Nature	14) Conscious Life/Freedom	14) Death Process/Dependence On Others
15) Mating	15) Romantic Love; Earned; Exchange of Objective Values; Mutually Enriching and Empowering	15) Love Play; Comfort and Security; Exchange of Subjective Values; No growth
16) Rewards of Biological Survival	16) Happiness/Wealth	16) Pursuit of Comfort and Security; Anxiety; Poverty; Envy

HOW NEO-TECH DIFFERS FROM ALL OTHER IDEA SYSTEMS
(from the article "Why Neo-Tech Succeeds When All Other Idea Systems Fail")

NEO-TECH IDEA SYSTEM	**OTHER IDEA SYSTEMS**
Offers honesty.	Offers "truth".
Guiltlessly recognizes and honestly creates values of prosperity, power, love.	Guiltily evades or dishonestly denies values of prosperity, power, love.
Requires no leaders, gurus, or followers.	Depends on leaders or gurus living off their followers.
The individual alone knows what is best for self.	Individuals are told by others what is best for self.
Depends on delivering maximum values to the broadest possible markets via business.	Depends on being accepted by peers, the media, or certain intellectuals.
Value to all. Wanted by all wanting prosperity, power, love. Every value producer benefits.	Value to idea soulmates. Wanted only by closed circles of soulmates. Others ignore. Few benefit.
Potential customers are all conscious beings wanting life.	Potential customers are soulmates wanting answers.
Tough, front-trench, high-effort value sell. No rest. Must always develop, improve, grow, decrease cost, increase value, push ahead. ...Self-esteem based on efforts made.	Wimpish, languid, low-effort value sell. Rest on laurels. Little more to learn or improve. Gentle, pipe-smoking professor aura. ...Self-esteem based on ideas held.
Dynamic, growing, fully integrated values dependent on honesty.	Static, dying, unintegrated values dependent on non sequiturs.
Free-market guiding pressures. Profit oriented. Depends on profit via delivering free-market values.	Academic guiding pressures. Non-profit oriented. Depends on tax money, contributions, or soulmate largess.
Integrated with the essences of life (effort and honesty) versus mysticism (laziness and dishonesty).	Not integrated with the essences of life (effort and honesty) versus mysticism (laziness and dishonesty).
Recognizes links to personal productivity, business, and happiness.	Evades or ignores links to productivity, business, and happiness.
Can stand firm with bulldog tenacity. Fully integrated basis. Can never be manipulated. Thus, works to eliminate mystics and neocheaters.	Cannot stand firm. No solid ground. Unintegrated, floating basis. Can be manipulated as non sequiturs to benefit mystics and neocheaters.
Rejects mysticism in self and others. Guiltlessly rejects attacks on values. Rejects mysticism as death-oriented.	Seeks acceptance of mysticism in self and others. Guiltily accepts attacks on values. Accepts mysticism as "spirit-oriented".
Self-esteem based on honest, productive efforts.	Self-esteem based on ideas held and personal acceptance.
Going toward mystic-free, openended prosperity, happiness, Biological Immortality.	Going nowhere, even sound Aristotelian systems as libertarianism and objectivism.
Leads to power, wealth, life.	Leads to little or nothing.

JUSTICE AT LAST
Abraham Lincoln (the Worst) versus Jay Gould (the Best)

The illusions or "feelings" arising from manipulations by neocheaters are usually the exact opposite of the facts. For example, contrary to the neocheaters' illusions, Abraham Lincoln was by far the worst, most destructive American president. Lincoln was not the emancipator of slavery. Instead, he was the father of long-range, Fabian slavery: In addition to his own created civil-war legacy of death and destruction, he created the mechanism to increasingly enslave honest people, especially the producers of values. Aided by his great rhetorical skills and demagogic deceptions, he was a grand master of non sequiturs and mystical illusions. Unable to earn honest power by competitively producing values, he created horrendous problems where none existed. ...Solely to usurp personal power, Lincoln killed more young men and destroyed more private property than all the other presidents combined.

With presidential power slipping in a divided nation, Lincoln instigated a bloody civil war for one and only one purpose: to expand his unearned power. Why? He needed to boost his sagging self-esteem. As with most master neocheaters usurping vast powers, he never hesitated using mass killings of innocent youth and wholesale destructions of private property in order to appear important and feel worthwhile. Once such killing starts, little difference exists if the killing required is one innocent life, or 600,000 in the case of Lincoln, or 40,000,000 in the case of Stalin and Mao. The amount of killing and destruction makes minimal difference to the neocheater when his "feelings" are at stake — when usurped power is needed to justify a parasitical life and faked self-worth. He will kill and destroy in direct proportion to the power he can usurp.

Lincoln needed to usurp more and more power in order to support an anxiety-ridden, pseudo self-esteem. Under the "emergency" guise of his own created civil war, he was the first President to conjure up "laws" to usurp both the life and property of every honest, productive citizen: He was the first to instigate (1) the immoral, unconstitutional draft* and (2) the immoral, unconstitutional income tax*. Lincoln was the seminal instigator of government-sponsored destruction of life, values, and property in America.

A close examination of history reveals the civil war had little to do with slavery. The issue of slavery was a non sequitur manipulated by an array of neocheating powercrats, authors, and journalists. Indeed, Lincoln actually opposed the abolition of slavery. In fact, leading abolitionists, such as William Lloyd Garrison, bitterly criticized Lincoln's opposition to abolition. Moreover, Lincoln explicitly opposed economic freedom in the South. For that freedom would have precipitated genuine, rapid freedom for slaves. Instead, he favored a gradual phasing out of black slavery over many decades in exchange for a gradual enslavement of everyone, especially the producer.* But Lincoln scrapped that plan for gradual power accumulation when he realized the immense power he could seize immediately through a civil war. Thus, Lincoln staged that bloody war solely to assuage his lack of confidence and boost his pseudo self-esteem by usurping giant doses of power. For, he was unwilling to exert sustained, business-like efforts needed to produce genuine, competitive values for others. And, genuine self-esteem comes only by producing competitive values for others without the use of force or coercion.

By not producing values, one loses self-esteem in becoming dependent on usurping values from the producers to survive. In a mystical world, the neocheater usurps values and power by having others view the world through his or her manipulated emotions and inverted illusions. The public responds to those calculated, inverted illusions by *feeling* President Lincoln was a great man and *feeling* "Robber-Baron" Jay Gould was an evil man. They feel and then believe their feelings are true even though the facts are the exact opposite.

In a Neo-Tech world, however, mystics and neocheaters are impotent. For, to be competitive, people must view the world through honest, objective facts. Indeed, facts, not manipulated feelings or inverted illusions, reveal that Lincoln, an anxiety-filled, unhappy, brooding, unloving man, delivered mass destruction to society with his legacies of the civil war, the draft, and the income tax. While Jay Gould, a consistently temperate, happy, cheerful, loving family man, delivered great values to society with his legacies of the transcontinental railroad system, the national telegraphic communication system, and the millions of productive jobs he ultimately created for others.

Lincoln, the value destroyer, needed the press and public to view him as a "great man". He needed to feel important to prop his pseudo self-esteem. So, to feel "secure" about his personal importance, he conjured up a war that killed 600,000 men. He then jeopardized the lives and property of future generations by establishing the unconstitutional draft and income tax. By contrast, Gould, a great value producer, needed no one's view to prop his genuine self-esteem. Thus, he ignored the press and paid no attention to their attacks or dishonesties. Gould's ignoring of the press is what infuriated all neocheating journalists, igniting their insecurities, causing them to attack Jay Gould with rabid dishonesty. They ignored his created values: thousands of jobs, great wealth added to society, transcontinental communications and transportation.**

Such gross inversion of the worst versus the best occur constantly in all mystical cultures. Gould-type inversions are today still aimed at the aggressive value producer: He is presented as an exploiter of society and is widely targeted for injury by the neocheating forces of government, religion, the academe, and the media. But, those seemingly formidable forces hold no real power. Indeed, Neo-Tech easily demolishes their illusions. Thus, with increasing tempo, Neo-Tech will drum out of existence all dishonest inversions of facts such as: Lincoln, "the heroic emancipator of slavery"; and Gould, "the archvillain Robber Baron". ...The aggressive value producers will be held as the precious good — the creators of jobs, wealth, values — the heroes of civilization.

> Honor paid to Lincoln and other destructive neocheaters through holidays, statues, portraits on stamps or money is an obscenity promoted by other neocheaters and involuntarily paid for by their victims. In a Neo-Tech society, honor would be voluntarily paid only to genuine heroes — mighty value producers such as Andrew Carnegie, Jay Gould, John D. Rockefeller, Henry Ford, Thomas Edison, Harvey Firestone, Howard Hughes, Ray Kroc, Harold Geneen, Boone Pickens, Donald Trump and other genuine heroes who have received unjust hatchet jobs by the neocheating intelligentsia.

---

*D.L. Lendt, "Demise of the Democracy", Tate University (1973); J.K. McNulty, "Federal Income Taxation of Individuals", West Publishing (1983); W.L. Garrison, "The Liberator" (1859-1865).

**M. Klein,"The Life and Legend of Jay Gould", The John Hopkins University Press (1986).

NEOTHINK, THE MIND OF THE FUTURE

The human mind has a limited storage and processing capacity. But Neothink, a discovery made through Neo-Tech, infinitely expands the capacity of consciousness to understand anything in existence. The Neo-Tech discovery of exchanging the conscious mind for the Neothink mind is equivalent to the discovery 3000 years ago of exchanging the bicameral mind for the conscious mind. And, as 3000 years ago, this exchange will occur swiftly, automatically regardless of what anyone does, says, or thinks. The pressure to convert to Neothink is competition. Those who do not convert cannot survive. Just as the bicameral mind could not compete and survive 3000 years ago. With Neothink, all mystics and neocheaters are finished. For, they will be ignominiously laughed out of existence.

Neothink is the development of new concepts over unlimited ranges of integration. That unlimited capacity is accomplished by dividing separate thoughts into two or more separate groups and then building each of those groups toward the maximum capacity of consciousness. Those groups of conscious thoughts can then be swiftly integrated into vast units of new knowledge and concepts far beyond the capacity of the human mind thinking as a single conscious unit. An example of Neothink through such maximum-capacity units is F. R. Wallace's work titled "Achieving and Surpassing Einstein's Ultimate Goal" presented to the Second Neo-Tech World Summit. In that work, 25 separate maximum-capacity thought units were developed and then suddenly integrated into spectacular, new knowledge far beyond the capacity of any single-unit thought of the conscious mind. Another Neothink work is Mark Hamilton's "The I & O Story" presented at the Third Neo-Tech World Summit. That masterwork delivers revolutionary business and management concepts that will someday dominate all future value production.

Neothink provides entirely different ways to look at nearly every important idea and concept encountered by conscious beings. For, since organized neocheating began about 2000 years ago, essentially all ideas and concepts have been integrated with the big-lie hoaxes of mysticism and altruism. Those hoaxes were and are still cleverly designed by neocheaters for usurping their livings from the producers. Thus, what appears to be two opposite choices in the prevailing mystical/altruistic context are not opposite choices at all. But instead, as revealed by Neothink, those supposed choices are always the same choice. For all their choices always support their mysticism and neocheating. Their choices are always the same, merely presented from different angles.

Neothink shows that the real choice is not between the various Hobson's choices of invalid mysticism, but is always between the clever dishonesty of neocheaters and the fully integrated honesty of Neo-Tech. Common, everyday areas of life in which startling new views and choices are revealed by Neothink include:

actors	education	losers	romanc
advertising	effort	love	sadness
aerobics	finances	management	science
alcoholism	food	mathematics	sense of life
anger	friendship	maturity	sexiness
autos	grammar	music	smiling
bars	guns	nature	sports
bankers	happiness	New York City	survival
business	health	numbers	taxation
children	hiring	nutrition	technology
clothes	immigration	pain	teenagers
competition	industry	pets	therapy
creativeness	jobs	photography	thinking
death	lawyers	police	values
diet	laziness	psychology	winners
drugs	life speed	reading	words

INDEX

created by
Sharon T. Smith
PROFESSIONAL INDEXING

— A —

Abacus, 255
Ability, 217
Abolitionists, 406
Abortion
   laws against, 207
   movement against, 173, 185
   rights to, 179
Absolutes, 7-9
Abstraction, 343
Abstract symbols, 351
Abstract values, 363, 369, 371
   vs. material (tangible) values, 365
Abuse of partner, 125-129
Academia, i, v, xv, 27, 65, 227, 231, 259, 307
   as envious malefactors, 329, 331
   intellectualism in, 259
   as neocheaters, 211
Achievement, 91, 315
   defined, xxxix
   as highest value, 27
Actions
   destructive, 83
   good and bad, 7, 9
   integration of with reality, xix
   objectively good or bad, 7
   rational, 3
   responsibility for, 85, 185, 245, 309, 363
   volitional, 85
Addictions, 133-137
   See also specific types
Adolescent sex, 113, 117-119
Adult-adult incest, 203
Adult-child incest, 203
Adult-child sexual relationships, 201, 203, 205
Adultery, 203
Aerobic exercise, 133, 135, 187
Aerobics, 133
Aerosols, 273
Aesthetic pleasure, 77-79
Africa, 45, 381-383
Age of Reason, 75, 177, 209
Aging, ix
   unnecessary, 113-115
"Aide," 343
AIDS, 91, 271
Airlines, 197, 199
Alcohol, 83, 187
   addiction to, 135
   government control of, 139
   laws against, 207
   and psychuous sex, 137-141
   and romantic love, 137-141
   as suppressor of happiness, 137

Aloneness, 161
   independent, 265
Alpha brain-wave condition, 426
Altruism, iii, xvii, xxiii, xxxi-xxxv, 29, 37, 43, 65, 263, 305, 307, 329, 331
   See also Platonistic philosophy
   Aristotelian view of, 21
   in businessmen, 253, 255, 257
   vs. capitalism, 257-267
   and compromise, 145
   defined, xxxi, xxxix
   elimination of, 197
   ethics of, 31
   and government, 273
   and Hitler, 359
   and intellectualism, 259
   and love, 191
   in modern times, 387
   myths about, 231
   vs. Neo-Tech, 335-337
   philosophy based on, 45
   Platonistic view of, 19, 193
   professional advocates of, xxxiii, xxxv
   and psyche death, 313
   vs. psychuous pleasures, 335-337
   religion as product of, 49
   and Roman Empire, 173
   and sense of life, 27
   tools of, 53
   and utopias, 385
   and women's rights, 207
   and word connotations, xxxix
Amateur hypnosis, 121
America, discovery of, 197
American Academy of Arts and Letters, 351
Amin, Idi, 277
Amoral values, 91
Anal sex, 203
Anarchy, 207
   Christian, 67
   vs. limited government, 213
   political movements based on, 269
Ancient Greece, 173, 209, 239
Anti-abortion movement, 173, 185
Anti-government movements, 269
Anti-individualism, 313, 387
Anti-intellectuals, xxv, 259, 329
   use of poetry by, 339
Anti-life character profiles, 291
Anti-life philosophies, 193, 389
   See also Platonistic philosophy; specific philosophies
Anti-obscenity laws, 251, 277-283
Anti-pornography movement, 173
Anti-prostitution laws, 165

Anti-sexual attitudes of Christianity, 173
Antitrust laws, 257
Anxieties, 315
Apartheid, 381
Aphorisms, 219
Aphrodisiacs, xlviii, 143
Appearance, 17, 131-133
Aquinas, Thomas, xiii
Arab dictatorships, 381
Arafat, Yasir, 277
Aristotelian philosophy, 59, 61, 317
   See also Aristotle
   and freedom, 251
   and happiness, 3
   history rewritten by, 197-201
   and human nature, 1
   and individual rights, 251
   and life style, 303
   and love, 3
   poetry based on, 345, 347
   and power, 239-245
   and prosperity, 3
   and reality, 3
   and word connotations, xxxix-xlvii
Aristotle, iii, xxi, 25, 161, 197, 337, 339, 400
   See also Aristotelian philosophy
   vs. Plato, 193-199
Army of Neo-Tech, 426
Art, 77, 339-351
   collectors of, 351
   fine, 343
   highs from, 187
   integrity of, 77
   law of, 351
   modern, 221, 343, 349-351
   Neo-Tech, 343
   objective evaluation of, 77
   objective standards for, 77
   objective value of, 79
   ownership of, 81
   response to, 77
Artificial highs, 189
Artificial sweeteners, 271, 273
Artistic/intellectual love, xi
Art of Loving, The, 41, 43, 47
Asceticism, xi, 173, 359
   Catholic, 73
   in Egypt, 69
Asia, 45, 261, 271, 381
Asiatic philosophies, 43
Aspartame, 271
Assertive effort, 249
Assertiveness, 303
Astrology, 5, 45, 53-63, 315, 353
Atheism, 53

of church officials, 259
and dictatorships, 51
Atheistic states, 53
Atkins, Robert C., 131, 133
Attorneys for mafia, v
Attractiveness, 35, 123, 157-159
Authority
control by, 1
dependence on, 335
external, vii, xvii, 21, 221
government, 65
judgment of, 243-245
as myth, 15
resistance to, 13
smallest unit of, 239-241
Automatic (bicameral, split) mind, vii
Automobiles, 197, 199
"Average individual," 151, 153
Awareness
mystical, 353-355
responsibility for, 353
self-. *See* Self-awareness
Ayatollahs, 331
in Iran, 53, 77

— B —

Babbitts, 307
Babies. *See* Children
Bad-thought (BT) jealousy, 105-111
defined, 107
BARRONS financial weekly, 213
Bastiat, Frederic, 400
Beaches, 231
Beauty, 125-129, 157
natural. *See* Natural beauty
Begin, Menachen, 277
Behavior traits of producers, 311
Benevolent termination of value-oriented relationships, 145
Bestiality, 203
Beta brain wave condition, 426
Better Business Bureaus, 329
Bible, xxv, 43, 49, 400
Bicameral (automatic, split) mind, vii
Bicycles, 255
Big business, 253
and capitalism, 251
Biological immortality, ix, 57, 61, 197, 199, 211, 271, 389-393
defined, 321
purpose of, 323
steps to achievement of, 321-323
Biological nature of man, 129, 135, 189, 221, 285
objectively good or bad actions based on, 7
Biological needs, xxix, 1, 15, 35, 213
defined, xxxix
Bio-rhythms, 353
Birth control, 75, 179, 279
Birth defects, 169
Bishops as atheists, 259
Black-African dictatorships, 381

Blackman, Justice, 283
Black rights, 183, 185
Blackwell, Elizabeth, 165
Black and white moral absolutes, 7-9
Blake, William, xi
Blaming others, 87
Blood sugar, 133
Blue laws of 1650s, 73
Bluenoses, 73
Body functions, iii, 131-133
control of, 137
Body-mind link. *See* Mind-body link
Body movements, 123
Boleyn, Anne, 73
Books
See also Literature; specific books
harmful, 41-45
on love, 297
on marriage, 297
on personality development, 297
positive-thinking, 37
self-improvement, 37, 39
on sex, 39-45, 297
valuable, 39-41
Bores, 161
Born-again Christianity, 77, 173
Boston Women's Health Book Collective, 133
Boulder City, Nevada, 239
Brain
See also Mind
activity of, 426
Brain cell death, 139
Brain patterns, 139
Branden, Nathaniel, 400
Breathing, 189
Brennan, Justice, 283
Bribes, 25, 27
Bridgeberg Books, 347
Bridge, Darlene, 347
Briefness of life, 321
Bruce, Lenny, 279, 281
BT. *See* Bad-thought
Buddhism, 63
Burden of proof, 45, 47, 273, 275
Burger, Justice, 281, 283
Buscagilias, Leo, 299
Business
big. *See* Big business
capitalistic principles in, 257, 259
collusion between government and, 255-257
defined, xxiii
as highest evolution of consciousness, xxiii
intellectualism in, 259
vs. mysticism, xxiii-xxvii
of Neo-Tech, 426
Neo-Teching, 257
Businessmen, 25, 27
altruistic, 253, 255, 257
defined, xxv

— C —

Caffeine
addiction to, 135, 141
breaking of addictions to, 141
as suppressor of happiness, 137
Callahan, Roger J., 85
Calvinist marriage, 73
Calvin, John, 73
Cambodia, 213, 305
Cancer
curing of, 137, 197, 271
elimination of, 199, 211
prevention of, 137
seeds, 1, 25
Capitalism, xiii, 65, 75, 183, 193, 195, 211, 361
See also Laissez faire
vs. altruism, 257-267
attacks on, 335
and big business, 251
vs. conservatism, 255
defined, xxxix
feminist view of, 185
and freedom, 183
freedom-oppression level under, 209
Neo-Tech, 245-257, 307, 361, 387, 391
and prosperity, 183
rise of, 177-179, 209, 345
and women's freedom and prosperity, 183
Capitalist Party of the United States, 213
Capone, Al, xxi
Carbohydrates, 135
diets of, 133
metabolism of, 131, 141
Cardinals as atheists, 259
Career housewives, 163, 165-171
Career mothers, 163
Career women, 163
Carnegie, Andrew, xxiii, 253, 406
Cars, 197, 199
Carson, Rachel, 261, 271
Carter, Jimmy, xxxi
Cartoonists, i, 345
CAS Happiness Diet, The, 137
Castro, Fidel, xxi, 53, 277, 305, 347
Casual hypnosis, 121
Casual sex, 35, 93-95, 117-119, 121, 141
vs. serious sex, 89
Catastrophes, 55
Catholic asceticism, 73
Catholic Church, 69, 71, 175
and art, 343, 345
leaders of as atheists, 259
view of women by, 185
Catholic Priest Association, 279
Causes, xvii
Celebrities, v, xv, 307
as social commentators, i
Celestial forces, 5, 55

Celibates, xi
Censorship, 207, 277-283
Certainty, 287, 289
Ceylon, 271
Change, 101
   capacity to, 153-155
   false, 153, 155
Chants, 221, 339
Character, 9, 125, 147
   of neocheaters, 291
Character development, 17, 93, 103, 123, 125, 147, 153, 155
   equality between men and women in, 161
Character traits, 123, 291
   See also specific types
   of producers, 311
Chemical preservatives, 271
Childbirth, 131-133, 169
Child of past, 3
Children, 165-171
   as burdens, 167
   externally produced, 169
   fear and understanding of death by, 321
   genetically controlled, 169
   individual rights of, 203
   love between parents and, 115-117
   as nonconsenting people, 205
   physical assault of, 117
   protection of from mystics and neocheaters, 227-233
   respect for, 117
   responsibility to, 385
   rewards of raising, 167, 169
   sex between adults and, 201, 203, 205
   world of, 169
China, 53, 213
Choice
   conscious, xxix
   between effort and laziness, xxiii
   free. *See* Free choice
   key, xix-xxiii
   mystically oriented, anti-life (Platonistic), 193
   philosophical, 193
   reality-oriented, pro-life (Aristotelian), 193
Chopin, xiii
Christ, 83, 197, 341, 347, 359
Christian anarchists, 67
Christianity, 67, 69, 75, 173
   anti-sexual attitudes of, 173
   born-again, 77, 173
   condemnation of emotions by, 83
   ethics of, 49, 303, 377
   freedom-oppression levels under, 209
   and guilt, 85
   oppression under, 67-77
   rise of, 175
   vs. romantic love, 209

Christmas Carol, A, 257
Chronic fatigue, 133
Chronic muscular tensions, 189
Chronology
   of Aristotelian history rewrite, 197-201
   of Christian oppression, 67-77
   of freedom, 207-211
   of oppression, 67-77, 207-211
   of women's potential, 171-185
Church, 207
   See also Religion; specific churches
   and art, 343, 345
   Catholic. *See* Catholic Church
   vs. Renaissance, 175
Church of Scientology, 47
Cigarette smoking, 141, 187
Cities, 305
City of God, The, 69
Civil War, 406
Classical composers, 343
   See also specific composers
Classical liberals, 249
Clergy, i, xv, xxvii, 219, 227
   See also Theologians
Cloning, 389
Closeness, 87
Coercion, 9, 89, 203, 205, 215, 219, 361
   elimination of, 381, 387
   government. *See* Government coercion
   and Supreme Constitution, 225
Colleges. *See* Academia
Cognitive-based psychotherapy, 107
Cohen, B., 379
Collectivism, xvii, 197, 313
   See also Platonistic philosophy
   elimination of, 197
   vs. individualism, 19-23
Combined-working type romantic relationship, 149, 151
Comfort, Alex, 39, 41
Commentators, xv
Commercial airlines, 197, 199
Commercial productivity, 163, 165
Common good, 247, 375
Communication
   levels of, 295-303
   open, 303
   in romantic love relationships, 303-305
Communication Map, 101
Communism, 51, 65, 193
Community standards, 281, 283
Compassion, 255, 263
Competence, 125, 135, 145, 187, 225, 247, 333
Competition, 231, 255, 337
   fear of, 183
   between governments, 213
   heterosexual, 125
   laws against, 257

   sexual, 123, 125
Comprachicos, 229, 231
Compromise in romantic love relationships, 145
Compulsions, 135
   See also specific types
Compulsive gambling, 141
Computerized ostracism, 197
Computers, 199
   interstellar, 61, 63
Comte, Auguste, xxxiii
Con artists, v
Concepts
   integration of, xxix, 7, 375
   thinking in, xxix
Conceptual mind, xxix
Confessions, 69
Confidence, 55, 301
Conflict of interest, 245
Conflict resolution, 99-101, 145
Consciousness, 19
Conscious choices, xxix
Conscious life, xi
Conscious loss of potency, 127
Conscious mind, ix
   and pleasure, ix
Consciousness, 27
   defined, xix
"Consciousness, The End of Authority," 235
Conscious thinking, xxix
Conscription, 21, 207, 253
Consenting individuals, 205
Conservatism, 245-257, 269
   vs. capitalism, 255
   and government-corporate collusion, 255
Constitution
   Supreme, 215-227
   U.S. *See* U.S. Constitution
Consumer-aid organizations, 329
Consumerism, 183, 255, 259, 261, 275, 307, 325, 331, 361
   envious malefactors in, 329, 331
Context, 373
Control, xi
   by authority, 1
   of body functions, 137
   government. *See* Government controls
   by human mind, 57
   of nervous system, 137
   of own destiny, 3-5, 55, 187
   of own future, 3
   of own self, 187
   of own well-being, 135, 137
Cooper, Kenneth H., 133, 135
Coordination, 189
Corporate collusion with government, 255, 257
Correction of errors, 101-103
Corruption, 27
Country vs. government, 207

Courtesans, 173
Courtly love, 71, 175
Court system, 213
  private, 197
Cox, Kenyon, 351
"Created logics," 195
Creation of existence, 47
Creativity, 91, 383
  individual differences in, 151
Credibility
  of feminists, 183
  of myths, 55
  of neocheaters, xvii, xxvii
Crime, 197
  elimination of, 197, 199
  organized, 141
  and race, 377, 379
  victimless, 277
Crime and Race, 379
Crime in the United States Uniform Crime Report, FBI, 379
Criminals, 217, 329
  neocheaters compared to, 51
Criticism, 289, 291
  avoidance of, 103
  of romantic love partner, 103
  unjust, 25, 111, 113
Crying, 359
Cuba, 213, 269
Cubism, 349
Cultural oppression of women, 171
Cyclamates, 271, 273

— D —
Dark Ages, 69, 171, 175, 207, 333
Das Kapital, 251
Da Vinci, Leonardo, xiii, 161
DDT, 261, 269, 273
Death, 197
  defined, xli
  emotional, 361
  finality of, 321
  and government, 269-275
  growth, 311-319, 361, 367
  life after, 321
  psyche, 311-319
  of romantic love partner, 97
Deception, 223, 253, 263
  mysticism as fertilizer of, xv
  religion based on, 181
Deceptive manipulation, 141
Decision making and emotions, 295
Default, xvii, xix, xxi, 323, 327, 335, 353
  mental, 335
  reasoning, xxxiii
Defense, 207, 217, 383
  national, 213
  Star-Wars, 59, 269
De la Boétie, Etienne, 13
Demagogues, 331
Democracy, 65, 193, 195, 213
Denial, 69

of emotions, 83
of feelings, 87
Dependence, 325, 373
  on authority, 335
  on government, 267, 269
  vs. independence, 247
Desirability, 301
Destructive actions, 83
Developmental thinking, 383
Dewey, John, 195, 231
d'Holbach, Baron, 400
Dialectical materialism, 195
Dickens, Charles, 257
Dictators, 51, 193, 277, 381
  See also specific dictators
  as envious malefactors, 327, 331
  envy tactics used by, 327
  poetry used by, 347
Diet, iii, 133-137, 185, 187
Dignity, 301
Disagreements, 99
Disarmament movement, 59
Disaster Lobby, The, 271
Disaster-oriented investments, 265
Discipline, Thought, and then Control (DTC) method, 143-144
  See also Control; Thought
Discourse of Voluntary Servitude, A, 13
Discovery of America, 197
Disease, 197
  cures for, 271
  elimination of, 199, 211
  mysticism, 1
  and pesticide bannings, 261
Dishonesty, xiii, xv, xvii, xlviii, 97, 135, 141, 223, 247, 275, 313
  and fighting, 99
  of media, 49
  rationalization of, 341
  truth rescued from, 257-263
Distortion
  of reality, 137
  of words, xiii
Division of labor concept, 161-165
Divorce, 75
  and Puritans, 177
  in rational, nonmystical relationships, 93
  reform in, 177, 179
Dogma elimination, 5-7
Dominance, 127
Dominant/surrender interaction, 127, 129
Doomsayers, 387
Doomsday Syndrome, The, 271
Douglas, Paul L., 233, 239
Douglas, William O., 283
Draft, 21, 207, 253
Drama, 77
  highs from, 187
Dr. Atkins' Diet Revolution, 131, 133
Drink, 187

See also Alcohol
Droughts, 263
Drugs, 83, 187, 189
  See also specific drugs, drug types
  addiction to, 135
  government control of, 139
  laws against, 139, 141, 207
  marketing of, 271
  and psychuous sex, 137-141
  research on, 271
  and romantic love, 137-141
Drunkenness, 189
DTC. *See* Discipline, Thought, and then Control
Du Pont, E.I., xxiii, 253
Duty, 21, 169
  to love, 115
Dying process, 113

— E —
Ear responsibility, 127
Earth exploration by other planets, 59-63
Ecologists, 259, 325, 361
  as envious malefactors, 329, 331
  envy tactics used by, 327
  pseudo, 43
Ecology, 255, 261, 307
  laws on, 271
  problems in, 271
Economic collapse, 263
Economic freedom, 179
Edison, Thomas A., xiii, xxiii, 161, 253, 406
Education professors as envious malefactors, 331
Education system, 195, 231
Educators, 231
Efficacious understanding, 15
Effort, xix, xxiii, 9, 97, 249, 369
  integration of time with, xxv
Effortless knowledge, 131
Egalitarianism, xvii, 43, 45, 51, 65, 145, 163, 191, 193, 285, 303, 309, 313
  See also Equality
  defined, xli
  elimination of, 337
  emotional, 297, 299
  envy tactics used in, 327
Egypt, 69
Ehrlich, Paul, 387
Einstein, Albert, xxiii, 161, 391
Elderly, 267, 271
Electrical brain patterns, 139
Electrical power, 197
Electrical-shock experiments at Yale, 13
Electronic transfer of mind contents, 389
Ellis, Albert, 41
Ellis, Havelock, 41, 117
Elman, D., 121

Emotional closeness, 87
Emotional conclusions vs. objective conclusions, 293-295
Emotional death, 361
Emotional egalitarianism, 297, 299
Emotional highs, 187
Emotional honesty, 87
Emotional needs, xxix, 35
Emotional requirements for psychuous pleasures, 35
Emotional stress, 303
Emotional tension, 189
Emotional well-being, 135
Emotions, 9, 25
  See also Feelings
  capacity to feel, 83
  Christian condemnation of, 83
  and decision-making, 295
  denial of, 83
  differences in men and women, 355-359
  fear of, 85
  fluctuation in, xiii
  guilt about, 25, 85
  guiltless acceptance of, 81
  guiltless feeling of, 81
  and intellect, 135
  moral judgment of, 83
  nature of, 185
  negative, 121, 185, 293-295, 303
  painful, 81
  positive, xlviii
  primacy of, xv
  reaction to, 295
  and reality, 83
  relationship of reason to, 107
  repression of, 83, 85, 185, 293-295, 303
  responsibility for, 25, 185-186
  suppression of, 83, 295
  understanding of in others, 355-359
  value of, 81-83
Encephalitis, 261
Encouragement, 371
Endorphin-producing exercise, 187
Ends and means, 13, 165, 205, 243
Energy, 133
  capacity for, 59, 63
  technology for, 199
Enjoyment, 191
Enlightened Greece, 173, 209
Entertainers, v, xv, 307
Enviers vs. producers, 331-335
Environmentalism, 183, 275, 331
  pseudo, 43
Environmental Protection Agency (EPA), 269, 273
Envy, 53, 147, 223, 247, 257, 309, 313, 315, 323-331
  concealing of, nature of, 325, 327
  cure for, 331-333
  defined, 105
  vs. jealousy, 325
  and laziness, 331-335
  tactics in, 327
EPA. See Environmental Protection Agency
Epigrams, 345
Equality, 151, 181
  See also Egalitarianism
  earned, 179
  government-enforced, 161
  of men and women, 161-165, 173
Equal love, 43
Errors
  allowances for, 103
  correction of, 101-103
  in judgment, 285-291
  relationship, 93-95
ESP. See Extrasensory perception
Ethics, 191
  altruistic, 31
  Christian, 49, 303, 377
  Judeo, 303, 377
  Judeo-Christian, 303
  religious, 49, 303, 377
Ethiopia, 263
Evans, Luther, 387
Evenly traded vs. fairly traded material values, 371
Evil, defined, 31
Evolution, 35
Exercise, 133, 135, 187, 189
Existence, 47
Existentialism, xiii, 9, 63-67, 77, 193, 195, 283
  defined, 67
Exologists, 331
Exorcism, 71
Exploration in Hypnosis, 121
External "authorities," vii, xvii, 21, 221
Externally produced babies, 169
Extrasensory perception (ESP), 57

— F —

Fabian slavery, 406
Facts and justice, 375-381
Factual view. See Aristotelian philosophy
Failure-to-judge syndrome, 283-293
Faint celestial forces, 5, 55
Fairly traded vs. evenly traded material values, 371
Faking
  of self-esteem, 31
  of sensuousness, 37
False changes, 153, 155
False-front illusion, 101, 103
Family love, xi, 367
Famine, 211, 261, 271
Famous quotes, 345
Famous women, 183
Fantasies, 121
  enactment of, 203
  sexual, 75
Fascism, xxxiii, 65, 193, 253
Fatigue, 133
Fatness, 131, 133, 135, 141, 231
FBI. See Federal Bureau of Investigation
FCC. See Federal Communications Commission
FDA. See Food and Drug Administration
Fear, 247
  of being hurt, 87
  of competition, 183
  of emotions, 85
  of freedom, 183, 313
  incest, 117, 201
  of independence, 313
  irrational, 85
  of losing happiness, 275
  in men, 303
  objective, 85
  of producers, 331
  of rejection, 87, 157
  of risk taking, 87
  subconscious, 275
  in women, 303
Fearlessness, 85
Federal Bureau of Investigation (FBI), 379
Federal Communications Commission (FCC), 269
Federal Trade Commission (FTC), 269, 273
Feedback, 353, 355, 365, 371
Feelings, 9, 79, 195
  See also Emotions
  acting on, xlviii
  deadening of, 83
  denial of, 87
  penetrated vs. penetrator, 355-357
  repression of, 99
  of social incompetence, 155-157
  subjective, 313
  understanding of in others, 355-359
Fein, Sinn, 277
Females. See Women
Feminists, 161, 163, 171, 179, 181, 183, 185, 211
  See also Women
  capitalism criticized by, 185
  credibility of, 183
  and government, 181, 183, 185
  as neocheaters, 179, 183, 185
  Roman, 173
Feudal hierarchy of social classes, 177
Fighting, 99
Finality of death, 321
Fine art, 77, 343
  See also Art
Firestone, Harvey Samuel, 253, 406
First Amendment, 237, 283
Fist fights, 357
Fitness, iii, 131, 133-137, 143
  equality between men and women in, 161

Five Minute Phobia Cure, The, 85
Fixed incomes of elderly, 267
Flagellation, 75
Flint, John, 233, 239, 400
Flynt, Larry, 281
Folk medicine, 255
Follett Publishing Company, 271
Food, 187
   gorging of, 189
   scarcity of, 271
Food and Drug Administration (FDA), 269, 271, 273
Food preservatives, 269
Force, xv, 9, 59, 65, 89, 193, 203, 205, 207, 215, 247, 263, 337, 339, 359, 363, 385
   advocates of, 249
   agents of, 223, 227
   government. *See* Government force
   group, 19
   initiatory. *See* Initiatory force
   legalized, 65
   as moral issue, 11
   and mysticism, 225
   and Supreme Constitution, 217-219
   threat of, 205, 215, 217, 247, 275, 363
Forced mediocrity, 27
Forcible rape, 201, 205
Ford, Henry, xxiii, 161, 253, 406
Ford, Henry III, 255
Fortune telling, 353
Fraud, xv, 5, 9, 45, 193, 195, 203, 205, 207, 215, 217, 225, 361, 363
   elimination of, 197, 199, 381, 387
Free choice, 223, 363
   defined, xix
Free-choice love, 179
Freedom, 5, 45, 99, 143, 187, 195, 227, 245-257, 277, 315, 387
   and Aristotelian philosophy, 251
   to be oneself, 101-103, 189
   and capitalism, 183
   to correct errors, 101-103
   defined, xli
   economic, 179
   fear of, 183, 313
   history of, 207-211
   individual, 211, 313
   of press, 49
   and psychuous pleasures, 1
   and reason, 183
   of women, 173-185
Free enterprise, 211
Free loaders, 5
Free love, 75
Free markets, 65, 197
Freud, Sigmund, 17, 117
Friendship, xi, 363
   and love, 111
   as necessary ingredient of romantic love, 367
   vs. romantic love, 365-373

Frigidity, 37, 41, 121, 125
Fromm, Erich, 41, 43, 47, 49
FTC. *See* Federal Trade Commission
Fun, defined, 95
Fundamental basis of romantic love, 147-149
Fundamentalist religion, 77, 173, 211
"Fundamental Principle that Determines the Long-Range Common Stock Value of a Corporation, The," 257
Fun-only sex. *See* Casual sex
Future, control of own, 3
Future potential aspect of romantic love, 149
Future romantic love, 181-185

— G —
Galileo, xxiii
Gambling, 141
Garrison, William Lloyd, 406
Geneen, Harold, 406
Gender use of "man," xxvii
Generic use of "man," xxvii
Genetically controlled babies, 169
Germany, 213, 269
Gestaltism, 63
Giftedness, 79
Giotto, 349
Goals of Neo-Tech, 426
God, 5, 47, 49-53, 231, 259, 315, 387
   See also Religion
   proof of existence of, 275
God-labeled government, 53
"Golden, The," 347
Golden Age of Greece, 1, 183, 197
Gold investments, 265
Good
   common, 375
   higher, 375
   understanding of, 373-375
Good and bad actions, 7-9
Good-thought (GT) jealousy, 105-111
   defined, 105
Gorbachev, 277
Gould, Jay, 25, 257, 406
Government, xxxv, 27, 129, 207, 217, 307
   See also specific types
   authority of, 65
   competing, 213
   corporate collusion with, 255, 257
   vs. country, 207
   death machines of, 269-275
   defined, xli
   dependency on, 267, 269
   equality enforced by, 161
   force-backed, 181
   God-labeled, 53
   limited, 213
   as mystical, 400
   as mystical hoax, 207
   as myth, 400

   nature of, 265, 267
   nonforce, 215, 361
   and Platonistic philosophy, 251
   power of, 55
   protection from destruction by, 263-269
   rationalizations for, 273
   schools run by, 195
   selling of property of, 215
   state-labeled, 53
   totalitarian, 213
   voluntarily supported, 213
Government coercion, 25, 27, 51, 165, 171, 181, 253, 269, 387
Government Company, 215
Government control, 1, 65, 245, 253, 255, 313, 329, 387, 389
   of alcohol, 139
   of drugs, 139
   of media, 49
   of women's equality, 173
Government departments and agencies, 269-275
   See also specific departments, agencies
   modus operandi of, 275
Government force, 11, 19, 21, 139, 163, 165, 171, 173, 193, 207, 245, 253, 257, 265, 269, 329
   and feminism, 181, 183, 185
   mass suffering and death from, 271, 273
Government oppression, 197, 245
   of women, 185
Government power, 129
Government regulation, 27, 253, 255
   See also Government control; Laws
   of drug research and marketing, 271
   ecological, 271
Government repression, 65
Goya, 349
Gracefulness, 189
Graham, Billy, 347
Graphology, 353
Grayson, Melvin J., 271
Greatness in women, 165-171, 379-381
Greece, 173, 183, 197, 209, 239
Group force, 19
Growth, ix, 87, 97, 99, 103, 119, 163, 165, 365, 367
   commitment to, 145
   death of, 311-319, 361, 367
   direction of, 143
   intellectual, ix, 145
   of mind, ix
   need for, 365
   personal. *See* Personal growth
   and poetry, 339
   of romantic relationships, 95
GT. *See* Good-thought
Guerrilla existence, 5
Guilt, xv, xvii, 17, 25, 51, 69, 129, 191, 333, 359

and Christianity, 85
about emotions, 25, 85
masturbation, 165
and preachers, xi
pushers of, 5
and religion, 49
and sex, 33, 67
Gypsies, 229

— H —

Hammond, William, 177
Hand-made goods, 255
Happiness, i, iii, ix, xiii, xxvii, 135, 215, 223, 333, 337
　Aristotelian view of, 3
　attacks on, xlviii
　cliches about, 17
　defined, xxxv-xxxvii, xliii
　destruction of by mystics and neocheaters, xix
　fear of loss of, 275
　goals for, 15
　inability of mystics to achieve, xvii
　vs. joy, 191
　judgment of others', 17
　vs. laziness, 426
　life-long, ix
　long-range. See Long-range happiness
　vs. misery, 305-311
　negative sources of, xxxvii
　oppression of, 67-77
　Platonistic view of, 3
　vs. pleasure, 191
　and productivity, 311
　"random-walk" capacity for, 153
　requirements for, 15
　responsibility for, 115, 385
　retention of, 29-31
　role of emotions in, 81
　romantic, iii, vii
　romantic love as source of, xi
　and self-esteem, 23-25
　short-term, xxxvii
　suppressors of, 137
　test for, 15-17
　as ultimate moral purpose, xxxvii
Hard (real) symbols, 351
Harmony in philosophy, 147
Hatred toward producers, 247, 331
Heads of states, v
　See also specific people
Health
　mental. See Mental health
　psychological, 137
　responsibility for, 115
Health, Education and Welfare Department (HEW), 269
Heart disease, 137
Hefner, Hugh M., 33, 279
Hellfire-and-brimstone religion, 49
Heraclitus, 197
Herbicides, 269, 271

Heroes, 329, 406
Herpes, 91
Heterosexual competition, 125
HEW. See Health, Education and Welfare
High-density environments, 305
Higher good, 375
Highs
　artificial, 189
　natural, 187-191
　reality, 187
Hippies in Egypt, 69
Hitler, Adolph, xxi, xxv, xxxi, 53, 161, 195, 249, 283, 347, 387
　as altruist, 359
　self-esteem of, 359
Hit & Run, 261
Homeric women, 173
Homosexuality, 125, 203, 205, 355
Honest fighting, 99
Honest thinking, 135
Honesty, xlviii, 9, 23, 43, 89, 93, 153, 155, 179, 183, 187, 243, 269, 299, 301, 321, 369
　in business people, xxv
　commitment to, 95, 99, 145
　emotional, 87
　and logical thinking, 335
　loyalty to, 97-101
　in romantic relationships, 99
　self-. See Self-honesty
Hook, Sidney, 195
Horizontal thinking, 201
　vs. vertical thinking, 383-385
Hormones, iii
Horoscopes, 353
Housewives, 163, 165-171
Howe, Woodson, 235
Hubbard, Ron, 47
Hughes, Howard, 25, 406
Hugo, Victor, xiii, 229
Humanism, 71
Humanitarianism, 263
Human nature, xxix, xlviii, 1-3, 39, 45, 191, 195, 375
　Aristotelian view of, 1
　biological. See Biological nature of man
　defined, xlv
　elements of, 5-7
　Platonistic view of, 1
　and Supreme Constitution, 225
　and survival, xxix
Human needs vs. human rights, 249
Humility, 3, 51
Humor, 201, 385
Hunger, 261
Hustler magazine, 281
Huxley, Julian, 387
Hypnosis, 121, 189-191
Hypocrisy, 247, 331
　of media, 49

— I —

Idealism, xiii
　irrational, xi
　rational, xi
Ideas
　irrational, xv
　Neo-Tech vs. other, 405
I Hate To Eat Diet, 137
Illness
　mental, 107
　and mind-body link, 137
Illusion, xvii, 101, 103
Immortality. See Biological immortality
Impersonal/automatic level of communication, 297
Impersonal/factual level of communication, 297
Impersonal/personal level of communication, 297
Imports, 255
Impotence, 33, 37, 41, 121, 125-129
Inadequacy, 147
Inalienable rights, 247
Inborn knowledge, 131
Incest, 117, 201, 203
　adult-adult, 203
　adult-child, 201, 203, 205
　as crime, 201, 203
　fear of, 201
　parent-child, 201, 203, 205
Incestuous marriages, 203-205
Incompetence, 45, 217
　social, 155-157
Indecent exposure, 279
Independence, 55, 97, 135, 143, 163, 165, 181, 247, 269, 315, 335, 369, 373
　vs. dependence, 247
　fear of, 313
Independent aloneness, 265
Independent judgment, 87-89
Independent thinking, 319, 335, 339, 341, 345
India, 381
Indian subcontinent, 271
Indian Union Carbide accident, 261
Individual differences, 91-93
　in creativity, 151
　in productivity, 151
Individual freedom, 211, 313
Individualism, xiii
　vs. collectivism, 19-23
　defined, xliii
Individuality, 179
Individual preferences, 93
Individual rights, 19, 65, 67, 91, 129, 139, 177, 181, 185, 207, 211, 213, 227, 281, 283, 383
　and Aristotelian view, 251
　of children, 203
　equality of, 151
　government oppression of, 139

as moral issue, 11
of Palestinians, 377, 381
as supreme, 361
and Supreme Constitution, 217
violation of, xxxiii, 165, 205
of women, 207
Individual-Rights Amendment to U.S. Constitution, 215
Individuals
"average," 151, 153
as highest value of universe, iii
as minority, 19
oppression of, 65
sovereignty of, 65
as supreme value, 339
Individual rights, 381
Individual uniqueness, 151-153
Industrial accidents, 261, 263
Industrialists, 253
Industrial-philosophy departments in businesses, 257
Industrial Revolution, 183, 345
Infallibility, 287
Infants. *See* Children
Infatuation, 289
Inflation, 253, 261, 267
Inheritance
laws on, 75
rights of, 177
Initiatory force, 21, 59, 83, 139, 195, 205-207, 213, 215, 217, 219, 335, 361
abolishment of, 225-227
elimination of, 197, 381, 383, 387
and Supreme Constitution, 225-227
Injustice rationalization, 341
Innocence, 325
Inquisitions, 71, 175, 209
Insects, 261
Insecurity, 105
Instinct, 129-131
Integrated, contextual truth, vii
Integrated philosophical systems, iii
See also Aristotelian philosophy
Integration
of body and mind. *See* Mind-body link
of concepts, xxix, 7, 375
and mind, 195
of philosophy with psychology and physiology, iii, vii
of reality, 15, 135
of time with effort, xxv
of words and actions with reality, xix
Integrity, 87, 93, 269
of art, 77
equality between men and women in, 161
Intellect
development of, 161
differences among individuals in, 93
and emotions, 135
Intellectual/artistic love, xi

Intellectual growth, ix, 145
Intellectually honest poetry, 343
Intellectual nature of man, 5-7
Intellectual needs, xxix, 35
Intellectual requirements for psychuous pleasures, 35
Intellectuals, 257, 259
in business world vs. in academic world, 259
defined, 259
as neocheaters, 375
reality-oriented, 373
social. *See* Social intellectuals
Intelligence and logical thinking, 335
Internal combustion engines, 199
Internal mysticism, 185-186
Internal Revenue Service (IRS), 269, 273, 275
Interplanetary travel, 199
Introspection, 97
Intuition, 243
Investments in gold and silver, 265
Involuntary ending of relationships, 97
I & O Publishing Company, xxiii, xxv, 233
Iran, 53, 269, 305
Iranian Ayatollahism, 77
Irrational fear, 85
Irrational idealism, xi
Irrational ideas, xv
Irrationality, xi, 63, 65, 245
Irrational relationships, xlviii
IRS. *See* Internal Revenue Service
Is Anyone Out There?, 57
Islam, 377
Israel, 381-383

— J —
James, William, 195
Jealousy, 105-111, 147
vs. envy, 325
nonsexual, 105
poison core of, 111-113
sexual, 105-111
Jesus, xxxi, 83, 161, 197, 341, 347, 359, 387
Jews, 375, 377
Johnson, Lyndon B., 249
Joint-working relationships, 149, 151
Jones, Jim, 347-349
Journalists, i
Joy
vs. happiness, 191
vs. well-being, 191
Joy of Sex, The, 39, 41
Juan, Don, 75, 121
Judeo-Christian ethics, 303, 377
Judgment, 243-245
of authority, 243-245
of emotions, 83
errors in, 283-293, 335
independent, 87-89
moral, 285, 293

of others, 283
of others' happiness, 17
of potential romantic-love partners, 289, 293
of power, 243-245
segmentalized, 283-293
traps in, 285-291
of value of relationships, 365
of volitional actions, 285
Justice, 45, 153, 179, 195, 369, 406
and facts, 375-381
vs. mercy, 377
social, 331
understanding of, 373-375
Justice Department, 269
Just laws, 207

— K —
Kantian-based philosophies, 51
See also specific types
Kant, Immanuel, xxi, xxxiii, 400
Kennedy, John F., 249, 347
Kennedys, 253
Key choice, xix-xxxiii
Khan, Genghis, xxxi
Khomeini-style terror governments, 211, 349
King Henry VIII, 73
King, Martin Luther, 347
Kinsey, Alfred Charles, 117
Knowledge, 195
effortless, 131
inborn, 131
interstellar, 61
pursuit of, 91
of self, 83
Knox, John, 73
Kramar, Henry, 71
Kroc, Ray, xxiii, 406
Kurtz, Paul, 387

— L —
Labor-saving devices, 333, 335
"Lady or man killer" syndrome, 125
Lafite-Cyon, Fracoise, 41
Laissez faire, 59, 183, 193, 195, 197, 251, 387
See also Capitalism
defined, xliii
Language, 373
Lateral thinking, 201
Laws
abortion, 207
antitrust, 257
drug, 207
ecological, 271
just, 207
moral, 207
pornography, 251, 277-283
prostitution, 165, 207
against voluntary sexual acts, 201-205
Laziness, xix, xxi, xlviii, 9, 195, 217, 221, 245-257, 309, 327, 335

...viers, 331-335
...appiness, 426
mechanisms of, 309
mental, 333, 335
and mysticism, 333
physical, 335
vs. productivity, 305-311
rationalization of, 337, 341
as root cause of evil, 335
Lees, Edith, 41
Legalized force, 65
Legal marriage, 119
Legal oppression of women, 171
Lenin, Vladimir, 5
Lethargy, 315
Liberalism, 181, 245-257, 361
classical, 249
neocheating, 171
Liberal media, 255, 261
envy tactics used by, 327
Liberated approaches to sex, 31
Liberation movements, 183
See also specific types
Libertarians, 269
mystically oriented, 265
Liberty. *See* Freedom
Life
See also Living
briefness of, 321
conscious, xi
defined, xi, xlv
purpose of, xxxvii
satisfaction from, 17-19
sense of. *See* Sense of life
standard of, 15
as supreme value, 321
value of, 91, 321-323, 391
Life-after-death myths, 321
Life-Lifting Capacity, 143
Life-long happiness, ix
Life-long prosperity, ix
Life style, 9, 303-305
See also specific types
Limited government vs. anarchy, 213
Lincoln, Abraham, 406
Lincoln Star, 235
Listening skills, 157
Literature, 77, 343
See also Books
highs from, 187
Living
See also Life
in the past, 3
in present, 5
in reality, 187
standard of, 211, 261
Logic, xiii, xxix, 9, 195, 243, 335, 345
defined, xlv
reality-oriented, 61
Loitering With Intent, 237
Lomans, Willie, 307
Long-range happiness, xxxvll,17,23
95, 131, 135, 333, 393

equality between men and women in, 161
and fraud, 5
Long-range planning, xxv
Losers, iii, xxv, 1
rejection of, 223
Love, ix, xlviii, 23
Aristotelian view of, 3
basic views of, 31
books on, 297
courtly, 71, 175
death of, 97
defined, xi-xiii
destruction of by mystics and neocheaters, xix
duty to, 115
equal, 43
fading of, 97
family, xi, 367
free, 75
free-choice, 179
friendship aspects of, 111
intellectual/artistic, xi
limitations of, 93-95
and Neo-Tech, xlviii
of parents, 115-117
Platonistic view of, 3
playboy view of, 33-35
religious views of, 33-35
role of emotions in, 81
romantic. *See* Romantic love
and sex, 73
testing for proof of, 111
types of, xi
understanding of, 373-375
Low blood sugar, 133
Loyalty
to honesty, 97-101
to rationality, 223
to truth, xix, 9, 17, 87, 91, 95, 97, 223, 235, 243, 311
Luther, Martin, 73

— M —

Maddox, James, 271
Mafia
attorneys for, v
members of, 329
Malaria, 261, 271
Malefactors, 323-331
Males. *See* Men
Malnutrition, 271
Malthus, Thomas, 387
Man
See also Men; Women
biological needs of, xxix
defined, xxvii-xxxiv
gender use of, xxvii
generic use of, xxvii
Manipulation
deceptive, 141
in sex, 119
"Man or lady killer" syndrome, 125

Man's nature. *See* Human nature
Manson, Charles, 161
Man Who Laughs, The, 229
Man-woman relationship aspect of romantic love, 149
Mao, xxxi, 53, 161, 283, 347, 359, 406
Marcuse, Herbert, 17
Marijuana, 137-141
Marital sex, 71
Marriage, 119
books on, 297
Calvinist, 73
church domination of, 69
as civil contract, 75, 177
incestuous, 203-205
legal, 119
plural, 203
Marshall, Justice, 283
Martyr attitude, 127
Marx, Karl, 195, 251
Marxism, xxxiii, 51, 263, 269, 305
Marxist-style terror governments, 211
Masochism, 83, 205
Mass murder, 51, 53, 83, 253, 263, 305, 347, 406
Mass production, 199
Master neocheaters, i, xxvii
defined, xxv-xxvii
elimination of, 397, 398-399
first identification of, 400
Picasso as, 349
Masters and Johnson, 139
Masturbation guilt, 165
Materialism, 195
Material (tangible) values, 359, 363, 365, 369, 371
vs. abstract values, 365
fairly traded vs. evenly traded, 371
Mathematics, 287
Mating behaviors, 129
Mead, Margaret, 387
Means and ends, 13, 165, 205, 243
Media, xvii, xxv, 25, 27, 49, 63, 211, 227, 283, 285, 307
as envious malefactors, 329
and envy, 325
envy tactics used by, 327
freedom for, 49
government control of, 49
hypocrisy of, 49
liberal. *See* Liberal media
poetry used by, 347
as professional neocheaters, i
Media commentators, xv
Media personalities, v
Medicine, 255
Mediocrity, 27
Meditation, 63
Mein Kampf, xxxi
Memoires vs. Massachusetts, 281
Men
characteristics of sought by women, xiii

desire for peaceful core in, 357-359
emotional differences between women and, 355-359
fear in, 303
nature of vs. female nature, 357-359
psychological differences between women and, 355-359
Menstruation, 131-133
Mental default, 335
Mental health, 17, 295
and self-esteem, 107
Mental illness and mysticism, 107
Mental laziness, 333, 335
Mental well-being, 135
Mercy vs. justice, 377
Metabolic problems, 131
Metaphors, 351
Metropolitan areas, 305
Michelangelo, xiii, xxiii, 345
Middle-of-the-roaders, 251
Milgrams, Stanley, 13
Military draft, 21, 207, 253
Miller vs. California, 281
Milton, John, 75
Mind, 55
See also Brain
bicameral (automatic, split), vii
conceptual, xxix
conscious. *See* Conscious mind
and control, 57
as "creator of reality," 195
cure of disease by, 137
electronic transfer of contents of, 389
growth of, ix
and happiness, ix
independent use of, 319
and integration, 195
as neuter, 161
pleasurable gratification of, ix
and pleasure, ix
potency of, 27
power of, 55
prevention of disease by, 137
rational, 5, 35, 335
rational use of. *See* Rational thinking
self-healing power of, 319
subconscious, 189, 295
Mind-body link, xi, 17, 35, 37, 135, 189
and illness, 137
Mind-body sensations, 189
"Mind over matter" concept, 137
See also Mind-body link
Minorities
individuals as, 19
rights of, 181, 185
Mirroring of another's qualities, 353, 355, 365, 371
Misery vs. happiness, 305-311
Modern art, 221, 343, 349-351
Modern romantic love, 179-181
Money and Neo-Tech, xlviii

Monogamous relationships, 91
Monopolies, 251, 253
Moral absolutes, 7-9
Moral issues, 9-15
See also specific types
Morality, xxiii, xxix-xxxi, 217
basing of on reality, 9
and business, xxiii
defined, xxxi, xlv, 221
of mystics, 221-223
of nonmystics, 223
of sexual attractiveness, 123
objective, 7, 9
and pleasure, 35
and sex, 35
subjective, 9
Moral judgment, 285, 293
of emotions, 83
Moral laws, 207
Moral purpose, xxxvii
Moral responsibility, 385
Moral standards, 205, 285
Moral values vs. personal values, 293
More Joy, 39, 41
Moslem dictatorships, 381
Mosquitos, 261
Mothers, 163
See also Parents
Motivation, 89
of relationships, 121
Mouth responsibility, 123, 185-187
Multi-partner relationships, 89-91
Murder, 203, 205
mass, 51, 53, 83, 253, 263, 305, 347, 406
Muscular tensions, 189
Museum of Modern Art, New York, 349
Music, 77, 343
See also specific types
highs from, 187
rock. *See* Rock music
unintegrated, 341
Mussolini, 347
Mutual seduction, 123
Mutual values, 147
Mystical awareness vs. self-awareness, 353-355
Mystical experiences, 187
Mystical values, 27
Mysticism, i, iii, xvii, xxxiii, 9, 49, 51, 53, 63, 77, 183, 195, 197, 259, 309, 315, 333, 337
See also Mystics; Platonistic philosophy
and addictions, 135
vs. business, xxiii-xxvii
defined, xiii-xv, xlv, 219
and destruction, 45-47
and disease, 141
as disease, xiii, xv
elimination of, vii, xlviii, 197, 225-227, 393, 397,

elimination of 398-399
as fertilizer of deception, xv
and force, 225
government as, 400
as harm to values, xlviii
internal, 185-186
and laziness, 333
in libertarians, 265
and mental illness, 107
nature of, 219-221
vs. Neo-Tech, 400
philosophical basis for, 193
rationalization of, 341
"scientific," 57
smoking, 187
spreaders of, xv
and Supreme Constitution, 219-221
symptoms of, xv
techniques of, 47-49
Mystics, xiii, xlviii, 153, 191, 211
See also Mysticism
dismissing of, iii
elimination of, 337
as envious malefactors, 327
and judgment of others, 283
and morality, 221-223
Neo-Teching of, 257-263
vs. nonmystics, xv-xvii
professional, 341
protection of children from, 227-233
unifying characteristics of, 45
use of poetry by, 339
Myths, 53-63
See also specific myths
altruistic, 231
of big business-capitalism link, 251
credibility of, 55
governments as, 400
life-after-death, 321
religious, 231
"scientific," 57

— N —

Nader, Ralph, xxi, 161, 253, 261, 329, 347, 359, 387
Naiveness, 325
National defense, 213
National Review, 215
Natural beauty, 123, 125, 157
relying on, 157-159
Natural body functions, 131-133
Natural catastrophes, 55
Natural giftedness, 79
Natural highs, 187-191
Natural phenomena, 129-131
Nature
biological, 135
of emotions, 185
of envy, 325, 327
forces of, 55
of government, 265, 267
human. *See* Human nature
of man. *See* Human nature

ticism, 219-221
  heating, 219-221
  of psychuous sex, 91
  of reality, 353
  of self, 353
  variables of, 5
Nazi Germany, 213, 269
Neck stiffness, 189
Needs
  biological. *See* Biological needs
  emotional, xxix, 35
  for growth, 365
  intellectual, xxix, 35
  physical, 19, 35
  psychological, xxix, 19, 35
  vs. rights, 249
Negative emotions, 121, 185, 293-295, 303
Negative sources of happiness, xxxvii
Neocheaters, xvii, xix, xlviii, 1, 31, 145, 153, 191, 249
  See also Neocheating
  abandonment of, 13-15
  academia as, 27, 211
  character of, 291
  common bond linking, v
  countering of, 233-239
  credibility of, xvii
  criminals compared to, 51
  dependence on, 335
  dismissing of, iii
  feminist, 179, 183, 185
  intellectuals as, 375
  and judgment of others, 283
  liberals as, 171
  master. *See* Master neocheaters
  media as, i
  mysticism as tool used by, xiii
  Neo-Teching of, 257-263
  vs. nonmystics, xv-xvii
  politicians as, 51
  protection of children from, 227-233
  psychologists as, 187
  self-esteem of, 265
  and Supreme Constitution, 221-223
  theologians as, 51
  therapists as, 109
  use of poetry by, 339
Neocheating, 197
  See also Neocheaters
  defined, xv, 219
  elimination of, xlviii, 225-227, 393, 397, 398-399
  essence of, 275
  nature of, 219-221
  rationalization of, 341
  and Supreme Constitution, 219-221
Neo-Tech, i, iii
  advantages of, 1, 401-403
  vs. altruism, 335-337
  army of, 426
  business of, 426
  defined, vii
  goal of, 426
  marketing of, xxv
  vs. mysticism, 400
  vs. other idea systems, 405
  political constitution for, 213-215
  and racism, 381-383
  silver bullet of, 426
Neo-Tech art, 343
Neo-Tech brain waves, 426
Neo-Tech capitalism, 245-257, 307, 361, 387, 391
Neo-Teching business, 257
Neothink, 137, 211, 398-399, 407
Nervousness, 157
Nervous system, 121
  control of, 137
Newspeak, 221, 373
New York City, 305
Nicaragua, 305
Nidal, Abu, 277
Nixon, Richard, xxxi, 249
Nobel-prize laureates, v
Nonconsenting people, 205
Nonconsenting sadism, 205
Noneuclidean mathematics, 287
Nonexactness, 343
Nonforce government, 215, 361
Non-integrated thinking, xv
Nonintimate sex, 93-95
Nonjudgable values, 91
Nonjudgmental values, 91
Nonmanipulative seduction, 123
Nonmarital sex, 117-119
Nonmysticism, xxiii
  defined, xix
  and morality, 223
  vs. mysticism, xv-xvii
  vs. neocheating, xv-xvii
  in relationships, 93
Nonproducers, 23
  as envious malefactors, 327
  vs. producers, 237
Non sequiturs, i, xv, 63, 219, 255
  See also specific types
  defined, i
Nonsexual jealousy, 105
November 3rd trap, 275
Nuclear-Decision Threshold, 59, 61, 63
Nuclear holocaust, 211
Nuclear power, 197, 199
Nuclear warfare, 59
Nude bathing, 279
Nude streaking fad, 281
Nutritionalists, 275

— O —

Obedience to Authority, 13
Obesity, 131, 133, 135, 141, 231
Objective-Aristotelian connotations of words, xxxix-xkvuu
Objective conclusions vs. emotional conclusions, 293-295
Objective evaluation of art, 77
Objective fear, 85
Objectively right or wrong values, 91
Objective morals, 7, 9
Objective principles, 315
Objective reality. *See* Reality
Objective standards for art, 77
Objective truth, 287, 341
Objective values, 325, 333, 359
  abstract expressions of, 343
  of art, 79
  attacks on, 335
Objectivity, 23
  defined, xlv
Occult, 315
Occupational Safety and Health Administration (OSHA), 269
"Old-time" religion, 49
Omaha World-Herald, 235
Omniscience, 287
O'Neill, George, 41
O'Neill, Nena, 41
O'Neill, Thomas "Tip," 253
Open communication, 303
Open Marriage, 41
Openness, 87, 99, 297, 299, 301
Opera, 343
Opinions of others, 87-89
Oppression, 253
  Christian. *See* Christian oppression
  government. *See* Government oppression
  of happiness, 67-77
  history of, 207-211
  of individual, 65
  of individual rights, 139
  of men, 207-211
  sexual, 127
  of women, 171, 173-185, 207-211
Oral sex, 203, 205
Organized crime, 141
Orgasm, 355
  psychological, 121
Orgies, 93
Original sin, 83, 315, 317
OSHA. *See* Occupational Safety and Health Administration
Ostracism, 197
Our Bodies, Ourselves, 133
Outside sexual affairs, 101
Ovid, 119
Ownership
  of another's life, 105
  of art, 81
Oxford English Dictionary, xiii

— P —

Packaged truth, 339, 345, 349
Pain, 83
  emotional, 81
Palestinians, 377, 381
Parables, 219, 341, 345
  defined, 341

Paradise Lost, 75
Parasiticism, 197, 309, 325, 373
   and envy, 327
Parents
   love of, 115-117
   as scapegoats, 115-117
   sex between children and, 201, 203, 205
Passion, xlviii
Past, 3
Patriarchal culture, 303
Peaceful core desire in men, 357-359
Peace movement, 59
Penetrated vs. penetrator feelings, 355-357
Peppers, Claude, 267
Performance anxieties, 33
Performing arts, 77
Personal appearance, 131-133
Personal growth, 101, 145, 147, 165, 167
   and poetry, 339
Personality, 93, 147
Personality development, 91
   books on, 297
Personality traits, 123
Personal level of communication, 297
Personal preference, 7
Personal values vs. moral values, 293
Personal worth, 151-153
Pesticides, 261, 269, 271
Philosophers, xxi, 231
   See also specific philosophers
   job of, iii
Philosophical basis for mysticism, 193
Philosophical choices, 193
Philosophical-ethical position, 191
Philosophical origins of power, 241-243
Philosophy, iii, 45, 337-339
   See also specific types
   anti-life, 389
   Asiatic, 43
   harmony in, 147
   integrated, iii
   integration of with psychology and physiology, iii, vii
   Kantian-based, 51
   practicality of, iii
   pseudo, 191
   for romantic love, 191-193
Philosophy professors as envious malefactors, 331
Phnom Penh, 305
Phobias, 85
Phoenician commerce, xxiii
Physical attractiveness, 157-159
Physical beauty, 125-129
Physical coordination, 189
Physical differences among individuals, 93
Physical fitness, iii, 131, 133-137, 143
   equality between men and women in, 161

Physical grace, 189
Physical laziness, 335
Physical nature of man, 5-7
Physical needs, 19, 35
Physical requirements for psychuous pleasures, 35
Physical senses, ix
Physical survival, 15
Physical tension, 189
Physical well-being, 135, 137
Physicians, 115
Physics, 287
Physiology, iii
   integration of with philosophy and psychology, iii, vii
Picasso, Pablo, xxi, 349
Piekoff, Leonard, 400
PK. *See* Psychokinesis
Planning, xxv
Planning commissions, 239
Plato, iii, xxi, 197, 337, 387, 400
   See also Platonistic philosophy
   vs. Aristotle, 193-199
Platonistic philosophy, 59, 63, 315, 337
   See also Plato; specific philosophies
   as basis for educational system, 195
   and government, 251
   and happiness, 3
   and human nature, 1
   and life style, 303
   and love, 3
   and mysticism, 339
   and power, 239-245
   and prosperity, 3
   and reality, 3
   and word connotations, xxxix-xlvii
Playboy Corporation, 33, 277
Playboy Forum, 33, 279
Playboy Foundation, 33, 277
Playboy magazine, 33, 277
Playboy philosophy, 277
   of love, 33-35
   of sex. *See* Casual sex
Playboy Press, 279
Pleasure, ix, xiii
   aesthetic, 77-79
   vs. happiness, 191
   of human mind, ix
   limitations of, 93-95
   and morality, 35
   psychuous. *See* Psychuous pleasure
   role of emotions in, 81
   of romantic love, xi, 31-33
   and senses, ix
   sexual, ix
   as sin, 71
   vs. well-being, 191
Plural marriages, 203
Poetry, 79, 221, 339-351
   anti-intellectual nature of, 339
   Aristotelian-based, 345, 347

   intellectually honest, 343
   personal growth blocked by, 339
   romantic love undermined by, 339
   seductive nature of, 341
Police protection, 213
Political cartoonists, i, 345
Political constitution for Neo-Tech, 213-215
Political science professors as envious malefactors, 331
Political systems, 213
   See also specific types
Politicians, i, xv, xxi, xxv, xxvii, xxxi, 19, 27, 49, 51, 65, 153, 211, 219, 227, 249, 263, 291, 361
   See also Government
   defined, xlv
   dependence on, 335
   elimination of, 337
   as envious malefactors, 327, 331
   and envy, 325
   envy tactics used by, 327
   nature of, 263
   poetry used by, 347
   self-esteem of, 265
Pope of 904 A.D., 69
Pope Clement VII, 73
Pope Innocent VIII, 175
Pope John Paul, xxxi
Popes, xxi, xxv, 71
   See also specific popes
   as atheists, 259
   as envious malefactors, 331
Popular causes, xvii
   See also specific types
Pornography, 75
   laws against, 277-283
   movement against, 173
   Supreme Court decision on, 1973, 251
Positive emotions, xlviii
Positive-thinking approaches, 37, 39
Possessiveness, 105, 107, 109, 147
Potency, 363
   loss of, 125-129
Pot, Pol, xxi, 277, 359
Poverty, 197, 211
   elimination of, 197
Powell, Justice, 283
Power, 239-245
   government, 129
   judgment of, 243-245
   and Neo-Tech, xlviii
   philosophical origins of, 241-243
Predestination, 315, 317
Preferences, 7, 9, 93
Premarital sex, 117-119, 203
Pre-Renaissance, 175
Present, 5
Preservatives, 269, 271
Press freedom, 49
Pride, xiii, 21, 65, 67
   defined, xlv

Principles, 243
  See also specific types
  objective, 315
Privacy, 169, 299, 391
Private courts, 197
Private property, 129
Private protection services, 197
Problem handling, 97-101
Producers, xxvii, 23-25, 27, 29, 45, 49, 51, 53, 129, 217, 221, 225, 249, 257, 305
  behavior traits of, 311
  character traits of, 311
  defined, xlv
  dedication to, copyright page
  vs. enviers, 331-335
  fear of, 331
  hatred toward, 247, 331
  as heros, 329
  independence of, 269
  vs. nonproducers, 237
  self-esteem of, 265
  self-image of, 307
Productive effort, 9
Productive individuals. *See* Producers
Productive work, 369
Productivity, 3, 9, 15, 23, 91, 135, 183, 187, 189, 217, 305, 369
  categories of for women, 163-164
  commercial, 163, 165
  as essential to life, 307
  and happiness, 311
  individual differences in, 151
  vs. laziness, 305-311
  and psychuous pleasures, 311
  vs. sacrifice, xxxiii
  and self-esteem, 17
Professional mystics, 341
Professional women, 163
Professors. *See* Academia
Prohibition, 141
Pro-individual sense of life, 27, 29
Pro-life choice, 193
Pro-life philosophy. *See* Aristotelian philosophy
Promiscuity, 83
Property rights, 21, 65, 75, 129, 139, 177, 207, 245, 247, 381
  equality in, 151
  of Palestinians, 377, 381
  and Supreme Constitution, 217
  violation of, 165
Prosperity, i, iii, vii, ix, 215, 245-257
  Aristotelian view of, 3
  and capitalism, 183
  cliches about, 17
  destruction of by mystics and neocheaters, xix
  and fraud, 5
  goals for, 15
  inability of mystics to achieve, xvii
  life-long, ix
  Platonistic view of, 3

psychuous, xii-ix
and reason, 183
requirements for, 15
Prostitution, 75
  laws against, 165, 207
Protection from government destruction, 263-269
Protectionism, 253, 275
Protection rackets, 273
Protection services, 197
Proximire, William, 267
Prurient interest, 281
Pseudo ecologists, 43, 259-261
Pseudo environmentalists, 43
Pseudo-intellectuals, xxiii, 329
Pseudo philosophies, 191
Pseudo sciences, 57
  See also specific types
Pseudo self-esteem, 331, 359
Psyche death, 311-319
Psychoanalysis, 353
Psychokinesis (PK), 57
Psychological differences
  among individuals, 93
  between men and women, 355-359
Psychological dominant/surrender interaction, 127, 129
Psychological health, 137
Psychological nature of man, 7
Psychological needs, xxix, 19, 35
Psychological orgasms, 121
Psychological requirements for psychuous pleasures, 35
Psychological well-being, 77
Psychologists as neocheaters, 187
Psychology, iii
  integration of with philosophy and physiology, iii, vii
Psychology professors as envious malefactors, 331
Psychosexual dominance, 127
Psychosexual virgins, 121
Psychotherapy, 107
Psychuous concept, i
  defined, vii, ix
Psychuous experiences, 37
Psychuous love, 33-35
Psychuous pleasures, iii, 23, 45, 81, 87, 89, 95, 99, 113, 121, 129, 131, 133, 135, 187, 189, 245, 299, 333, 337, 363, 369
  achievement of, 95
  vs. altruism, 335-337
  and children, 167
  for couples with children, 167
  equality between men and women in, 161
  freedom as requirement for, 1
  and physical fitness, 135
  political constitution for, 213-215
  and productivity, 311
  as reality high, 189
  requirements for, 35

vs. sensuous behavior, 35-37
vs. sensuous pleasures, ix-xi
Psychuous sex, 23, 33-35, 37, 89, 95, 119, 123, 125
  capacity for, 37
  defined, ix
  and drugs, 137-141
  intensity of, 37
  nature of, 91
Public schools, 195, 231
Puritans, 73, 177, 209
Purpose, xxxvii

— Q —
Qaddafi, 277
Quackeries, 353
Quantum mechanics, 287
Quotations, 221, 345

— R —
Race and crime, 377, 379
Rachmaninoff, xxiii
Racism, 183
  Neo-Tech solution to, 381-383
Rand, Ayn, xxi, xxiii, 183, 185, 187, 400
"Random-walk" capacity for happiness, 153
Rape, 201, 203, 205
Rapid hypnosis, 121
Rather, Dan, xxi
Rational action, 3
Rational best interest, 61
Rational idealism, xi
Rationalists, xiii, 75, 177
Rationality, xiii, xxiii, 87, 187, 189, 249
  defined, xlv
  loyalty to, 223
Rationalizations, xxxiii, 63, 219, 247, 333, 341, 349
  for government, 273
  of laziness, 337
Rational mind, 5, 35, 335
  See also Rational thinking
Rational relationships, xlviii, 93
Rational self-interest, 245, 247, 315, 377
Rational thinking, 15, 335, 353
  See also Rational mind
  commitment to, 95
Reactionism, 385
Real (hard) symbols, 351
Reality, ix, 195, 219, 259, 287, 317, 375
  ability to perceive, 269
  acting in concert with, vii, xlviii
  Aristotelian view of, 3
  as basis of truth, 339
  defined, xxxv, xlv, 3
  distortions of, 137
  effectiveness in dealing with, 23
  and emotions, 83
  evasion of, xv, 219

faking of, xv
and human nature, 39
identification of, 135
integration of, 15, 135
integration of words and actions with, xix
mind as creator of, 195
morals based on, 9
nature of, 353
negation of, 65
obscuring of, iii
Platonistic view of, 3
sense of living in, 187
transcending of, 349
understanding of, 39
"Reality-creating" approach, 195
Reality highs, 187, 189
Reality-oriented choice, 193
Reality-oriented logic, 61
Reality-oriented philosophy. *See* Aristotelian philosophy
Reality-oriented intellectuals, 373
Reality/self-interest premise, iii
Reason, xxxi, 9, 49, 55, 183, 195
 capacity for, 51
 default of, xxxiii
 defined, xlv
 and freedom, 183
 and prosperity, 183
 relationship of emotions to, 107
Red China, 53, 213
Reflecting of another's qualities, 353, 355, 365, 371
Reformation, 73
Regulation. *See* Government regulation
Rehnquist, Justice, 283
Reich, Wilhelm, 17
Rejection
 fear of, 87, 157
 of losers, 223
 of utopias, 387
 value of, 155-159
Relationships
 See also specific types
 errors in, 93-95
 irrational, xlviii
 love. *See* Love; Romantic love
 monogamous, 91
 rational, xlviii
 romantic. *See* Romantic love
Religion, xxxv, 5, 45, 51, 53, 67, 129, 179, 193, 197, 207, 217, 291
 See also God; specific religions
 basis of, 45
 deceit-based, 181
 decline of, 177-179
 defined, xlv
 and envy, 325
 ethics of, 49, 303, 377
 and freedom-oppression level, 209
 fundamentalist, 77, 173, 211
 Jewish, 377
 leaders in, v, xxxi
 "old-time," 49
 of oppression of women, 185
 overall effect of, 35
 power of, 55
 vs. renaissance humanism, 71
 rise of, 209
 and sex, 33-35
Religion professors as envious malefactors, 331
Religious ascetics, xi
Religious automatons, 349
Religious experiences, 187
Religious myths, 231
Rembrandt, 349
Renaissance, 71, 183, 209, 343, 345
 vs. Church, 175
 humanism, 71
Repression
 of emotions, 83, 85, 99, 185, 293-295, 303
 government, 65
Republic form of government, 65
Resentment, 25, 53, 147, 223, 313
Resistance to authority, 13
Respect, 89
 for children, 117
Responsibility, 99, 245-257
 for actions, xix, 309, 363
 for awareness, 353
 and business, xxiii
 to children, 385
 of emotions, 185-186
 for happiness, 115, 385
 for health, 115
 for judgment errors, 289
 moral, 385
 mouth, 185-187
 for own actions, 85, 185, 245
 for own emotions, 25
 for own life, 385
 for own self, 309
 for own well-being, 363
 of parents, 169
 for problems, xv
 self-. *See* Self-responsibility
 for well-being, 115, 245, 385
Reuben, David, 39
Reverse infatuation, 289-291
Rights
 black, 185
 inalienable, 247
 individual. *See* Individual rights
 minority, 181, 185
 for minority groups, 19
 vs. needs, 249
 privacy, 391
 property. *See* Property rights
 women's, 185
Rights movements, 165, 181, 183
 See also specific types
Risk taking, 87
Robber barons, 257
Rockefeller, John D., 25, 161, 253, 406
Rockefeller, Nelson A., 255
Rock music, 221, 339, 341
 and thinking, 341
Role playing, 101
Romance, xiii
Roman Empire, 67, 179, 209
 decline of, 173
 women in, 173
Roman pagans, 67
Romantic happiness, iii, vii
Romanticism, xi, xiii
Romantic love, ix, xi, 81, 83, 87, 89, 125, 143-145, 293, 363
 attacks on, xlviii
 benefits of, 31-33
 and children, 167
 vs. Christianity, 209
 combined-working type, 149, 151
 communication in, 303-305
 competition in, 231
 compromise in, 145
 vs. conservatism, 245-257
 defined, xlvii
 and drugs, 137-141
 earned, xiii
 ending of, 97
 equality between men and women in, 161
 exchange of values in, 359-363
 and fear of being hurt, 87
 finding partners for, 155-159
 and fraud, 5
 vs. friendship, 365-373
 friendship as necessary ingredient of, 367
 fundamental basis of, 147-149
 future, 181-185
 future potential aspect of, 149
 growth of, 95
 honesty in, 99
 inability of mystics to achieve, xvii
 judgment of potential partners for, 289, 293
 vs. laziness, 245-257
 vs. liberalism, 245-257
 man-woman relationship aspect of, 149
 modern, 179-181
 money in bank, 99
 multi-partner relationships in, 89-91
 objective standards for, 289
 philosophy for, 191-193
 pleasures of, 31-33
 and poetry, 339
 political constitution for, 213-215
 rise of, 209
 segments of, 147-149
 separate-working type, 151
 sharing in, 299
 as source of happiness, xi
 standards for, 145-147

symbols in, 351
twentieth century, 179
types of, 149-151
value-oriented, 95
waxing and waning of, xiii
Romantic Period of 19th Century, xi
Rome, 69
Roosevelt, Franklin D., xxi, 249
Roosevelt, Theodore, 87
Rousseau, Jean Jacques, xi
Rules elimination, 5-7
Russia, 51, 53, 213, 269, 381

— S —

Saccharin, 271
Sacrifice, xxxi-xxxv, 3, 19, 21, 37, 45, 51, 193, 315, 331, 335, 337, 359, 385
  avoidance of, 29
  defined, 11
  as moral issue, 11
  vs. productivity, xxxiii
  self-, 19, 21, 335, 359
Sadism, 83, 205
Sanger, Margaret, 75
Santa Claus, 231
Satisfaction from life, 17-19
Scapegoat role of parents, 115-117
Schweitzer, Albert, xxxi, 43, 161
"Scientific mysticism," 57
"Scientific" myths, 57
Scientology, 47, 65
Scrooge, Ebenezer, 257
SDI, 59, 269
SEC. *See* Securities and Exchange Commission
Secret of Non Sequiturs, The, i
Secret sexual affairs, 99
Securities and Exchange Commission (SEC), 269
Seduction, 119-123
  mutual, 123
  nonmanipulative, 123
  for serious sex, 123
Seductiveness, 121, 123
  of poetry, 341
Segmentalized judgment, 283-293
Self-appointed advocates, i
Self-awareness, 65, 81, 187, 189, 295
  vs. mystical awareness, 353-355
Self-confidence, 301
Self-deception, 97
Self-defense, 59, 207, 383
Self-discovery, 145
Self-doubt, 315
Self-earned values, 153
Self-effort and logical thinking, 335
Self-esteem, 15, 51, 77, 81, 95, 125, 145, 189, 225, 247, 369
  and addictions, 135
  Aristotelian view of, 3
  and casual sex, 33, 93-95, 117-119
  equality between men and women in, 161
  faking of, 31
  and happiness, 23-25
  of Hitler, 359
  and honesty, 17
  of housewives, 165
  and independent judgment, 89
  and jealousy, 105
  of Lincoln, 406
  and mental health, 107
  and mind, 55
  as moral issue, 11
  and morality, 9
  and mysticism, 45
  and myths, 57
  need for, 35
  of neocheaters, 265
  of nonproducers, 53, 309
  of politicians, 265
  of producers, 265
  and productivity, 17
  pseudo, 331
  as psychological need, 19
  and religion, 45
  and revealing of self, 297, 301
  and sloppiness, 131
  of theologians, 331
Self evaluation test, 23-25
Self-expression, 123
Self-healing power of mind, 319
Self-honesty, 9, 299
  and logical thinking, 335
Self-hypnosis, 121, 189
Self-image, 307
Self-improvement, 103
  books of, 37, 39
Self-interest, 245, 247, 315, 377
Self-interest/reality premise, iii
Selfishness, xiii, 315
  defined, xlvii
  vs. selflessness, 27-29
Self-knowledge, 83
Selflessness, 51, 191, 331
  defined, xlvii
  vs. selfishness, 27-29
Self-love, 15
Self-made qualities, 151
Self-protection, 59
Self-responsibility, xv, 63-65, 95, 97, 115, 137, 187, 225, 245, 247, 249, 309, 321, 335, 353, 387
  See also Responsibility
  as envious malefactors, 327
  and logical thinking, 335
Self-sacrifice, 19, 21, 335, 359
Self-sufficiency, 15, 135, 163, 331, 333, 335, 361, 369
Self-torture, 69
Self-worth, 135, 151-153, 223
  See also Self-esteem
Sense of life, 25, 325
  altruistic, 27
  in art, 77, 343
  defined, 27
  and humor, 201
  pro-individual, 27, 29
Sense of living in reality, 187
Senses, ix
Sensuosity, ix-xi
Sensuous behavior vs. psychuous pleasure, 35-37
Sensuousness, 121, 123
  defined, ix, xlvii
  faking of, 37
Sensuous pleasures vs. psychuous pleasures, ix
Sensuous projection techniques, 123
Sentimentalists, xi, xiii
Separate-working type relationships, 151
Serious vs. casual sex, 89
Sermon on the Mount, 83
Sex
  adolescent, 113, 117-119
  adult-child, 201, 203, 205
  anal, 203
  basic views of, 31
  books on, 39-45, 119, 297
  casual. *See* Casual sex
  and Christianity, 67-77, 173
  defined, xi, xlvii
  fantasies about, 75
  Freudian view of, 17, 19
  fun-only. *See* Casual sex
  and guilt, 33, 67
  hard symbols for, 351
  laws against, 201-205
  liberated approaches to, 31
  limitations of, 93-95
  and love, 73
  manipulative, 119
  marital, 71
  and morality, 35
  nonintimate, 93-95
  nonmarital, 117-119
  oral, 203, 205
  parent-child, 201, 203, 205
  playboy view of. *See* Casual sex
  premarital, 117-119, 203
  psychuous. *See* Psychuous sex
  religious views of, 33-35
  sexual attractiveness, 123
  voluntary, 201-205
  women as objects of, 357
Sex American Style, 279
Sexual affairs, 99
  outside, 101
Sexual attractiveness, 35
Sexual competition, 123, 125
Sexual fantasies, 203
Sexual impotence, 33, 37, 41, 121, 125
Sexual jealousy, 105-111
Sexual liberation, 209
Sexually liberated women, 33
Sexual oppression, 127
Sexual pleasures, ix
  faking of, 37

Sexual revolution, 77, 179
Sexual roles, 125-129
Sexual surrender, 127
Sexual value system, 93
Sharing, 299
Sharon, Ariel, 277
Shepard, Thomas R., 271
Shiits, 349
Short-term happiness, xxxvii
Shyness, 155-159
Sickness and mind-body link, 137
Silent Spring, 261, 271
Silver bullet of Neo-Tech, 426
Silver investments, 265
Sin, 85, 315, 317
　original, 83
　pleasure as, 71
Sincerity, 299
Singles bars, 161
Singles clubs, 159
Skid-row inhabitants, 329
Skinner, B.F., 387
Slavery, 5, 253
　and Civil War, 406
　Fabian, 406
　and suicide, 275, 277
　totalitarian, 5
Sleep elimination, 199
Slogans, 221, 341, 345
Sloppiness, 131
Smoking, 187
Social classes, 177
Social commentators, i
Social incompetence, 155-157
Social "intellectuals," 49, 65, 153, 283, 285, 291, 331, 361
　attacks on capitalism by, 335
　dependence on, 335
　elimination of, 337
　as envious malefactors, 329
　and envy, 325
　envy tactics used by, 327
　poetry used by, 347
Socialism, 65, 193, 255
Social justice, 331
Social policies, 263
Social science, 21, 373
Social science professors as envious malefactors, 331
Social Security, 215
Social status, 183
Socrates, 197, 337
Sodomy, 279
Soft (unreal) symbols, 351
Songs, 221
　See also Music
　lyrics of, 339, 341, 345
South Africa, 381-383
Southeast Asia, 271
Sovereignty of individual, 65
Soviet Union, 51, 53, 213, 269, 381
Spark, Murial, 237
Speculation, 265

Spencer, Herbert, xiii
Spirits, 231
Spiritual, defined, 77
Spiritual well-being, 77
Split (bicameral, automatic) mind, vii
Spontaneous humor, 201
Sprenger, Jacob, 71
Sri Lanka, 261, 271
Stalin, Joseph, xxi, xxxi, 53, 161, 249, 283, 406
Standards
　community, 281, 283
　of life, 15
　of living, 211, 261
　moral, 205, 285
　objective for art, 77
　romantic love for, 145-147
Starvation, 271
Star-Wars defense system, 59, 269
State, 53
State-labeled government, 53
Statism, 315
　and envious malefactors, 327
Status, 183
St. Augustine, 69, 75
Steam engines, 197
Stewart, Justice, 283
Stiffness in neck, 189
St. Jerome, 71
Stoneley, J., 57
Streaking fad, 281
Strength, xiii
Stress, 303
"Striving for approval" approach, 39
St. Simon, 69
St. Thomas, 71
Students' whims, 195
Subconscious absorption
　of negative information, 127
　of unjust criticism, 111, 113
Subconscious fear, 275
Subconscious form of negative-feedback self-hypnosis, 121
Subconscious loss of potency, 127-129
Subconscious mind, 189, 295
Subconscious negative effects of repressed emotions, 185
Subjective feelings, 313
Subjective morals, 9
Subjectivism, 9
Suez Canal, 343
Suffering, 261
Sugar
　addiction to, 135
　blood, 133
　breaking of addictions to, 141
　destructiveness of, 229, 231
　as suppressor of happiness, 137
Suicide, 5, 275-277
Superstitions, 221
Suppression of emotions, 83, 295
Suppressors of happiness, 137
Supreme Constitution, 215-227

Supreme Court anti-obscenity decision, 251, 277-283
Surrender, 317
　sexual, 127
Survival, xxix, 51, 129
　and human nature, xxix
　physical, 15
Sweeteners, 271, 273
Swinging, 93
Symbols, 351
System of Nature, The, 400
System of Positive Polity, xxxiii

— T —

Taboos, 201-205
　See also specific types
　incest, 117, 201
Tangible values. *See* Material values
Tastes, 93
Taxation, 51, 205, 253, 267
　abolishment of, 197
　and art collection, 349, 351
　elimination of, 215
Technology, xiii
　defined, xlvii
Tension release, 189, 191
Terminal illness, 275, 277
Terror governments, 211
Terrorists, 277
Terror theocracy, 211
Terror totalitarianism, 5
Testosterone, 139
Tests
　happiness, 15-17
　for humor, 201
　for proof of love or fidelity, 111
　psychuous capacity, 37
　self evaluation, 23-25
Theistic dictatorships, 51
Theists, 275
　as atheists, 259
Theme, 77
Theocracy, 211
Theologians, xxi, xxvii, 49, 51, 65, 145, 153, 283
　See also Clergy
　attacks on capitalism by, 335
　Christian, 67
　defined, xlvii
　dependence on, 335
　elimination of, 337
　as envious malefactors, 329, 331
　envy tactics used by, 327
　poetry used by, 347
　self-esteem of, 331
Therapists, 297
　as neocheaters, 109
Therapy
　cognitive-based, 107
　failure of, 187
Thinking
　in concepts, xxix
　conscious, xxix

creative, 383
developmental, 383
and God concept, 55
honest, 135
horizontal. *See* Horizontal thinking
independent, 335, 339, 341, 345
lateral, 201
logical. *See* Logic
non-integrated, xv
process of, 53
rational. *See* Rational thinking
and rock music, 341
vertical. *See* Vertical thinking
Time
integration of with effort, xxv
wasting of, 157
Titian, 349
Tobacco, 187
breaking of addictions to, 141
Toledano, R. De, 261
Totalitarianism, xxxiii, 5, 51, 55, 89, 213, 387
leaders in, 53
slavery under, 5
Transcendental meditation, 63
Transcending of reality, 349
Transfer-payment services, 215
Travel to other planets, 199
Truth, 9, 209, 219, 243, 345
integrated, contextual, vii
loyalty to, xix, 9, 17, 87, 91, 95, 97, 223, 235, 243, 311
objective, 287, 341
packaged, 339, 345, 349
reality as basis of, 339
rescue of from dishonesty, 257-263
Twentieth century romantic love, 179
"Two worlds" concept, xxvii

— U —
UFOs. *See* Unidentified flying objects
Ultimate battle, 269, 275
Uncertainty, 287
Underachievers, xxv
Underground existence, 5
Understanding, 15
Unidentified flying objects (UFOs), 5, 53-63
Unilateral disarmament movement, 59
Unintegrated music, 341
Union Carbide, 261
Union leaders, xv
Uniqueness of individuals, 151-153
Universities. *See* Academia
University professors. *See* Academia
Unjust criticism, 25, 111, 113
Unnecessary aging, 113-115
Unreal (soft) symbols, 351
U.S. Constitution
First Amendment to, 237, 283
Individual-Rights Amendment to, 215
Utopias, 387

— V —
Value
of life, 91, 321-323, 391
of rejection, 155-159
Value-attack techniques, xvii
Value-oriented relationships, 95
benevolent termination of, 145
Values
abstract. *See* Abstract values
achievement as highest, 27
amoral, 91
defined, xlvii
destruction of, 31
discovery of mutual, 147
exchange of in romantic love, 359-363
and individual differences, 91-93
material. *See* Material values
moral vs. personal, 293
mystical, 27
mysticism as harm to, xlviii
nonjudgable, 91
nonjudgmental, 91
objective. *See* Objective values
self-earned, 153
sexual, 93
tangible. *See* Material values
Value-scale of judgment, 293
Vandalism, 83
Vanderbilt, Cornelius, 253
Van Gogh, xi
Variables of nature, 5
Venereal disease, 91
See also specific types
Verbal fighting, 99
Verdi, 343
Vertical thinking vs. horizontal thinking, 383-385
Victimless crimes, 279
Victorianism, 75, 177, 179, 209
decline of, 177-179
Virgins, 121
Vlahoulis, Thomas P., 233, 235, 237
Volitional actions, 85, 285
Voluntarily supported government, 213
Voluntary ending of relationships, 97
Voluntary sexual acts vs. unjust laws, 201-205

— W —
Wars, 27, 51, 83, 197, 253, 273
elimination of, 197, 215, 227
nuclear, 59
Wasting of time, 157
Watergate tapes, 249
Welfare, 215
Well-being
control over, 135, 137
vs. joy, 191
vs. pleasure, 191
responsibility for, 115, 245, 363, 385

Western world democracies, 213
Whims, 195, 243
White, Justice, 283
White, Tom, 235
Why of universe, 47
Wife-beating, 69, 175
"Willed realities," 195
Winners, iii, xxv, xlviii, 1
Wishes, 243, 313
Witches, 71-73, 175, 209
Wolfgang, M.E., 379
Wolsey, Bishop, 73
Women
See also Feminists
career, 163
Catholic view of, 69
characteristics of men sought by, xiii
Christianity's view of, 69
economic freedom for, 179
emancipation of, 177-179
emotional differences between men and, 355-359
equality of with men, 161-165, 173
famous, 183
fear in, 303
freedom of, 173-185, 207-211
government oppression of, 185
greatness achieved by, 165-171, 379-381
individual rights of, 207
liberation of, 173
nature of. *See* Human nature
nature of vs. male nature, 357-359
oppression of, 173-185, 207-211
potential of, 171-185
productivity categories for, 163-164
professional, 163
as property of men, 69
psychological differences between men and, 355-359
and Puritanism, 75
rights of, 185
as sex objects, 357
sexually liberated, 33
subjugation of, 209
voting by, 75, 177
Words, 373
distortions of, xiii
Wordsworth, William, xi
Worldwide economic collapse, 263
Worth, 151-153
self-. *See* Self-worth
Write-in ballots for Supreme Constitution, 227

— XYZ —
Yale University, 13
Zen Buddhism, 63
Zionism, 377, 379, 381
Zoning, 239, 241

Opportunities Available

The Neo-Tech Research and Writing Center is seeking high-energy people integrated with Neo-Tech. Available are opportunities to learn the business of collapsing mysticism, starting from janitorial, clerical, secretarial levels and rising to any level. Sex, age, experience, race, location (including foreign countries and languages) are no barrier. Energy, honesty, enthusiasm, and attitude are everything. Every Neo-Tech owner who writes to John Flint at the address shown on page 155 of the Neo-Tech Instructions will eventually be approached about working with the Neo-Tech Center.

Neo-Tech Owners May Obtain The Complete
Neo-Tech Reference Encyclopedia

The mighty Neo-Tech Reference Encyclopedia is sold *only* to owners of the Neo-Tech Discovery. The quarter-million-word Neo-Tech Reference Encyclopedia backs every Neo-Tech Advantage. In addition, that Encyclopedia includes a comprehensive survey of 3000 books published since 2 BC with over 200 book analyses worth thousands of dollars. Those analyses utilize a rating system that grades every contribution and error in each book. Those analyses also save hundreds of hours in reading time and library searches. Owners of the Neo-Tech Discovery may acquire the complete, typeset, 480-page copy of the Neo-Tech Encyclopedia for $59.95 postpaid from John Finn at his address shown below.

Neo-Tech Owners May Obtain The
Original 192-Page Neocheating Manuscript

Those interested may also acquire F. R. Wallace's original Neocheating manuscript. This manuscript shows the origins of the Neocheating discovery first uncovered at the fever-pitched poker tables in Las Vegas. This manuscript includes the complete details of neocheating in cards with 35 photos demonstrating the actual Neocheating techniques. You may acquire this manuscript for $39.95 postpaid from John Finn at his address shown below.

Neo-Tech For Your Children, Parents, Kin,
Friends, Business Associates, Employees, Customers

Neo-Tech Owners wanting to share the values of Neo-Tech with those they care for may purchase the manuscripts at special prices for giving or reselling. As a Neo-Tech owner, you may acquire the complete, two volume Neo-Tech Discovery (I-V) at the repeat-order price of $49.95 postpaid or three complete sets for $100 postpaid (below wholesale) from **John Finn, Box 19358B, Las Vegas, NV 89132**. They can be shipped to you or drop shipped to whomever you wish in the USA or Canada without extra charge (all foreign shipping include an extra $6.95 per package). This offer is open for 90 days after you receive Neo-Tech. Send credit-card number with expiration date or your check or money order made out to "Neo-Tech".

Please do not send other correspondence or mail concerning Neo-Tech or I & O Publishing to John Finn. For such mail cannot be processed through his name and address.

NEO-TECH

Neo-Tech is fully integrated honesty: Neo-Tech is a fully integrated matrix of new techniques and technology that identifies mysticism and eliminates neocheating everywhere. Neo-Tech is the entelechy of prosperity and happiness through effort and honesty — through elimination of mysticism and neocheating. Indeed, Neo-Tech is the eliminator of mysticism and neocheating. ...Neo-Tech guiltlessly delivers earned money, power, and romantic love.

NEO-TECH BRAIN WAVES

Human-brain-activity conditions fall into two categories: (1) The alpha-brain-wave condition — a passive condition achieved while day dreaming, watching television, being spaced-out on loud rock music or drugs. (2) The beta-brain-wave condition — an active condition achieved during conscious, wide-range, integrated thought (beta-plus). Mystics seek to exist in the alpha brain-wave condition. Neo-Tech people seek to live in the beta-plus brain wave condition. ...People dominated by mysticism generally live with miserable government faces and sour ennui. Has anyone ever seen a destructive government bureaucrat with a genuinely radiant, happy face? (I & O offers $100 to photograph such a face.) Indeed, such people by nature hate life. For, they live by attacking and destroying values. By contrast, Neo-Tech people live with innocent, clean minds. For, they live through cheerful productivity. They live by producing competitive values for others and society.

LAZINESS VERSUS HAPPINESS
NEO-TECH'S SILVER BULLET

Surrendering to laziness versus high-effort pursuit of value creation are the two opposing actions that determine the quality of all human life. And ironically, laziness and value creation are the two ideas most feared, evaded, and distorted by mystics and neocheaters, ranging from Marxist-Leninist murderers to objectivist-libertarian underachievers. Thus, the two aspects of Neo-Tech feared most by mystics and neocheaters are: (1) Neo-Tech's explicit identification of laziness as the root cause of all mysticism and neocheating; and (2) Neo-Tech's explicit identification that the sole, moral purpose of human life is to achieve abiding happiness. And that happiness is achieved only through the exertion of rational thought and effort needed to create competitive values wanted by others. ...Neo-Tech and business are the antithesis of mysticism and neocheating. Moreover, Neo-Tech is the silver bullet that will end all mysticism and neocheating to yield abiding prosperity and happiness for all human beings.

THE BUSINESS OF NEO-TECH

The business of Neo-Tech is to cure the disease of mysticism and eliminate its symbiotic neocheaters worldwide.

THE GOAL OF NEO-TECH

The goal of Neo-Tech is to end the 2000-year hoax of mysticism and eliminate neocheating in order to achieve commercial biological immortality with prosperity and happiness for all honest, productive people.

THE NEO-TECH ARMY

The Neo-Tech army is growing. It has no budget and needs no money. It has no property and needs no weapons. It has no generals, leaders, authorities, gurus. It has no soldiers, followers, servants, slaves. Everyone in the Neo-Tech army is a supreme commander-in-chief who takes orders from no one and gives orders to no one. The Neo-Tech army never takes life — only gives life. With each individual marching to his or her own step forever into the future, the Neo-Tech army is already the most powerful movement on earth. This army is on the move against all mystics and its symbiotic neocheaters.